BAD SEEDS IN THE BIG APPLE

BAD SEEDS IN THE BIG APPLE

BANDITS, KILLERS, AND CHAOS IN NEW YORK CITY, 1920-1940

PATRICK DOWNEY

CUMBERLAND HOUSE
NASHVILLE, TENNESSEE

PUBLISHED BY CUMBERLAND HOUSE PUBLISHING INC.
431 Harding Industrial Drive
Nashville, TN 37211-3160

Photos credited to the Mike Web Collection are courtesy of Mike Webb, www.crimecollectibles.com; photos credited to the Ransom Research Center are courtesy of the Harry Ransom Humanities Research Center, University of Texas at Austin.

Cover design: Gore Studio, Inc.
Text design: John Mitchell

Library of Congress Cataloging-in-Publication Data

Downey, Patrick, 1968-
Bad seeds in the Big Apple : bandits, killers, and chaos in New York City, 1920-1940 / Patrick Downey.
p. cm.
Includes bibliographical references and index.
ISBN-13: 978-1-58182-646-3 (hardcover : alk. paper)
ISBN-10: 1-58182-646-X (hardcover : alk. paper)
1. Crime—New York (State)—New York—Case studies. 2. Criminals—New York (State)—New York—Case studies. I. Title.

HV6795.N5D69 2008
364.1092'27471—dc22

2008002765

Printed in the United States of America

1 2 3 4 5 6 7—14 13 12 11 10 09 08

For Amy, Ellie & Jack.
Life is good.

Contents

Foreword

Obviously crime pays, or there'd be no crime.
— G. Gordon Liddy

When John Dillinger, "Pretty Boy" Floyd, Bonnie and Clyde, and other "motorized bandits" robbed banks, fought running gun battles with lawmen, and traveled along midwestern back roads under cover of night, their style of banditry was hailed by the press and the FBI as a new and alarming by-product of the Great Depression. It appeared to be yet another example of a social phenomenon showing its dark side: Prohibition had left a legacy of Tommyguns, the St. Valentine's Day Massacre, and deaths from bad hooch, and now the Depression was baring its teeth by unleashing deadly bunches of have-nots, mostly rural in origin, who robbed from the rich and gave to themselves, the "deserving" poor.

In reality, the bandit gang dates back to the early days of U.S. history, when highwaymen ambushed solitary carriages and stagecoaches on lonely country roads. As the cities got bigger and the population denser, streets, alleys, and loot-rich warehouses became the new hunting ground. In *Bad Seeds in the Big Apple*, Pat Downey provides shocking proof that in New York City during the 1920s and '30s, the bandit was as much a part of the cityscape as Times Square and Gramercy Park. Antics pulled by loft workers, stickup artists, porch climbers, and payroll thieves were a staple of the daily newspapers, whereas in New York at least, gangsters and bootleggers had to kill or be killed before they drew similar attention: the funerals of Frankie Uale (often Yale), Nate "Kid Dropper" Kaplan, and Wild Bill Lovett received broader coverage than their crimes. It wasn't until the 1930s that the names of gang leaders like "Legs" Diamond, Vannie Higgins, and "Dutch" Schultz became as big a name in the press as they did in the streets.

Both the famous and the forgotten have their crimes revisited in *Bad Seeds in the Big Apple*. The mad love life and violent murder of Benita Franklin Bischoff, alias Vivian Gordon, the murder sprees of teenaged cop-killer Francis 'Two-Gun' Crowley, the cocky serial stickups of Cecilia Cooney ("the Bobbed-Haired Bandit") and her faithful husband Ed—all are here, and they join other killers and holdup artists who were forgotten the moment they entered either a cell or the death chamber at Sing Sing.

New York City witnessed many accomplishments between 1920 and 1940: the opening of the New York World's Fair, the completion of the Chrysler and Empire State buildings, and the formation of the New York Rangers, to name a few. But at the same time, future mob informant Joe Valachi was perfecting his skills as a killer for the Genovese crime family, ex-Gophers gangster Vincent Gaffney was hacked to death behind the Seeley Bottle Works, and Gerald Chapman, the "Gentleman Bandit," progressed from thieving to murder, a transition that landed him on the gallows at the Connecticut State Prison.

Some were famous for fifteen minutes. Others became popular, glamorous figures whose trials drew capacity crowds and whose graves became a magnet for tears and flowers. Their stories are presented in this eye-opening volume, which affirms historian Edward Gibbon's oft-repeated saying, "History is indeed little more than the register of the crimes, follies, and misfortunes of mankind."

— *Rose Keefe*

Author of *Guns and Roses: the Untold Story of Dean O'Banion,*
The Man Who Got Away: the Bugs Moran Story,
and *The Starker: Big Jack Zelig, the Becker-Rosenthal Case,*
and the Advent of the Jewish Gangster

Preface

History dictates that, in regard to crime, the 1920s belong to gangsters like Al Capone, who rode the wave of Prohibition to new criminal heights, and that the 1930s belong to bank robbers like John Dillinger. History also dictates that the latter acted in small bands and generally operated in the Midwest, and that these roving gangs of bandits were the result of the Great Depression. This, however, isn't true. The bandit gangs weren't a midwestern phenomenon brought on by the Depression; they were nationwide, and they had been around for years.

Just as Prohibition made the United States a veritable gangster's paradise, so to did the lack of quality security make America's cities and towns bandit paradises. Long before electronic money transfers, armored cars, and direct deposits, cash was delivered by hand. Once a week the thousands of businesses operating in New York City had to pay their employees, which meant a trip to the bank to pick up the thousands of dollars that would subsequently be doled out to the workers in individual envelopes. Two company men with a satchel brimming with greenbacks were no match for four or five well-armed bandits. The pickings were good.

Not all bandit gangs went in for cold hard cash. Some were loft burglars, stealing valuable goods such as furs and silks that could later be sold to a fence. Some, like the Whittemore Gang and the band headed by George Cohen and Sol Brofman, specialized in robbing jewelry stores. Others kept to the tried-and-true method of simply running into a store or gas station with a handgun and demanding money.

The idea for this book was hatched while researching my first book, *Gangster City: The History of the New York Underworld 1900-1935*. While poring through newspaper articles about the organized crime figures and bootleggers of the 1920s and '30s, I continually came across the actions of those profiled in this book. Back then more newspaper ink was given to bandits than bootleggers. For the most part, prior to 1930, even at the height of Prohibition, unless a bootlegger was killed, he seldom made the papers. The trials and tribulations of bandits, on the other hand, made for great copy. In fact, many of the members of organized crime who are now infamous were little known in there own time. For example, Brooklyn mob boss Frankie Uale (often Yale) appeared on Page One of the *New York Times* once, and that was when he was killed. However, "super bandit" Gerald Chapman and the aforementioned Richard Whittemore each made some forty appearances each on the *Times'* front page.

As the early 1930s rolled around, the mobsters began to get their due. "Legs" Diamond dominated the dailies, and the other gangsters of his time didn't do too badly either. Vincent "Mad Dog" Coll, Vannie Higgins, "Dutch" Schultz—all became fodder for the reporters, but they shared the headlines with the likes of Vivian Gordon and Francis "Two-Gun" Crowley.

In New York City, however, the 1920s belonged to the bandits. Seemingly every day there were reports of a payroll robbery or jewelry store heist. Between 1923 and 1925, if you were talking about the Diamond brothers, you were discussing Morris and Joseph, not Jack and Eddie. It's hard to believe now, but there was actually a time when New York City (and most other major U.S. cities) was infested with small gangs of men, armed to the teeth, who robbed and murdered on a daily basis.

Yes, New York had its bootleggers and organized crime figures, but it also had so many other wicked characters that it makes one wonder how this era could be considered by some to be "the good old days." Since the two former groups have been explored in numerous tomes, the goal of this book is to fill in the rest of the Big Apple's criminal landscape during the years between the World Wars. In it you will find the marquee names of the day as well as some of the smaller operators and some whose stories are just plain interesting. One thing all of these ne'er-do-wells had in common is that, whether for a single day or an entire year, they were the talk of the town.

Acknowledgments

The following folks have assisted me with this book, and for that I am grateful: Mario "the Chicago Encyclopedia" Gomes, Mike Tona in Buffalo, author and pal Rose Keefe, "man of a thousand photos" Mike Webb, Rick Mattix, Ellen Poulsen, and William J. Helmer. Thanks also to Leonora Gidlund and the staff at the New York City Municipal Archives, as well as the staffs at the Monmouth County Library in Manalapan, New Jersey, and the New York Public Library.

BAD SEEDS IN THE BIG APPLE

GENTLEMAN GERALD

AND THE DUTCHMAN

"I have never killed anybody, and I think it's pretty rotten
to slaughter me for something I didn't do."

— GERALD CHAPMAN

I n the latter half of the nineteenth century, a young couple by the name of
Chartres emigrated to New York City from County Cork, Ireland, to start a
family and seek the American dream. Had the customs agents known what
was in store for the couple's middle child, they no doubt would have sent the
family straight back to the Emerald Isle. To Ma and Pa Chartres, he was their son
George, born in August 1887, but to 1920s America he would be known as Gerald
Chapman, notorious "master criminal" and "super bandit."

Mr. and Mrs. Chartres, however, wouldn't live to see their son reach the height
of infamy. They died about four years after George was born. Although they surely
would have been ashamed of George's life choices, they probably would have
found some consolation in the fact that their errant son was also extremely well
read, could discuss history and philosophy at length, and wrote poetry.

After the death of their parents, George, his older brother Thomas, and a
younger sister went to live with their aunt and uncle, Katherine and John Con-
nors. His siblings were good kids, but George took to crime early in life. In 1902,
at the age of fourteen, he was arrested for robbery and sent to the House of
Refuge. His aunt managed to get him paroled and sent him back to school for

two years, after which he became, like his brother, a plumber's assistant and gas-fitter. Though he worked at a respectable job during the day, at night George could be found in the city's poolrooms and dance halls consorting with other young hooligans. He was also operating as a prowler on upper Park Avenue.

His modus operandi was to grab a newspaper and search the classified ads for people looking to rent furnished rooms or sell furniture. If he found one that caught his fancy, he would answer the ad, and if there was anything of value, he would come back at night and steal it.

In 1907 he was again arrested for robbery and sent to prison. During sentencing the judge told him, "You're a fit candidate for the electric chair." But the prophetic statement fell on deaf ears. After serving fourteen months, George was paroled and got a job as a secretary but was arrested for stealing $115 from his boss. On September 22, 1908, he was sentenced to three and a half years and shipped off to Sing Sing, the state prison near Ossining. A month later he was transferred to Auburn Prison, where he remained until the spring of 1911.[1]

Back on the outside, George got a job as a streetcar conductor but was fired when it was discovered he was an ex-con, so he went back to robbing houses. By this time he had adopted the name that would follow him to an early grave, Gerald Chapman. He also had expanded his territory and was hitting homes in towns as far away as Poughkeepsie, New York, and Stamford and Danbury, Connecticut.

In New York City, Detectives James Brennick and James Morell were charged with bringing Chapman in, and they caught up with him in a Harlem boarding house on October 28, 1911. The detectives entered the building and started up the stairs just as Chapman, carrying two suitcases, was descending. Seeing the lawmen, he threw his cases at them and made a run for the roof but was grabbed on the fourth floor. After a brief fight he was subdued and taken to the police station, where Chapman said he would rat out his partner if the cops would go easy on him. A deal was struck, and soon the two detectives, with Chapman handcuffed to Brennick, were on their way to the apartment where the bandit's accomplice lived.

When they arrived, Morell stayed out front while Brennick and Chapman went inside. Chapman's pal wasn't there, so they waited. After a while Chapman complained that he was getting sick and pleaded with the detective to take the cuffs off so he could go to the bathroom, which was located on the second floor in the rear. Brennick knew better than to remove the cuffs but agreed to take Chapman to the restroom. As both men squeezed inside the small space, a bag concealed in Chapman's waistband slipped out and fell to the floor, revealing several watches, gold stickpins, and various other pieces of jewelry.

"Oh, so that's what you've been hiding," Brennick said, leaning over to pick up the evidence. As he did so the butt of his pistol protruded from behind his coat and Chapman grabbed it. Sticking the gun in the detective's stomach, he said, "Now, take off those cuffs or I'll blow you to the devil." Having left the keys with his partner, and gambling that Chapman wouldn't shoot, Brennick said, "No, I won't take 'em off. You just shoot. You're harnessed to me for good, whether I'm dead or alive." He then grabbed the gun and a scuffle ensued. "I'll shoot," Chapman kept repeating. "You're afraid to," the detective laughed back.

While they were wrestling, Brennick kept kicking the bathroom door over and over again, and finally the landlady came up to see what the fuss was about. When she opened the door and saw the gun, she immediately started to run away, but Brennick yelled, "He won't shoot! "I'm a detective. I've got him. Now, madam, grab his throat and choke him until his tongue hangs out."

The landlady complied, and while she choked Chapman the detective gave him a few punches to the face to take the fight out of him. Back at the station, Chapman was charged with felonious assault, assaulting an officer, grand larceny, and bringing stolen goods into the state. Chapman returned to Auburn Prison in 1912 to serve a ten-year sentence.[2]

It was in Auburn that Chapman met a criminal who would have a great impact on his life. George Anderson, called "Dutch" because of his strong Danish accent, was born Ivan Dahl von Teler to a well-to-do family in Denmark circa 1880.[*] Well educated, he was multilingual and a self-described bachelor of the arts and translator of literary masterpieces. With a fondness for high culture and good living, Anderson moved to America's Midwest when he was about twenty years old and, although his mother believed he was a successful businessman, turned to a life of crime.

In addition to fine hotels, "Dutch" also patronized some of this country's finest penal institutions, including the Illinois State Prison in Joliet. Eventually he headed to New York, where he served a term for forging money orders. In 1917 he ended up in Auburn for robbing a safe in Rochester, and it was about this time that he came to know Chapman. Since Anderson was well educated, he was able to pass his time in prison tutoring his fellow inmates. Chapman worked in the library and became an avid reader. Sharing common interest, the two convicts became friends, and in 1919, when both were paroled, they moved to the Midwest and became bootlegging partners operating between Detroit and Toledo, Ohio.[3]

By 1920 Chapman and Anderson were back in New York, living the high life with their bootlegging profits. In August the duo hooked up with another ex-con they knew from Auburn, Charles Loerber, and invited him to take part in a job they were preparing to pull. The plan was to rob a U.S. Mail truck loaded with cash and

---

[*] This information came from his lawyer. Other sources give his nationality as Swedish.

bonds. They had an inside source who could tip them off as to which truck would be carrying the loot, and once the truck was identified, they studied its movements. To determine the best place to rob the vehicle, the hoods followed it several times on foot and in a car, from the time it left the post office until it reached its final destination, noting how fast it went and how the driver reacted to traffic.

On the evening of October 24, 1921, the plan was put into motion. The trio drove to the downtown post office in a green Cadillac and waited for the mail truck. The postal vehicle left at its normal time, and while driving up Broadway the driver checked his rearview mirror and saw the sedan pulling up, with Chapman standing on the running board. As the truck approached Leonard Street, a cab shot out from a side street and forced it to stop. The driver would later say he was certain whoever was in the the taxi was in on the job.

When the truck came to a halt, Chapman jumped onto its running board with a gun and ordered the driver to turn onto Leonard Street. When he did, Anderson jumped out of the sedan with a gun and kept the driver covered. The bandits then led the driver to the rear of the truck and made him open it and get inside. They put a bag over the man's head, and after deciding which mailbags to take, tossed them into the Cadillac and quickly disappeared.

After the theft, Chapman, Anderson, and Loerber drove to a farm in Lake Ronkonkoma, Long Island, and hid the loot in a barn. The take was approximately $2.4 million in bonds plus some cash. Loerber received $6,000 in cash and $400,000 in bonds. A quarter of the loot was to go to the inside man, post office employee Jeremiah Savelli.[4]

The bandits struck again less than two months later, on December 1, at Niagara Falls in upstate New York. Joining the trio was another hoodlum named Ludwig Schmidt, a German immigrant who went by the name of "Dutch Louis." This time the target was the American Express Company.

On the day of the heist, three American Express employees left the company building pushing a hand truck bearing two strongboxes containing $40,000 in cash, money orders, and railway checks, and headed to the train station where the money would be shipped. As they prepared to cross the street, they found themselves surrounded by three armed men. Two of them, Chapman and Anderson, forced the employees to walk to the wall of the train station and do an about-face, while the third man stood back and kept his eye on things. When the employees raised their hands, Chapman, not wanting to attract unwanted attention, ordered them to put their hands down.

While this was happening, a fourth bandit loaded the strongboxes into the thieves' getaway car. As soon as he was done, Chapman and Anderson backed toward the car, keeping the American Express employees covered, and all four robbers piled inside and made a clean getaway. Although this second robbery didn't garner as much attention as the mail truck robbery had, it would eventually lead to the bandits' capture.[5]

As postal inspectors diligently worked to solve the most infamous crime in post office history, Chapman and Anderson returned to New York City, where they moved into the Hotel Berkeley with their ill-gotten spoils and settled into a life of fake respectability. Dressing in fine suits set off by stylish spats and walking sticks—not to mention a monocle for Chapman—neither man would have been mistaken for a thief. Adding to the façade, they used their associate Loerber as a chauffeur, and on any given day he could be seen driving the bandits around, either in Chapman's black and yellow $7,500 Pierce-Arrow or Anderson's Packard.[6]

Things were moving along smoothly for the bandits until March 1922, when Loerber made a grave mistake: he paid his rent with some of the American Express traveler's checks from the Niagara Falls job. On March 4, when his landlady went to a department store and tried to make a purchase with one of the stolen checks, she was immediately arrested and detained until the authorities were certain she'd had nothing to do with the robbery. The landlady did, however, drop a dime on Loerber, and a detective hired by American Express named Gordon McCarthy arrived in New York to investigate.[7]

Later that spring Chapman and Anderson moved to the exclusive Gramercy Park section of Manhattan, with the former posing as a successful businessman and the latter as a professor.

Living with Chapman at this time was his young girlfriend Betty, who was described as an attractive, petite girl about fifteen years his junior. The neighbors knew them as Mr. and Mrs. G. Vincent Colwell, and for a short time Anderson lived with the couple before getting his own apartment in the area. Betty later denied knowing how her "husband" and his cohort earned their living, saying that she assumed all of their out-of-town appointments were business related. Although they patronized some of Manhattan's better nightclubs, Chapman and Betty's favorite rendezvous was an Italian restaurant in Greenwich Village, where they would while away the hours in clever conversation under a dense cloud of tobacco smoke.[8]

While Chapman and Anderson were living the high life, the post office's investigation was beginning to bear fruit. In April some of the stolen bonds surfaced in Detroit after the duo used them as a $10,000 deposit on some real estate. Officials interviewed the realtor who had accepted the bonds, and he described one of the men as a stout fellow with glasses and a German accent. This brought to mind "Dutch" Anderson as a possible suspect since the inspectors had dealt with him in the past when he was arrested for forging money orders. Back in

New York City, postal authorities employed a former convict named Edward Rose as a stool pigeon and underworld spy. Rose had done time with Anderson, so he was directed to dig around and see if he could learn anything. He was able to locate "Dutch," and police put a tail on the bandit.

More of the stolen bonds turned up in New York in a sting operation set up by postal inspectors. A fake office was opened, with an agent posing as a crooked broker. He was contacted by an actual crooked broker named Louis Wolf, who sold him some of the bonds. Wolf was arrested, but the inspectors weren't any closer to getting the real thieves.[9]

In early June, Detective McCarthy from the American Express Company, possibly with the assistance of Edward Rose, the post office's underworld pigeon, was introduced to Loerber. Posing as a stickup man from the Midwest, McCarthy was trying to determine if Loerber was one of the American Express bandits or just a fence. Through Loerber, McCarthy met Chapman and Anderson, and they both bought his act as well. Throughout June they all partied together at some of New York's best hotels and night spots.

Hoping to catch the bandits with the hot traveler's checks, McCarthy let it be known that he had contacts in Toledo who could handle such stolen commodities. Taking the bait, the bandits gave McCarthy $21,000 worth of bonds on June 28 for his imaginary confederates and let him know that if things worked out, there would be thousands of dollars more. Realizing he was on to something much bigger than just the Niagara Falls robbery, McCarthy took the bonds, which proved to be from the Leonard Street mail truck robbery. He then alerted the postal inspectors.

A couple of days after they gave McCarthy the bonds, however, something made the robbers suspicious, and on the evening of July 2, 1922, they demanded that McCarthy return them. Playing along, the undercover detective agreed to wire Toledo for them. The following day the bandits met McCarthy in upper Manhattan, and their suspicions were aroused even more when they noticed a carload of detectives passing by. "Better give us your gun before one of those bulls finds it on you," one of the hoods told McCarthy, who had no choice but to comply.

At about noon, the detective was sitting with Chapman and Anderson in one of their cars waiting for Loerber, who was eating in a luncheonette. Thinking that he may be in serious trouble with the bandits, McCarthy stepped away and phoned another detective, telling him that if he didn't call back in fifteen minutes, the cops should go in and make the arrests. Messages were quickly relayed, and the detectives wasted no time in swooping in for the catch, apprehending Loerber as he stepped out of the restaurant and nabbing Chapman and Anderson while they sat in the car.[10]

After being processed at the local precinct house, the trio was hustled down to the postal inspectors' headquarters at Manhattan's General Post Office.

Although the bandits remained mum about the stolen bonds, Chapman and Anderson had no qualms about discussing almost anything else. "Why, these fellows are the most polished men we have run across in a long time," a postal inspector said later. "One of them was quoting Walt Whitman to us at length this evening, and at intervals they exchanged remarks showing more than a casual knowledge of medieval history."[11]

Because of his apparent sophistication, Chapman would be dubbed "the Gentleman Bandit" in press accounts. He also would be stuck with the moniker "the Count of Gramercy Park," although he never tried to pass himself off as royalty.

While the questioning continued, officers raided the Gramercy Park apartments and took Betty and one of her friends into custody. In addition to twenty suits of clothing and two automatic pistols equipped with silencers, inspectors found $400,000 worth of the Leonard Street bonds and $3,000 worth of traveler's checks from the Niagara Falls job in Chapman's flat.[12]

Around 10 p.m. at the General Post Office, Chapman was left alone in the room where he was being questioned, and when his interrogator returned, the bandit was gone. The only avenue of escape was through a window; however, the room was on the third floor and jumping to the street was not an option. Looking out on the street, the officer didn't see a body, so he raised the alarm and all hands went searching for the escaped outlaw.

Chapman was on the ledge, looking for some way to make it to the ground. Unable to find one, he found an open window and climbed through it into a vacant office, where he managed to hide himself behind some boxes. After a brief search of the premises, he was recaptured. As a result of Chapman's disappearing act, all three bandits were chained to their chairs for the remainder of their stay.[13]

When the trio stood trial the next month, Loerber pleaded guilty and became a witness for the government against his two associates. Chapman and Anderson claimed Loerber and two other men actually had committed the crime, and that he had come to them to dispose of the bonds. Their long police and prison records worked against them, however, and on August 23, 1922, both were found guilty and sentenced to twenty-five years in the Atlanta Federal Penitentiary.[14]

When Chapman and Anderson arrived in Atlanta, they kept pretty much to themselves as they knew that stool pigeons were around and authorities would be interested in anything they might have to say. Over time, however, Chapman befriended an inmate named Frank Grey, whom he deemed a "right guy." Both men were in the hospital ward—Chapman claimed he was there because he was diabetic—and after about three months Grey came up with an escape plan.

Outside the hospital was the courtyard, which was surrounded by the prison walls. On top of the walls were guard towers and searchlights. The cord for the searchlights passed through a tree on the way to the power box, and the tree was in what was called the "tuberculosis camp," which was in the courtyard. The plan was to saw through the bars of a prison hospital window and shinny down a rope made of sheets to the courtyard. Once they were in the yard they would signal a confederate in the tuberculosis camp who would short-circuit the searchlight cord. Then, when the compound was dark and the guards were looking to see what had happened, they would throw a rope ladder over the wall and escape. The break would take place at 3 a.m. because every morning at this time the guard in the hospital unit went downstairs to wake the convicts who worked in the kitchen, leaving only a nurse, who was also a convict, in charge.

Some help from the outside was needed. Chapman had two guns smuggled into the facility at a cost of $1,500 each, and it was arranged for some civilian clothes to be waiting for them in a secluded spot outside the prison wall. The convicts managed to steal some saws, and Grey went to work on the window bars whenever an opportunity presented itself. They also managed to procure a thirty-five-foot rope ladder complete with a grappling hook.

Finally, on March 27, 1923, Chapman and Grey decided to make their move. After the guard left for his 3 a.m. rounds, the duo went to work. They didn't trust the nurse on duty, so they bound and gagged him. The pair removed the bars from the window and slid down a sheet to the first-floor level, where another sheet was tied to a window bar, and they slid down it to the yard. Moving along the wall, they made it to the area where the rope ladder had been stashed and signaled their pal in the tuberculosis camp that they were ready to go. The electrical cords in the tree had been skinned to expose the wire within, and the convict dropped another piece of wire onto the exposed portion, shorting out the lights in the yard. While the guards ran to investigate, Chapman and Grey threw the ladder over the wall and climbed their way to freedom.[15*]

Once outside the prison walls, they ran to the nearby woods, where the change of clothes was waiting for them. As they were changing, the prison sirens began to go off, and the escapees ran into the nearby neighborhood of Lake Wood Heights and approached a house. The homeowner, Henry Edwards, had heard the sirens had stepped outside expecting a search party to pass by, but he found Chapman and Grey instead. "We will give a thousand dollars if you'll hide us in your house," one of them said. But Edwards replied, "I can't be mixed up in any business of this kind." That wasn't the answer the convicts wanted to hear.

"Then come with us," one of the escapees said, sticking a pistol in Edwards's ribs. "If you don't come with us, and if you make one single outcry, you are a dead

---

* This was Chapman's account of the escape. Authorities said he bribed his way out and that the ladder, tied sheets, etc. were just a ruse to cover it up. Chapman would later scoff at that statement, saying prison officials didn't want to admit he and Grey had outsmarted them.

man. If we are captured, they are going to capture your dead body with us." At this point Edwards's wife began to approach. "Tell her to go back," the gunman whispered. "Tell her that if she tells a soul, she will have to pay for it with your life."[16]

The trio left Edwards's house and started to walk toward a streetcar stop. As they passed a neighbor standing on his porch, one of the convicts asked Edwards, "Do you know that man?" When he responded in the affirmative, the hoodlum told him, "If you speak to him, if you look at him, we'll blow your brains out." The escapees and their captive made it to the streetcar, and Edwards was forced to cough up the fare. After a short ride, his captors allowed him to get off, warning him not to say anything.

While on the streetcar Chapman and Grey noticed a man in a taxi driver's uniform and hired him to take them toward the town of Athens. The hack noticed the men were carrying guns, but he also noticed they were carrying large quantities of cash. His greed overcame his fear, and he agreed to take them on the long trip. A few miles outside of Athens, he dropped them off, returned to Atlanta, and reported the affair.[17]

Early the next morning, the convicts jumped a freight train but were put off between the towns of Colbert and Hull. Afterward, the conductor told a Colbert cop about the two men, saying he thought they may have been the prisoners who had escaped from the Atlanta penitentiary. The officer drove along the road running parallel to the tracks and saw two men walking. When he hollered for them to stop, they pulled out their guns and started shooting. The cop returned fire until he was out of ammunition, then went back to town for reinforcements.

A posse consisting of local citizens and three lawmen went back to the scene of the firefight and found Chapman hiding in a cotton patch. Choosing to shoot it out, the convict stood up and began to fire. The posse responded with a barrage of their own, and Chapman dropped to the ground with three bullet wounds. Grey was found later, hiding in a clump of bushes with a jammed gun. Chapman was sent to a hospital in Athens with two bullet wounds to the arms and one to the kidneys, while his pal was sent back to Atlanta.[18]

Chapman was placed in St. Mary's Hospital, where an around-the-clock watch was maintained by a guard from the Atlanta pen named W. S. McCarty. Also in the hospital was another convict from Atlanta, Joe Morrillo, and his personal guard, Harry Bishop. In another room was Athens motorcycle cop William McKinnon, who was recovering from an accident. Chapman's condition was bad, but he wouldn't necessarily need to be healthy for his next escape.

Whether he bribed his way out of Atlanta is debatable, but there can be no doubt that he bought his way out of the Athens hospital. A day before his second escape, two unknown men, later identified as New York hoodlums Dominick

Didato and Abe Silverstein, were seen driving around town in a Packard with "bags of money" as well as Chapman's nurse, Cora Ramey.[19]

On the evening of April 4, all was quiet at the hospital. Officer Bishop was guarding Morrillo in his room, and McCarty was with Chapman. Just before 9 p.m. McCarty left and would say later that he had asked Bishop to keep an eye on Chapman's room and not let anyone in or out except the nurse and doctor. Shortly after nine o'clock the nurse went in and checked Chapman's vital signs, noting that his temperature was 100.3 degrees. At 9:50 p.m. the doctor went in to check on him and found that he had escaped, using his clothes and blankets to construct a makeshift rope.

The police surmised he had climbed out the second-story window, lowered himself thirty feet to the ground, and escaped. Right away there were doubts about how someone with a fever and wounds in the arms and kidneys could have managed such a feat. Adding insult to injury, the bandit also had helped himself to some of Officer McCarty's clothes.[20]

Lawmen poured into town, and the manhunt was on. Since he was wounded and only had about a fifty-minute head start, the authorities deduced that Chapman was still hiding somewhere in Athens. McCarty was sent back to Atlanta under a heavy veil of suspicion. The following night there were two nurses on duty, and one of them heard someone in the hospital basement and went to tell Officer Bishop, who was still guarding Morrillo. Bishop and two nurses went into the basement and saw a man sitting in a wheelchair. Having left his gun upstairs, Bishop grabbed a poker and demanded, "Who are you? What are you doing?" When he received no response, he told the nurses, "Give me my gun and he'll answer."

At that, the man in the wheelchair asked, "Don't you know me, Mr. Bishop?" The stunned guard exclaimed, "Why, it's Chapman!" Upon hearing that the man was the notorious escaped con, one of the nurses grabbed Bishop around the neck and screamed, "Don't let him get me!" Bishop later said that while he was wrestling with the nurse, Chapman was able to escape. Amazingly, the officer expected everyone to believe the story, and what's even more amazing is that they did.[21]

Why Chapman was in the basement of the hospital the evening after his escape has never been adequately explained. Some believe that he never went out the window, knowing that in his condition he would be captured quickly, and instead chose to stay in the basement until he could make his getaway. Chapman's own unbelievable story is that he did in fact jump from the hospital window and wandered around town in a weakened condition before returning to the hospital's boiler room to warm up. Once he was rejuvenated by the heat, he again ventured outside and found an abandoned house in which to hide for the entire next day.

The second night found Chapman once again chilled to the bone, so he returned to the hospital boiler room, where he was found. After this escape he managed to collapse outside a whorehouse run by the proverbial madam with a heart of gold, who took him in and nursed him back to health. Unfortunately (or conveniently for Chapman, should anyone want to check his story), the fallen angel died shortly thereafter.[22]

In an account given six years after the event, William McKinnon, the motorcycle cop recovering in the hospital at the time of the escape, stated that while Bishop was dealing with the hysterical nurse, Chapman walked out of the hospital to a waiting sedan, escorted by the other nurse, who was trying to get him to go back to his room. He also stated that Chapman's nurse, Cora Ramey, later told him that the outlaw was there waiting for her because she was going to dress his wounds. When the others showed up, he walked back out to the car and was whisked away. Whatever the reality of the situation, it was apparent that the bandit had spread a lot of money around to ensure his escape.[23]

Eight months after his partner escaped, "Dutch" Anderson tunneled his way out of the Atlanta penitentiary at about 4 p.m. on December 30, 1923. The bandit had made friends with a couple of inmates in the tuberculosis camp who had cut a trapdoor in the floor of their tent and begun to dig their way out. The tunnel eventually measured fifty feet long and ran eight feet under the main wall. After it was completed, Anderson, the two tubercular convicts, and Anderson's old pal "Dutch Louis" Schmidt, who had subsequently been captured for the Niagara Falls job, all crawled through the tunnel to freedom.[24]

Chapman and Anderson reunited on the outside, and one of the hideouts they used on and off from April until August 1924 was a little farmhouse on the Ohio-Indiana border a few miles outside of Muncie. The owners, Mr. and Mrs. Benjamin Hance, were well aware their guests were criminals, as boarding members of the underworld was their business. As a result, there was no need for Chapman and Anderson to hide what they were, and they left the tools of their trade in plain sight for all to see and even took target practice with their guns.[25]

On Saturday April 5, 1924, Chapman popped up in Steubenville, Ohio, where he entered a car dealership at about 10 p.m. He was "exceptionally well dressed," remembered the young woman who worked there, and approached a Lincoln sedan. Chapman mentioned that he lived up the street, but the woman knew he was lying. When he asked her if the car he was looking at was locked, she said that it was but that she could get the key. However, before she had a chance to retrieve it, Chapman said, "That's a damn good way to keep the car," and walked out. The dealership closed, but when it reopened on Monday, a Lincoln touring car that had not been locked was missing.[26]

According to Chapman, he and Anderson were engaged in bootlegging at this time, and in June they both went back east to try to set up a delivery site and a storage depot for booze in Boston, and to drum up some customers. They got in touch with thirty-two-year-old Walter Shean, the black sheep of a well-to-do family and an underworld figure in Springfield, Massachusetts. They told him they were looking for customers who could buy booze in shipments of 200 and 300 cases at a time. Shean was unable to find an outlet for their hooch, but his relationship with the hoodlums prospered and he became their contact in Massachusetts. Shean would later insist, however, that he had no idea that the two men, posing as Waldo Miller and Dr. Johnson, were in fact the notorious Gerald Chapman and "Dutch" Anderson.[27]

He also would say that on Saturday evening, October 11, 1924, Chapman, driving the stolen Lincoln from Steubenville, picked him up and asked him to join him on a trip to Hartford, Connecticut. On the way, Chapman said that whenever bootlegging got slow, he had to "swing on a little peter," which was underworld parlance for blowing safes. Shean asked if Dr. Johnson (Anderson) also blew safes, but Chapman said no, he was the safe-blower. The two stopped in Hartford for gas, then continued to the town of New Britain, Connecticut, where Chapman entered the Davison & Levanthal Department Store. After about five minutes he returned and said, "Everything's all fixed."

They continued to Waterbury, where Chapman met with some people and then drove himself and Shean to the outskirts of the town of Meriden, where they stopped at the Old Colony Inn, had dinner, and took a couple of rooms for the night.

At 5:30 the next morning Chapman woke Shean, and they headed back toward New Britain. During the drive, Chapman informed Shean that he was going to rob the safe at Davison & Levanthal. Before pulling into town, Chapman stuffed a pistol into his waistband and handed one to Shean, telling him to do the same and advising that he should pull his belt tight, because in the past he (Chapman) had dropped a gun down his pant leg. They pulled into town early that Sunday morning, and Chapman parked the car down the street from the department store. Grabbing a briefcase and a package, he left Shean in the car and made his way to the store.

Chapman went around back and let himself in through the rear door. Once inside, he went to the front door and cut off the security bolts and opened all the windows to the fire escape so that he would have a number of exits available if he needed to make a quick getaway. After about an hour Chapman returned to the car and told Shean, "I want you to come with me. I've had some trouble with a sucker down there."

The two men entered the store through the rear door, but this time they were seen by a man who worked in a stable across the alley. Suspicious, he called the store's proprietor, Mr. Davidson, and asked if he had scheduled any workers to come in that morning. When Davidson said no, the stable worker replied, "You'd better tell police headquarters then, because I just saw two men go in the back way, and they're in there now." Davidson quickly called the police, and five officers were dispatched.

Once inside the store, Chapman and Shean went to the mezzanine level, where the latter could see that one safe had already been blown. Chapman asked Shean to hold his briefcase and also gave him some money from the first safe. At this point, Shean began to get cold feet, and he told Chapman, "This is too dangerous for me." Chapman replied, "What is the matter with you? Are you getting a little kinky? There may be two or three coppers around here, but that doesn't amount to anything." Shean, however, wasn't buying any of it, and he hightailed it out of the store and returned to the car.[28]

When the five officers arrived, they split into two groups, Officers Atwater and Skelly would enter through the rear, while the other three would enter through the front door. But before the three officers had a chance to reach the front of the building, Atwater and Skelly made their way inside, alerting Chapman to their presence. As Atwater walked through the door, Chapman came running down the stairs with his gun drawn. Atwater jumped behind a counter just as the bandit fired at him, but his leap to safety left Skelly exposed, and he caught the bullet in the stomach. As Skelly collapsed, Chapman ran past the counter and out through the front door and disappeared down an alley. Shean was captured as he was getting into the car. A search of the vehicle turned up a bag of safecracking tools, $200 in cash, an unfired pistol, a rifle, and two sawed-off shotguns.

Skelly was taken to the hospital, and Shean was brought to his bedside. Skelly identified him as the man who had shot him but said that he had been wearing a different-colored hat. The lawman died a short time later, but because of his comment about the hat and the fact that the gun the police found in the car was unfired, investigators felt Skelly had been mistaken. Shean was questioned at great length and kept his mouth shut, but after a while he caved in and identified Chapman as his accomplice. Chapman succeeded in making a getaway but was named as the killer of Officer Skelly.[29]

About a month after Skelly's murder, New York City police were ordered to clean up the city for the holidays. This meant any known hoodlum was arrested on sight and tossed in jail for the duration, whether he deserved such treatment or not. On November 17, two detectives recognized a thug named George Stuyvesant and placed him under arrest. Originally from Troy, New York, Stuyvesant was missing an eye, the result of a shootout the previous year with a couple of cops in Harlem. That wasn't his first gun battle with police; he also had been arrested in 1920 after wounding two officers when they came to question him about a Pennsylvania bank robbery.

The detectives brought the hood back to the station and charged him with a holdup they knew he hadn't committed, just to keep him off the street. Stuyvesant was then taken to police headquarters, where some of the cops immediately noticed that he fit the description of the safecracker who had killed Officer Skelly.

Authorities in New Britain, Connecticut, were notified and came to the city with the stable employee who had witnessed the break-in. Stuyvesant was placed in a lineup with other thugs, and the witness picked out the one-eyed desperado without hesitation. Although he denied being involved in the murder, the prisoner reportedly admitted during interrogation that he knew Shean. The New York police went on to say that authorities in New Britain had given out Chapman's name right after the murder so the real murderer would think they were on the wrong trail.[30]

Since he was wanted in the East, Chapman returned to the Midwest, where he, "Dutch" Anderson, and bandit named Charles "One Armed" Wolfe continued with operations. With Shean locked up, detectives searched his place of business and uncovered loot as well as weapons. On one container holding a number of stolen fur coats was a mail tag with the return address of a house in Muncie, Indiana. Detectives in that city were alerted, and they set up a stakeout in the hotel across the street from the house to keep an eye out for Chapman. As it turned out, Chapman was staying at the same hotel and was spotted visiting the house.

When Chapman left the hotel the next morning, Sunday, January 18, 1925, the two detectives on the stakeout immediately called police headquarters and reported the bandit was on the move. One detective waited for reinforcements while the other tailed Chapman. Within minutes Captain Puckett arrived at the hotel with another officer, and they began searching the area for their quarry, whom they spotted a few minutes later walking down the street. The cops pulled to the curb, and as they approached Chapman, one of the lawmen, hoping to catch him off guard, asked if he knew where a certain doctor's office was located. Realizing what was happening, Chapman went for his gun and was able to fire one ineffectual shot before being punched in the mouth and subdued. A search of his person turned up close to $5,000 in cash, two bottles of nitroglycerin, and $3,000 in bonds.[*31]

---

* Another theory holds that he was turned in by someone he trusted. When first arrested he was told he had been double-crossed by a friend.

Other than admitting that he was Gerald Chapman and damning "the man who turned me up for blood money," the bandit said little else to his captors. Knowing his propensity for escape, the detectives transferred him to the Marion County Jail in Indianapolis where federal authorities could take charge. The feds asked him what he had been up to since his escape from Atlanta and questioned him about a number of robberies that had been credited to him. "It doesn't matter what I'm guilty of, or what I'm not," he replied. "I've got twenty-five years to do [referring to his previous sentence], and that means life to me. What is it going to get me if I talk? You've got me; you ought to be satisfied."[32]

The following day Chapman was placed in handcuffs and cuffed to a U.S. marshal, who took the bandit to the police station for new Bertillon pictures and measurements (the Bertillon Method was a rather imperfect system used by police of the period to identify suspected criminals). Once word spread that the most famous criminal in the country was in their station house, virtually the entire Indianapolis police force gathered around to look him over and talk to him. "You get credit for a lot of big robberies in the dispatches. How about them?" one of the officers asked. With a smile, Chapman replied, "Oh, that's customary, giving me credit for everything that happens."

When he learned of the bandit's capture, a Connecticut state's attorney, Hugh Alcorn, a personal friend of then-President Calvin Coolidge, indicted Chapman for the murder of Officer Skelly.[33]

Wearing handcuffs and leg irons, Chapman was escorted to the train station and loaded on board for his trip back to Atlanta. In an attempt to thwart any escape or rescue attempts, every depot the train pulled into was crawling with squads of armed men. The journey went without a hitch, and soon Chapman was once again behind Atlanta's walls and settled into solitary confinement to finish his original sentence.[34] Two weeks later, on February 5, however, things changed dramatically for the bandit.

"I was taken out of my cell one day." Chapman later explained. "In fifteen minutes I was on my way to Connecticut. I had no word from the warden or from anyone." By 8 a.m. the convict was heading north. The following afternoon his train pulled into New York City's Penn Station, and without any fanfare, Chapman and his guards were taken by cab to Grand Central Station, where they had to wait two hours for the train that would take them to Hartford.[35]

February 13 found Chapman in court to hear the indictment against him. Also in court that day was Walter Shean, who had turned state's evidence. Chapman remained cool and paid no particular attention to Shean, who trembled slightly and had tears in his eyes. State's Attorney Alcorn refused to let Chapman plead to the charge and pleaded not guilty on his behalf, meaning that if the jury found against him, the bandit would hang. When asked if he had legal counsel, Chapman replied in "cool, low tones," "Yes, but I have not had an opportunity to consult with him."[36]

On March 24, 1925, the media frenzy that was Chapman's trial began in Hartford. Every day the courthouse was packed with members of the press and spectators straining to hear the parade of witnesses brought in to testify. The coverage was such that *Time* magazine, ranting against the press's tendency to glorify crime, commented, "With the customary exception of the *Christian Science Monitor* and a few others, every newspaper of any dimensions east of the Mississippi set aside one or more columns a day on Page 1 for glowing accounts of the trial . . ."[37]

In the procession of witnesses for the prosecution was the young lady from the car dealership in Steubenville where Chapman had stolen the Lincoln in which Shean was subsequently captured. When asked how she could be sure that Chapman was the man who had come by that night nearly a year earlier, she said, "I remembered him because I thought he was a very unusual customer. He had piercing eyes and high cheekbones and a profile you could never forget." This remark elicited a sly smile from the vain hoodlum. The proprietor and waitress from the Old Colony Inn also were brought in to testify that Chapman had eaten dinner and spent the night there.[38]

The next witness didn't help Chapman's case at all. It was Ben Hance, the man who had put up Chapman and Anderson in Indiana. Hance had made the trip alone because, fearing reprisal from the underworld, Mrs. Hance refused to come with him. She actually called the local police a number of times while her husband was at the trial to say that men were watching her house.[39]

When he arrived in Hartford, Hance said he thought the world of Chapman and was only testifying against him because he had to. Once he was on the stand and face to face with the bandit, he "shrank under Chapman's stony glare." Chapman's stare was unable to quiet Hance, though, because when he was shown the guns and tools used in the New Britain job, he admitted to having seen them in the presence of Chapman and his associates, although he couldn't say for sure to which gang member they belonged.[40]

Shean was placed on the stand and gave the history between Chapman and himself as well as details of the Davison & Levanthal shooting. After his first day of testimony it was reported that a local movie house had shown a newsreel about the case—and that when Chapman appeared on screen the audience broke into cheers and applauded, but when Shean was shown on screen the cheers quickly turned to boos and hisses.

Wrapping up the prosecution's case was a witness who said he had heard the shot and saw Chapman run from the store holding a gun, and two ballistic experts who testified the bullet that killed Skelly had been fired from the same gun found on Chapman when he was captured in Muncie.[41]

It was then the defense's turn. The lawyers brought in two of their own bal-listics experts, who denied that the bullet had been fired from the gun found on Chapman in Muncie. The defense attorneys also brought in the witness from the stable who swore that he had seen Shean and another man enter and exit the department store a number of times, and that the man he had seen with Shean was not Chapman. Shown a picture of Stuyvesant, whom he had picked out of the lineup in New York and who was released after Chapman's capture, the wit-ness once again identified the hoodlum as the man he had seen with Shean.[42]

Chapman took the stand in his own defense, stating that he had been in Brooklyn the weekend of the murder. (Three witnesses had previously testified to this; however, one was a fellow inmate of Chapman's from Atlanta, a fact the prosecution would use against him in summations.) Chapman also said it wasn't uncommon for Shean to use his Lincoln when he wasn't around.[43]

The trial came to a close on April 4, and the twelve male jurors were given their charge and retired to discuss a verdict. When court was reconvened to hear their decision, Chapman rose, holding his hands at his side. "Gentleman of the jury," the judge intoned, "how find you the defendant, guilty or not guilty, as charged in the indictment?" "Guilty of murder in the first degree," the jury fore-man replied. Showing no expression, Chapman simply licked his lips and crossed his arms over his chest.

State's Attorney Alcorn asked that sentence be read immediately, but one of Chapman's lawyers asked for a thirty-minute recess to write a motion to have the verdict set aside. The judge granted his request, and Chapman was led down-stairs by his guards where he was questioned by reporters. "It is what I expected. It was inevitable," he told them, adding, "The jurymen were prejudiced before they went into the jury box by the publicity I have had. The newspapers have made me out a 'super bandit,' an arch-criminal. They have not convicted the accused, but a man named Chapman."

Thirty minutes later Chapman was back in court facing the judge. Chap-man's lawyers submitted their motion to have the conviction set aside, but it was quickly overruled. Chapman was then brought before the judge, who, after making some official statements, turned his eyes to the condemned man and said, "Gerald Chapman, have you anything to say why sentence of death should not be pronounced against you?" In a low voice the bandit replied, "I have noth-ing to say." "The sentence of death is this," the judge continued. "You, Gerald Chapman, are remanded to the custody of the warden of the state prison . . . until the twenty-fifth day of June 1925, upon which day, before the hour of sun-rise, within the prison walls . . . you shall be hanged by the neck until you shall be dead."

Keeping his cool, Chapman did an about-face and started to walk out of the courtroom with his guard. As he passed his lawyers' table he motioned to the hall with his head and said, "Come on." As they were walking out, his primary lawyer, named Groehl, said, "I'm sorry Chappy." "That's all right," Chapman replied. "You did the best you could."[44]

The public was not happy with the outcome of the trial, mostly because they looked on Chapman as an antihero but also because thousands of dollars had been lost on wagers. Bookies were getting two-to-one odds against a first-degree murder conviction. So strong were the feelings for Chapman that the car dealership in Steubenville from which he had stolen the Lincoln, and whose employee had testified against him, was set on fire.[45]

Ben Hance, who became a trial favorite, couldn't gush enough about his relationship with the condemned man. "I don't know whether you can imagine Chappy feeding chickens on an Indiana farm, but that is what he did many times," he said. Basking in the attention, he went on to describe how helpful Chapman had been around the house and also lent credence to Chapman's literary attributes by mentioning that "the man was a steady reader. He read every book in my house." He concluded by saying, "No one can ever tell me that the man I knew as Tom Miller on my farm out in Indiana should be hung. He was a right smart man and the finest to me, Mrs. Hance, and the kids that I ever knew. I only testified against him as I had to when the Muncie cops came to get me."[46]

Even the judge who sentenced Chapman to death genuinely seemed to like the bandit. "It is unfortunate that he has not used his obvious natural talents in a better way," he said. "He was a likeable man and, had he worked along different lines, would have been useful to society."[47]

The day after his conviction, more than the usual amount of fan mail arrived for the condemned man, much of it from female admirers and some from anonymous men who said they had committed the crime themselves. Hearing that at one time Chapman had been a Catholic, a man identified as a prominent member of the Catholic Church gave one of Chapman's lawyers a beautifully made crucifix to deliver to the bandit. When presented with it, Chapman looked at it and said, "Very pretty. Will you be good enough to return this to whoever sent it with my sincere thanks. I am not, you know, the repentant thief."[48]

Shean also received some communications, but they were not as benign as those Chapman got. Shean's came in the form of death threats. Although he was in the clear for the murder, he feared being convicted as an accomplice to burglary and sent to prison, where he no doubt knew he would meet a squealer's fate.[49]

As Chapman sat in his cell reading, his lawyers prepared briefs for an appeal and searched for witnesses and evidence that would clear their client in a second trial. They also believed they had a good chance of keeping him from the gallows by arguing that the State of Connecticut had no legal right to put Chapman to death before he finished serving his twenty-five-year term in Atlanta. The lawyers reasoned that the only way their client would be able to get out of serving his federal sentence first would be to have President Coolidge pardon him. And should Chapman receive such a pardon (which was likely because Coolidge was a friend of State's Attorney Alcorn), a precedent already had been established whereby a man had the right to reject a pardon and serve out his sentence.

Chapman was spared the death chamber that June as the first of his three reprieves was granted. His lawyers now had until December 3, 1925, to make an appeal to the state supreme court.

On August 14, 1925, five months after Chapman was found guilty, Ben Hance and his wife were speeding along a highway five miles southwest of Muncie. Another motorist said the Hance auto seemed to be racing with a coupe. Farther down the road the coupe pulled ahead of the Hances' car and forced it to stop. Both doors of the coupe flew open, and "Dutch" Anderson jumped out of the driver's side while Charles "One Armed" Wolfe jumped out of the other. Ten feet away, the Hances emerged from their car.

A few words were exchanged, and then Anderson and Wolfe raised their pistols. Barefoot, her worst fears being realized, Mrs. Hance began to run. Her horror didn't last long. Before she made it a few feet, a bullet slammed into her head, killing her. Mr. Hance began to wrestle with Anderson, and a few shots were heard before Hance, who had been wounded, jumped over a fence and tried to make a getaway in a cornfield. "Dutch" fired more shots at him, and Hance collapsed after running about twenty-five feet.

The town marshal was called, and when he arrived he found Mr. Hance was still alive. "He stayed at my home. I told on him," the dying man babbled. "They shot me—Charles Wolfe and 'Dutch' Anderson." Hance asked for Detective Puckett from Muncie and was taken to the hospital, where he died a short time later. After the double murder, rumors spread that Hance had not only been a witness at Chapman's trial, but he was also the man who had put the finger on him. It was also rumored that Hance may have cut a deal with Detective Puckett, the man who arrested Chapman, in exchange for exoneration in a larceny case.[50]

When informed by his lawyer that the Hances had been murdered and that Anderson and Wolfe were the prime suspects, Chapman jumped to his friend's defense. "I've known Anderson a long time, and he's incapable of such a rotten deal, particularly after the kind treatment Mrs. Hance accorded Anderson and myself when we stayed with them," he said. He went on to say that he harbored no hard feelings against the couple and understood that Hance had been forced to testify against him because the police had something on him. Chapman suggested that the killers may have been neighbors of the Hances who feared what they could tell the police about their activities.[51]

After the Hance murders, the heat was on to find "Dutch" Anderson. He immediately was blamed for robberies in several of states, and police in Toledo and Detroit said they had come close to nailing him. Although he was credited with bank jobs that netted thousands of dollars, his downfall came as a result of attempting to pass counterfeit money. At the end of October 1925, the bandit, who was known to frequent the finest hotels and restaurants, was in Flint, Michigan, trying to pass some bad money to a keen-eyed shopkeeper. When the clerk realized the bills were bad, Anderson knocked him down and ran from the store.

A week later, on November 2, with a fake bankroll of $2,000, "Dutch" popped into the Lake Michigan shore town of Muskegon and used a fake twenty-dollar bill to purchase a box of candy at a restaurant. The proprietor's wife thought the bill was counterfeit and took it to a nearby bank where her suspicion was confirmed. She then took it to the police station, and Detective Charles Hammond was dispatched to bring in for questioning the man who had given it to her.

The restaurant owner's son pointed out Anderson in a drugstore. Detective Hammond approached him and, tapping him on the shoulder, said, "I want to ask you a few questions. Come with me to headquarters." Anderson made no objections and walked out with the officer. Because of "Dutch's" easygoing disposition, Hammond didn't feel the need to handcuff him for the walk to the police station. But as they were passing an alley, Anderson seized the opportunity and dashed into it. Hammond gave chase, and after a few feet "Dutch" stopped, drew his gun, and fired. The shot missed, and he once again began to run. After a few feet, he stopped, turned, and fired, but his second shot also missed and the chase continued. This sequence was repeated three times.

Finally, as Hammond was gaining on him, Anderson stopped against a wall. As the detective was about to grab him, Anderson fired into his stomach. Mortally wounded, Hammond grabbed the pistol and wrestled it out of the bandit's hands. Anderson jumped over the wounded detective and tried to make a run for it, but Hammond was able to squeeze off two quick shots. The first went through "Dutch's" right hand; the second struck him in the back. One report states that when another officer ran up, Hammond said, "Get him. He got me." At that point, the officer allegedly pumped another bullet into the prostrate bandit.

Anderson was taken back to the police station, where he died, and Hammond was rushed to the hospital, where he succumbed to his wound. Twenty-four hours later, Anderson was identified and one of the biggest manhunts in U.S. history was over.[52]

On November 23, 1925, three weeks after Anderson was killed, President Coolidge officially pardoned Chapman for the Leonard Street mail robbery, which allowed the State of Connecticut to move forward with his execution. Chapman's lawyers again received a stay of execution in order to take the case to the circuit court of appeals in New York City. The court upheld the ruling, which had Chapman's legal team again seeking a reprieve in order to take the case to the U.S. Supreme Court.

They were granted a sixty-day stay, but on March 15, 1926, the Court decided that a federal offense couldn't block an execution for murder, and Chapman's legal team was out of alternatives. April 6, 1926, was the date set for the bandit's execution. When given the news, the condemned man said, "All I can say is that, as Gerald Chapman, I didn't expect anything else, but as a man, I had hopes."[53]

With no more legal maneuvers at his disposal, the only thing Chapman could do to save his life was petition the state Board of Pardons for a commutation of his sentence to life in prison. Nine hours before he was scheduled to hang—and after attorney Groehl had done his best—he was allowed to petition the board himself. Chapman never raised his voice or let the strain of impending death show during his speech. In fact, his plea was more a diatribe about why he felt his trial had been unfair, chiefly because of the overly ambitious efforts of State's Attorney Alcorn. "Mr. Alcorn said I didn't protest my innocence," he railed. "Well, I don't think I could protest loud enough out of solitary confinement to be heard a great distance." Needless to say, the Board of Pardons was not moved by his sarcasm.[54]

Although Chapman was to be hanged, his was not to be a traditional gallows execution. The so-called "super bandit" was going to be the first person executed by the Connecticut State Prison's new state-of-the art hanging machine. A noose would be placed around Chapman's neck, and at the push of a lever, a weight would be released, causing him to be jerked off the ground, breaking his neck.

The execution was the biggest media event in prison history up to that time. A couple of days before it was to occur, the waiting room of a prison official's office was turned over to eight telegraph operators who would tap out an estimated 120,000 words about the hanging. The Postal Telegraph Company and AT&T both strung extra telegraph wires so that newspaper correspondents from throughout the East and Midwest could communicate the details of Chapman's demise.[55]

On the night of April 5 between 1,500 and 2,000 people gathered outside the Connecticut State Prison to await Chapman's execution. One of those on hand was his sister, who tried to gain access to the prison to see the condemned man one last time, but she was turned away. "I am Gerald Chapman's sister. Can't I go in?" she pleaded, but the guard on duty would have none of it, "Yes, and I am Queen Victoria. Go back across the street," he snapped.[56]

At one minute before midnight, about thirty witnesses, half of them newspapermen and half police or prison authorities, were allowed into the death chamber to view the spectacle. At four minutes and ten seconds past midnight on April 6, with his hands bound in front of him, Gerald Chapman entered the death chamber preceded by a priest and flanked by guards. Chapman reportedly wore a slight grin and maintained his cool demeanor as he looked over the witnesses, almost as if searching for someone in particular, perhaps his sister.

Only the sound of pencils scribbling on paper could be heard in the death house. The State of Connecticut forbade final statements by condemned men, so there would be no speaking of any sort. Two guards stepped up behind Chapman and strapped his arms to his side as a third placed a black bag over his head. Next, a noose was placed around his neck and adjusted. Then, with a nod from the deputy warden, the warden pushed the lever with his foot, and Gerald Chapman was jerked twelve feet into the air. Fifteen seconds after entering the room, "the Gentleman Bandit" was dead.[57]

The rope of the hanging machine was slackened at a snail's pace, which resulted in Chapman's corpse swaying back and forth throughout the nearly nine-minute descent before two doctors were able to officially pronounce him dead. His body was then placed in a large wicker basket and sent to a local funeral home. Eight hours later Chapman's lawyers and sister showed up at the funeral parlor and escorted his remains to a nearby cemetery. To throw off reporters, the casket was taken out the back door and placed in a van instead of a hearse. The group then left for the cemetery without fanfare.

To thwart the curious and the macabre, America's number-one bandit was buried in an unmarked grave. As the gravediggers were finishing the hole, the coffin was opened and the mourners took a final look at their brother and client. Chapman's sister then knelt beside the burial spot as the plain oak box was lowered into the ground. Before she could finish her final goodbye, however, a group of photographers came barging into the area. Emotionally distraught, the bandit's sister screamed hysterically and ran from the site to a waiting car.[62] Even in death, Gerald Chapman was a victim of his fame.

LET'S MISBEHAVE

"Outside of this bandit business, I'm a good girl . . . "
— CECILIA COONEY

When Ed and Cecilia Cooney decided to start pulling robberies to get money for their soon-to-be-born child, little did they know that Cecilia would become a national phenomenon. In retrospect it was inevitable; after all, New York City had never known a female bandit. She came on the scene at the perfect time, because women were exerting themselves in American society like never before. In the presidential election of 1920 women voted for the first time, and less than four years later one was running around Brooklyn with a gun, putting the fear of God into men. And if that weren't audacious enough, she also had bobbed hair—and even may have smoked! Welcome to the Roaring Twenties, where hemlines rose and nineteenth-century sensibilities fell.

Though the jobs the Cooneys pulled didn't earn them much money, the publicity they received was worth millions. During their crime spree people couldn't wait to discover this Jazz Age she-bandit's true identity. If one couldn't find a story on the real "Bobbed-Haired Bandit," there probably was one on the many impersonators—both male and female—who tried their luck at the robbery game during the four months the Cooneys kept the Brooklyn police running in circles. After their capture, a New York daily newspaper paid Cecilia $1,000 to write her personal story while she sat in prison waiting to learn her fate. Since gunmen were a dime a dozen, no one cared what Ed had to say, so it is Cecilia's version of events that fills out the story.

Like the majority of the New Yorkers who chose a life of crime, Cecilia Roth was born into poverty, in her case, in Greenwich Village in 1904. By the age of fourteen she was living on her own and supporting herself by working long hours at a box factory until she took a job at a laundry. Although the job meant being on her feet from 8 a.m. until 5:30 p.m., it provided her with an extra $3 a week, upping her weekly take-home pay to $15. She stayed at the laundry for two years before taking a less strenuous job at a lightbulb factory, and although that job was easier for her, her take-home pay was reduced to $12 a week.[1]

In early 1923 Cecilia met Ed Cooney through a friend, and a relationship soon blossomed. After a short engagement the couple was married on May 18, 1923, and moved into a furnished room. Even though he had a police record, Ed had gone straight and was making $30 a week as a welder. He told Cecilia that he didn't want his wife working, so she quit her job. The couple managed to get by on Ed's wages, but that fall Cecilia learned she was pregnant, and the additional expenses that were sure to come began to weigh heavy on their minds.

The thought that their baby would be born in a small furnished flat didn't sit well with the Cooneys, especially Cecilia, who had grown up with nothing and desperately wanted to buy what every mother with means bought for their babies. Day after day Ed read newspaper accounts of the many robberies taking place in the city, and one night he told his wife, "Look here, Cecilia, I've been thinking about how we might get more money, and there's one way, all right, we might do it." He went on to say that many people were making loads of money by pulling holdups, and that if they could pull off a couple of high-paying ones, they would be all set. Cecilia didn't have to be asked twice.[2]

At first the couple only talked about it, but once their minds were made up, Ed went about setting them up for the crime spree. The first order of business was obtaining guns. Ed already owned a .25-caliber automatic, which he gave to Cecilia, and he went to a couple of stores in Brooklyn to buy more weapons, but they wouldn't sell him any. His luck wasn't any better in the Bowery, where he was turned down by a pawnshop proprietor. However, a man in the shop overheard their conversation, followed Ed outside, then took him into a doorway and sold him two pistols.[3]

The couple decided they would rob groceries and drugstores. To prepare, Cecilia read crime magazines to pick up the correct lingo that would help her in her role—basically traditional phrases like "Stick 'em up quick!" Once Ed got back home with his new hardware, the couple conducted some rehearsals in their flat. Ed stood behind the table posing as a clerk, and Cecilia walked up and asked for a dozen eggs. While Ed pretended to get the eggs, his wife pulled out the automatic and let loose with her bandit jargon.[4]

Transportation to and from the jobs wouldn't be a problem. Since Ed was a good employee, his boss let him keep keys to the garage and allowed him to use the company car. On several nights the couple drove around looking for an easy target.[5]

On the night of January 5, 1924, Ed went to the garage and picked up the car. He returned for Cecilia, and they cruised the streets looking at different shops to rob before deciding on the Roulston grocery store. Looking in the window, they saw there were only clerks inside, no customers. They also looked up and down the block and saw very few people walking around.

So, according to their plan, Cecilia walked into the store first, approached the manager, who was near the register, and ordered a dozen eggs. While the clerk was getting them, Ed walked in and stood a little behind his wife. As the clerk pushed the eggs across the counter toward her, Cecilia took a couple of steps back, drew her .25, and shouted, "Stick 'em up quick!"

The shocked manager at first remained still but then raised his hands as ordered. At this point, the robbery almost stalled because Cecilia didn't know what to do next. However, Ed, who was holding a pistol in each hand, jumped into action, yelling for the clerks to go to the back of the store. Once the men had been herded to the rear, Ed told his wife to cover them while he rifled the register and the safe, which was conveniently open. Having control over the six clerks sent Cecilia on a power trip.

"For once in my life I was boss," she said later. "Here were six of them, afraid to move, afraid to do anything except what I told them. And they so big and me so little."[6] After Ed filled his pockets he yelled to the clerks, "Don't any of you make a move! And if you want your head blown off, just try to follow us out." None of the clerks felt the need to test Ed's resolve. Cecilia walked out first and jumped in the car, then Ed piled in over her, put the car in gear, and pulled away.

The couple drove in silence for a while until Cecilia couldn't take it anymore and whispered, "Was it all right, Ed?" Her husband reached over and patted her on the knee. "Sure, kid," he told her, "you're a peach." After making guesses about how much their heist had netted, they returned the car to Ed's workplace and then went home.[7]

When they arrived, they slid a chair under the knob of the front door and covered the window before Ed dumped the loot onto the bed and began to count it. Excited, he got mixed up and had to start over, but the final count was $688. That Monday, he took a half-day off and the couple went out and found a nice apartment. The day after that, Ed took more time off and he and Cecilia went shopping for furniture. Like kids in a candy store, they went overboard and ordered a dining room set, bedroom set, a sideboard, and everything else a house needs. They managed to rack up a thousand-dollar bill and decided to put some money down and pay off the rest in monthly installments.[8]

About a week after the move and spending spree, the Cooneys realized they couldn't keep up their new lifestyle on $30 a week. Ed was the first to broach the subject of pulling another job. "You saw how easy it was," he said. "But we didn't get enough; we got to do it again. Maybe we can get a big roll, and then we'll quit and be square." Once again, Cecilia didn't have to be asked twice. "Sure, Ed, it's all right, whatever you say."[9]

The following Saturday, January 12, found the couple once again patrolling the Brooklyn streets looking for another target. Before long Ed pulled up in front of an A & P store. "This'll do," he said. This time they walked in together, but Ed stayed toward the back as Cecilia went up to the counter and ordered a dozen eggs.

This job mirrored their previous one; the only difference was that there were two older customers, a man and his wife, in the store. When Ed pulled out his guns and ordered everyone to the rear, the woman, who was hard of hearing, had to ask her husband what was going on. When he told her a robbery was in progress, she decided that she didn't want to be involved and attempted to leave. Ed politely, yet firmly, stopped her and made her join the rest of the hostages. Once again Cecilia covered everyone while her husband rifled the cash register. When he'd emptied it, they exited the store, got back into the car, and drove away.

There had been no safe at the store, and after driving a few minutes, Ed said, "Kid, we didn't get much that time—less than a hundred dollars, it looked to me [the official amount was listed as $113]. We got plenty of time and everything is set. Let's try another." About twenty minutes later they pulled up in front of another grocery store and repeated their routine. This time their take was $250.[10]

After the two robberies the Cooneys went home to bed. As he had done the previous Sunday, Ed went out to buy some newspapers. The first week's heist had received a small write-up, but after the back-to-back robberies the media coverage was much different. The papers were all talking about the "Bobbed-Haired Bandit," some calling her "a dope fiend" and the "leader of an underworld gang."

Cecilia thrived on the attention. "I danced around the room," she said later. "Who'd have ever thought that little old Cecilia Cooney, working in a laundry at twelve dollars a week, would be all over the front pages of the newspapers like that! Gee! I felt big!"[11]

Ed, however, wasn't exuding the same enthusiasm, and Cecilia figured he was upset because he wasn't getting the same attention she was in the papers. Ed was relegated to "male companion," and not much was being said about him. Sensing he was jealous, Cecilia began to kid him, but he let her know the real reason he was so morose: one of the newspaper stories said the police had been issued orders to shoot to kill. Cecilia's elation quickly subsided, and then she threw up. Perhaps it was pregnancy hormones, because a few hours later she was dancing around again.[12]

Whatever fear the two may have had was trumped by their desire for easy money. Three days later, on January 15, they robbed a drugstore. Since Ed had had trouble opening some of the cash registers during their earlier heists, Cecilia walked to the counter and asked for change to make a phone call. When the clerk opened the register, she drew her gun and demanded cash. This robbery netted about $60.[13]

In their haste to put an end to the publicity-generating crimes, the police arrested a woman named Helen Quigley and declared that the "Bobbed-Haired Bandit" mystery was over. Ed and Cecilia didn't mind one bit. They figured this would take the heat off of them and that Quigley would never be convicted. However, witnesses from some of the early capers identified her as the woman who had robbed them, so things didn't look good for Ms. Quigley. The Cooneys decided they couldn't stand by while an innocent girl took the rap for their crimes, so they wrote a letter to the police:

> Leave this innocent girl alone, and get the right one which is nobody but us. We are going to give Mr. Hogan manager of Roulston's on Seventh Avenue another visit, as we got two checks we couldn't cash. Also ask Mr. Bohack's manager did I ruin his cash register. I will visit him again as I broke a perfectly good automatic on it. We defy you fellows to catch us.

Because the letter mentioned specifics about the heists that only the real robbers would have known, Quigley was exonerated.[14]

Meanwhile, the Cooneys continued their work and on January 20 pulled a job that netted them $160. They pulled three more holdups over the course of the next month that brought in just under $100 apiece. By this time, the Brooklyn police had established a "Bobbed-Haired Bandit" squad, and since grocery stores were the main target, undercover men were stationed in and around the local food markets.

Realizing this, the Cooneys switched tactics. On March 4 they robbed a man of cash and jewelry worth either $1,100 or $1,500, depending on the news source. The victim, Louis Pfeiffer, a restaurateur, had just put his car in the garage, and when he turned toward the street the couple was waiting for him. Cecilia placed her gun in his side and ordered him to put up his hands and keep them up as Ed helped himself to his watch and chain, diamond stickpin, diamond ring, and $300 in cash. Pfeiffer went to the police and made a report, and his descriptions matched others that witnesses had given but added another intriguing element. He was fairly certain that the woman who had held him at gunpoint was pregnant.[15]

All during the crime spree Ed continued working at the garage from 7 a.m. to 5 p.m. Each morning on his way to work he would stop by his mother's home for coffee. "We talked about the 'Bobbed-Haired Bandit,'" she would say later, "and he joked about her and said that she was 'pretty slick.'"[16]

On March 6 the Cooneys hit a drugstore, and this proved to be their most nerve-racking stickup. They looked inside the store and it appeared to be empty, but right across the street was an armory where 150 police reservists were drilling. Deciding it was too risky, the couple pulled around the corner to talk things over but after a few moments decided to go ahead with the crime. Five minutes later they pulled up to the pharmacy, left the car running as usual, and went inside. This time, though, they switched roles.

"Let me have a tube of your best toothpaste," Ed said to the proprietor. When the man turned to get the paste, Ed whipped out his pistol and told him, "Well, never mind the toothpaste. Stick up your hands and keep them up." He then ordered the owner to the rear of the store.

Ed noticed two telephone booths in the store, each occupied by a woman, that he and Cecilia hadn't seen from the street. He tapped on the glass and made the women join the owner in the back. Cecilia then appeared with two guns and covered the women as Ed ordered the proprietor to open the safe. At this point, two men walked in off the street and Cecilia quickly herded them into the back room with the others. When the man finally opened the safe, there was nothing in it of value, so Ed then went for the cash register.

As he was working on the register, the owner's wife came downstairs from their apartment above the store. At gunpoint, she too was forced to join the others in the back. Ed pocketed the dough and Cecilia told the captives, "The first person to make a sound before twenty minutes will die." Hurrying out the door, she joined Ed in the car and they drove off.

The take amounted to a measly $35 for this job, despite all the trouble. The big losers, however, were the police. Once again the "Bobbed-Haired Bandit" had foiled hundreds of officers and pulled a heist right under the noses of 150 of them. After this raid the Cooneys felt Brooklyn had become too hot, so they took a break. They informed the police of their hiatus with another letter:[17]

> We are taking a vacation. But we'll be back on the job again. And if any cops interfere we will shoot them.[18]

The Cooneys went to Falls River, Massachusetts, and then to Boston. Perhaps more than Cecilia, Ed realized that their days as bandits were numbered. While lamenting their predicament to Cecilia one night, he told her, "We got to pull one more big one, careful and different and then blow." As usual his wife complied, "All right, Ed, anything you say."[19]

The plan was to rob the National Biscuit Company, which was right down the street from where they lived. The couple returned to New York City and took a room at the Times Square Hotel in Manhattan, signing the register as Mr. and Mrs. Parker from Boston. They had decided to take their expected windfall from the National Biscuit Company and flee by boat to Jacksonville, Florida, where Ed had spent some time when he was in the Navy. He felt the couple could do well there. They bought tickets for the trip, and then Ed called a touring-car service and ordered a chauffeured limousine, which they intended to use to reconnoiter the area.

The limo arrived and the driver was a rather large man named Arthur West. The Cooneys told him they wanted to see the Brooklyn Bridge and tour some of the borough in general. West drove them to Brooklyn, and they told him to pull over near the National Biscuit Company. Ed got out and walked around a bit, looking inside the building and getting a lay of the land. When he returned to the car Cecilia asked him what he thought. "It's all right, I guess, but there's a lot of people in that office, a lot of clerks and a lot of Janes pounding on typewriters."

They told West to drive to Prospect Park where, unbeknownst to the chauffeur, his clients were looking for a secluded place where they could waylay him and steal the limo before pulling the heist. Cecilia couldn't help but feel important riding in the back of the touring car:[20]

> It was fine, going through Brooklyn that way—me now riding in a limousine where I used to work in a laundry.[21]

After seeing everything they needed to see in Brooklyn, the Cooneys returned to their hotel in Manhattan. They decided the best thing to do with West was to tie him up and keep him in the back seat while they knocked over the biscuit company. Ed went out and bought some rope so Cecilia could practice tying him up. Although the rope was strong, it proved to be too thick and Ed managed to slip out each time without much trouble. He went out again and bought some picture wire, and when Cecilia tied him up this time the wire cut into him as he struggled to get free. Now they were all set.[22]

The next day, April 1, 1924, when West picked them up, the couple told him they wanted to return to Prospect Park. When they arrived at the designated location Ed tapped on the glass and told the driver to stop. Cooney got out and, after looking around to ensure that nobody else was around, drew a gun and stuck it in the driver's side. He told West to get in the rear with Cecilia and then joined them. Since West was a bit rotund and Ed was no slouch himself, the rear passenger compartment was pretty crowded. Cecilia tried to tie the chauffeur's hands behind his back, but he was so big she had to tie them together in front of him. West was forced to lie on the floorboard while Ed tied his legs together.

Once the driver was taken care of, Ed climbed into the front seat and headed for the National Biscuit Company. With West trussed up on the floorboard there was nowhere else for Cecilia to put her feet but on the captive driver. This afforded the she-bandit one more power trip:

> I had to move my feet so he could turn and I got to looking down at my own feet. I had on new high-heeled pumps and pretty stockings and they looked so little with him all hunched there that I thought how funny it would be if I put one of them on his neck like Cleopatra I once saw in the movies. And the more I thought of it, the more I couldn't help doing it, so I put one foot easy and rested it right on his neck, and then I pressed the heel down a little, but not enough to hurt him.[23]

The bandits soon arrived at the biscuit company and both jumped out of the limo. "You stay here and watch this guy, and if he opens his mouth, you know what," Ed told his wife. This was a bluff, because they were both going inside for the robbery.

Cecilia entered first, followed by Ed. This was Cecilia's first look inside the building, and she was a little concerned because it was a lot bigger than she was expecting and there were many people around. She was starting to wonder if they would be able to pull off the robbery when a clerk approached. Cecilia asked to see the cashier, and when he arrived she handed him an envelope, which contained a blank piece of paper. As he opened the envelope, Cecilia drew her gun and Ed pulled out his two pistols and barked at the crowd, "Hands up, everyone, and make it snappy!"

The employees quickly complied and the bandits began to herd them into a small room. While Cecilia continued getting everyone into the room, Ed went for the safe but found nothing of value ($5,000 had been removed and placed *under* the safe until it could be delivered to the bank). As the last of the clerks began to enter the room, he made a grab for Cecilia's gun. They wrestled for a moment and then the girl bandit fell over backwards and fired a shot. The clerk quickly jumped into the room with his colleagues and pulled the door shut.

Hearing the shot, Ed ran over and saw his wife on the floor and the door closing. He fired two shots through the door, and both he and Cecilia heard a man scream. Ed went to help his wife up, but she assured him she was OK and they both walked out to the car and drove away. Little did they know that when Cecilia fell she dropped a little black book containing the addresses where she had lived.[24]

Frightened and afraid they had committed murder, the Cooneys drove to a subway stop and ditched the car, with West still tied up in the back, and caught a train to the city. They went straight to the pier and boarded the boat that would take them to Florida, and didn't come out of their cabin once during the entire trip. The Cooneys arrived in Jacksonville with less than $50. Grabbing a cab, they asked the driver to take them to a boarding house, and he delivered them to a dump worse than any place they'd ever lived in New York.[25]

The botched robbery and sudden departure marked the beginning of the end for the Cooneys. Witnesses agreed that the "Bobbed-Haired Bandit" was indeed pregnant, and the police now had Cecilia's book of addresses and began to trace the couple. And if this weren't enough, another clue fell into the cops' lap.

The day after the National Biscuit fiasco, John Schwartz popped into the police department to file a complaint. He said that when he went to the Cooneys' apartment to collect the April installment on the furniture he had sold them, he found the place vacant. The detectives went to the apartment, and the landlady told them the couple had moved out in a hurry on March 31, and that Cecilia was going to have a baby.[26*] When the Cooneys signed for the furniture, Ed had given his mother as reference and Cecilia had listed her previous landlord. The detectives visited Cecilia's landlady first.

The landlady, Mrs. Gallagher, didn't have many nice things to say about her former tenant. She said that she was sure Cecilia had stolen $20 from her purse and a silver picture frame worth $40. As a consequence, Mrs. Gallagher was more than happy to give police a photo she had of Cecilia.

Investigators dug up Ed's police file, and when they showed his mug shot and the picture of Cecilia to the witnesses in the National Biscuit Company heist, they all agreed the Cooneys were the bandits.[27] Their next stop was Ed's mom's house, but when detectives questioned her she said she had no idea where her son and his wife were. She said Ed had stopped in two days earlier and said the cops were after him and that he and Cecilia were leaving town. She said Ed had told her he hadn't done anything but that the cops were going to lock him up for months on suspicion. The detectives put a twenty-four-hour watch on Mrs. Cooney's apartment and started a waiting game.[28]

On April 10 Cecilia began having severe pain, but they were afraid to go to the hospital. After a while Ed thought his wife was dying, and he got a neighbor woman to stay with her while he went to fetch a doctor. The doctor admitted Cecilia to a sanitarium where she gave birth, about a month prematurely, to a baby girl on April 12. Since the couple didn't have any money, Cecilia was forced to leave after two days. They ended up in a new rooming house that was even worse than the first one.[29]

---

* There was no shortage of clues. Someone who knew Ed from the neighborhood saw him running out of the biscuit company, and a neighbor who had seen the couple with a large wad of bills had actually contacted police earlier, but the tip was never followed up.

Any thoughts the new parents might have had about going straight were dashed on April 16 when Ed picked up a newspaper and made a beeline back home. There on the front page were both their names and pictures. The Brooklyn police had cracked the case and sent wanted circulars throughout the country. Hospitals had been alerted that Cecilia was expecting a baby, and police were told that Ed may seek work at garages.[30] The next day, desperate for cash, Ed wired his mother:

> Baby is sick STOP Send money to Sheehan 514 Ocean Avenue Jacksonville Fla. — Ed[31]

The message, sent in vain as the baby died that same day and was buried two days later, never reached Mrs. Cooney. When the telegraph delivery man showed up to the apartment, the detective on duty went up, flashed his badge, and seeing that the message was for Ed's mom, signed for it.[32]

Authorities in Jacksonville were notified that the famed "Bobbed-Haired Bandit" and her "companion" were in their city and that New York City detectives would be down on the next train. The next evening Detectives Gray and Casey arrived and were greeted by the local police. They immediately went to the boarding house on Ocean Avenue and surrounded it.

Gray and Casey went to the front door and rang for the landlady. When she answered, they said they wanted to see the Sheehans. The landlady told the detectives their baby had died the previous day and that they had moved out. They contacted the undertaker who had buried the infant and were sent to the sanitarium where Cecilia had given birth, where they obtained the couple's new address. At 1 a.m. on April 21 police surrounded the house and the detectives rang the bell. The housekeeper opened up and the police showed her the pictures of the Cooneys and said they wanted to speak to the Sheehans. "One flight up, in the rear apartment," she told them.[33]

The detectives made their way upstairs, and as they stood outside the Cooneys' apartment they could hear Ed talking. They knocked on the door and shouted, "Police! Open up!" There was no response, but they heard rustling noises inside. As the cops began to break down the door, Ed told Cecilia that he should kill her and then himself, but she quickly talked him out of it. The detectives burst in with guns at the ready, and the Cooneys had theirs in hand as well. "Don't shoot and we won't," Cecilia said. The detectives ordered the couple to drop their guns, and they complied.

Ed and Cecilia were allowed to dress and were taken to police headquarters, where they were questioned about the shooting at the National Biscuit Company. Both took credit for shooting the employee, hoping to spare the other from the electric chair. But once it was learned that the clerk would survive,

Cecilia admitted that it was her husband who had fired the shots that wounded the man.[34]

The Cooneys waived extradition and were soon headed back to New York with the arresting detectives. On the way the bandit couple confessed to most of their jobs, which pleased the detectives, who told them that they would get lighter sentences if they confessed and didn't bother with a trial.[35]

After news of the arrests spread, Cecilia's previous landlords were interviewed. It appears that Ed was always well liked but his wife was not. Her harshest critic was the aforementioned Mrs. Gallagher, who accused Cecilia of stealing from her. "I didn't like the girl, for she was too bold," she said, "but I did like Mr. Cooney and I'm sure now his wife had a bad influence on him."[36]

Ed's mother didn't go as far to blame everything on Cecilia, but she staunchly defended her son as she tearfully told reporters:

> "I don't believe he did it. I don't believe it. . . . Eddie was always a good boy. . . . I didn't know he was going to get married until a few days before the wedding when he told me he was going to marry a very nice girl. . . . I told him I was not pleased because she is a German girl and I would liked him to marry one of his own kind because he is an Irish-American boy. I have only seen his wife three or four times, not often enough to know whether or not I like her."[37]

When the public learned which train was carrying the famed "Bobbed-Haired Bandit," a large mob was on hand trying to get a look at the she-bandit and her "companion" when they pulled into the station in Philadelphia. This was only a precursor of what awaited them at New York City's Pennsylvania Station. Realizing she was going to be the center of attention, Cecilia asked and was permitted to doll herself up as much as possible.[38] At about 11 a.m. the train pulled in and thousands of people crowded the platform hoping to catch a glimpse of New York's most notorious gun girl. Just prior to their arrival, President Coolidge had left the station, and although a crowd had come to see the president, Cecilia drew a much larger audience.[39]

A cordon of cops cleared a path and flash bulbs popped like crazy as Cecilia was escorted off the train. At first the young girl appeared nervous amid the crush of the mob and the blinding lights, but once the crowd got a look at her they began to cheer. Cecilia's disposition quickly changed and she smiled and had something smart to say to anyone who had a question for her.

"Why did you start this thing?" a detective asked. "There was no one to stop me," she quipped. "There were ten thousand of you, and look how long it took you to get me." When asked what she thought would happen next, she said, "I may get out this week and then I'll go to the circus." Asked about the death of her baby, she replied, "Too bad."[40] Her flippant responses didn't win her any fans. In fact, her cavalier attitude so soon after the baby's demise made her appear cold and uncaring. Cecilia would address this in an exposé that would later appear in the *New York American*:

> Just the same I smiled and kidded. And some of those sob sisters said I was hard boiled. What did they want me to do? Bust out crying on their shoulders, maybe and tell them the sad story of my life so they could write it down? Just the same I got some pride, and that's why I smiled and kidded.[41]

The detectives battled through the crowds and finally got the Cooneys into a cab, but before they could take off for Brooklyn a young man ran up waving a piece of paper that turned out to be a writ of habeas corpus. "Who the hell are you?" one of the detectives demanded. "I'm Samuel Liebowitz, their attorney."[42] The lawyer and the lawmen argued for a bit, and Liebowitz finally convinced them that they would be breaking the law if they returned to Brooklyn, so they went to the Manhattan District Attorney's Office. At the court Liebowitz began to argue for his clients, saying, "Your Honor, this girl has a perfectly good and substantial defense, even though she did commit these robberies. If what a Jacksonville man said is true, this girl has a perfectly legal defense. We want him as a witness and want to tell our own story to twelve men in open court."[43]

The prosecution answered with, "We understand, Your Honor, that the defendants have no counsel." The judge asked the Cooneys if they had hired Liebowitz, and both said no. Then they were asked if they wanted him for a lawyer, and again both said no. Case closed. Liebowitz pulled out a document saying that he had been hired by Ed's brother, but nobody paid him any attention.[44]

Ed and Cecilia were finally taken to Brooklyn where another mob awaited, albeit not as big as the one at Penn Station nor as benign. There was no cheering or applause this time, just catcalls and rude comments.[45] Once inside the courtroom, they came face to face with their victims. Nathan Mazzo, the National Biscuit Company employee whom Ed had wounded, came in and placed his hand on Cecilia's shoulder. "That's the 'Bob-Haired Bandit,' all right," he said. The Cooneys smiled at each other and Cecilia spoke up. "Mazzo, I'm sorry you were shot. It was all a mistake," she said. A female witness to the robbery came in and, seeing Cecilia, said, "You're the girl who held us up." Cecilia responded, "You're right. I'm the famous 'Bobbed-Haired Bandit.'"[46]

While the Cooneys sat in prison waiting to be sentenced, Cecilia signed a contract with the *New York American* and was paid $1,000 (more than they made during their crime spree in their estimation) to tell her life story. Nobody was interested in what Ed had to say. Just before her life story went to press, the Cooneys began to rethink their guilty pleas, and Cecilia summoned Sam Liebowitz. At first the counselor was reluctant because of the way he previously had been dismissed, but he agreed to see her. After a couple of days and a few meetings with the lawyer, Cecilia petitioned the court to change her plea to not guilty by reason of temporary insanity. After consulting with Liebowitz she justified her change of heart, telling reporters, "I was rushed off my feet. I had no time to think or to consider what to do. I hardly knew what was being said to me or what I was doing. From the time I was placed under arrest until I was committed to jail, I was never left alone a minute."[47]

The court denied Cecilia's request because the couple had willfully turned down the chance for legal counsel when they were arrested. The judge had also questioned them privately afterward to make sure they wanted to enter guilty pleas. Psychiatrists, however, were brought in to determine if Ed and Cecilia were in fact mentally impaired. This put off their sentencing for a little more than a week.[48]

On April 28, 1924, the first installment of Cecilia's life story hit the streets. In it she owned up to her actions but made no apologies for why she committed her nefarious deeds:

> When I went into that first store and said, "Stick 'em up," I wasn't seeing diamond ear rings and gin and jazz and a good time—I was thinking of pretty little pink shoes, pink leather baby shoes like I saw once in a window . . . and I was thinking, If I can get away with a big wad once and quit, maybe this baby that's coming won't have the rough time I had.[49]

From the get-go, Cecilia used her unborn baby as an excuse for her crimes. After speaking with her, the warden of the Raymond Street Jail, where she was being held, commented, "Her statement that she embarked on a criminal career to get money for an expected baby is not convincing. From talks I've had with her I believe she is a product of poverty and that a desire for fine things inspired her to join her husband in these robberies."[50]

Using her exposé to gain public support and sympathy, Cecilia claimed that she was a good girl with few bad habits:

> So help me, I've never had a drink or smoked a cigarette. . . .[51]

It was reported, however, that both she and Ed had smoked a great deal on the train ride into town,[52] and while shooting the breeze with reporters a few days before here saga was released to the public, she said to photographers who asked here to pose for some pictures. "What's in it for me?" When one of them offered her $25, she laughed him off, saying, "Piker, that's only cigarette money."[53]

For the first time Cecilia also started talking about her past and her parents. She said she had been born on the Upper East Side and added:

> My father was Michael Roth, a truck driver. He was an honest man. He worked hard for poor pay. My mother was Anna Roth. She couldn't work outside the home. She worked hard enough at home, having nine babies.[54]

She also went on about the hard life the family had led, but after her sisters started working and bringing home some money things started to get better. Unfortunately, however:

> Papa got sick and had to quit worker, mama got sicker. Why string it out? In six months of each other they both died.[55]

Any sympathy gained from the story of her parents' tragic deaths was lost about a week later when they turned up very much alive. "Well, what of it?" Cecilia retorted when told they had been found. "Isn't there enough disgrace on my family without dragging my old mother and father into it, too?"[56] They had not seen Cecilia in four years, and most likely their daughter lied not to spare them any embarrassment but because she was embarrassed by them and by her childhood. When the backgrounds of her father and mother, now fifty-nine and fifty-four, respectively were checked, it was found that Cecilia had been born not on the Upper East Side but in an East Village basement. Her father was hardly the hardworking truck driver she claimed; he was an alcoholic who hardly worked at all. Any money that came into the household was provided by Cecilia's mother, or, sadly, by the Roth children who were forced to go out on the streets and beg.[57]

Michael Roth had been arrested a number of times before Cecilia's birth for being a drunk and a lousy parent. There were times when the Roth children were given clothes by charities only to have their parents sell them.[58]

At the age of four, Cecilia was taken from her mother and father by the Children's Society of New York. She was returned to her mother on December 17, 1908. Neighbors soon found the young girl abandoned in the furnished room where her mother had left her three days before. After this episode she was sent to live with an aunt in Brooklyn. Several times her mother picked Cecilia up and took her into Manhattan, where she would sell her daughter's clothes and send her back to the aunt in rags.[59]

With the true story of her life now available for public consumption, one wonders what would have happened if Cecilia had said yes when she first arrived in New York and was asked if she wanted Sam Liebowitz as her lawyer. Between her unpleasant upbringing and her pregnancy, it's not hard to imagine a jury letting her off the hook.

In subsequent installments of her biography, Cecilia left out some things that wouldn't reflect well on her. Whereas she spoke of being on her own at a young age and working hard jobs, she failed to mention that she was on her own because she had moved out of her sister's house at the age of sixteen because her older sibling was critical of her staying out late with and bringing home sailors.[60]

When it came to Ed, Cecilia said they had started going together around October 1922, but when the police initially identified the couple as the bandits and Cecilia's previous landlords were interviewed, it was learned that she had rented a room with a man named Bill Cherison, who posed as her husband, from March 1922 until April 1923, a month before she married Ed. Bill actually didn't live there; he just stopped by every night from about 8 to 11 p.m. The family that ran the boarding house thought it odd that Cecilia's husband didn't stay the night but figured it had to do with his work. Plus they really liked Bill. He brought the kids nuts and dried fruit and took the father fishing. Sometimes the couple would go out and sometimes they would stay in Cecilia's room and listen to jazz records and dance.[61] Since Cherison and the sailors didn't really fit well with the image Cecilia was trying to portray, she understandably left them out of her life story.

On May 6, 1924, the Cooneys arrived at court to receive their sentences. Each got ten years. Cecilia's parents showed up at court, but she either didn't see them or ignored them. As she and Ed were walking to the van that was going to take them back to jail, Cecilia spotted one of her sisters and told her to claim her seal skin coat from the cops. Someone in the crowd asked Cecilia how she felt. "Fine," she responded. She was asked about her parents, said she didn't see them, and didn't respond when she was asked if she wanted to. Ed told her to keep quiet, but Cecilia continued to wave and yell goodbye to the crowd as the van pulled away.

Back at the jail Cecilia was asked about the sentencing. "I expected the limit and I got it," she said. "I was not disappointed. I thought the judge would give me a lecture, but he didn't. I deserve what I got." One reporter even thought to ask Ed for his opinion. "I'm glad it's all over," he said. "I liked the way the judge spoke. I'm glad he didn't bawl us out. We were treated all right all the way through. Both of us are going to start all over again when we get out."[62]

When they were back in their cells Cecilia seemed to understand that the ride was almost over and that ten years in prison was a reality. The normally vivacious young woman broke into tears and refused to see anyone.[63]

With their departures for prison looming, Cecilia sent a letter to the warden of the Raymond Street Jail asking that she be allowed to see Ed one more time before he left for Sing Sing, saying:

> I know that seeing me smile before he leaves will make him feel a bit better. He loves to see me smile. It will help to keep him up.[64]

The warden allowed the Cooneys one more visit on May 8, the day Cecilia was to depart for Auburn Prison. As it turned out, Cecilia was the one who needed help "keeping up." Her mother arrived to say goodbye, and all the young bandit could do was weep. The scene was repeated when a sister arrived to say goodbye as well. The warden then came in and told Cecilia that the keeper and matron from Auburn had arrived for her, and once again the flood gates opened. He kept his word, though, and brought Ed in so they could say their farewells.

Husband and wife at first just stared before running into each other's arms and crying. Ed spoke first, saying, "It'll be a long, long time, a long time before I see you. But we got to make the best of it." Cecilia tried to work up a smile but only cried instead. "Yes, we got to," she said, "but the time ain't going to be so long, Ed. We'll soon be together." After this, they went off into a corner and kissed and cried some more until the warden informed Cecilia that it was time to go. Cecilia insisted that the $980 remaining from her newspaper money be given to Ed or at least held for him, and as she was being escorted away, she managed to smile one more time.[65]

Cecilia was taken from Brooklyn to Manhattan and spent the night in the Jefferson Market Jail before heading to Auburn on May 9. Her departure was kept a secret, and the throngs that had been on hand to greet her when she arrived in the city a few short weeks before were absent. Later that afternoon Ed was transferred to Sing Sing to start his sentence.[66]

The next day the final installment of Cecilia's life story ran in the *American* and she summed up her predicament with:

> It's easy to be sorry and figure out how wrong you were, when everything is too late.[68]

Ma Flanagan's Boys

*"I class them [the Flanagan brothers] as the toughest,
bravest outlaws I ever had the misfortune to meet."*
— Captain Cornelius Willemse, NYPD

Known as the Four Fierce Flanagans, brothers Tom, Frank, Marty, and the youngest of the quartet, "Baby" Joey, were a gang of desperadoes who operated with various other gang members in New York and New Jersey to pull off a number of robberies. They were best described by New York Detective Cornelius Willemse, who, in his memoir, *Behind the Green Lights*, remembered them as "real hard, tough men, that quartet, never equaled here or in Chicago in the daring and skill of stickup and payroll raids." Conversely, the *New York Herald* described them as "personable figures, always well dressed and debonair in their bearing."

Tom appears to have been the been the first of the brothers to venture into crime—or at least to get caught at it—and was arrested for robbery in 1909 and sent to the Elmira Reformatory for a stretch of five years. He was released early but arrested again on May 29, 1912, for robbery and sent back. In the years before World War I, Tom became known as an "auto-bandit," a term used at the time to describe robbers who used the relatively new automobile in the commission of their crimes. Although police believed he participated in the robbery of the American Can Company payroll on June 5, 1914, it wouldn't be until the following year that he was arrested and subsequently jailed for an "auto-robbery."

At 11 a.m. on June 8, 1915, Thomas Boyd, superintendent of the Borden Condensed Milk Company, and George Listhardt, the company's cashier, climbed into a buggy along with the week's receipts of $8,500. The pair left the company, which was located in the Bronx at 180th Street and Park Avenue, and headed for the bank. Two blocks down the street, as they passed three men lurking by a footbridge that crossed a railroad ditch, one of the trio grabbed the horse's bridle while the other two charged the buggy.

"Hold up your hands!" one of the men yelled, as the other approached Boyd from behind and struck him over the head, knocking him out of the buggy. Listhardt grabbed the money bag but was struck in the face and also knocked to the street. "I've got the money," the first bandit shouted, and the three hoodlums darted across the bridge as Listhardt began to chase them.

One of the robbers turned and fired two shots at the cashier and then ran toward a large touring sedan. Seeing his confederates coming, the driver, cigar in mouth, calmly got out of the car and turned the crank to start the motor. Two of the bandits jumped into the tonneau, but the third fell down, so his associates jumped out and pulled him inside. Once all were aboard, the sedan roared off but ran into a telephone pole a block away. The vehicle was drivable, but as the driver was pulling away, he clipped a little girl. Although the facts weren't given, Tom and an accomplice were arrested later that night. (In press reports, Tom was identified as James Flanagan.)

On March 10 of the following year Tom was sentenced to twenty years in Sing Sing for the robbery. The Flanagan brothers had good contacts, however, and after Tom had served about two years, he was granted a pardon by New York Governor Al Smith.[2]

Frank was the next Flanagan brother to gain notoriety when he was arrested in June 1919 for murdering bartender Patrick Mulhearn in an uptown saloon. Found guilty, he was shipped off to the Sing Sing death house to await execution. While behind bars Frank gave a little family history, no doubt trying to win some sympathy:

> "I was three years old when I came from Ireland with my mother and father. There were fourteen of us children and two adopted ones. My father was a drinking man. . . . We were very poor, and after I had been to school three years I left at the age of ten and went to work as a wagon boy in a department store."[3]

As Frank's execution date drew near, brother Martin, who in addition to being a thief was also proprietor of the Blue Bird Café where infamous New York

City gangster Monk Eastman met his demise on Christmas 1920, worked tirelessly to get his brother a retrial. Finally, two days before Frank was set to "ride the lightning," he was granted a reprieve and a new trial. Miraculously, Marty had dug up a number of witnesses who swore that Frank had been with them on the night of the murder at a party honoring returning war veterans. Frank was found innocent this time and, commenting on his brush with death, said, "I never quite lost hope, though it was dreary enough at times. But when the day of my execution was just two days off, and no word of hope had reached me from outside, I made up my mind to go through with it without a murmur, though I was dead sore all the time."[4]

With his newfound liberty, Frank returned to society, but his narrow escape from the electric chair caused either the press or the underworld to christen him with a new sobriquet: "Death House" Flanagan.

Back on the streets, Frank continued his life of crime. In November 1920 a messenger carrying a satchel containing $60,000 worth of diamonds was accosted at the corner of Forth-seventh Street and Seventh Avenue by four men who grabbed the gems, jumped into a cab, and escaped. Frank was arrested for the job, but nothing came of it.[5]

The banditry continued into the next spring when, on May 24, 1921, "Death House" and his cousin William, known as "Lightning Harry" (perhaps one of the two adopted siblings), attempted to rob a man named George Hatchett. But Hatchett was a tough guy himself and ended up shooting William in the neck and keeping his cash. Both Flanagans were captured after the robbery attempt but never charged.[6]

The summer of 1921 saw Tom's last big heist when he; gang affiliate James Breen, who like Tom had a long police record; and three others (whether any were Flanagans is unknown) took part in a brazen robbery. At 11:30 on the morning of July 11, George Schneider, cashier for the Horton Ice Cream Company at 205 East Twenty-fourth Street, and Thomas Duffy, assistant superintendent of the plant, were leaving the building with a canvas bag containing $20,000 in cash and another $17,000 in checks for deposit. The two men took an elevator down to the loading dock where a car was waiting for them. As Schneider climbed into the back seat, someone called to Duffy, who turned to see who wanted him.

As he did, four men, two on each side, ran up to the car and pointed their pistols at the cashier's head while a fifth man stationed in the middle of the street hollered to the numerous Horton employees around, "Don't anybody move!" One of the gunmen grabbed the money bag, and then, covering the workers with their pistols, the robbers all backed up toward a Buick parked across the street. At this point, an employee made a move and one of the bandits fired a shot at him.

As the thieves sped away, a Horton truck driven by Floyd Bates, who had been an ambulance driver in World War I and was accompanied by another employee, Milton McRoberts, began to chase them. The bandits turned onto First Avenue, with the Horton truck closing in. Heading north, both vehicles had to contend with horse-drawn wagons, pillars of the elevated train that stood there at the time, and pedestrian traffic. The ice cream truck continued to gain on the bandits' car, which careened onto Twenty-sixth Street and headed toward Second Avenue, where it turned again, continued north, and swerved onto Twenty-seventh Street. In the middle of the block, with the Horton truck right on their bumper, the robbers pulled over.

As soon as the ice cream truck came to a stop, the gunmen jumped out of the Buick and fired six shots which perforated the vehicle. One of the bullets narrowly missed Bates, who was saved by his steering wheel. As the gunmen piled back into their car, one of them yelled to the two would-be heroes that if they continued the chase, the bandits would shoot to kill. Bates and McRoberts decided not to press their luck. A month later Tom Flanagan was picked up by police, and Horton cashier George Schneider identified him as the leader of the robbery gang.[7]

Although Tom was in prison, it was business as usual for his brothers. On December 3 the gang stole the payroll of the Weser Brothers Piano Manufacturing Company, but it was a job three weeks later, on December 22, that received the most notoriety.

A little before 2 p.m., in a taxicab that had been stolen just a few hours earlier, seven men pulled up in front of the Phipps tenement homes in an African-American section of Manhattan known as San Juan Hill. Five of the men got out of the cab and entered the foyer of the rental office. Getaway driver John Little remained in the vehicle while James Breen stood alongside the cab as a lookout. Four of the men remained in the foyer while the fifth entered the office and cased the premises as he spoke with the rental agent. The bandit, described as well dressed, asked the female agent, who sat behind a five-foot-high iron gate, about a family who supposedly lived in the tenements.

While the agent searched the books for the nonexistent family, the bandit was able to see the piles of rent money laying on her desk. The agent told the man that the family he sought had never lived in the Phipps development. He graciously thanked her and left the office as she went back to counting the rent money. A few minutes later all five men returned, each armed with a pistol and all but one wearing a handkerchief over his face.

"Shut up. Don't make a sound," the man with the bare face said as he approached the iron gate, "We ain't going to hurt you. All we want is the jack [money]." He handed his pistol to an accomplice and jumped over the gate, landing on the woman's desk. Retrieving his pistol, he placed it against the woman's head and threatened to kill her if she didn't open the safe. As the agent unlocked the safe, the man let his accomplices inside to collect the other rent money.

As the robbery was taking place, Charles David, a former police officer from British Guiana who lived in the Phipps tenements and worked as a watchman, was on his way home for lunch when he saw the cab outside the building. Since taxis seldom came to his neighborhood, he found it odd that it would be idling at the curb. He found it even stranger that Breen, a well-dressed young white man, would be pacing outside the apartments, furtively looking about. So instead of entering his building, the watchman hung back to see what was transpiring.

After cleaning out the rental office of $800, the bandits stepped back into the foyer and removed their masks as they left the building. David saw them exit and caught the last man taking off his handkerchief. Realizing that a robbery had taken place, he ran up his stoop and drew his gun as the bandits got into the cab. As Breen ran to the vehicle and stepped on the running board to pile inside, David fired, hitting him in the side. The force of the bullet spun Breen around, but he jerked out his pistol and returned fire, nicking the watchman's arm. David squeezed off another shot, this time hitting Breen just below the heart, causing the bandit to collapse onto the sidewalk. Two of his cohorts stuck their guns out the car windows and began firing at David, who continued shooting at the cab, his shots perforating the vehicle but hitting no flesh.

Leaving Breen to his fate, the robbers pulled out onto Sixty-third Street and took off toward West End Avenue just as a policeman who had heard the shooting rounded the corner. The officer yelled for the cab to stop and fired a number of ineffectual shots at its tires as it sped past him. With the taxi gone, the cop approached Breen, who managed to prop himself up on an elbow and fire two shots at the policeman. Both missed and the cop ran up and kicked the pistol from Breen's hand, then rushed the gangster to the hospital, where he died upon arrival.[*]

As Breen was making his last stand, the getaway car turned onto West End Avenue and began heading downtown. The bandits soon saw Officer Patrick Monahan, responding to the police call, ahead of them and fired a barrage at him, but all of their shots missed. Monahan returned fire and one of his bullets struck the driver, Little, in the upper lip and exited out his right cheek. The impact caused Little to swerve, but after a moment he regained control of the car. Monahan commandeered a vehicle and gave chase, following the bandits' machine as

---

[*] The next day, George Schneider and another Horton Ice Cream Company employee went to the morgue and identified Breen as one of the holdup men from the July 11 robbery.

it started to turn onto Fifty-sixth Street. Little was growing weak from loss of blood and couldn't complete the turn, resulting in the car crashing into a truck.

The robbers jumped out of the disabled vehicle and calmly walked away, assisting Little, who was holding a handkerchief to his face. As they walked down the street a cop passed by on the opposite side and, oblivious to the melee that had just occurred, figured that Little had been in a fight and decided to continue on his way. He changed his mind, however, and as he began to approach the group the bandits quickly took off running. The officer ordered them to stop and fired a shot when they continued to flee.

He gave chase and quickly captured Little and held him until Monahan arrived. The other five bandits escaped. Little was taken to a hospital and questioned while doctors patched him up. He refused to answer any questions, and when the doctor was finished treating him the cops took Little back to the police station for additional grilling instead of sending him to the hospital ward at Bellevue.[8]

Nineteen twenty-two would prove to be a bad year for the Flanagan brothers, for by its end one would be in prison and one would be dead. "Baby" Joey, however, was the first to have a run-in with the law. At 5 a.m. on March 11, he and two associates were standing at the corner of Eighth Avenue and Forty-ninth Street when they were noticed by a passing detective. The lawman figured it was a little odd for three men to be around that early, so he approached them, got their names and addresses, and asked a couple of questions, which they satisfactorily answered. The detective suspected they were up to no good, however, and he let them go on their way but discreetly began to follow.

The men went to the address on Amsterdam Avenue that Joey had given him and went inside, so the detective left, figuring he had been wrong about the trio. Later that afternoon, however, he learned that a clothing store in the vicinity of Eighth and Forty-ninth had been robbed. Remembering the three men from the morning, he and three other detectives went to Joey's place and set up a stakeout.

At 9 p.m., after a group of young men had entered the building, the detectives followed them up to a third-floor apartment and tried to get in. They were told the room was a private club and that they couldn't be admitted unless they were card-carrying members. In lieu of membership cards, the detectives drew their pistols and forced their way inside, where they found Joey and his pals along with the swag from the clothing store. Even though he was caught red-handed, Joey managed to beat the rap.[9] He wouldn't be as fortunate the next year, however, when he was arrested for taking part in a robbery in New Jersey and sent up the river.

On June 20 Frank took part in a robbery that would end up costing him seven years in prison. The target was the $5,000 payroll of the I. Lewis Cigar Company in Newark, New Jersey. That afternoon Harold Lewis, son of the proprietor, along with his brother Donald and an employee named Ross Dimms, had picked up the money at a local bank and were heading back to the factory when Harold, who was driving, realized they were being followed by five men in a touring car. "These fellows are holdups," he told his companions. "I'll put on full speed and dash up to the factory door," he told Dimms, adding, "you jump out with the satchel, and Donald and I will try to prevent them from following you into the factory."

Dimms never had a chance. The bandits were right on their tail, and as they pulled up to the factory and Dimms jumped from the truck, three gunmen were able to cut him off while a fourth covered the Lewis brothers. "Drop that bag and beat it inside," one of the robbers demanded. When Dimms dropped the bag, one of the bandits picked it up and ran to the touring car while the others kept the victims covered. Once the money was aboard, the other gunmen jumped inside the vehicle and waved goodbye to the Lewis brothers as they made their getaway.[10]

Frank subsequently was arrested for the robbery and went on trial in January 1923. At one point he was removed from the courtroom for becoming "boisterous" when a prosecutor brought up the Mulhearn murder from 1919. His claims of innocence fell on deaf ears, however, and he was sent away to the state prison at Trenton. After his release around 1928 he faded into obscurity.[11]

About the time of the cigar company robbery Tom Flanagan was in court standing trial for his participation in the $37,000 Horton Ice Cream Company robbery. He was found guilty, but because he was smart enough to had hired Jimmy Fallon, one of the Big Apple's top attorneys, he was able to get off on a technicality. While Tom was awaiting his sentencing hearing, Fallon pointed out that the prosecutor had referred to his client as a "notorious criminal" without any legal right to do so—and as a result Tom got to walk.[12]

That legal loophole would be Tom's last piece of luck, however, because five months later, on November 30, 1922, he was at "Yumpsy" Cunningham's saloon when somebody shot him in the chest. Some of his cohorts placed him in a cab and sent him to his father, who called the police, who in turn rushed the dying gangster to Bellevue Hospital.[13]

The aforementioned Captain Willemse arrived at the hospital just as the gangster was receiving the last rites and rushed to his bedside hoping to obtain a deathbed confession. After the priest finished his business, Willemse stepped up and said, "Hello, Tom, I'm sorry. You're in bad shape, the doctor tells me. What happened?" Seeing the lawman, the gangster retorted, "What the hell do you want? Get away from me, you son of a bitch!"

Willemse tried again. "Tom, you're going before your Maker in a few minutes where there won't be any Fallon to defend you," he said. "You've had the last rites. Come on, step out clean." But "Turk" Flanagan was a gangster through and through. "You son of a bitch, I'll tell you nothing," he growled. "You framed me and many others. I'll take care of this myself, and if I kick off, what the hell do you care?" With that, Willemse left the room, but he wasn't ready to give up.

Hoping to catch Flanagan off guard he sent in another detective, one unknown to Tom, dressed as an orderly to try to pry some info out of him. The man entered Tom's room and whispered in his ear, "Say, Tom, some of the mob's outside. They want to get the lowdown on who gave you the works. They can't come in with all the bulls here. They want you to tell me." Flanagan saw through the ruse, however, and with as much anger as a dying man could muster said, "Why, you son of a bitch, go outside to that big bum Willemse. I'm no rat, you bastard."

Shortly after that, Tom started to fade fast, so Willemse ran back into the room and began to throw names at him in hopes of seeing a flicker of recognition on his face. But Tom, by now unable to speak, "stepped out" without betraying the criminal's code of silence.[14]

By the late 1920s two of the remaining Flanagans, Frank and Martin, the latter of whom had done a stretch for robbing the Rockefeller Institute, seemed to have learned that crime doesn't pay. Both apparently went straight and faded from public view.

Joey, on the other hand, having been released from prison sometime around 1928, continued his life in the underworld and, like his brother Tom, paid the ultimate price. On Sunday morning, November 17, 1929, a churchgoer leaving his apartment found what he believed to be a man sleeping off a drunk in the hallway. He stepped over him and went to church. When the man returned after the services and the "drunk" was still there, he kicked him a couple of times to rouse him. When there was no movement, he lifted the prone man's fedora and discovered the truth of the situation.

The "drunk" was "Baby" Joey, who had been drilled in the temple on a "ride job" and dumped in the tenement hallway sometime between 4 and 8 a.m. Although he was no longer actively involved with his brothers, he was keeping the family image alive, it seems, for the *New York Herald* reported that when he was found he was elegantly dressed in a dark-brown suit, gray overcoat, and tan kid gloves.[15]

4

Two Worthless Diamonds

*"Perhaps no crime ever was committed in Brooklyn which
so shocked and outraged all our people as the one for which the
four men just sentenced are to pay the penalty."*
— BROOKLYN SUPREME COURT JUSTICE JAMES CROPSEY

O n the morning of November 14, 1923, sixty-four-year-old William Barlow, a retired police officer, and twenty-four-year-old William McLaughlin, both messengers for the West End Bank in Brooklyn, left the bank with more than $43,000 in cash to be deposited in the Irving National-Columbia Trust Company. Since robberies were so commonplace, Barlow and McLaughlin used a decoy method when transporting money. Barlow would fill his money pouch with newspapers while McLaughlin would take the actual cash, wrap it in newspapers, and wrap that with an oilcloth so that it appeared he was carrying a set of tools. He would walk about ten paces behind Barlow, so that if Barlow were held up by robbers McLaughlin would be able to escape with the money. This morning the messengers, both armed, left the West End Bank and boarded the elevated train, taking seats on opposite sides of the car.

The news everyone was talking about concerned a payroll robbery the previous day in which robbers had stolen more than $18,000 from the Ward Bakery in Brooklyn. When he'd read the newspapers the night before, Barlow told his family, "If they ever hold me up I'm going to give them the battle of their lives, if I get the drop on them." Before making their morning trip to the bank, a cashier reminded the messengers of the Ward robbery and told Barlow that if anyone tried to rob them, they should just give up the money. But Barlow and McLaughlin laughed off the warning, tapping their pistols and saying that if it came down to it, they would fight it out.[1]

Little did McLaughlin and Barlow know, however, that a group of desperadoes had been meeting on and off at a bungalow in the Bronx for the past month devising a way to separate them from their money. But for all the time the thieves spent strategizing, their plan was shockingly and horrifically simple—and this was the day they would put it into effect.

When the bank messengers arrived at their stop, they exited the train and, with Barlow in the lead, descended the stairs to the first landing. Before they made it to the exit door, which led to the steps to the street, a man walked up to Barlow and shot him point-blank in the face. Another shot plowed into his arm. At the same time, another gunman fired at McLaughlin, hitting him in the arm and chest. "My God, my God," McLaughlin gasped, as he stumbled across the platform into the arms of a bystander and died.

The bandits grabbed the messengers' packages and hurried down the stairs to a waiting Cadillac. One of the gunmen was running so fast that he passed by the car and had to turn around. Once both men were in the car, it sped off, followed by a Ford sedan that would be used, if necessary, as a crash car to ensure that the killers escaped.

As soon as the robbers got into the Cadillac, their plans began to unravel and mistakes were made that would lead authorities to identify them within hours. In the back seat they opened both packages and tossed aside the decoy newspaper, tore open the oilcloth covered with McLaughlin's blood, and pocketed the money. In their frenzy to escape, the bandits turned down a street that was under repair and found themselves blocked by a cement mixer. Panicking, the men jumped from the vehicle and attempted to remove its license plates. They were able to remove the back plate but couldn't get the front one off, so they left both behind. Most incriminating were the bloody fingerprints left inside the car by one of the bandits.[2]

The police found the abandoned Cadillac and through the bloody fingerprints were able to identify twenty-eight-year-old Morris Diamond, who was a relatively new denizen of the underworld. Unlike most criminals, he had actually had a good childhood. Reared in Bensonhurst, his father owned a box factory and the family never wanted for anything. Known as "Whitey" because of his blonde hair, Morris was considered one of the best high school athletes in the area and showed great prowess on the football field. He was patriotic as well; ten days after the United States entered into the World War he enlisted and was sent to Europe.[3]

His life, however, had taken a turn for the worse when he returned from the war. In 1919 his father died of cancer, and the family, racked with hospital bills, was barely able to keep the box factory afloat. More tragedy followed when Morris's young wife died, leaving him to raise their five-year-old son. Not long after Morris became a widower his name began to appear on police blotters. He was arrested in Brooklyn in June 1922 for carrying a pistol and followed that up in November with an arrest in Danbury, Connecticut, for stealing a car while armed with a pistol. The latter arrest resulted in a six-month prison term. He was arrested again in Brooklyn the following August for assault and robbery but was released for lack of evidence.[4]

After Morris's prints were found in the abandoned Cadillac, detectives immediately staked out the Diamond home, but their surveillance proved fruitless. Their quarry had already hightailed it to Philadelphia with his twenty-two-year-old brother Joseph who, Morris would later insist, had been the driver of the crash car during the heist. The brothers checked into a posh Philly hotel and Morris got in touch with a showgirl he had previously met in New York. He told her to grab a friend and meet him and his brother for a good time.

The night after the murder Morris and Joseph were living it up in the City of Brotherly Love with the showgirls, but guilt was already eating away at Joseph. During the evening he leaned over to his date and said, "Listen, they say a woman can't keep a secret, but I'll trust you because I know you will keep my secret." Although he was sober, Joseph was talking loudly, so the girl suggested they go somewhere quiet. They ended up back in Joseph's room where he broke down and told her the whole story.

As he paced back and forth, he told the girl how the brothers had turned to crime to help pay their father's medical bills, and he also mentioned Morris's misfortune with his wife. He then went into detail about the murders, after which Joseph fell to his knees, professed his love for the girl he'd known for approximately three hours, and asked her to marry him, promising that they would start a new life together. At this point Morris came into the room, and the girl asked if what his brother had said was true. Morris laughed nervously and told her Joseph was delusional and that "arrangements were being made to have him treated by a specialist."[5]

After about a week of enjoying the high life in Philadelphia, Morris bought two train tickets for Cleveland. Joseph wanted to go back to New York, however, so the brothers split up and the older sibling went to Ohio by himself. A few days later police picked up the Diamonds' trail in Philadelphia and, with the help of the showgirls, learned that one or both of them had gone to Cleveland. Morris made things easy for the police by making a big mistake in Cleveland.

Working in tandem, New York and Cleveland detectives began searching hotel registries and discovered, much to their surprise, that Morris had signed into a hotel under his real name. A porter tipped the detectives that Diamond was planning to take a train to New York that evening after he attended a football game. This gave them the time they needed to lay a trap, and so one detective waited at the front desk while another kept watch on the eighth floor where Diamond's room was located.

After the game Morris came back to the hotel and stopped at the front desk to check out. The detective got on the elevator with him, and when they stepped out on the eighth floor he signaled to his partner. As Diamond put the key in his door, they came up behind him and poked him with their guns. "What do you want me for?" a panicked Morris asked. "You know why," one of the detectives replied. He did indeed know why. "Well, I guess I better go back to New York with you," Diamond said, giving up peacefully.[6]

Once Morris was captured, Joseph turned himself in under the pretext that he was innocent and simply wanted to clear himself. But with constant questioning, and faced with witnesses, both Diamonds broke down and admitted being involved in the heist. To separate themselves from the killings and hopefully save themselves from the electric chair, the brothers claimed lesser roles in the job. Morris said he had been the driver of the Cadillac, and Joseph, both insisted, hadn't even been there; he'd simply supplied one of the stolen cars used in the robbery. It wasn't long before they started to rat out their associates. They named John Farina, George DeSaro, and another man as the actual triggermen.

After the Diamonds started to sing, other arrests quickly followed. On November 28 Anthony Pantano, and old school friend of Joe's, was picked up at 2:45 a.m. as he tried to enter his home. The brothers declared he was the idea man. A former employee of both the West End Bank and the Irving National-Columbia Trust Company, Pantano had contacted them and, for a slice of the profits, provided them with inside information about the money transfer. Or so the Diamonds said.

Once in custody, and realizing the brothers had put him there, Pantano told police, "The Diamond boys say I cooked this up, eh? Well, they're two damned lousy liars. *They* cooked it up." According to Pantano, he had run into his old pal Joe at the West End Bank, and under the guise of buying his car Joseph had taken him to a bungalow in the Bronx. This was just a ruse, however, because the whole gang was there, including hardened gunmen John Farina and George DeSaro, one of whom stuck a pistol in Pantano's ribs and said, "Now you know all about the transfer of this money. Give us the right steer and we'll fix you up. If you give us a bum steer, we'll kill you." So, under duress, Pantano explained how McLaughlin and Barlow worked. Or so he said.[7]

After Pantano was picked up, police raided the Bronx bungalow. In addition to being the place where the West End job was planned, the bungalow also was used by John Farina and his brother Anthony in their bootlegging enterprise. The raid on the house netted Nicholas "Cheeks" Luciano, whose moniker was the result of a long scar on the right side of his face, Angelo Farina, and another man not involved in the robbery. "Cheeks," who worked with John Farina, stole one of the cars that was used in the robbery.[8*]

A lucky break for detectives led to the capture of John Farina. On December 8 two Hoboken, New Jersey, detectives investigating a robbery happened to be at the intersection of Newark and Clinton streets when they overheard a woman mention to a friend that she new a guy with lots of money who was setting sale for Italy the next day. Intrigued, the detectives picked her up and learned during her interrogation that she had been talking about John Farina. They informed the New York Police Department and a detective was sent over.

Investigators got an address out of the woman and immediately went there, arriving at about 5 a.m. They were greeted at the door by a young woman who insisted that only her brother was at home, but they brushed past her and found Farina in bed with a .45 under his pillow and a .38 in his coat pocket. Two other men and another gun also were found on the premises.

Farina claimed he was John Seters, a simple laborer from Plainfield, New Jersey. What about the guns? Well, actually he was a bootlegger and needed to protect himself. When the detective produced a picture of John Farina, he looked at it and said, "It looks like me. But it's some other guy, not me. You've got the wrong bird." But when the detective produced a card with Farina's fingerprints, "Mr. Seters" mumbled a few incoherent words and then he admitted who he really was. That was all the information the cops got out of him, however. He didn't fold like his confederates. "It's no use," he told his captors. "you can't make me talk. Do your damnedest and see."[9**]

Just before the trials the police tried to get all four prisoners to come clean with matching confessions, but the Diamonds stuck to their story, Pantano stuck to

---

* During the trial Luciano testified that Morris Diamond actually had stolen the car in question but that he had taken the rap for him.

** George DeSaro successfully sailed to Italy, supposedly on the same ship on which Farina had booked passage.

his, and Farina was no help whatsoever, saying, "You punks can cut my head off before you'll get a damned thing out of me."[10]

Morris was the first to go on trial, on February 4, 1924. The case was pretty much open and shut and Morris knew it. As the jury entered into deliberation he was overheard saying, "I guess my goose is cooked. Looks like there'll be a crepe on the door pretty soon." Much damaging evidence came from "Cheeks" Luciano, who assured the jury that the Diamond brothers, Farina, and George DeSaro had all been involved in the robbery. He also said that after the murders Morris had asked him if he'd heard anything about the job, and when he told him that he hadn't, Morris went on to say: "We tried to get it [the money] away from them, but they wouldn't give up and we had to pop them off." Needless to say, the verdict was guilty of murder in the first degree.

Joseph went on trial on February 13. One witness stated unequivocally that he had seen Joseph shoot one of the messengers. Hearing this statement, Joseph's mother and sisters began to scream and called the witness a liar. They were quickly removed from the courtroom and the trial continued. "Cheeks" Luciano testified that Morris had told him the day of the murder that Farina and DeSaro had done the killing. But it didn't matter, for the jury took just forty minutes to reach the same verdict that had been returned against Morris.

Less than a week later, on February 18, Farina went on trial, but in the end the jury took more than four hours to find him guilty. Pantano was placed on trial and also found guilty, mostly as a result of testimony by "Cheeks" Luciano, who said he had witnessed the former bank employee willingly provide inside information to the robbery gang.[11]*

On March 3, 1923, the quartet was returned to the courthouse for sentencing. All received the death penalty. As the condemned men were marched out to the van that would take them back to the Raymond Street Jail, Joseph was heard to say, "Well, that's that." As the van's door was being closed, Pantano yelled to the sizable crowd that had assembled to see the bandits, "Goodbye, you fortunate people. Good luck to you."

When they arrived back at the jail the warden told them, "Well I hope you fellows get new trials." But Morris was pessimistic. "No," he said, shaking his head, "I guess it ain't going to be. This is the last. I don't ever expect to come back to Brooklyn." The necessary paperwork was taken care of at the Raymond Street Jail and the four men were taken to Grand Central Station for the train

---

* Luciano claimed afterward that his testimony regarding Pantano was false, which moved Governor Al Smith to grant him clemency from execution since he had not been proven guilty beyond doubt.

ride to Sing Sing. To avoid the crowds they were sneaked in a side entrance at 1:30 p.m. to await the 2:04 p.m. train that would take them to their doom. A large number of thrill seekers purchased tickets for Yonkers, the train's first stop, just so they could get a look at the bandits. The cops were wise to them, however, and whenever anyone came into the car containing the robbers, they were ushered out again.

Little else transpired on the train ride, aside from idle chatter between the guards and the bandits and some newspaper reading. When they arrived in Ossining two girls were on hand and waved to the Diamond brothers, which cheered them up momentarily. Then the group piled into a couple of taxis for the short drive to the Sing Sing death house.[12]

John Farina managed to get a second trial, during which "Cheeks" Luciano took the stand and said he had perjured himself at the first trial and that Farina was not part of the robbery gang. But on cross examination he admitted he was lying, and Farina was again found guilty. For his perjury, Luciano was sentenced to a five- to ten-year term at Sing Sing.

The Diamonds and Farina were scheduled to walk the final mile on Thursday, April 30, 1925. The night before, the trio understandably had difficulty sleeping. Morris complained that he'd had to listen to a guard walking up and down the hall throughout the night, and Farina complained of having a flashlight shined in his cell whenever a guard passed by.

Later that day, as Farina was being transferred to the pre-execution chamber, a guard relieved him of two oranges he was carrying and noticed that they were stuck together. As it turned out, they were connected by a bone-handled toothbrush the killer had filed to a sharp point. It was his intention to kill himself as soon as his family completed their final visit. Farina's family was supposed to have visited the previous day but postponed their trip until the end, throwing a monkey wrench in his plans. Farina did, however, assure the keeper, "If I had a visit yesterday, you would have been saved a job tonight."

The condemned were given the black outfits they would be wearing to their deaths, and they had the backs of their heads shaved where the straps of the electric chair would be attached. They visited with their families, and as dusk approached each had his final meal. Joseph didn't have much of an appetite and so only had some cheese, bread, and coffee and spent most of the time smoking. His brother had fried eggs, French fries, fruit, bread, butter, and coffee. Farina dined on lamb chops, potatoes, bread, butter, and coffee.

When the designated time arrived, Morris was the first to go. He entered the death chamber at 11:05 p.m. and was given a chance to make a final statement. He started off by saying he felt he had deserved a better trial because of his service during World War I. His speech then became inaudible until the end when he raised his voice and said, "Here and now, face to face with my Maker, I state that Joe was innocent, that he was not there. The state's witnesses were paid perjurers. My sister and her lawyers hold the real truth about this. It should be investigated." He was then strapped into the chair and executed.

At 11:17 p.m. Joseph was brought in and, like his brother, used his final statement to proclaim his innocence, closing with, "Many men have died on the gallows, many men have been executed, and many men have protested their innocence. I am innocent of this crime. If I am guilty, may my soul burn in hell. I was convicted on perjured testimony. May God be my judge. Goodbye." He was pronounced dead at 11:25 p.m.

Three minutes later Farina entered the chamber, puffing on a cigar. A guard went to take it from his mouth, but he clenched down on it even harder and snarled at him. When he got to the chair he removed the cigar and asked for permission to speak as the others had done. With permission granted, he simply said, "I ask for forgiveness, just as any man would ask for forgiveness." As he was being strapped in, he managed a half smile and said, "Goodbye, all." Then, a moment before the switch was pulled, he uttered his last words: "Well, here goes nothing."[13]

Urban Cowboys

"Prison isn't such a bad place."
— Arthur Rothermel

In the mid-1920s Police Commissioner Richard Enright established a detective school for the New York Police Department and let it be known to the "old school" detectives that they could adopt the new methods or face the consequences. A number of the veteran detectives chose the latter and found themselves walking a beat while graduates of the new school took their jobs. A detective's number-one resource is the stool pigeon, and it takes years for detectives to cultivate a reliable network of stoolies. So when the veteran detectives were relieved of their duties, coincidently, or as a result of the shake-up, arrests diminished and robberies increased.

One of the robbery gangs flourishing at this time was the "Cowboy" Tessler mob, which just as easily could have been referred to as the Rothermel Gang and was credited with an astonishing eighty-one holdups over the course of some eight months. This outfit's trademark was using pistols equipped with silencers. The cash robberies the gang pulled were small time, namely drugstores, gas stations, and subway kiosks, but its members also dealt in jewels, furs, and basically anything else they could turn into cash.

The gang's namesake, twenty-five-year-old Frank "Cowboy" Tessler, had everything going for him. His parents ran a produce business and had managed to send him to Columbia University. After school he had become a furrier and ran a legitimate business for about two years. But in early 1925 he was approached by a denizen of the underworld who wanted to move some hot furs, and from there Tessler veered off the straight and narrow onto a path of crime.[1]

The mob, including fences, had about eleven members and rented an entire floor of a loft building under the name Edwards and Brown where they stored loot as well as merchandise brought in from outside the city to be resold. Of the latter, the gang received $1,000 worth of hot hardware from Stamford, Connecticut, each week. The loft also doubled as a shooting range where gang members practiced their aim with their silencer-muffled handguns.[2]

The hoodlum who approached Tessler most likely was one of the Rothermel brothers. Fred and Arthur (who also went by the alias Leslie) Rothermel were career criminals, and by all rights the gang should have gone by their name. Unlike Tessler, the Rothermels had grown up poor. According to their older sister, who described their upbringing to a judge in hopes of getting them more lenient sentences, their parents died when both were babies and "we had to do without what a lot of people had. We were penniless then. Why, we even had to borrow money to bury our father."[3]

Born sometime around 1898, Fred had the longer career, having orchestrated a failed bank robbery on March 19, 1919. Along with two associates, Henry Berman and David Brownstein, Fred had driven from Manhattan to Freeport, Long Island, where he'd found a bank he felt was ripe for the picking. There was a steady drizzle the day the trio pulled into town in a convertible. The streets were deserted because of the inclement weather, but the boys, who were not wearing overcoats, didn't go unnoticed. One of those who looked on with raised eyebrows was a bank clerk, who wrote down the car's license plate number as two of the bandits entered the building.

One of the men pulled out a ten-dollar bill and asked that it be changed into "little ones." Then he and his cohort pulled out pistols and ordered everyone to put up their hands. They grabbed almost $3,200 in cash (missing another $5,000 that was nearby) and backed out of the bank. Getting back into the car, one of the robbers yelled that if anyone tried to follow them, they would shoot.

The police were notified and the description of the car and the license plate number were transmitted across the island. In Queens a cop was speaking with a salesman named Abraham Such, who was sitting in his car when the bandits whizzed by at more than sixty miles per hour. The cop jumped into Such's car and gave pursuit, the vehicle was no match for the bank robbers' machine, so he commandeered another auto, which was able to over take Rothermel and his cronies. Forced to the side of the road, the bandits jumped out of their car. One of them pulled a pistol, but before he had a chance to shoot, the officer opened fire on the trio. Rothermel dropped to the ground with a bullet to the lung as his pals ran across a field into the surrounding woods.

At this point Abraham Such arrived on the scene and pulled his car alongside Dave Brownstein, who was running down the road. Realizing that Brownstein was one of the bandits, Such offered him a ride. "I've got to get to New York in a hurry," Brownstein told him, and the salesman said he would take him to the nearest streetcar. But when Brownstein jumped in, Such proceeded to take him to the nearest cop. Back at the police station the bandit spilled the beans on his partners, and Berman was arrested later that night as he was entering his house.[4]

After the botched robbery Fred Rothermel was sent to Sing Sing to serve a sentence of from ten to twenty years. However, because of the early retirement of experienced keepers taking advantage of a new pension plan, Fred would taste freedom, albeit briefly, by taking advantage of the inexperienced replacements. The keepers' first mistake came when Fred and two other convicts were ordered to fix a leak on the prison roof. Normally convicts serving long sentences are not allowed to do such work since escape is possible. While working on the roof on December 4, 1920, Fred told the keeper that he needed to go downstairs for a tool and was granted permission. Instead he walked over to the roof of the warden's house, entered the building through a cupola, and made his way downstairs and out the front door.

After about ten minutes the keeper realized Fred wasn't coming back and sounded the alarm. Fred managed to evade his pursuers for the rest of the day, but that night he was captured by the warden, Lewis Lawes, himself near the Rockefeller estate. Rothermel told the warden that he had taken off because he felt that he'd gotten a "raw deal" with his sentencing.[5]

After serving five years Fred was released. It was determined that because of the lung wound he'd received in 1919 it would have been cruel to keep him in prison where he was more apt to contract tuberculosis. By 1925 Fred and his younger brother, twenty-two-year-old Art, whose record consisted of an arrest in 1921 for grand larceny for which he received a suspended sentence, were back in business. Along with their new partner Tessler and the rest of the gang, they managed to operate unmolested by the police for nearly eight months, pulling as many as four jobs a day.

Two of the more infamous jobs credited to them resulted in the death of one victim and the wounding of another. The former took place on July 2, 1925, when the gang invaded the Pefka Brothers fur store. The company's namesakes and their employees were tied up, and one of them, Abe Pefka, also was blackjacked. While on the ground Abe began to groan, and "Cowboy" told him, "Damn you, keep still." The furrier continued to groan, so "Cowboy" kicked him in the ribs and stomach. The groaning did not abate, so Tessler shut him up permanently with five shots from his pistol. The second shooting took place on September 1, when Tessler and Fred Rothermel entered a dentist's office and robbed him of $165 in cash and another $135 in jewelry. At some point "Cowboy" shot a patient in the back.[6]

To combat the dramatic increase in robberies the police organized "the fence squad" and chose to head it former Detective Richard Oliver, who had been demoted to patrol duty to make way for new officers who had been trained in the latest crime-solving methods at Commissioner Enright's detective school. Oliver was said to have more underworld sources than any other officer, and in a matter of a few weeks he was on to the Tessler Gang. Soon the detectives were aware of two garages the gang used to alter and store the stolen cars they used on their jobs, as well as the warehouse where they stored their goods and took target practice.[7]

On September 30, 1925, the authorities made their move and arrested "Cowboy" and gang members Moe Auswaks and Louis Austen at one of the garages. One of the Rothermel brothers was supposed to have been there as well, but he left just before the raid. At the station Oliver asked Tessler if he had anything to say about the Pefka murder. "Say, what do you think, that I'm going to tie the straps on myself? They pay men to do that in Sing Sing," he replied. "But I'll tell you about the stickups. I pulled off fifty-one of 'em and had you cops running around in circles."[8]

A subsequent search of Austen's apartment turned up bales of wool worth $5,000. Later, twenty of the reported eighty cars the gang had stolen were located in New York and surrounding states. The arrests were not publicized for fear of tipping off the rest of the gang that the police were on to them.[9]

About a week later, on October 6, gang member Murray Markine was driving a stolen car containing Art Rothermel and his moll Rose Hameline. They were spotted by a motorcycle cop who soon gave chase down First Avenue. As Markine tried to lose the cop, Rothermel fired ten shots at him from a pistol equipped with a silencer and then three more from a "loud speaker" (pistol without a silencer). The officer was able to catch the car, but Rothermel managed to escape on foot. Markine was booked for driving the stolen vehicle; Rose was booked for carrying a knife and was bailed out.[10]

Markine expected the gang to bail him out, too, but after eight days he realized nobody was coming to his rescue and he decided to squeal. He wasn't going to talk to just anyone however. "No deputies," he said. "This is for the D.A. himself or nobody."[11]

Markine was able to fill in the pieces the fence squad lacked. He named all the gang members and gave all the pertinent addresses used by the gang. He also mentioned that it was Art Rothermel who had fired the thirteen shots at the motorcycle cop. Since ten of the thirteen shots had been fired from a pistol equipped with a silencer, the cop, Officer Gemmerich, thought he'd been fired on just three times. "My God," he exclaimed when told the truth, "I never knew how near death I was."[12]

Armed with the addresses, the police began to stake out all of the gang's known hangouts. The first member to go down was Fred Rothermel, on October 16 when he was located at a bakery he regularly patronized. The police didn't want to take a chance that anyone who knew him would see the arrest being made, so they waited for him to leave and tailed him for ten blocks before cuffing him. At four o'clock the next morning, brother Art and Rose Hameline were approaching her apartment when a detective stepped up and knocked Art out with a pistol butt to the chin before the bandit knew what hit him.[13]

At the station Art claimed his name was Walsh, although the police knew better. Rose said he hadn't shot at Gemmerich, the motorcycle cop, but when it looked as if the cops were going to charge Rose with the shooting, Art admitted he was the culprit.[14]

The next two gang members to get caught were Peter Stroh, who altered the stolen cars and moved some of the jewelry, and Joe Silverberg, the getaway driver. Police found them at a café and followed them as they got into a car and drove off. After a few blocks the hoods realized they were being followed and led the police on a fifteen-block car chase before being overtaken and surrendering without a fight.

The final gang member captured was Zany Englescher, who had joined the outfit the previous May after being fired from the William Armstrong Publishing Company, which published racing information. He got in touch with the Tessler Gang and explained how to steal the firm's $9,000 payroll. The heist was successful, and Zany was welcomed into the outfit as a "visit man." As such, he would "visit" the places the gang intended to rob to learn as much as he could about their security and banking habits.[15]

Once all the gang members had been rounded up, victims came in to identify them. "Cowboy" seemed to enjoy the attention and projected a calm, cool demeanor. A chain smoker, he sat back, flicking his ashes in a fancy manner as witnesses paraded by. The Rothermel brothers, on the other hand, stood by sullenly and shot menacing looks at the witnesses. According to the D.A., while a number of people had no problem identifying Tessler, several didn't identify the Rothermels until they were out of the room because they had been frightened by their mean appearance.

After the witnesses were through, the gangsters were led one at time into the grand jury room where they were presented to, among others, reporters, members of the district attorney's staff, and detectives. "Cowboy" was introduced to the crowd and the story of his killing of Pefka was told, after which the bandit bowed and smiled to all in the room and was then ushered out. He was followed by one of the Rothermel brothers and then the other, neither of whom shared Tessler's amiable disposition.[16]

In the end, "Cowboy" Tessler and the Rothermels pleaded guilty to robbing the dentist's office on September 1. Fred Rothermel was looking at thirty years behind bars, fifteen for the new robbery plus the fifteen he still owed on his parole. Art received eighteen years. Tessler's sentence wasn't mentioned in the press, but after he pleaded guilty to robbery he was indicted for the murder of Abraham Pefka. On March 10, 1926, however, the D.A. dropped the case, citing a lack of evidence. It seems that before "Cowboy's" arrest, Pefka's brother had picked another hoodlum out of a lineup and identified him as the killer. The hood subsequently was exonerated, and the D.A. felt the furrier's testimony wouldn't hold up in court.[17]

Bum, Killer, and Ice Wagon LLC

Bum" Rodgers, "Killer" Cunniffe, and "Ice Wagon" Crowley were three desperadoes who brought much grief to the police and society as whole during the 1920s. Rodgers was a lifelong criminal and onetime member of the Car Barn Gang, famous for not one but two escapes from police custody. Cunniffe and Crowley were ruthless bandits capable of committing heinous acts. The three would forever be tied together because of a prison escape.

John J. Rodgers was born on February 17, 1894, the youngest of four sons. A sister rounded out the Rodgerses' children. John's earliest years were marked by tragedy, as his father died while he was still a baby and his sister was killed in a sledding accident when he was five. After the death of her husband, Mrs. Rodgers went to work as a cleaning woman to support the family and earned extra money at night by taking in washing. Neighbors remembered her as "working her fingers to the bone." As a result of her labors, her youngest son was left on his own. Supposedly his older brothers were charged with supervising him, but it wasn't uncommon for young John to be found hanging out unattended on the stoop of the family's building.[1]

Before long John began to stay away from home and exhibit anti-social behavior. When he was nine his mother could no longer control him and turned him over to the authorities. He was labeled incorrigible and sent to the Catholic Protectory for more than two and half years. The stay apparently did little for his rehabilitation, however, because two months after his release on April 5, 1906, he was arrested for trying to pick the pocket of a man sleeping in Central Park. This resulted in a two-year stretch in the House of Refuge.

The month of April would prove to be a prominent one throughout John's early career. He reentered society on April 25, 1908, but his freedom was short lived. On November 20 of the same year he was arrested for larceny. Although the charges were eventually dropped, he was sent back to the House of Refuge for another three months for violating his parole. The next year was no different, for on April 9, after a brief few months on the outside, he was again arrested for picking pockets. This time he was sent to the state reformatory for a year.

By the time he was sixteen, Rodgers had spent a quarter of his life in some form of detention, and the trend would continue for the rest of his days. On April 3, 1912, he was arrested for carrying a blackjack. Prosecuted as an adult, he was shipped off to Sing Sing to serve three years and four months. When his term expired, he returned to the Upper East Side of Manhattan, where it was said he became a member of the Car Barn Gang.[2]

Although the gang never attained the status of other New York City gangs like the Hudson Dusters or Gophers, the Car Barn Gang did achieve notoriety in 1910 when it posted a sign forbidding any cops to venture into its territory—the area of Ninety-sixth and Ninety-seventh streets and Second Avenue. Of course, police officers accepted the challenge and fights ensued. Like the city's other street gangs, the Car Barn Gang was defunct by the end of World War I.[3]

While April was always his unlucky month when it came to arrests, Rodgers, who was now stuck with the moniker "Bum," allegedly because of his slovenly appearance, was apprehended on March 5, 1918, for assault and battery and received his longest term ever, fourteen years, and was sent back to Sing Sing. "Bum" would serve just two years and four months, however, because his mother came to his aid. One of her former cleaning patrons was a state representative, and she pleaded with him to go to bat for her son. The politician went to Governor Al Smith, who commuted "Bum's" sentence, and he was released on August 11, 1920.[4]

Upon his return to the city, Rodgers left his old stomping grounds for Manhattan's West Side. More arrests followed in 1921, one for burglary and one for carrying a knife, which resulted in a three-week stint on Blackwell's Island. Although he was exonerated of the burglary charge, he was sent back to Sing Sing on January 14, 1922, to finish his original sentence for violating his parole. "Bum" argued that since he'd been acquitted of the charge on which he was arrested, he should be released. He eventually was, but not until the spring of 1924.[5]

The parole board no doubt regretted its action when on July 13 of that year "Bum" and his pal Vincent McCormick were involved in the shooting of a police officer. Rodgers and McCormick were in the process of either trying to rob or kidnap a cabaret singer named Florence Hart in a tenement building when they were scared off by a resident. Detective James Lynch saw the pair run from the building to a taxi and speed away. Jumping on the running board of a police car, Lynch gave chase. The squad car overtook the taxi at the corner of 112th Street and Fifth Avenue.

When their vehicle came to a halt, McCormick drew his pistol and pulled the trigger, but his gun misfired. "Bum" went for his pistol, but the detective shot him in the leg before he had a chance to use it. An ambulance was called and both crooks were treated, "Bum" for his bullet wound and McCormick for injuries he sustained while "attempting to escape."[6] Both gunmen ended up at the prison on Welfare Island with a young psychopath named James Cunniffe, with whom "Bum" would forever after be associated.

Cunniffe was nicknamed "Killer," a fitting sobriquet because of his utter disregard for human life. His partner in crime was his lifelong pal and fellow psychotic William "Ice Wagon" Crowley. The two Irish hoods had grown up together on the Manhattan's West Side where, according to Cunniffe's brother, "they were tough as kids and tougher as men."[7] The duo started out providing protection for low-level crap games before forming a gang that supplied the same service for established gambling joints. They also maintained a presence at lucrative taxi stands in the area of Columbus Circle, keeping out the cabs that didn't pay for the privilege of using the high-traffic stops.[8]

Cunniffe and Crowley eventually graduated to bank robbery. One job attributed to them was the robbery of the First National Bank of Bellmore, Long Island. At 12:20 p.m., on April 4, 1924, two well-dressed men, probably Cunniffe and Crowley, entered the bank. Because it was the lunch hour only one teller was on duty and the other employees were either out of the building or lunching behind closed doors. One of the men approached the teller and asked for change while the other sauntered over to the door leading to the vault and teller area. Assuming the door was locked, the man began to climb over the railing as his confederate, who was waiting for change, whipped out a pistol and, knowing that every teller had a foot alarm, softly said, "Step back, girlie, or I'll shoot you. Don't step on anything. Don't holler. Don't do anything."[9]

At this point three more bandits entered the bank, and one of them, Frank "Ghost" Kiekart, took up a lookout position by the door while John Slattery and Ambrose Ross went behind the counter and began to load money into a sack. Another bank employee was forced to come out of a back room and sit with the teller. As the robbery was taking place one of the gunmen asked, "What'll we do with the two dogs?" (meaning the bank employees) and was told to "put the dogs in the cellar."[10]

As the workers were being marched into the basement, bond salesman Ernest L. Whitman pulled up outside the bank and Kiekart, per the plan, fired a warning shot inside the bank to let the others know someone was coming and that it was time to go. Oblivious to what was going on inside, Whitman entered the bank's vestibule and was shot four times by Kiekart and another bandit as the gang ran outside to the getaway car.

As driver Benjamin Haas pulled out, some bystanders dashed into the street to get the vehicle's license plate number. To ward off the onlookers, the bandits knocked out the rear window of the sedan and fired a rifle at them. Undaunted, three young men jumped into a Ford and attempted to follow the robbers but quickly changed their minds when another shot from the rifle whizzed past them.

The bandits zig-zagged their way across Long Island to throw off the police and eventually dumped the car just four miles north of Bellmore where another vehicle was waiting to take them back to the city.[11]*

After the Bellmore job Cunniffe was arrested on a lesser charge and sent to the prison on Welfare Island along with Rodgers and McCormick. In addition to being home to a prison, Welfare Island was also the site of several hospitals, which meant there was a constant flow of pedestrian traffic.

While in prison the desperadoes managed to become trusties and obtained jobs in the hospital ward. At 1:30 a.m. on January 19, 1925, the three men passed through an outer room in the medical ward into a back room. The nurse on duty in the outer room was familiar with them, so she didn't think anything out of the ordinary was taking place. Once inside the back room the men squeezed through a window, climbed over the bars that covered only the lower half of the window, slid down a rope until they were ten feet above the ground, and let go. Nobody saw them drop, and since the island had a sizable civilian population they were able to walk to the river, jump into a boat, and paddle to freedom.[12]

The first known job pulled by "Bum" Rodgers after his escape took place on March 7, 1925. As two employees of the Wadsworth Hardware Company of Valley Stream, Long Island, were walking to their place of business with the company's $700 payroll, a car pulled to the curb and "Bum" and an accomplice jumped out with guns at the ready and ordered them to put up their hands. The bandits took the envelope containing the money, jumped back into their car, and sped away.[13]

---

* Within a month Slattery and Ross, who had supplied the car for the job, were captured after police traced the vehicle to them. They were sentenced to life in prison.

Three months later, on June 30, "Bum" was posing as police officer and trying to shake down the proprietor of a Harlem restaurant for $1,000 at gunpoint when John Casey, a New York City patrolman on his way to work, passed by. Looking inside the restaurant, the officer recognized the wanted felon and went toward him. Rodgers turned his gun, fired twice at the cop, then hightailed it out of the restaurant and down the street. Casey returned fire but only managed to nip the hoodlum in his finger.

Casey chased Rodgers into a tenement and up to the second floor where "Bum" dashed into an apartment. The officer entered the flat just as Rodgers was climbing through a window onto the fire escape. As this was taking place Jacob Weingold, another off-duty cop who lived down the street and had heard the shots, grabbed his gun and came running. He saw "Bum" making his way down the fire escape and ran up as Casey was leaning out the window yelling for the fugitive to drop his gun. "Bum" dropped his gun but immediately jumped on Weingold, who managed to keep hold of the desperado until Casey made his way down to help.[14]

This time "Bum" was shipped off to the prison at Auburn, New York. In December of the same year he was brought back to New York City and sent to Mineola, Long Island, to stand trial for the $700 payroll robbery in Valley Stream. He was found guilty of the robbery, and another fifteen years were added to the seven he already faced. "Bum" had no intention of serving out his term, though, and a plan was in the works to free him.

On December 14, 1925, after the business in Mineola was wrapped up, "Bum" was handcuffed to Auburn Prison's deputy warden, Edward Beckwith, and driven into Manhattan by a Long Island detective. As the detective dropped the two off at Grand Central Station, he warned the deputy warden to be careful with Rodgers since he was "clever and dangerous." Beckwith, unimpressed, said he could "handle him all right."

A few moments before the train reached its first stop at the 125th Street station, "Bum" began complaining that he was hot and asked to take off his jacket. Beckwith looked around to make sure everything was all right and then unlocked the cuffs from his wrist. "Bum" took off his coat, folded it neatly, placed it in the upper rack, and then sat back down. Beckwith took off his coat and did the same. As the train was pulling into the station, Beckwith went to reattach the cuffs to his prisoner when someone from behind knocked him unconscious with an iron bar.

"Bum" and two cohorts ran down the aisle of the car, knocking down a brakeman who tried to block their way. When they jumped onto the platform, another railroad employee, assuming they were pickpockets, tried to stop them but was put out of commission with a kick to the stomach. The trio then ran down the stairs of the platform into a waiting taxi and escaped.[15]

Months went by and police found no trace of Rodgers. Because of the Welfare Island breakout, it was believed that McCormick and Cunniffe were the two men who had helped "Bum" escape. Although a raid on a New Jersey house and garage in July 1926 was said to yield the "Bum" Rodgers Gang's arsenal, as well as a few members and some of the loot from robberies, police really didn't come close to locating the escaped criminal or any of his known cronies, i.e., McCormick and Cunniffe, but that autumn things would take a dramatic and deadly turn.

Although "Bum" was hiding, Cunniffe and Crowley were preparing for what would prove to be their bloodiest job. Seeking more lucrative returns for their efforts, "Killer" and "Ice Wagon" set their sights on mail and payroll robberies. Though more dangerous, the profits from these jobs could be astronomical.

Their first attempt was to take place on October 4, 1926, but things went awry from the beginning and resulted in no payoff and the murder of two innocent people. The plan was to hijack a mail truck transporting securities and other valuable negotiable papers from New York City to an airfield five miles away in New Jersey. The gang was going to use two cars to overtake the truck, but before they had a chance to set the plan into motion one of the cars, a Pierce-Arrow containing two of the gangsters and the hardware that would be used for the job—six sawed-off shotguns, pistols, ammo, and wire cutters to be used on the locks of the truck—crashed into a ditch.

Three local teenagers drove up and helped the two very well-dressed men get the car back onto the road. One of the two gangsters offered the boys a drink of whiskey, and when they declined he gave them $2 and asked them to go up the road and fetch some ice cream, telling them they could keep the change. The lads drove off to get the ice cream, but on their return trip they saw the Pierce-Arrow coming toward them in the opposite lane and it careened across the road and hit them head-on.

The cars crashed in front of a farmhouse, and the hoodlums demanded that the farmer lend them his car so that they could go to the police and report the "accident." The farmer refused just as another farmer drove up, saw the damaged vehicles, and asked if he could be of assistance. The two bandits quickly jumped into his back seat and asked to be taken to the police station. Before they pulled out, however, the first farmer yelled a warning to his friend not to take the men anywhere and the teen whose car had been hit told the robbers, "You might as well stay here and straighten this thing out." Getting a bad feeling about his passengers, the Samaritan said he wanted to check his taillights but took the keys out of the ignition and ran into his friend's house.

Just then a sedan containing Frank Kearney, his wife, and his fifteen-year-old son, Robert, pulled up to see if they could be of help. The first farmer again yelled, "Don't take those men any where!" But the gangsters were getting desperate and one of them jumped on to the running board of Kearney's car. The forty-three-year-old Kearney immediately pushed him off the running board, and the bandit began to curse at him. Kearney got out of his car to deal with the man, but before he could do anything the gangster pulled out his pistol and fired a shot into his chest. As Kearney dropped to the ground the gangsters jumped into his car and sped off with his family. After the vehicle traveled about 150 yards Robert Kearney was tossed out with a bullet in his head, and after another 100 yards his mother was thrown onto the roadway. The killers managed to drive another 200 yards or so before slamming into a telegraph pole.

One of the gunmen was slightly wounded during the shootings and his face cut by windshield glass when the car hit the pole. The bandits ran to the nearest house and begged for a ride to the hospital. Two people in the house agreed to take them and they piled into a car, but a quarter-mile down the road the two were forced out at gunpoint. The gangsters sped off but broke through a railroad crossing trying the beat a train, which actually nicked the rear end of the car.[16] The hoodlums managed to elude police and ditched the car in Newark, New Jersey.

Robert Kearney succumbed to his head wound in the hospital, and his mother, who survived her tumble from the moving car, looked through a book of mug shots and identified Cunniffe as the man who had killed her son and husband. With the positive identification of "Killer," "Bum" was erroneously declared his accomplice. Knowing that one of the bandits had caught a face full of windshield, the police asked area doctors to report anyone who might show up with facial lacerations.[17]

After the Kearney debacle, the gang went on to its next venture, another mail truck robbery, and this time managed to pull it off in brazen fashion, although once again much innocent blood was spilled. The men to be involved in the job came together about a month beforehand to discuss the heist. The robbers included Cunniffe; Crowley; their confederates from the Bellmore bank job, Frank "Ghost" Kiekart and Ben Haas; and three new toughs, Canice Neary, Will Fanning, and Daniel Grosso.

On the morning of October 14, 1926, a mail truck at the Federal Reserve Bank in New York City was loaded with, among other paper valuables, the $160,000 cash payroll for the Singer Manufacturing Company. Its destination was the Elizabethport Banking Company in Elizabeth, New Jersey. While the truck was being loaded in the city, in Elizabeth a blue Studebaker driven by Canice Neary and containing "Ice Wagon" Crowley, "Ghost" Kiekart, and Grosso pulled to the curb at Elizabeth Avenue near Sixth Street. A black Packard driven by

Haas and containing Cunniffe and Fanning pulled to the curb farther back on Elizabeth Avenue.

About a half hour later, at 9:20 a.m., while the city of Elizabeth was going about its morning routine, the mail truck, driven by John Enz with security man Patrick Quinn riding shotgun, came rumbling down the street followed by its police escort, a motorcycle cop named Jacob Christman. When the truck and its escort passed the Packard, Haas pulled out behind the motorcycle cop and began to follow. Just as the truck was pulling into the intersection Neary pulled out from the curb, cutting it off. The truck came to a halt and the bandits jumped into action.

Grosso, armed with a Thompson submachine gun, sprayed the cab with bullets, killing Enz. Haas floored the Packard and plowed into the police motorcycle, sending Christman tumbling to the ground. Jumping from the sedan, Cunniffe shot the prostrate Christman for good measure, making sure he didn't cause any trouble, and then proceeded to cut the lock off the back of the truck. To thwart any would-be heroes, Fanning, also armed with a machine gun, stepped out of the car and began to blast indiscriminately up and down the street. Back up front, security man Patrick Quinn leapt from the truck's cab and began to fire at the robbers, but he was no match for Crowley, Kiekart, and Grosso, who knocked him out of the fight with bullets to his legs and wrist.

Once Cunniffe threw the mail sacks into the Packard, the gangsters piled into their respective cars and made a clean getaway. Rendezvousing at Cunniffe's Newark apartment, the gang divided the loot, which amounted to $20,400 per man. The gangsters then went their separate ways.[18]

From the get-go authorities correctly named Cunniffe as a chief suspect but, again, wrongly assumed that Rodgers had taken part. With their shares, Cunniffe, accompanied by his moll Frances Harris and "Ice Wagon" Crowley, headed for Detroit and rented an apartment in the Highland Park district on October 17. Neighbors described them as being well dressed and well behaved, but the quiet life would not last long.

In the early morning hours of Halloween, Highland Park police were called to investigate a shooting at the Highland Court apartments. Officers Ernest Jones, Ephraim Rancour, and Elmer Redman arrived and, assisted by tenant Jesse Wickam, a former cop, knocked on the door of the apartment where the shooting reportedly had occurred. Crowley answered the door wearing only a robe and underwear but had his right hand behind his back. "What's the trouble, buddy?" Jones asked. "Nothing at all," the hood replied. "What's all this shooting about?" Jones continued. "It's about this," Crowley said, jerking his pistol from behind and blasting Jones in the forehead at point-blank range.

Firing indiscriminately at the rest, he managed to hit Rancour in the shoulder and Wickam in the face.

Luckily for the surviving men, Crowley's gun jammed and he made a break for the bedroom to get another one but never made it. Redman and Rancour were able to get their pistols into action, and their bullets cut the desperado down in the hallway. The coroner would find six bullets in "Ice Wagon," the last couple fired into his prostrate body by an enraged Rancour.

When the cops entered the bedroom they found Cunniffe and his girlfriend dead on the bed wearing only their underwear. "Killer" had seven bullets in him and Frances two. What caused the falling out between the lifelong friends is unknown, but alcohol probably played a part as two empty bottles of champagne and a pint of whiskey were found on the premises. Ten thousand dollars in cash was on the kitchen table, leading authorities to believe the fight had been over the division of loot.[19]

The three bodies were sent back east. Frances ended up in Newark, where she came from, and Cunniffe and Crowley, their final night not withstanding, were buried as they had lived—side by side. As an interesting side note, the Detroit police reported that Crowley had scars on both cheeks, and witnesses to the Elizabeth robbery noted that one of the gunmen had a first-aid dressing on his face. Though circumstantial, this leads one to believe that Crowley most likely was the gangster whose face had been gashed in the car crash during the melee when the Kearneys were killed.

Less than a month after Crowley and Cunniffe were planted together, the intensive manhunt for "Bum" Rodgers came to an uneventful climax in a Bronx rooming house. On November 25, 1926, Detectives William Wallace and Ed Byrnes were staking out the tenement where "Bum's" wife, Kitty, had been living with her parents. At 1 a.m., they saw Kitty in a taxi along with another woman (who turned out to be her sister) and a man, who the detectives assumed was Rodgers but actually was Marty Madden, the brother of West Side mobster Owney "Killer" Madden.

The detectives followed, and at the intersection of Lexington and Ninety-sixth Street they cut off the taxi, jumped out with guns drawn, and approached the vehicle. They ordered the women to get out and yelled for Madden to stay inside. Marty either didn't hear the order or disregarded it, because he started to get out of the car, and Wallace, still assuming that Madden was Rodgers and knowing "Bum's" proclivity for shooting, fired into the cab. The shot missed Marty but slightly wounded the driver.[20]

After Kitty was apprehended the detectives went back to stake out her parents' home to see what sort of reaction the family would have to her arrest.

Wallace and Byrnes saw a man leave the apartment and tailed him to another tenement in the Bronx. Through some detective work they discovered "Bum" was staying in one of the apartments. Wallace went to the Bathgate Avenue police station to get reinforcements, and soon the neighborhood around the apartment building was swarming with cops. In addition to covering all possible escape routes on the ground, police stationed armed officers on nearby roofs, fire escapes, and at the elevated train station to await the shootout they were sure would come.

At 7:10 a.m. Wallace, Byrnes, and three other detectives made their way up to "Bum's" sixth-floor flat and jimmied the door. Once inside, they went into the first bedroom they came across and found James Pacificio and Helen Gershowitz, whom they took under control. As other cops began to climb in from the fire escape, Wallace and the other detectives entered the next bedroom and found the subject of their manhunt, looking emaciated and unkempt, sound asleep. Wallace grabbed one of Rodgers's arms and another detective grabbed the other. "Bum" woke up and pushed himself upright, which resulted in his being smacked on the forehead with the butt of a police pistol.

"You are a bum, all right; you look the part. You've grown a mustache," Wallace said to the scruffy, unshaven bandit. "What about all that money you're supposed to have?" "Oh, the newspapers have been printing lots of stuff that's not so," Rodgers replied. "For one thing, I haven't left New York since I escaped. I have been around here all the time." The lawmen again pressed him about the money. "Here's all the money I have," he said, reaching for his pants, out of which he pulled a single penny. A subsequent search proved that was in fact all the money he had.[21]

While "Bum" was being restrained in bed, a detective searched under the pillow and mattress for his gun, which was eventually found in a dresser drawer. The police felt fortunate to have conducted the raid when they did because an alarm clock next to the bed was set to go off at 7:30 a.m. and "Bum" had told them that if he'd had the chance to use his gun, he would have.

Back at the station Rodgers was questioned about a number of things, including his relationship with "Killer" Cunniffe. "I hadn't seen Cunniffe since a few days after I escaped that time [meaning the breakout from Welfare Island with McCormick]. He was a good fellow, all right, but too fond of taking people at their face value and talking to them. He wasn't safe to be with. He was too good natured."[22]

Rodgers also was asked who had helped him escape from the train. "You know better than to ask me that," he replied. He did, however, give the six addresses at which he had stayed since his escape and also talked about his life in hiding. "Say, I've lived on a crust of bread," he said. "I've been reduced to the direst poverty. The poorest of the poor gave to me, people who couldn't afford to give me a cent." He also said he had a radio and that he had listened to the police bulletins about him. When asked why he had stayed in the city, he said, "Why did I stay in New York? Well, this is a nine-day town, and I thought after a while the papers would not be printing my name and I could do something and get away to the west."[23]

The next day authorities decided to charge "Bum" with violating the Sullivan Law, which carried a mandatory life sentence since he was a four-time offender. When told that he would be spending the rest of his life behind bars, the bandit replied, "Gee, that's a tough break."[24]

Although District Attorney McGeehan considered Rodgers a "rat," after hours of questioning the well-read hoodlum he couldn't help but be impressed with "Bum's" smarts. "He's a remarkably intelligent man," the D.A. said, "and mentally, at least, he is no bum."[25] McGeehan went on to say that he believed the bad man must have studied law because he was just as knowledgeable as some of the D.A.'s assistants. This was no doubt a result of Rodgers's habit of reading as much as four hours a day. It was a trait he had picked up from Gerald Chapman, whom he had known during a previous incarceration at Clinton Prison in Dannemora.

Though Rodgers would talk for hours about himself—"I'm a bum from drink. Most of the trouble I've had, I got in when I was half stewed."[26]—the questioning always came back to the train escape and who his accomplices were. "I'd sooner die on the rack than tell who helped me escape," he said. When asked if it had been Cunniffe and Crowley, he responded, "They're both dead. I could blame it on them and no one would be the wiser, but they had nothing to do with it. Why drag in dead men?"[27]

Rodgers was found guilty of gun possession and ended up back at Dannemora after a brief stay in Sing Sing. On January 14, 1931, with a noose he had fastened out of a shirt tied around his neck, "Bum" Rodgers stepped onto a stool, tied the other end of the shirt to a ceiling fixture, and escaped prison one final time.[28]

The Daly Show

"Yes, certainly I did it. I shot both of them.
But I wish I'd stuck to stealing tires."
— Frank Daly

J ust over the northern boundary of the Bronx sits the town of Mount Vernon, and east of that is New Rochelle. The latter was the home of David DeMaio, who was labeled the "Bootleg King" of that Westchester County town. DeMaio got greedy and tried to augment his rumrunning profits by orchestrating what he thought would be an easy robbery. Little did he know his "sure thing" would result in four deaths.

Since he lived in New Rochelle and was known in the surrounding area DeMaio wouldn't actually take part in the job, so he ventured into New York City to put a gang together. The target was the payroll for a construction company working in the village of Pelham Manor. Five men were brought together for the job: John "the Dope" Marino, Salvatore "Solly Cheesecake" Melito, Joe Mazza, Jimmie Lipso, and Frank Daly. The six men rendezvoused at the Daylight Bakery on Manhattan's Upper East Side to plan the heist. The logistics were all set and the robbery was planned for early summer; however, when the day came, the paymaster didn't show up at the designated time and the men bailed.[1]

About a month later DeMaio approached the bandits with another scheme. He told them that every morning at 2:30, a trolley car nicknamed "the Owl" because of its early run time left the New Rochelle terminal en route to its final destination at 241st Street in the Bronx. The important piece of information was that an inspector for the trolley company rode the car every day to Mount Vernon where he would hand over the previous day's earnings to another inspector. DeMaio also mentioned that because of heavy Sunday traffic, the inspector could be expected to carry about $3,500 in cash on Monday.[2]

After driving out to reconnoiter the route, the bandits hatched a plan. Daly, who had the most nerve among the group, was in charge of the actual robbery. He, Lipso, and Mazza would board the train at its first stop, rob the inspector, and force the motorman to stop the car at a designated spot outside Mount Vernon where Marino and Melito would be waiting in a car. The five of them then would drive to New York City to meet DeMaio and split the loot.

On July 25, 1925, "the Owl" left New Rochelle and made the first stop. Two men got off as Daly, Lipso, and Mazza climbed aboard and seated themselves in different parts of the car so it wouldn't appear they were together. About fifteen minutes into the ride, as the trolley passed the bandits' sedan, Daly got up and walked to the front of the car, followed by his cohorts. The inspector was sitting directly behind the motorman filling out some paperwork when Daly pulled out his gun and ordered him to hand over his three sacks.

At first the inspector seemed to think it was some sort of joke and didn't comply, but then, realizing the gravity of the situation, he went for his hip pocket. Daly fired into him and then ordered the motorman to stop the car. Chances are the trolley driver didn't understand what was going on because he didn't stop right away, so Daly blasted him as well. When the man collapsed, engaging the ironically named "dead-man's brake," the car came to a halt. The bandits grabbed the satchels, jumped off the trolley, and dashed for the getaway car. As they roared off, Daly fired an errant shot at a pedestrian he mistook for a police officer.

Marino, the driver, was extremely nervous and began taking turns on two wheels. After one such turn he was unable to regain control of the Cadillac and slammed into a bridge, rendering the car useless. The bandits had only put a little more than a mile between them and the trolley car, and now they were on foot. They grabbed the loot and headed for some nearby woods where they split up. It was about this time they realized DeMaio's information was a little off. One of the inspector's bags was filled with canceled transfer tickets and the other two contained only about $1,700 between them, most of it in silver. As they ran through the woods, they periodically had to jettison some of the coins to lighten the load.[3]

Back in New York City, DeMaio was growing restless waiting for his confederates, so he jumped in his car and drove to the site of the robbery to see what had happened. En route he came across the smashed Caddy and began to get nervous. It had been only a few minutes since the crash, but a cop was already on the scene and waved DeMaio over, telling him to go to the nearest police call box and report the accident to the station. DeMaio went to the call box and pretended to phone the station, then returned and told the cop no one had answered. After that, he drove home.

Meanwhile, the other hoodlums were frantically trying to get back to the city. Marino and Daly stuck together and got lost. They ended up hiding in a hole that was being dug for a new sewer and spent seven hours listening to and, when the sun came up, watching the search parties hunting for them. At about 10 a.m. they decided to chance it and climbed out of the ditch and walked to the nearest train station. Sure that someone would report two men covered with dirt, they nervously boarded a train and surprisingly made it back into town without any trouble. The two separated after the train got into the city, and there was no rendezvous with the rest of the gang.

Searchers recovered about $1,400 of the stolen loot in the woods, meaning that, at best, a couple of the bandits were able to split $300—$150 for each of the men on the trolley who died of their wounds.[4]*

While the hoodlums were making their way back to the city, Captain Michael Silverstein and Lieutenant Herman Mattes of the New Rochelle Police Department traced the license plate of the Cadillac, which they were sure would turn out to be stolen. Since it was a New York City plate, they contacted police headquarters there, and Detectives Thomas Martin and Steven Donohue were assigned to the case. The car belonged to a woman named Edna Baltimore, and the four lawmen paid her a visit. She denied any knowledge of the crime, saying that she always kept the car in a garage and hadn't used it in several days.

Shortly after meeting with Ms. Baltimore, Detective Martin remembered that she was married to an ex-con named John "the Dope" Marino, and they decided to question her some more. When they returned, Ms. Baltimore had a visitor, Marian Mooney, who the detectives knew was married to an ex-con named Joseph Ryan but also played around on the side with a hoodlum named Frank Daly.

The women were grilled but denied knowing anything. However, since they were both involved with known criminals, and Edna's car was linked to a murder case, the cops arrested them and brought them back to Mount Vernon.

---

* Daly later said his take amounted to $35.

Although Edna Baltimore and Marian Mooney swore they knew nothing about the robbery and that their men hadn't been involved, the fellows were nowhere to be found. With the help of a stool pigeon, Martin and Donohue learned that a girlfriend of Marino's was in the hospital with a serious condition. Detectives staked out the girl's room, and soon letters started to arrive from Ohio signed by "J." The writing was compared to samples of Marino's that had been obtained from Edna's apartment and it was determined that Marino was indeed writing the letters. The detectives were then informed by the stool pigeon that Marino was being supplied with money by a syndicate of gangsters.

Authorities in the Buckeye State were asked to keep a lookout for "the Dope," but he wasn't found. Time continued to pass and the New York detectives began to get frustrated. Finally, about two weeks after the murders, detectives received a break when Marino sent his girlfriend a letter that ended with, "See you soon." On August 10 the stool pigeon told the detectives that Marino was back in town, and on the following day the hospital received another letter from the bandit—and this one had an address on it. The apartment was staked out, and on August 13 Marino was arrested while leaving.[5]

Looking at the electric chair, Marino quickly turned state's evidence and ratted out the whole gang. David DeMaio, who never went into hiding and was confident that his associate would never squeal, was picked up at his house on August 16. Things were finally coming together when the stool pigeon dropped a sweet piece of news into the detectives' ears: Frank Daly was hiding out at a farmhouse in Westport, Connecticut.

Joined by Silverstein and Mattes from Mount Vernon, Detectives Martin and Donohue went to Westport, where they hooked up with four local officers and set out for the farmhouse. They found it about midnight and figured they would have a better chance of taking Daly without a firefight if they waited until sunrise to make their move. At 5:15 a.m., as the sun was coming up, all avenues of escape from the house were covered.

Donohue and one of the local cops kicked in the rear door and made their way to Daly's room, where they found the fugitive sitting on his bed smoking a cigarette.[6] They arrested him without any trouble. Daly spoke freely about the killings, saying the inspector had thought he was kidding when he tried to hold him up, but "when the inspector saw I was serious, he moved his hand toward his hip pocket, and then I plugged him. Then I told the motorman to stop the car, and when he didn't do so, I shot him, too."

Waiving extradition, Daly was brought back to Mount Vernon and joined Marino and DeMaio in the White Plains County Jail, although the three men were held in separate cells. On the way, Silverstein spoke with the young killer and

asked him what he would have done if any of the passengers had tried to interfere. "I'd have shot them, too," he replied. When the detective said, "I guess you
know what this means," Daly responded, "Sure I know. The chair. I'm not afraid
to face what others have faced."[7]

On Wednesday, October 14, 1925, Daly was put on trial and two days later was
convicted of murder in the first degree, which of course meant what he already
knew: the chair. His sweetie Marian Mooney was on hand, and when the verdict
was read she wailed, "Oh Frankie, Frankie!" The judge was forced to bang his
gavel and demand order when her sobs disrupted the proceedings. Outside in the
anteroom the twenty-two-year-old slayer's mother was apprised of the situation
and she fainted. Frank, on the other hand, retained his cool.[8]

After Daly it was DeMaio's turn in the courtroom. Since he actually hadn't
taken take part in the crime, he was confident he would be exonerated. But on
November 27, after both sides had made their summations, it took the jury just
fifteen minutes to find New Rochelle's "King of Bootleggers" guilty of first-
degree murder. The defendant was dumfounded and his wife passed out.[9]

DeMaio joined Daly in Sing Sing's death house, and the lawyers for both men
went to work to save their clients from the electric chair. As Daly's appointment
with the Grim Reaper approached, he made a statement saying that DeMaio had
not been involved in any way in the trolley car robbery. The job, according to
Daly, was actually planned by another man, Dominick Tremarco, and he signed
an affidavit stating such. On July 24, 1926, DeMaio's counsel pleaded with the
state supreme court to grant a stay of execution so that Daly could be questioned
in hopes that the information gained would be enough to secure a new trial for
their client. The court, however, said that DeMaio had been found guilty fair and
square and that the Tremarco business was just a ruse on Daly's part to save himself from the chair.[10]

Told that his stay had been denied, Daly remained calm. He was visited by
Marian Mooney for the last time later that day but spent his remaining two
hours with a priest. Then, at 11 p.m., he walked into the death chamber and met
his Maker.[11]

Even though the Tremarco affidavit hadn't been enough to save Daly,
DeMaio felt sure it would at least cast some doubt on his own guilt and he would
be granted a reprieve. "Twelve men have I seen go out of this place," he told
reporters. "Eight of them have been electrocuted. Twelve have gone, and I will
be the thirteenth. I'm Italian, and I admit I am superstitious, but this one time I
am not."[12] His lawyer petitioned the state supreme court for a new trial because
of the new evidence offered by Daly, and he also sent the affidavit to the governor hoping that he would show clemency.

On August 19, less than a month after Daly's execution, DeMaio almost fainted when he was told the court had denied a stay. Unlike Daly, the thirty-three-year-old DeMaio spent his last day in anguish. His family made a final visit, and as the hour of death grew ever closer, his uneasiness grew. Two men were scheduled to die that night, and since the other had steady nerves it was decided that DeMaio would go first to spare him any additional anxiety. Up until the end, DeMaio maintained his innocence: "Frank Daly, who died for this crime, swore I was innocent before he died, and I feel that I should be able to live for my family's sake." The law, however, did not agree.[13]

THE CANDY KID

> *"I considered myself above law and order."*
> — RICHARD REESE WHITTEMORE

J ust about two weeks before Gerald Chapman walked the last mile, Jazz Age America was introduced to a new, self-proclaimed "super bandit" in Baltimore-born-and-bred Richard Reese Whittemore. Until his capture he was known only to the police of his hometown in Maryland, but after he and his gang were captured in New York City it became apparent just what a desperate group he and his cohorts were. With a penchant for fine clothes and Cadillacs, the Whittemore Gang stole an estimated one million dollars' worth of jewels in a crime spree that lasted about a year.

The Whittemore saga begins at the start of the twentieth century when Richard was born on September 8, 1900,[*] one of three children in a working-class Methodist family. His father was a mechanic, and although they were not rich the

---

[*] Various dates have been given for his birth. This date was taken from his death certificate but is suspect because the math doesn't work. He was executed on August 13, 1926, and gave his age as twenty-five years, eleven months, and twenty-seven days. Another source gives his birthday as December 9, 1898. Census data only adds to the confusion as he didn't make an appearance until the census of 1910 in which his age was listed as seven years, indicating he was born around 1903.

Whittemore house was not wanting. Richard appears to have had some mental defect from the get-go, possibly kleptomania. One social worker stated that he would steal anything, whether it had value or not. Like other youngsters, he attended classes during the week and could be found belting out hymns on the weekend at Sunday school. Apparently he missed the whole "Thou shall not steal" lesson, because at the age of nine he came home from a church social with eight spoons, two hymn books, and some communion glasses. When his mother found them, she immediately returned the items.

There is also a story that, at the age of eleven while his family was visiting some friends, he found a gun in a drawer and ran to the kitchen door and fired it. The police were called, and while no charges were pressed since nobody was hurt, Richard received a lecture from the judge. As he was entering his teen years, Richard was a compulsive thief, and the local police already knew about him because he continually stole from stores. Oddly, whenever the police confronted him he would admit to the crime and they would take him home, and his parents would either return the merchandise or pay for it.

As a teenager he began spending less time at home and more time with a gang of kids from the bad side of town. His evenings were spent hanging out, getting into fights, and getting into other kinds of trouble. When he was fourteen he was placed in a reform school, and after a year it was declared that the boy had been straightened out and he was sent home. Now that Richard was fifteen, his father was able to land him a job as a mechanic's apprentice.

Around this time Richard became reacquainted with a young girl named Margaret Messler, with whom he was smitten. He originally had met her at school, but when he was sent off to reform school, any interaction ended. Now back home with disposable income from his job, Richard rekindled the romance. Before long he fell back in with his delinquent friends and had resumed his old habits. By 1916 his parents had had enough, and labeling him as an "incorrigible," they had him placed in Baltimore's St. Mary's Industrial School. A year later he was out and back with his street gang. Margaret was also waiting for him, and the romance continued.[1]

When World War I broke out Richard joined the Coast Guard after the Navy refused him because of poor eyesight. However, his compulsion for taking things that didn't belong to him got the better of him and he ended up in the Portsmouth Naval Prison for stealing. After serving his term he was given a dishonorable discharge.[2]

After his stint in the Navy, Whittemore returned to Baltimore and married Margaret. The young couple then journeyed to New York City where in 1919 the bridegroom was convicted of burglary in Yonkers and sent to the Elmira Reformatory for a year. While there he met another young man named Anthony Paladino, who would one day become a member of his gang. Upon his release in 1920 Whittemore returned home to Baltimore and put together a new mob.

In October 1921 he was arrested for burglarizing a Baltimore house and sentenced to a three-year term in the Maryland Penitentiary. While there Richard met two men who would have an impact on his future: brothers Leon and Jacob Kraemer. With ties to "Dopey" Benny Fein on the Lower East Side, they were described by the head of New York City's detective division as "two of the best safe robbers in the country."[3] Leon also had a record in Europe, and in 1915 both were deported from London as undesirables. In 1916 they were arrested for attempting to rob a safe in Baltimore and sentenced to ten years in the pen, where they subsequently met Whittemore.[4]

While in prison Richard exhibited good behavior and was rewarded with a job in the hospital ward, and after serving three years he was granted a parole in May 1924. After his release he went back to Baltimore and returned to crime. This time he formed a gang with William "Baltimore Willie" Unkelbach and a junkie named Milton "Shuffles" Goldberg. Together they stole some Internal Revenue Service badges and began to shake down saloonkeepers in Baltimore and Philadelphia. It was in Philly that detectives raided an apartment on January 15, 1925, and found Richard, his wife, Margaret, and three others. During the raid Margaret passed two pistols to the men and tried to fire one herself, but the detectives were able to thwart the group. Because of her fierce actions Margaret was christened "the Tiger Girl" by police. One of the gang members turned state's evidence, and Richard and the others were sent back to the penitentiary for fifteen-year terms.[5]

On February 20, two weeks into his sentence, Richard purposely burned his hand and, with a piece of pipe concealed in his overalls, was sent to the hospital ward. Since he was known as a model prisoner from his previous term, no one thought a guard was needed to escort him. He crossed the prison yard to the building housing the medical center where sixty-year-old guard Robert Holtman opened the door for him. Whittemore received the necessary attention to his hand, and as he was leaving, Holtman turned to open the door for him again—but this time Richard took the pipe out and smashed it into the guard's skull. He then helped himself to the unconscious guard's money, prison keys, and a pistol. A trusty who witnessed the attack was forced at gunpoint to open the door leading to the street.[6]

Once outside the prison, Richard made his way to a bus stop and took a coach to the outskirts of Baltimore, where he hid out for two days before heading into Philadelphia on a truck hauling bootleg booze with a pal named "Chicago Tommy" Langrella. In the interim Holtman succumbed to his head wound, making Whittemore not only a robber and escaped convict, but a murderer as well.[7]

Whittemore stayed in Philadelphia long enough to grow a beard, and after dying his hair and beard red, he headed back to Baltimore with Langrella and hooked up with Unkelbach, Goldberg, and new gang members Simon Gilden and Edwin "Spike" Kenny. They committed their first robbery on March 11, when they robbed a bank collector of $11,000.[8]

After the robbery Whittemore spent time traveling between Baltimore, New York, and Cleveland. While in New York City he got in touch with the Kraemer brothers, and a new gang embarked on a career as jewelry store bandits. Whittemore and the other Baltimore men were the muscle and gunmen, while the Kraemers brought experience and beneficial contacts to the mob. They knew which places to hit and which fences would take the loot.

In May 1925, as the new gang was preparing for its first known job, Whittemore ran into his old Elmira pal Anthony Paladino and chitchatted for a bit. On May 8 he showed up in Paladino's Little Italy neighborhood with Goldberg and Unkelbach, and they took Paladino on as a gunman.[9]

The next day, with Unkelbach at the wheel of a stolen Cadillac, Goldberg, Whittemore, and Paladino headed toward the Ross Jewelry Store at Grand and Forsyth streets. When they arrived, Goldberg jumped out and took up a guard position outside while Whittemore and Paladino headed inside. Unkelbach stayed in the Caddy and kept the motor running.

Upon entering the store the two hoodlums pulled out guns, and Paladino cowed the three people inside into a back room where he handcuffed them while Whittemore cleaned out the safe and display cases. Carrying two black suitcases containing the loot, the bandits jumped into the car and Unkelbach drove to a corner near Paladino's house. The three men jumped out and took the jewelry to the latter's mother's home at 78 Mulberry Street while Unkelbach went to dump the car. About twenty minutes later Goldberg went out to get the fence while Whittemore and Paladino took the satchels to the St. George Hotel, where the robbers and the fence had scheduled a rendezvous. The fence arrived and, after a bit of haggling, agreed to give them $12,000 for the haul.[10]

That summer the gang rendezvoused at a hotel in Coney Island while Jacob Kraemer cased the Stanley Jewelry Store at 125th Street and Seventh Avenue. On July 16, with a new wheelman named Nate Weinzimmer, the gang took off in a stolen Packard for Harlem. Upon arrival Nate stayed with the car while Jacob took his position as lookout. Whittemore and Paladino then entered the shop, followed by Goldberg and Leon Kraemer. The gunmen forced the store's occupants to a room at the rear while Kraemer began collecting the loot. As the robbery was wrapping up, Jacob entered with another employee at gunpoint and put him with the others. When all the jewelry had been collected, they ran out to the Packard and returned to Coney Island. Jake Kraemer had a fence waiting, and the bandits sold him the loot for $15,000.[11]

Autumn brought more jobs as well as murder and attempted murder. On October 29 bandits robbed an armored car in Buffalo, New York, of $93,000, killing two bank employees and seriously wounding a third. Although Gerald Chapman's pal "Dutch" Anderson was initially given credit for the job, it was Whittemore who would eventually stand trial, although he probably had nothing to do with it.

Two days after the Buffalo job Whittemore was also involved in the attempted murder of one of his hometown pals, Edwin "Spike" Kenny, whom he shot at a roadhouse on the outskirts of Baltimore. According to Paladino, the shooting was a personal affair that took place when Richard, maniacally overprotective and jealous of his wife, felt his friend had either made a move on or slighted her in some way at a Halloween party. "Spike" was shot and left for dead, but as the story goes, when Richard learned "Spike" was only wounded and recuperating in a hospital, the hotheaded gunman went there to finish the job, telling the staff on duty that if Kenny were not sent out to the street he would come in and shoot up the place. Nothing happened as Whittemore was finally calmed down by his wife.[12]

The gang pulled three more jobs that fall. Paladino walked into the Ernest Jewelry Store at 566 Columbus Avenue to case the place that was to be the gang's next target. He asked to see a cigarette case, and after leaving a $3 deposit and a fictitious address met Jake Kraemer down the block. But when he told Jake it could be an easy score, Kraemer said, "Don't bother with that for a couple of days."[13] He had another target picked out—the Lindhous jewelry shop on Thirteenth Street and Sixth Avenue.

For two days Jake watched the shop, noting how many people were there at certain times and trying to determine the best time to hit the place. After two days he was joined by Paladino and Whittemore at closing time to give the store a final once-over. Paladino went inside to check things out, and this time he put down a deposit on a ring while casing the store. It was determined that the robbery would take place just before closing time on November 23 using the same crew from the Stanley job.

At the appointed time, the four gunmen entered the store and Paladino and Goldberg once again corralled the employees into a rear room. One man tried to fight, but Paladino smacked him over the head with his pistol butt. As Leon Kraemer and Whittemore were collecting the jewelry, Paladino and Goldberg tied up the employees with twine. After a few minutes they heard a woman screaming, and Jake Kraemer appeared with two women that he'd had to bring in from outside at gunpoint. Paladino told them to be quiet, and then they were tied up. The bandits made their getaway with between $75,000 and $100,000 in jewelry, which they sold to a fence for $12,000.[14]

A few weeks later, on December 2, the gang went back and hit the Ernest Jewelry Store on Columbus Avenue. It was basically a reprise of the Lindhous job, complete with a would-be hero getting smacked over the head and Jake Kraemer having to escort someone off the street at gunpoint. However, the major differences were that somehow the alarm was tripped—in vain, however, because the bandits made a clean getaway—and Jake was only able to sell the take for a paltry $3,000.[15]

The Lindhous job was followed by another small-time theft in which a store owner was followed after withdrawing some merchandise from the vault of the Harriman National Bank. They followed the man's chauffeur-driven car, and when it pulled over and the man got out, they ran up, stole the merchandise, and made their escape. However, all that they got were watches, penknives, and cuff links that brought in a small payoff.[16]

On December 22 one of Whittemore's Baltimore buddies, Simon Gilden, was found in lower Manhattan with a bullet in the back of his head.[*] On December 23 another robbery was committed at a jewelry manufacturing plant at Fulton and Nassau streets, but the proprietor managed to close the safe and protect $50,000 worth of uncut diamonds before the gang could get to them. Seeing this, either Leon Kraemer or Whittemore knocked the man over the head with a pistol, saying, "Take that for closing the safe door." Another employee went to close the second safe and got the same treatment. The bandits were able to get just $10,000 worth of goods from the second safe, which amounted to only a few hundred dollars per man after being sold.[17]

Although 1925 ended on a sour note with three small jobs, 1926 started off with the biggest haul of the gang's brief career. Jake began shadowing Albert Goudvis, the senior proprietor of Goudvis Brothers Diamond Merchants. As part of his daily routine Goudvis would take uncut diamonds from the vaults of Harriman National Bank at Fifth Avenue and Forty-fourth Street and walk to his firm on Forty-eight Street. Since traffic was so heavy on Fifth Avenue it was decided to hijack Goudvis in front of 14 West Forty-eighth Street before he made it to his place of business.

On January 11, the morning of the job, Weinzimmer pulled up in front of the predetermined address and waited while Whittemore and Leon Kraemer walked up and down Forty-eighth Street. In other strategic locations along Forty-eighth and the corner of Fifth Avenue were Paladino, Goldberg, and Unkelbach, who was

---

[*] Although Whittemore was assumed to have been Gilden's killer, there is no actual proof. The dead man, along with "Shuffles" Goldberg, was said to have been involved with bootleggers in Baltimore, Philadelphia, and New York, so his murder could have been the result of any number of things. Lending credence to the Whittemore angle is that he told police during his interrogation he had lost a considerable sum of money investing in a bad bootlegging venture, which could be seen as a motive. Another possible motive was provided by Baltimore authorities who stated that Gilden had been spotted making visits to the D.A.'s office there and word made it back to the gang.

brought in for the job. The men were waiting to see Jake Kraemer come up the street because right behind him would be the jeweler. Finally, after an hour's wait, they saw Kraemer turn the corner, followed by Goudvis and one of his associates.

As soon as the jewelers hit the mark, four of the gunmen fell on them. They didn't give the victims a chance to surrender the merchandise; they just bashed both men over the head with their pistols and grabbed the satchel containing the diamonds. Goudvis was knocked cold, but his associate managed to get up and stumble a few feet before collapsing. The men who took part in the robbery jumped into the car and sped off as the others just disappeared in the crowd.

There were many witnesses who began to yell for the police, and a former cop named George Helwig, who worked as a security guard, was able to empty his pistol at the escaping Cadillac.** Two other cops also managed to fire at the auto before it finally made a clean getaway. The most brazen of the mob's jobs also turned out to be its most lucrative. The gems stolen were worth around $150,000, and after they were sold each bandit walked away with $12,000.[18]

As spring of 1926 approached, New York detectives were aware that the Whittemore mob was responsible for a number of gem thefts in the city. About March 1 they received word that Goldberg had returned to the city, and on March 3 two detectives traced him to the Hotel Empire and put a tail on him. Before long "Shuffles" jumped into his Cadillac and drove to an Upper West Side apartment which detectives learned had been rented two weeks earlier by Whittemore. The lawmen followed the bandits for a little over two weeks until they were sure they could pick up the whole gang. They decided to make their move on March 18.[19]

That night detectives tailed Whittemore, Goldberg, and Leon Kraemer to the Chantee Club and waited outside as the bandits entered the nitery at about 10 p.m. About five o'clock the next morning the hoodlums emerged and drove off in their Caddy, and the detectives once again followed but lost them on Fifth Avenue. That afternoon detectives spotted Whittemore in the company of Pasquale Chicarelli, brother of one of the Chantee's owners, and a bandit pal named Bernard Mortillaro. They followed them to the Astor Hotel, where they had dinner. The bandits then made a forty-minute stop at the Loew's Arcade before driving to a house on Mott Street, where they stayed for an hour before heading back to the Chantee .

The trio arrived at about 3 a.m. and after two hours and ten minutes piled back into the Cadillac and drove up Broadway to a restaurant on Eighty-sixth

---

** Exactly a month later, on February 11, 1926, Helwig disappeared after telling his sister, with whom he lived, that he was going for a walk. His employers said he'd seemed depressed, but his sister felt certain he was the victim of foul play. A theory arose that he had been bumped off by the Whittemore Gang because he could identify its members; however, on May 4, his body was fished out of the East River and he was declared a suicide.

Street, then headed back downtown. About this time Whittemore realized they were being followed and fired a shot at the detectives, who returned fire and forced the bandits' car to the curb at Columbus Circle where the hoods surrendered without any more trouble.[20] Back at the station, Whittemore admitted he was surprised that he'd allowed himself to be caught. "I never figured you guys would get me," he said. "I always thought I could shoot my way out if it came that. But I didn't after all."[21]

Authorities in Baltimore and New York City wanted Whittemore, but the police in Buffalo asked that he be sent there first to stand trial for the October 29, 1925, armored car robbery in which two guards were killed. Gerald Chapman's former accomplice "Dutch" Anderson and his associates initially were suspected, but when witnesses were shown a picture of Whittemore after his arrest, a couple agreed that Richard had been one of the participants, even though they had previously identified someone else.

When asked if he would rather stand trial in Buffalo or Baltimore, Whittemore responded, "Oh, what's the difference? I don't care what they do."[22] While the authorities were working out where he would be tried first, Whittemore's father, Rawling, came to visit him at the Tombs (his mother died of tuberculosis in 1918). At first Richard refused to see him but gave in after his keepers goaded him a bit, telling him that he was being unfair since his father had traveled all the way from Baltimore to see him.

Before he went in to see his son, Rawling was corralled by the assistant district attorney, who told him he should try to get his son to tell all. When brought face to face, father and son were a bit apprehensive. They shook hands, and all that a visibly upset Rawling could say at first was, "My son, my boy." After some small talk, Richard could see his father was still upset and said, "Now, don't take on so. You can't blame yourself for the position I am in. It was in me and had to come out."[23]

Rawling tried to get his son to open up, but he refused. He did add, however, "If they turn my wife out in the street, I'll tell the works—the whole works—and it will startle New York."

As Rawling was leaving the prison, reporters questioned him about his son. "What can I say?" He told them. "I have nothing to say. I'll do all in my power to aid my son. All these stories in the newspapers can't be true. They have pictured my boy as being as bad as Jesse James."[24]

Meanwhile, the police were continuing their work. Unkelbach had led them to the apartment of the gang's fence, Joseph Trop, at 156 Second Avenue, where they arrested him with $20,000 in jewelry and two guns. He claimed to be a jeweler and when asked where his office was, he replied, "In my hat."[25]

When Trop was brought to the station, Unkelbach was there. "Hi Joe," he said, but the fence ignored him. "You know me," he insisted, "I was introduced to you by Jack Kraemer." "Oh, yes," Trop replied simply. The forty-year-old fence told police he had been born in Russian Poland and knew the Kraemer brothers in Warsaw. He came to America in 1912 and became reacquainted with the brothers on the Lower East Side in 1916. He admitted to being introduced to the Whittemore mob but denied ever buying anything from them. He also admitted being friends with rumrunning mogul and former Lower East Side tough "Waxey" Gordon.[26]

After much deliberation New York Governor Al Smith decided that Whittemore would be extradited to Buffalo instead of Baltimore. The reasoning was that if Baltimore should fail to secure a guilty verdict, New York would have a difficult time getting the bandit back; however, if Buffalo failed, he could easily be extradited to the Big Apple.[27]

On April 1, Whittemore was taken to Buffalo. "There will be no chance of his escape," a detective told reporters before they left for Grand Central Station to catch the train. "He'll be carried into Buffalo either dead or alive." He went on to explain that two detectives would be shackled to Whittemore at all times and added, "If, under these circumstances, he wants to take a chance, we are ready. We all know how to shoot. He will be executed immediately."

Then, with a guard handcuffed to each of Whittemore's hands and ten others along for support, the group left for the station. On the way there was a cordon of photographers, and the gangster desperately tried to kick one of them. On the train detectives asked him to explain his actions. "I recognized him," he said. He's the bird who took my wife's picture when I told him not to. I wish I killed him."[28]

When he arrived in Buffalo, Richard released a statement to the press through his lawyer which read:

> I am not an angel, but I wish the people of Buffalo to know that neither I nor any of my pals had anything to do with the Bank of Buffalo job. The only thing I ask from the city is that it retain its reputation of fair play and justice and give me a fair and impartial trial, free from prejudice and passion. If I am given that, I am sure I will be acquitted.[29]

While preparations for the trial took place Richard was housed in the Erie County Jail. He received considerable mail, including a letter that contained complete floor plans of the jail and a package of stationery from Baltimore with saw blades inside. Authorities intercepted these and concluded both had been sent by deluded fans of the robber and not gang members.[30]

About two weeks later the trial began and the prosecution was hell-bent on putting Richard away. After a few days he received a letter from Margaret, who was following the trial in the papers. In part, she wrote: "O, daddy, my heart is almost broken. O, how I love you. I am worried to death for fear they may frame you the way they did [Gerald] Chapman."[31] On April 12, Margaret was released from prison and went to Buffalo with Richard's father.

Margaret needn't have worried about the trial's outcome. Prosecutors built their case around the witnesses who had at first identified another hoodlum as one of the robbers before changing their minds and saying it was Richard. The jury was unable to come to a verdict, leading the judge to dismiss them, and Whittemore was acquitted. When the decision was announced, the hundreds of people who had packed the courthouse began to cheer. As Richard was escorted from the courtroom men threw their hats in the air and numerous women and young ladies tried to shake his hand. They also cheered for Margaret as she left the building with tears streaming down her cheeks. "I'm tickled to death," she told reporters. "That's all I can tell you. I never thought they would convict him. Oh, I'm so happy."[32]

The next day a jubilant Richard was playing pinochle with detectives on a train heading back to New York City. As if rehearsing for his upcoming trial, he told the guards that he had killed Holtman in self-defense during his jailbreak. "That guard was a bad guy," he said. "He had already killed three prisoners before I killed him. I had just been sentenced to sixteen years' imprisonment at the time, and you know my disposition—I wasn't in a very good humor. I was also just out of the hospital and not feeling any too good, and I wasn't going to let him knock me around.

"I was standing with a negro prisoner in a place where we prisoners had no right to stand," he continued. "I saw the guard approaching, and I knew I was in for it. So I picked up a piece of iron bar and hid it inside my coat. When the guard reached us, he started an argument and struck me. Then he reached for his gat. I knew he would shoot, so I let him have it."[33]

To avoid another "Bum" Rodgers-type escape, six guards were stationed at the 125th Street stop for the three-minute layover before heading to Grand Central Station. While the train sat in the station, Richard waved to a group of girls who were part of a group that had come to see the famous hoodlum. When the train reached its final destination and the group began walking toward the street, Richard, enjoying his fame, said to the detectives, "Well, the rubberneckers will get another chance to give me the once-over. And I suppose I'll be greeted with the usual barrage of camera flashlights." The cameras were there, and he proved much more amiable than he had been before leaving for Buffalo, but the large crowds he was expecting were nowhere to be seen. "Where are they?" the disappointed robber asked his captors. "They must be hungry and at supper."[34]

In response to a reporter's query about whether he'd rather go on trial in Baltimore or New York City, Richard said, "I can beat the Baltimore charge. At least I'll never hang for it, because the only witness they have against me is a negro—

and you know how much the word of a negro, especially a convict, goes down there. Even if I was convicted, I'd only get a life term, and a life term, after all, is not as bad as the bit I might get in New York for those stickups."[35]

Two days after arriving in New York City, Whittemore was back on a train to Baltimore. When he and his escorts arrived at the station, some 500 people had gathered to catch a glimpse of him. But while the crowds in Buffalo had cheered for him, those who turned out in his hometown were less jubilant. They stood and stared in silence, an ominous prelude of things to come.[36]

Three weeks after his arrival, Whittemore was ushered into a courtroom to hear whether the jury believed the killing of the prison guard was an act of self-defense or premeditated murder. The fact that the jury only needed an hour to come to a decision was not a good sign. With his wife and father seated behind him, Richard stood to hear the verdict read aloud: "Guilty of murder in the first degree."

Whittemore showed no emotion, but Margaret stood up, sobbing, made a reach for him, and fainted. Rawling Whittemore and a woman picked her up and laid her on a bench. The courtroom was silent as the judge released the jury and said that he would not pass sentence until the next week. He then ordered the prisoner to be taken back to his cell. Whittemore's cheeks turned red as he was led from court, and when he passed the state's attorney who had prosecuted him, Richard spat in his face. This caused a collective gasp in the courtroom, but the attorney took it in stride and said with a smile, "That's the highest compliment I've had paid me in a long, long time."[37]

Both of the predictions Whittemore had made to New York detectives regarding his trial in Baltimore couldn't have been more wrong. Not only did the jury believe the sole witness, but "the Candy Kid" was sentenced to death by hanging.

All attempts to get his sentence commuted failed, and Whittemore was scheduled to die on August 13, 1926, at 12:08 a.m. There had never been such a high-profile execution in Baltimore, and it became a festival of the macabre for those so inclined to partake. Hundreds of people came to the prison to be a part of history. Many loitered around the prison walls, while several other young men and women sat in their cars joking, playing ukuleles, and singing. For those wanting an ice cream or soda, vendors were on hand to oblige.[38]

At 3 p.m. Margaret, her mother, and Richard's father and brother pushed their way through the crowds into the penitentiary and were given sixty minutes to say goodbye. As time was running out Margaret asked if she could be alone with Whittemore in his cell, but her request was denied. In their final moments together they would be divided by a row of double bars and chaperoned by a guard. Richard maintained his composure, but Margaret sobbed uncontrollably. Trying to console his wife, Richard said, "Don't mind, Marge. They've got it in for me, and they're going through with it. Be brave. My last thoughts will be of you."[39]

When the guard informed the group that the hour was up, Margaret went into hysterics, screaming, "Reese, Reese I won't leave you. I can't live without you." Richard's father and brother escorted her into the hallway, where she approached another guard and pleaded, "Won't you let me kiss him goodbye? Please! I shall never see him again." Although touched, the guard said it was against the rules and indicated to the men that they should take her away. Richard spent the remainder of the evening reading newspapers and talking to guards. "Everybody in the world is against me," he told them, "but I'm going to show them that I can die game."[40]

Later, the prison chaplain came by to offer some spiritual comfort, but Whittemore wouldn't have any. Though he wasn't interested much in what the clergyman had to say, Richard did have a Bible, which he gave to one of his guards shortly before walking the last mile. "There isn't much I can give anyone," he told him, "but I want you to have this Bible as a gift from me." The guard thanked Whittemore and asked how much of it he had read. " I finished a hundred and eighty-two pages," the condemned man answered. "I wish I had time to read it all, but—" He concluded the sentence by shrugging his shoulders. Just before midnight the warden came to his cell with some guards to shackle him for his walk to the gallows. Before he was put in restraints, Whittemore shook hands with each of the men and even thanked the warden for being so kind to him.[41]

At 12:03 a.m. the door to the death chamber opened and Richard was led up the gallows and placed on the trapdoor. At this point two guards approached with a gray hood. Before they placed it on his head, Whittemore was allowed to speak. "I wish to say goodbye," he said. "That's the best I can wish to anyone." He then managed to crack a smile as the hood was placed over his head.

Once all was in place, the warden signaled a man in another room to spring the trapdoor, and Whittemore dropped. It took fifteen minutes, but doctors finally declared "the Candy Kid" dead. Afterward, as the undertaker was preparing the body, he found a newspaper photo of Margaret pinned to the dead man's shirt. Later that morning Whittemore's corpse was removed to his brother's house, where it would remain for two days until the funeral. When the body arrived, Margaret again went into hysterics.[42]

More than a thousand people gathered for the funeral, and as Richard was being lowered into the ground his mother in-law said, "I hope that the ones responsible will find, if they ever attempt to kiss their wives, that Reese's spirit will come between them and separate them." Her daughter then threw two roses into the grave and, again becoming hysterical, attempted to throw herself in as well.[43]

9

RED SCARE

"On my dying oath, that's the man that plugged me."
— CECIL LINDERMAN IDENTIFYING MIKE MCKENNA

ailing from the West Side of Manhattan, the McKenna brothers, John and Michael, were another team of bandit siblings who left their mark on New York City. By the mid-1920s John, who like his brother was called "Red" in the press, was wanted by New Jersey law enforcement authorities. On September 17, 1921, he and an accomplice had robbed a man of $1,100 in the town of Matawan. John was quickly captured and after pleading guilty was sentenced to hard labor "for a period not exceeding fifteen years nor less than ten years" and shipped off to the New Jersey State Penitentiary at Trenton.[1] On July 14, 1924, he somehow managed to escape from a warehouse.

Mike McKenna also had a record, having been arrested for a robbery in Brooklyn in 1922 for which he served less than seven months of a one-year sentence. This was followed by two more arrests that were dismissed. Then, on January 24, 1924, he was sent to Sing Sing for a term of two and a half to five years for grand larceny.[2]

The jobs the McKenna Gang is known to have pulled began on March 8, 1926, when Mike, James Nannery, Peter Powers, Harry Lucasik, and another man robbed a well-known restaurant called the Hofbrau Haus. The bandits entered the establishment at 3 a.m. and immediately saw cashier Hilda Diamant holding a bag containing $600. Hilda quickly figured out what the men wanted and yelled a warning to the other employees. Her husband, who was the head waiter, came running to her aid and was quickly knocked out by a blow from a blackjack. Two other employees also tried to help, but they also were blackjacked into submission. Mrs. Diamant was then taken into the back room, where Lucasik forced her to open the safe. The bandits helped themselves to the weekend's receipts of $8,460 before making their escape in a waiting auto.[3]

With the success of the Hofbrau Haus job, another popular restaurant, Reuben's, was targeted. At 4:15 a.m. on March 22 four men, all well dressed, entered and took a table near the door. One of them ordered a steak. Two of the fellows walked up to the cashier's cage while a third went to the middle of the room and yelled, "Stick 'em up!" As a busboy bolted for the door, he was pistol-whipped. One of the bandits jumped over the counter and went for the safe, which contained $6,000. The cashier tried to stop him, but he too was pistol-whipped. The robbers collected the money, and as they were backing out of the place, they told the rest of the staff, "Now, if you guys try to follow us, we will fill you full of lead."

The bandits then ran outside to the car and drove off. However, a taxi was parked nearby and the driver, who had witnessed the whole thing, began to follow them. A block later he saw a patrolman and filled him in on the situation. The officer jumped on the running board of the cab and the chase was on. With one hand holding onto a strap inside the cab, the officer opened fire on the robbers' car as it made its way across town. But just as the cab was gaining on the thieves, it was cut off by a milk truck. The taxi driver tried to pull around the vehicle and catch up, but he eventually lost the bandits, although the officer was able to get off a few more shots.[4]

The gang's crime wave continued into the spring when the desperadoes ditched restaurants in favor of payrolls. On May 18, 1926, Samuel Grossman was sitting in his parked Nash on the Upper West Side reading a pamphlet when he suddenly got the feeling that something was wrong. He looked up and saw Harry Lucasik pointing a gun at him. "I just want to borrow your car," Lucasik said as Grossman began to inch away from the door.

Moments later John McKenna, John Werner, and James Nannery surrounded the car, McKenna and Nannery brandishing guns. Grossman was told to hop in the back seat. With Grossman sandwiched between McKenna and Nannery, Werner jumped behind the wheel and Lucasik rode shotgun. McKenna and Nannery each held a pistol to Grossman as the car rolled through Central Park to the Upper East Side. Werner stopped at 160 East Eighty-fifth Street, and McKenna got out and surveyed the building. He yelled back to his companions, and

Lucasik took Grossman into the building, where the bandits walked him to the end of the hall, robbed him of $42, and told him to stay where he was.[5]

Lucasik and McKenna jumped back into the car, and Werner drove the four blocks to that day's target, the General Baking Company. Werner stayed behind the wheel while the other three entered the front door, blew past the saleslady on duty, went to the rear of the showroom, and climbed the stairs to the office. With guns drawn, they took all the employees by surprise, ordering them to "stick 'em up," which they did. "Up on your hind legs and face the wall," McKenna barked, and again the employees did as they were told.

As the bandits turned their attention to the safe, which was conveniently open, the company's telephone operator attempted to plug his phone line into the switchboard, but "Red" saw him and ran over and knocked him unconscious with a pistol blow to the head. "Ain't you guys ever going to learn?" he said as the operator dropped to the floor. The bandits continued to scoop up the money, $6,800 in total, but soon heard footsteps approaching the office. "Red" pressed himself against the wall as another employee, oblivious to what was going on, walked in. McKenna jabbed his gun in the man's back and made him join the others against the wall. When all the money was in their possession, the bandits beat a hasty and successful retreat.[6]

About three hours after the robbery, the police found the robbers' abandoned Nash and impounded it. They found a fingerprint on the windshield, which turned out to belong to John Werner. Once he was arrested he ratted out his three accomplices.[7]

Detectives picked up John McKenna's trail on the Upper West Side, where he lived and frequented many of the saloons. It was at one such watering hole that the cops captured "Red" and Nannery on June 29. Once in custody McKenna admitted his part in the robberies and ratted out Lucasik but not Nannery. Although Werner identified the latter man, apparently no witnesses were able to do so, because he was released on July 3. McKenna admitted he had taken part in the General Baking Company job and that his share of the loot amounted to $1,600. He had some other news for the police as well.

Although he had been a wanted man for two years, McKenna had been visiting his brother Willie, who was incarcerated at Clinton Prison in Dannemora, and brother Mike at Sing Sing. He also mentioned that he had witnessed a murder. On May 29, he had been at a speakeasy called the Owls Club when Frank "Rags" Looney, the proprietor of another saloon, was shot. With a bullet in his chest, "Rags" had staggered out of the bar and dropped dead in the street. McKenna swore that he'd had nothing to do with the murder and just happened to be there when the shooting occurred,[8] but nonetheless he was sent to the

Tombs Prison in lower Manhattan. About two weeks later, on July 10, Michael was released from prison and returned to the city.

The day after Michael's release, the law finally caught up with Harry Lucasik. While detectives were staking out a garage Lucasik was using, they saw Lucasik and Peter Powers pull in. They planned to follow the pair to see if the hoodlums would lead them to any more bandits who could be picked up on suspicion, but the two gunmen managed to elude them. No harm done, however, as the detectives simply returned to the garage and picked up the men when they came back for their car. Powers was released, but witnesses from the General Baking Company, as well as Samuel Grossman, identified Lucasik as one of the bandits. Remarkably, he was released on bail.[9]

Michael McKenna probably visited his brother at the Tombs and was told to get in contact with Nannery and the rest of the gang still at large. The first order of business was to try to break his brother out of prison. On July 14 John was scheduled to be taken in a patrol wagon to the Harlem Court for arraignment. The bandits learned there would be just one keeper to handle John and two other prisoners when they arrived at the courthouse. The plan was for someone to secretly give John an iron bar, which he would smuggle uptown and at the earliest opportunity smack the keeper over the head and escape.

The first part of the plan went off without a hitch. The weapon, wrapped in newspaper, was delivered to John, and he was able to get it into the black mariah. However, before he made it to Harlem Court, a snitch in the prison blew the whistle on him, and when he arrived uptown, detectives were waiting for him. They frisked him as soon as he got out of the wagon, but finding nothing, they rightfully assumed he had hidden the weapon in the wagon as it was pulling up.[10]

Although the breakout had been botched, the gang's next robbery was planned. The crew consisted of the recently liberated Mike McKenna, Nannery, Peter Powers, and William Reichel, a known gunman with a stretch in Sing Sing under his belt. Whether he was one of the gang's previous members or had been brought in for this job is unknown. Rounding out the crew was the fifth member, who managed to remain anonymous. The target chosen was the Reid Ice Cream Company in Harlem.

Just after 4 p.m. on Sunday, July 25, the bandits pulled up in front of the ice cream plant and McKenna, Nannery, Powers and Reichel got out, leaving the fifth man at the wheel. The four hoods made their way to the first-floor offices and Reichel took up a position outside while the other three went in and surprised the lone clerk. The employee was ordered to raise his hands, and one of the robbers told him, "Keep quiet or we'll blow your head off." The clerk raised his hands and was ordered to open the safe. Powers stuck his gun in the clerk's stomach and told him he'd better do as he was told. The clerk opened the safe, and Powers grabbed a box containing $6,000 in cash and another $7,000 in checks. Then for no apparent reason the bandits began to beat the clerk. The office manager, who heard the melee and ran into the room, was jumped and given the same treatment until he was unconscious.

With McKenna covering their retreat, Reichel, Nannery, and Powers ran down the stairs and out to the waiting car. While "Red" was making his dash, Cecil Linderman, one of the company's delivery men, surmised something wasn't right and tried to stop McKenna, who shot him in the belly. Pushing the wounded man aside, "Red" jumped into the car.

Once the bandits were on the road things went from bad to worse. Trying to put as much distance between themselves and the ice cream plant as possible, the getaway driver sped downtown, weaving in and out of traffic. He took a turn too fast and the auto went up on two wheels, and when it came down the driver lost control and careened into a fire hydrant.

Water was spurting everywhere as a crowd began to form to see if the occupants were all right. As the hoods began climbing out of their car, three off-duty cops who were nearby pushed their way through the crowd. Knowing nothing of the robbery, the officers figured the men were accident victims and offered their help. The robbers, however, were taking no chances and opened fire, causing pandemonium. With women and children screaming, the cops drew their guns and shot at the fleeing bandits, all of whom except Peter Powers escaped by running into nearby buildings. Powers was captured in a tenement hallway with two fully loaded revolvers and $600 in cash.[11]

Police questioned the three Reid Ice Cream employees who had witnessed the robbery. While going through the rogues' gallery, wounded driver Cecil Linderman picked Mike McKenna as the man who had pulled the trigger. The cops began searching for McKenna but weren't too concerned when they couldn't find him because they new exactly where he would be that Friday, July 30. The detectives charged with bringing him in showed up at the New York State Prison Parole Commission and simply waited for him to report. When "Red" showed up, the detectives grabbed him, thwarting his attempt to pull out his automatic.

Booked for violating the Sullivan Law, Mike was taken to the hospital and paraded in front of Cecil Linderman. "I know I am on my death bed and that I am dying," Linderman said when confronted with McKenna. "I swear by all that's holy that you are one of the bandits." He then went on to finger McKenna as the triggerman. Realizing that if Linderman died he'd be looking at the electric chair, McKenna replied, "You want to be careful and not pick an innocent guy." "You're the man," Linderman insisted moments before passing out.[12]

After exactly twenty days of freedom following a two-and-half-year term at Sing Sing, "Red" McKenna joined the other "Red" McKenna in the Tombs. Once the victims of the Reid caper had identified him as one of the bandits, robbery and assault were added to the list of charges against him. A little over a week later Linderman died of his bullet wound and McKenna was charged with his murder.

Both McKenna brothers were now safely tucked away in the Tombs, but Michael's darkest hour still lay before him. John asked the warden if he could be put in the same cell as his brother, and the warden allowed it. The McKennas befriended inmate Peter Heslin, who was facing the electric chair for the murder of a police officer. Through Heslin they became acquainted with one of the Tombs' keepers, Tom Colton, or "Old Tom," as he was known to the prisoners. "Old Tom" wasn't above providing favors for a fee, and over the course of the summer Mike and John used him to sneak thousands of dollars as well as whiskey into the prison.[13]

Heslin and the McKennas began to discuss another breakout, and Heslin said he had a pal named John Hogan who would "go the limit" for him and supply some pistols, saw blades, and a rope ladder for an escape. On Friday, September 10, an employee of the city board of transportation whose office was across the street from the Tombs, was working late and looked out the window to see some men hiding a rope and a block and tackle underneath a pile of rubbish outside the prison's outer wall. He quickly notified the police, who came and confiscated the items.[14]

A little more than twenty-four hours later, on Sunday morning, an officer walking his beat saw five men (a sixth was sitting at the wheel of their sedan) place a package in a garbage can approximately two blocks from the Tombs. As the cop approached, the five men took off running and the driver of the sedan began to pull off; however, the officer jumped on the car's running board as it began to speed down the street. The driver hit the gas and made a semicircle, which sent the policeman flying off the car, which then slammed into a light pole.

As the driver jockeyed the vehicle around, the officer threw his nightstick through one of its windows and began firing on the car as it pulled away. Another patrolman heard the shots and was able to squeeze off a few rounds of his own before the car made a successful getaway. The second patrolman saw the men who were trying to escape on foot and managed to capture one of them—Peter Heslin's pal John Hogan. The package in the garbage can was found to contain two pistols and twelve hacksaw blades.[15]

The kibosh was put on the breakout and before a new plan could be formed, Peter Heslin was shipped off to the Sing Sing death house. The date also was drawing near when John McKenna would be sent to Clinton Prison at Dannemora to begin his twenty-year stretch for the General Baking Company job, so the brothers needed to move quickly.

According to John, "Old Tom" smuggled $6,800 into the prison for the brothers, and Michael gave the keeper $2,300 to deliver a package containing pistols.[16] Before the guns could be delivered, however, John was sent to Dannemora. Michael would have to find some new accomplices, and it just so happened that the Tombs recently had become home to some desperate jewel thieves and killers who were looking for a chance to break out . . .

From Maiden Lane

to the Tombs

O n July 19, 1926, a gang consisting of bandits from Chicago and New York City converged for what, for some of them, would be their final job. The brains behind the gang was twenty-nine-year-old Solomon Brofman, a product of New York's Lower East Side who specialized in planning jewelry store robberies as opposed to taking part in the act itself.

Brofman studied how jewelers approached other gem dealers to buy unset stones and final pieces. Posing as a jeweler, he would talk dealers into displaying their whole stock of diamonds, making mental notes of where the stones were kept. Sometimes he would bring one or two of the holdup men with him on his final visit to the targeted jewelry store so they could get a better idea of its layout. He would devise the whole scheme and then drill it into the heads of the bandits.[1]

Brofman's main companion was twenty-seven-year-old Chicago gunman George Cohen, whose record dated back to April 27, 1920, when he was convicted of armed robbery. More recently, in September 1925, the bandit had shot a police officer and been indicted for assault with intent to kill. Able to post a $25,000 bond, he hightailed it to New York City.

There were a number of men involved with the gang from time to time, although they may have not taken part in every job. From Chicago were Cohen's brother Abraham; thirty-six-year-old Robert Berg, a lifelong bandit; and Isadore "Harry" Alderman. Representing New York in addition to Brofman were Benny

Mintz, the gang's wheelman, and Hyman Amberg, both from Brownsville, Brooklyn. As a base of operations the gang used the East Village apartment of Joseph Herbsman.[2]

The mob's final job, which would become known as the Maiden Lane Robbery, after the name of the street where the store was located, was a daring one considering that it took place in a ninth-floor office of a building that was rigged with a burglar alarm which, if tripped, would cause all avenues of escape to be shut down in a matter of minutes. All the due diligence work had been done, but in the end it would be a couple of careless mistakes that did the gang in.

For three weeks beginning in late June the bandits had been posing as jewelers, conning an actual jeweler named Abraham Faigin into believing they were going to make a large purchase. On the first visit Brofman and Cohen said that they wanted to purchase a large diamond ring. Faigin showed the pair a doozy priced at $3,500, and Cohen said he thought that was a fair price and would return to pick up the piece. A week later the imposters showed up to take another look at the ring. Cohen asked Faigin if he could use his phone to call another client. The jeweler agreed and made a mental note of the number. Cohen agreed to buy the ring and said he and his partner would return the following week with the money.

The next week, on July 19, the two bandits called on Faigin and offered him a check for the ring, but the jeweler said that since he didn't know them they would have to pay cash. The men said they understood, and Brofman said he would go to the bank to get the cash while Cohen remained at the office. A while later Brofman called the jeweler and said he'd been delayed at the bank but would return in about ten minutes. Cohen told Faigin he would run down and see if he could help his partner.

A few minutes later Cohen returned with Berg and Isadore Alderman in tow. He entered the office, pulled out a pistol, and ordered Faigin and Faigin's assistant to raise their hands. The robbers forced them into chairs and bound and gagged them. Another man entered to purchase a watch and was tied up as well. Once all were bound, Cohen reached into Faigin's coat and pulled out a wallet containing $75,000 in diamonds. There was a momentary pause as the bandits considered the safe, but Cohen said, "We've got enough; you two fellows beat it."

Cohen stood guard over the captives as his partners walked down the hall. Once he heard the elevator operator close the gate and knew is friends were on their way out, he slipped into the hallway after telling the hostages they would be shot if they didn't stay put for ten minutes. Not wanting to push their luck, the three captives waited a few minutes before triggering the alarm. As Cohen was making his way downstairs the entire building went into emergency shutdown. The building superintendent and the elevator operator, who had just reached the first floor, went to pull down the gate over the stairwell. As they were doing this, Cohen appeared, casually walking down the stairs.

"Where are you going?" the superintendent demanded. "I'm going out," Cohen responded. "Not until I find out who you are." As soon as the words had left the super's mouth, the female elevator operator grabbed the bandit's coat lapels. "Well, I'm going out just the same," Cohen growled as he pulled out his pistol and knocked the elevator operator on the wrist. The young woman grabbed him with her other hand, but he pushed her off. Cohen rammed his pistol into the superintendent's body, backing him up, and then made a break for the door. The super and the elevator girl began to chase him, so Cohen turned and fired an ineffectual shot at them. The hallway was crowded with employees returning from lunch, and Cohen cleared a path for himself by threatening all with his pistol. He made it outside, ran into a building across the street, and disappeared.[3]

Faigin told detectives investigating the robbery how the two bandits had posed as jewelers and visited him a number of times. He also told them about the phone call that Cohen had made on a previous visit and, yes, he remembered the phone number. The detectives traced the call to a studio apartment in midtown Manhattan and found that it was owned by a music teacher who had sublet her home for the summer while she was in Europe. The apartment was empty, and the rental agent told detectives that two men claiming to be Texas Rangers had lived there for three weeks but had just moved out—coincidently the same day the robbery took place. "They told me they were here for a month to study New York detective methods in order to introduce them in Texas," the agent said.

The detectives searched the apartment, and it looked as if the bandits had left without a trace until one of the officers emptied a wastebasket and discovered Cohen's second mistake. At the bottom were bits of paper the detectives painstakingly put back together like a puzzle. One of the documents turned out to be a bank deposit slip for someone named George Mitchell. The detectives went to the bank and found there was indeed a depositor named George Mitchell, and they were a bit stunned to learn that he had opened the account using references from a number of well-to-do people in Chicago.

Knowing that criminals sometimes had good connections, the detectives delved further into George Mitchell's banking history. They asked the bankers if they had anything more on Mitchell, and they produced a check he had made out to a New York City hotel. The detectives went to the hotel and began to ask questions about Mitchell and learned that he shared a room there with another man. Feeling certain that he was one of the bandits, they went up to Mitchell's room to confront him. Neither man was in, so the cops let themselves into the room and began checking out the premises. Inside some bags they found two pistols and what was known as a "bootlegger's cannon"—a 28-gauge double-barreled shotgun with its stock and barrels cut down so it could fit into a coat pocket. Confident that they had their man, the detectives turned off the light and waited.

After about two hours they heard a key in the door, and when it opened a man entered and turned on the lights. Suddenly, Sol Brofman had four pistols pointed at him. "Stick 'em up!" one of he lawmen shouted. The bandit put up his hands, and cuffs were placed on his wrists. "Are you bulls?" Brofman asked. When they confirmed that they were, he praised his captors, saying, "Well, I congratulate you. You've certainly done good work on this case." One of the detectives tried to respond, but Brofman cut him off. "No, I mean it," he said. "You've certainly done good work on this case." The bandit continued to compliment the detectives on their work but was finally told, "Keep your mouth good and shut now."[4]

The lights were again doused, and five long hours passed before another key was heard in the lock and a repeat of Brofman's capture took place. This time it was George Cohen who found four pistols pointed at him. "What's all this about?" he demanded. "We want you for that Maiden Lane job on Monday and a couple of other things," one of the detectives replied. Then they showed him the sawed-off shotgun and asked him where he'd obtained it. "I got nothing to say to you fellows," Cohen replied."[5]

Brofman, on the other hand, had plenty to say. He had no problem telling about jobs he had participated in, nor did his conscience prevent him from implicating Cohen and others. After just forty-eight hours, the police had solved not only the Maiden Lane robbery but the gang's numerous other jobs.

With Brofman's loose tongue and the help of witnesses, the gang's list of offenses was chronicled. The first job credited to the gang was a low-paying robbery of a pawn shop. Jacob Woldar, the proprietor, had just opened his shop and was holding $350 in cash when three armed men walked in. Woldar immediately stepped on the alarm button, which started the bells above the shop door to start ringing. One of the gunmen struck him on the head while another grabbed the money, then they all beat a successful retreat.[6]

Not all jobs had gone as planned, however. One of the well-planned capers that went awry took place on December 10, 1925, when the gang attempted to rob the pawn shop of Jacob Levin. At about 10 a.m. as the proprietor and his son were minding the shop, a young man entered and plunked down a five-dollar bill and a pawn ticket for a ring. The elder Levin went to the safe to fetch the ring as two more men entered.

"That's him," one of the newly arrived men said, referring to the first customer. "We are detectives," one of them said as he flashed what appeared to be a badge. They asked the proprietor and his son if they could identify the young man as the original owner of the ring. Both said no. The original customer began to argue with the "detectives" when two other men entered and appeared to be waiting their turn. After a bit more chatter one of the "detectives" asked the younger Levin if anyone else was in the shop, and when told they were alone said, "Well let's have done with this nonsense and get down to serious work."

With that, the original customer whipped out a pistol, grabbed young Levin by his necktie, and attempted to pull him over the counter. The young man was able to break free and dove behind the counter. He popped back up in a flash with a pistol in his hand and began firing at the robbers, who were caught by surprise and hightailed it for the door as bullets smashed into the windows around them. Levin chased the bandits all the way to their car and fired a few more shots as they drove away. One of the hoodlums returned fire from the auto, but his shot only shattered a display case. Not only did the bandits fail to get any loot, they left behind the five-dollar bill the first man had placed on the counter. "That will help pay for the windows" the elder Levin told reporters.[7]

About two weeks later the next job planned by Brofman went much better. Under the guise of being jewelers, Brofman and other gang members visited the shop of Herman Goldberg, a wholesale jeweler, to barter over some gems. After a handful of visits they hatched a plan and on December 27, as Goldberg and his employee were assisting two customers, four men knocked on his door, which was always locked to prevent bandits from walking in.

Recognizing the men, Goldberg unlocked the door and let them in. The hoodlums immediately drew pistols and ordered everyone in the shop to raise their hands and go into a rear room. Goldberg hesitated, so two of the bandits knocked him out with blows from their guns and carried him to the back while their confederates emptied the safe of approximately $61,000 in gems. The bandits then made a clean getaway.[8]

On January 31, 1926, the gang pulled another Brofman-planned caper. One of the bandits knocked on the door of the Lerner Brothers & Buxbaum jewelry shop, which, like Goldberg, also kept its door locked to keep out robbers. When an employee opened the door, one of the gang members whipped out a pistol and held the door open for three gun-wielding thugs to enter. "Throw up your hands and don't make any goofy remarks," the lead bandit barked. Three employees and a handful of customers were herded into a back room while the display cases were cleaned out. Unfortunately for the bandits, they were unable to open the safe.

Hearing some sort of commotion, the jeweler next door meandered over and popped his head in the door to see what was happening. The bandit on guard duty smashed him over the head with his pistol, knocking him unconscious. Even though they couldn't get into the safe, the hoodlums managed to escape with $18,000 in merchandise.[9]

Two days after Valentine's Day 1926, Raphael Kleinman, a jewelry salesman, stepped into a restaurant and took a seat. A minute later one of the restaurant's proprietors walked in with more than $800 in cash to pay some bills. He handed $500 to his partner and left $340 on the counter. Moments later Hyman Amberg ran in waving a shotgun and yelled for everyone to stand up and raise their hands. He was followed by four more gunmen, two with sawed-off shotguns and two with pistols. The quartet started to herd all the patrons into the kitchen while Amberg ordered Kleinman to get up and stand by the cashier.

As he walked him over, the gunman noticed the $340 on the counter and pocketed it. (The proprietor had tossed the other $500 aside when the men entered.) The two owners were then ordered to go into the kitchen with the others. The one who had tossed the money didn't move fast enough and was hit over the head with a pistol butt and dragged into the kitchen. Kleinman was now alone with three of the gunmen. Amberg ordered him to hand over his diamonds, but the salesman professed he had none. Knowing Kleinman was lying, Amberg ordered his two associates to tear off the man's pants. They complied and found a money belt around the salesman's waist, and hanging from it was a chamois bag containing $28,000 worth of diamonds. The bandits grabbed the jewels, backed out of the restaurant, and escaped.[10]

Brofman's next brainchild took place on February 17, when a Cadillac containing six men pulled up in front of Jacob Brill's jewelry store. Four of the bandits entered the store, where they found Brill's son by himself. The leader asked if it would be all right if they waited inside for a friend, but before young Brill could answer all four men pulled out pistols. "Stick up your hands and hand over the key to that safe," the lead desperado demanded. Brill raised his hands, and two of the gunmen ran around the counter and grabbed the key. Either Brofman hadn't done his homework or the bandits weren't concerned, because when they opened the safe they failed to disconnect the alarm system, which began ringing above the store's door, causing shopkeepers up and down the street to come outside and start yelling for the cops.

"Hurry up, make it snappy," the leader barked at the gunmen cleaning out the safe, which contained seven trays that each held forty-eight diamonds. As the bandits ran out of the store with $39,000 in loot, they ran smack into a woman who began to scream. "Keep your mouth shut or I will blow you to pieces," one of the robbers told her. She quickly became quiet and was told to beat it, which she did immediately.

Three people in a neighboring doorway were yelling for the police, so the crew's leader trained his gun on them and thundered, "Get back into the store or we will blow you up." When he reached the getaway car and started to get inside, a witness threw a hammer at him from a second-story window. It missed him but landed in the vehicle's back seat. As the hoodlums sped away, they passed a cop responding to the commotion who managed to get off a few shots at the getaway car, but to no avail.[11]

July 22, 1926, the day after Cohen and Brofman's arrest for the Faigin robbery, Aaron Rodack opened his jewelry store, no doubt savoring the news of the two diamond bandits's capture. Rodack was no stranger to armed robbers. Twice before holdup men had descended on his shop demanding precious stones and twice he had driven them away with the business end of his .45. In 1924, the first time bandits had entered his store with guns drawn, Rodack picked up his gun and charged them, firing as he advanced. The gunmen fired some shots but ran outside with Rodack in pursuit, firing at their retreating car until his clip was empty.

Having stood up to gunmen and won, Rodack became somewhat of a local celebrity and was dubbed "the Fighting Jeweler." "They'll never get anything from this shop while I'm alive," he told all. He also believed his actions would protect him from further robbery attempts. "They know I mean business," he said. "They know I will shoot. Now they will leave me alone."[12]

Apparently not all hoodlums got the message, because on January 18, 1925, another batch of bandits poured into his store ordering him to put up his hands. Once again he grabbed his .45 and another firefight broke out as he charged his enemies. Like the first time, he chased his adversaries outside and emptied his clip as they drove away. Unlike the first time, however, they pulled away leaving one of their own lying on the sidewalk with a belly wound that would prove fatal. Once again Rodack "the "Fighting Jeweler" was lauded for his actions, but killing a man did not sit well with him and he didn't bask in the praise as he had the first time.[13] Business, however, went through the roof.

Even though he was adversely affected by the death of the gunman, Rodack didn't let his vigilance drop so on that July morning when another raiding party came through his door at 10:15, he once again grabbed his .45 and started banging away. A gun battle ensued that left Rodack's employee, Sidney Freifield, fighting for his life with two bullet wounds to his body. As he had done before, Rodack charged the gunmen and chased them from his store.

Hearing the exchange of gunfire, those in the neighborhood quickly figured "the Fighting Jeweler" was once again battling hoodlums, and they watched as the robbers ran from the store without any loot. Rodack got down on one knee and began firing at the hoods as they got into their sedan. He managed to wing one, and the others helped him into the car. Once inside, the robbers unleashed a volley of gunfire as they sped away. Two of the shots smashed through shop windows and a third struck Rodack in the head, killing him.[14]

The positive press the police had received for snagging Cohen and Brofman was quickly doused by Rodack's murder. Fortunately for them, Brofman's squealing would lead to the resolution the police desired. While ratting out his confederates, Brofman said a man named Benny Mintz had been the driver for his gang as well as "the official chauffeur for all the holdup gangs in New York."[15*]

In addition to the police, a group called the National Jewelers Crime Commission also wanted the bandits responsible for Rodack's death and hired Pinkerton detectives to work with New York detectives in capturing the desperadoes. The Pinkertons learned that Mintz and four others were involved in the robbery of a crap game in Brooklyn on August 9. Mintz, however, wasn't the getaway driver—a man named John Silverman was behind the wheel, and Mintz stayed in the front of the apartment building as a lookout while his four accomplices made their way to the rear apartment where the game was in progress.

"Hands up," the bandits ordered, and all but two men complied. The two who didn't were subdued with pistol butts. While the robbery was in progress a gunman hired to protect the game snuck out the back, came around the front of the building, and opened fire on the bandits as they made their getaway. One of the bullets struck Mintz in the arm, and when the Pinkertons learned he was being treated by a doctor in Manhattan, they began to stake out his office. On Monday, August 23, Mintz was grabbed while leaving the doctor's office.[16] Keeping the bandit's capture a secret in hopes of picking up the rest of the gang members before they got wise, the cops brought Mintz to police headquarters where he was interrogated with fists and a rubber hose.[17]

Whether under duress or to save his own skin (probably a little of both), Mintz admitted that he had driven the car during the botched Rodack job and that the gunman who fired the fatal shot at "the Fighting Jeweler" was Brooklyn thug and sometime Cohen and Brofman associate Hyman Amberg. He also stated that after the shooting they had driven to the East Village, where they dropped off gang member William Green, wounded by Rodack's barrage, at a hospital before dumping the car.

Four days after Mintz was picked up, Amberg decided it was a good time to leave town and hopped a boat for Albany. Unfortunately for the twenty-two-year-old, detectives already had a line on him and took off for the state capital in a car. At Poughkeepsie, Amberg disembarked and boarded the *Empire State Express*, riding the train the rest of the way. Detectives somehow caught wind of the change, and when the bandit alighted at 2 p.m. at Albany's Union Station,

---

* Mintz told detectives that he always kept eight to ten stolen cars in garages throughout the city. He would use the car parked closest to the site of the planned robbery and afterward would drop the bandits at a safe place and then ditch the car.

they were waiting for him. Amberg was taken to the local police station and questioned for seven hours. The killer said nothing and was driven back to Manhattan, where he was questioned relentlessly for fifteen hours straight but would only tell his interrogators, "I've got nothing to say."[18]

The detectives drove him to his house and searched the premises for evidence but found nothing but the gunman's mother, who stated that her son had been at home with appendicitis at the time of the Rodack murder and since then had been recovering from an appendectomy. Back at the station, Amberg still refused to talk, saying, "I'm too sick to listen to you fellows. I know nothing, so what's the use of asking me questions?"[19]

The police kept hammering away, and through a combination of perseverance and sleep deprivation, they finally got the confession they were after. On August 31 Amberg was charged with homicide in connection with the Rodack murder and joined Mintz, Cohen, and Brofman in the Tombs.

The next member of the gang to get pinched was thirty-six-year-old Robert Berg, who was traced back to his native Chicago and arrested on September 22 with thousands of dollars in loot from the robberies. He was held on a $150,000 bond and fought extradition to New York. The Big Apple won out, however, and he arrived in the city on October 13. Berg was reported to have made a deal with the police whereby he would confess to the Faigin robbery and assist the cops with capturing the other bandits still at large. He then rejoined his pals in the Tombs.[20]

Autumn found a number of hardened criminals in the Tombs, including the the the Cohen/Amberg bunch and the notorious McKenna brothers and various members of their gang. The police managed to thwart a September 10 escape attempt by the McKennas that was orchestrated by inmate Peter Heslin (see Chapter 9). Since that time, Heslin had been shipped off to Sing Sing and a new plan had been devised. Now joining the McKennas on the breakout attempt would be Hyman Amberg, Robert Berg, McKenna Gang member Peter Powers, and two other inmates.

According to John McKenna, "Old Tom," a keeper at the Tombs who sold his services to the inmates, had smuggled $6,800 into the prison for the brothers, $2,300 of which was given to "Old Tom" to deliver a package containing pistols. But before the weapons could be delivered, John McKenna was sent to Dannemora, leaving six men in the breakout party. The plan called for the prisoners to pretend to be sick, and when they were all in the physician's office, which was twenty feet from the main gate, they would pull out the guns hidden in their clothes, overpower the guards, and make their break.

At about 2:50 p.m. on November 3, 1926, the men began to feign illness and asked to be sent to the infirmary. It was decided that they would be sent in two groups of three. Amberg, Mike McKenna, and Berg were the first ones to be let out of their cells and led to the doctor's office. When they arrived, the doctor was attending another convict, so the inmates were left outside his door. Spotting gatekeeper Louis Lorch with his key in the gate, they seized the opportunity, whipped out their weapons, and made their move.

"Louis, you [expletive], open that door!" yelled Berg, who was leading the charge. "You go to hell," Lorch responded, grabbing the key and running for safety. Hearing the commotion and wondering what was happening, the warden stepped out of his office and was immediately cut down by a hail of bullets. Realizing that they wouldn't be able to exit through the main gate, the three desperadoes ran past the mortally wounded warden and made their way out into the courtyard, where there were two guardhouses and another gate that led to freedom.

Unfortunately for the escapees, the guards, Murphy and O'Connor, were away from their posts. With nobody to open the gate for them, the convicts jumped behind a coal pile to decide on their next move. By this time, the police realized an escape was in progress and began to mobilize. Murphy and O'Connor quickly returned to their posts, and the escapees opened fire on them. O'Connor dropped with a bullet in his side before reaching the guardhouse. Murphy made it, but as he was returning fire a bullet passed through his mouth and entered his brain. The convicts rushed the guards to get their keys but were forced to back behind behind the coal pile by a volley of shots from other officers.

Amberg and his cohorts retreated to an area out of the guards' view and tried to come up with another plan. Nearby was a ditch in which an electrician named Thomas Kelly, who had witnessed the shootout, was hiding. The gunmen eyed him suspiciously, but Amberg told the others not to blast him. "Is there any chance of me getting out of this?" the electrician asked Amberg, who suggested that he lie low in the ditch. Kelly followed his advice.

With options quickly running out, a desperate Amberg ran to the nearest wall and unsuccessfully tried to scale it. As he did so he noticed that workers in a nearby building were watching from an office window. He raised his gun as if to shoot at them, and they all ducked out of sight. After a few moments they looked down again, and this time Hyman laughed and waved at them and yelled something inaudible, waved again, and then turned his attention back to the task at hand.

By this time more police, armed with machine guns, began to take up positions in the neighboring buildings and rained gunfire on the convicts. Amberg and McKenna ran into a guardhouse for safety and called for Berg to join them. Realizing the futility of the situation, the bandit, bleeding from a head wound, stood erect, squared his shoulders, clicked his heels together, and placed his gun to his head. "Don't do that!" yelled Amberg, "We got a chance!"

This momentarily stopped Berg, but then with mind made up, he repeated the exercise, placed the gun to his head, pulled the trigger, and . . . *Click!* Nothing happened; his gun jammed. So while bullets ricocheted around him, Berg fidgeted with his weapon and finally, on the third attempt, succeeded in sending a bullet into his brain that blew him over in a near somersault.

Meanwhile, Amberg and McKenna were running low on ammunition as volleys from the police were increasing from inside the prison and from windows and fire escapes from the neighboring buildings. Needing more firepower they ran to their fallen comrade and Amberg pried the pistol from Berg's death grip. Just as he grabbed it a bullet struck him in the hand, but he managed to pass the gun over to McKenna as they ran back to the safety of the guardhouse and started blasting away at the officer who had shot Amberg.

Initially, the escapees were battling pistol against pistol, but now they had to contend with shotguns and machine guns as well. With a steady stream of lead from the latter holding the prisoners in place, the guards prepared to rush the convicts. Back in the guardhouse Hyman, like Berg, realized the futility of the situation and, like his confederate, chose the same way out, minus the military fanfare. Hyman simply stepped into the door and shot himself in the head. The force of the bullet blew him back into the arms of McKenna, who quickly pushed him out the door and then, standing in the same spot, placed a gun to his head.

By this time, however, the gunfire was so concentrated that police couldn't tell if the bullet that went into McKenna's head was his own or had been fired by one of the officers. Once all three men were down, the cops came over and found that "Red" was still alive and sent him to the hospital, where he died the following day. An examination confirmed that he had died by his own hand. The police slowly made their way about the yard, unsure whether any more armed escapees were lurking about.

Sensing the shootout was over, Thomas Kelly, the electrician, raised his head from the ditch. One of the officers saw his noggin and took a shot at it. Kelly hit the dirt again as other cops opened fire. Trying to send a message that he wasn't a convict, he raised his shovel—which was shot from his hand. Hearing that the cops were preparing to charge the ditch, Kelly began to yell that he was a laborer. The police ordered him to come out with his hands up. He did, and all went well.

Officer Murphy was killed on the spot, and his partner, O'Connor, was sent to the hospital in critical condition but later recovered. Before succumbing to his wounds, the warden was pleased to learn that his slayers were either dead or dying. He was visited at the hospital by his boss, the commissioner of corrections, and proudly reported, "Commissioner, not one of them got away. They shot me. Please break the news gently to my wife." He died a short time later.[21]

Don't Cry Out Loud

"They wept like babies."

—A DETECTIVE'S DESCRIPTION OF THE OBERST GANG
IN A POLICE LINEUP

As a bandit's bullet plowed through Aaron "the Fighting Jeweler" Rodack's head on July 22, 1926, a gang of seven armed thugs was preparing for what would prove to be another botched robbery resulting in death. Not to mention their final job. The gang was a confederacy of young hoodlums who modeled themselves after the Whittemore Gang, even though none were actually hardened criminals like those whose exploits they tried to emulate. All came from respectable families, and the leader, Phillip Oberst, was described as soft spoken and having good manners; he had even attended high school, where he studied engineering.

The target that day was a private bank owned by John Liccione and located in an Italian neighborhood in the Bronx. Oberst was the first bandit on the scene. He showed up about an hour before the job was to be pulled and had left the rest of the gang at the rendezvous in Manhattan's Chelsea district. To the gang leader's chagrin, two large payrolls had been withdrawn, reducing the $50,000 take he was expecting to $12,000.

Driving the getaway car would be the mob's wheelman, Peter Mahoney. The twenty-one-year-old still lived at home, and every morning he left his house at eight o'clock to fool his mother into believing that he held a job. He even went so far as to contribute $2 a week to his Christmas Club account at the bank. Providing guard duty that day would be Frank Kerrigan. A year younger than Mahoney, he was a former three-card monte dealer who had graduated to running dice games. He previously had been arrested in a police raid at a hotel and now was following his friends into armed robbery.

Joining Oberst on the inside would be twenty-five-year-old Peter "Pete the Polack" Baranowski. The oldest of the bunch, Pete's record dated back to 1924, when he served two days for disorderly conduct. That was followed by a thirteen-month stretch for carrying a gun. He also had been arrested and released for a robbery the previous April. Another inside man would be twenty-year-old Bernard Frankel, known as "Frenchy," who was on parole from the New York City Reformatory for shooting a man in a poolroom three years earlier. Like Mahoney, he also had a nonexistent job. He told his mother he was going to go into the bootlegging business, but she insisted that he keep his $20-a-week imaginary job as an elevator operator.

The other gunmen who would be on the inside were Leo Hecker and Jimmy O'Connor, both twenty-one. The former had done a stint at Elmira after being arrested at the furniture company where he worked. He would find out where the furniture was to be delivered, then beat the delivery men to the address and sign for it.

According to the plan, to be as inconspicuous as possible, some of the gang members arrived at Liccione's bank by subway, some by taxi, and a few rode with Mahoney in the getaway car. Once everyone was on hand, Mahoney took a ride around the block to make sure the coast was clear. When he returned and signaled all was well, each man put on a pair of blue driving goggles and went into action. Kerrigan took up his position outside the bank with his .45 pistol as Oberst and the others entered with .45's drawn. "Hand's up!" one of them ordered, and immediately the proprietor's nephew, Manleo, and another clerk dropped to the floor as the bandits opened fire, slightly wounding a third clerk who didn't hit the deck quickly enough.

As the bandits tried unsuccessfully to open the cashier's gate, Manleo Liccione crawled to a desk where a revolver was stashed. Retrieving the pistol, he fired three shots into the air and sent another over the bandits' heads causing the gang to panic and retreat. Out on the street the gunmen waved their guns at pedestrians to clear a path to the getaway car. Kerrigan jumped into the front seat, followed by Frankel, Hecker, and O'Connor. Baranowski stopped outside the bank and continued to shoot inside until Oberst signaled for him to get in the sedan. "Pete the Polack" jumped into the back seat, closed the door, and crouched on the floorboard. Oberst jumped onto the running board as the car pulled away. As the gang leader was opening the rear

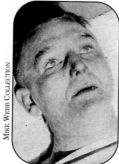

• *"Gentleman Bandit" Gerald Chapman (top) progressed from thievery to murder, which landed him on the gallows at the Connecticut State Prison (below). His longtime accomplice was George "Dutch" Anderson (left), whose death by police bullets in 1925 ended the largest manhunt in U.S. history until that time.*

• *Pulling robberies made diminutive Cecilia Cooney (bottom left, with husband Ed) feel like a big shot. Dubbed "the Bobbed-Haired Bandit" because of her coiffure, she got most of the attention in the papers, while Ed was relegated to "male companion."*

All photos are from the Author's Collection unless otherwise noted.

• *Brother Tom (top left), was one of the Four Fierce Flanagans, a gang of desperadoes described variously as "hard, tough men" and "well dressed and debonair."*

• *The Diamond brothers, Morris and Joseph (top right) were executed for a poorly executed robbery. They were joined in the West End Bank fiasco by bootlegger and gunman John Farina (above left).*

• *The "Cowboy" Tessler mob was credited with committing an astonishing eighty-one robberies in eight months. The photo at right above shows Tessler flanked by gang members Moe Auswacks and Louis Austen. Also part of the gang were Fred Rothermel (right) and his brother Art's moll Rose Hameline.*

NEW YORK EVENING JOURNAL • • America's Greatest

3 ESCAPED MEN ARE STILL AT LIBERTY

3 WHO ESCAPED FROM WELFARE ISLAND

JOHN J. ROGERS   VINCENT M'CORMICK

Wide Search for Desperadoes Who "Walked Off" Welfare Island So Far Futile.

The wide hunt that is being conducted to-day for the three desperadoes who virtually walked off Welfare Island so far has proved futile. The ease with which the fugitives made their escape has occasioned much comment among penal authorities and the demand that this island be given up as a place to confine prisoners.

Both Commissioner Wallis and Warden McCann are in favor of giving up Welfare Island over entirely to either the Department of Welfare, for exclusive use of its hospitals and home for the aged, or to the Department of Correction to be occupied exclusively by the penitentiary and prison ward. They favored moving of the penitentiary, however, and suggested Riker's Island as a proper location.

"The penitentiary of Welfare Island has passed its usefulness as a place of penal correction," Commissioner Wallis said. "Prisoners should be kept busy at work, both for their own benefit and to reduce the cost of their upkeep. Humanitarianism does not require that prisoners be kept idle or coddled. I would like to take the penitentiary to Riker's Island and establish factories there where the prisoners would be employed eight hours a day."

ALL HAVE RECORDS.

The escaped men all have long criminal records and all have warrants awaiting their re-arrest upon release after serving their present

terms. They are believed to have escaped by an unguarded stairway leading to the Queensboro Bridge.

Leaving the prison ward after the check, they went into an adjoining room, and, tying a clothesline around the top of the bars, which protect only the lower half of the windows in the administration building, where the prison ward is located, on the second floor, they lowered themselves. The rope reached half way to the ground and they dropped the rest of the distance.

They are: John J. Rodgers, alias "Bum Rodgers," thirty-two years old, a lather, of No. 222 East Ninety-fifth street; Vincent McCormick, alias "Paul" McCormick, twenty-eight years old, a plumber, of No. 446 East One Hundred and Thirty-fifth street, both convicted of assault, and James Cunniff, twenty-six years old, a clerk, of No. 493

JAMES CUNNIFF

• Bandit John Rodgers (top left) allegedly acquired the nickname "Bum" because of his slovenly appearance. He met psychopathic "Killer" Cunniffe (above center) at the prison on Welfare Island. Rodgers, Cunniffe, and Cunniffe's equally psychotic pal "Ice Wagon" Crowley (above right) would be forever linked by a prison escape. Among members of the Crowley/Cunniffe gang was Frank "Ghost" Kiekart (above left).

• *Bootlegger David DeMaio (above) came up with the idea to rob a trolley car inspector en route to the Bronx with the previous day's receipts. He enlisted five men to handle the ill-fated job (clockwise from top right): Jimmy Lipso, Joe Mazza, John "the Dope" Marino, Salvatore "Solly Cheesecake" Melito and the nervy Frank Daly (below, being escorted from his cell). The inspector and the train's motorman were killed, but while Daly confessed to the slayings, both he and DeMaio went to the chair.*

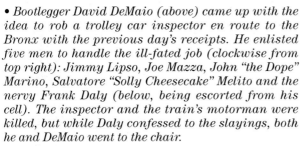

• The Whittemore Gang stole over a million dollars' worth of jewels during a yearlong crime spree. Top from left are leader Richard Reese Whittemore, "the Candy Kid"; his wife, Margaret, christened "the Tiger Girl"; and associate William "Baltimore Willie" Unkelbach. The mob portrait above includes (from left) Bernard Mortillaro, Pasquale Chicarelli, Leon Kraemer, Jacob Kraemer, Anthony Paladino, Milton "Shuffles" Goldberg, and Whittemore.

• Bandit brothers John and Michael McKenna (above left and right) both went by the moniker "Red." Among members of the McKenna Gang, which moved up from restaurant heists to payroll robberies, were Harry Lucasik and Peter Powers (far left and left). The McKennas eventually ended up sharing a cell in the Tombs Prison.

• *The robbery of jeweler Abraham Faigin was the last job pulled by Chicago bandit George Cohen and his New York City counterpart Solomon Brofman (above left). Among the crew were (clockwise from right) Chicagoan Robert Berg and Brooklynites Hyman Amberg and Benny Mintz. After their arrest, a detective (top right) examines the gang's arsenal.*

• *An attempted breakout from the Tombs in November 1926 by Mike McKenna, Hyman Amberg, Robert Berg, and two others sparked a bloody shootout that was a news photographer's dream. The final toll was five dead, including the prison's warden, a guard, and three of the hoods: McKenna, Amberg, and Berg, who took their own lives.*

SURRENDERS TO PRIEST

William Hoey, wanted for the murder of Policeman Daniel J. Neville, and Father Cashin, Catholic chaplain at Sing Sing, to whom he surrendered yesterday. Hoey told Father Cashin he feared a beating from the police. The priest brought him to the District Attorney, to whom Hoey admitted he was in the lot on Eleventh avenue when the officer was killed.

•When members of the Oberst Gang (above) were seen crying and whimpering after being taken into custody, the press tabbed the mob the "Cry Baby Bandits." From left are Leo Hecker, Frank Kerrigan, Phillip Oberst, Peter Mahoney, and Bernard Frankel.

• Junkie and cop-killer William Hoey (left) surrendered to a priest to avoid a beating by the NYPD.

• By all accounts, robbery gang leader Thomas "Red" Moran (below) was crazy as a bedbug.

Police Slayer Threatens Suicide

BANDIT SAYS HE HAS SILVER PLATE HERE

HANDCUFFED SO THAT HE CANNOT RAISE HANDS ABOVE CHEST

- "Radio Burglar" Paul Hilton (above left) was a music lover as well as a cop-killer.

- Bandit James Nannery (right) was dubbed "New York's Most Desperate Criminal," although the official record doesn't support the appellation. He and pal Eddie "Snakes" Ryan (above center) broke out of Sing Sing by climbing over walls that had been left unguarded, swimming the Hudson River, and catching a freight train into New York City.

- After a botched holdup of the Bronx National Bank in Westchester, John Bolling (below, with bandaged head) and James Nannery are surrounded by arresting detectives who inspect the bandits' hardware.

Police Batter Armed Bandits; Block Bank Holdup

• *Sexy extortionist Vivian Gordon (top left) was killed by Harry Stein and Sam Greenberg (top center and right) in a car provided by underworld hanger-on Harry Schlitten (above left). John A. Radelof (above right) was Vivian's lawyer and the instigator of her death.*

• *Unknown car thief Francis "Two-Gun" Crowley (above left) became one of New York's most notorious killers, but it was his dramatic capture, witnessed by thousands (right and below), that made him famous.*

• *Crowley's foster brother John (above center) died in a shootout with a cop, which may have kindled Francis's hatred for the police. Francis's burgeoning criminal career was almost sidetracked by love when he met Helen Walsh (above right), but when she turned down his marriage proposal, "Two-Gun" by his own admission began drinking and went back to his old gang in the Bronx.*

The scene of the battle at 303 West 90th street. Tear gas may be seen over the roofs.

• *Perhaps miffed by Francis's reconciliation with Helen Walsh, girlfriend Billie Dunne (above left) blew the whistle on "Two-Gun" Crowley (above). She worked at a taxi-dance joint with Virginia Joyce Brannen, a party-girl "cut up" who took her last joy ride with Crowley and his pal Rudolph "Fat" Duringer (below left).*

• *After Duringer's capture, he admitted to killing Virginia and showed detectives (left) where he and Francis had dumped her body (below).*

• *Criminal prodigy Roy Sloane (right) managed to talk his way out of prison . . . and into the sights of gangster shotguns outside a speakeasy called the Mad Dot Boat Club (below). An artist's rendering (above) depicts the ambush that cut down the former college student, who died in a hospital an hour later.*

• *The authorities thought Leonard Scarnici and his gang had committed several bank robberies, but he admitted to only two. His final bank job, which would lead to his demise, took place in May 1933 in the upstate town of Rensselaer. Pictured above at right are Scarnici gangsters (standing from left) Anthony Reino, Charles Herzog, Leonard Scarnici, Philip Zeigler, and Fred Prentl. Seated are Eleanor Scarnici (left) and Emma Reino. A detective (above left) checks out the gang's weaponry and other tools of the trade.*

• *After the death of her notorious husband Vincent "Mad Dog" Coll, queen of the molls Lottie Coll (below) formed a mini-gang with gunmen Joe Ventre and Al Guarino (below at right).*

• *A $427,000 armored car heist outside Brooklyn's Rubel Ice Plant in April 1934 was the largest cash robbery in history up to that time. The bandit team included Bernard McMahon and Percy "Angel Face" Geary (top from left), brothers John and Francis Oley (center from left), and Harold "Red" Crowley (seated at left below with John Oley after their prison break).*

- "Red" Crowley (above) also took part in the July 1933 kidnapping of John J. O'Connell Jr., the nephew of two Albany political bosses.

- At left is a machine gun left behind by the bandits after the armored car robbery in Brooklyn.

- The gang's rendezvous after the heist was a boarding house run by landlady-to-the-underworld Madeline Tully (below left), who harbored the Arsenal Gang, among others.

- The FBI's capture of kidnappers Harry Brunette and Merle Vandenbush (below center and right) sparked a war of words between bureau Director J. Edgar Hoover and the NYPD.

• *After snatching gangland bookie Bart Salvo (top left), Al Stern (top center) and his gang learned the hard way not to kidnap mob guys. The Mafia caught up with gang members Benny Holinsky (top right) and Frank Dolak (above left), but Edward Knott and Louis Ellbrock (above center and right) were more fortunate.*

• *David "the Beetle" Beadle met his end outside the Spot bar (right) on the West Side waterfront where nine years earlier he had gunned down the three Lawlor brothers.*

door, his pistol went off and the bullet struck Baranowski in the neck and traveled down his spine.

Paralyzed from the waist down and bleeding, Baranowski told his companions that he believed he was dying. About a mile from the bank, Mahoney stopped and everyone but he, Oberst, and the wounded man got out of the car. Baranowski was then driven to Manhattan, where, thinking they were near a hospital, Mahoney and Oberst lifted the semi-conscious gangster out of the vehicle and deposited him on the curb. "Don't worry, I'll not squeal,"[1] was the last thing they heard their friend say. The two bandits then dumped the sedan and returned to the rendezvous where they met up with the others and commiserated about the loss of their pal.

It wasn't long before "Pete the Polack" was discovered and an ambulance called. At the hospital detectives began to pump him for information about the Rodack heist. Since witnesses said they had seen the jeweler wound one of the bandits during his final charge, the cops felt sure Baranowski was their man. Pete denied that he'd had anything to do with the job, saying he had been shot in a bootleggers' fight at the corner of 149th and Third Avenue.

"Why did they shoot you?" a detective wanted to know.

"They thought I ratted, and they done [sic] for me,"[2] the gunman responded. When asked why his cohorts had driven him across town, the bandit just shook his head. The cops looked into his story and discovered there had been no shooting at the location he described, so they continued to press him on the Rodack murder, which he continued to deny any participation in until his death that afternoon. "Pete the Polack" was loaded into a hearse—which, coincidently, also contained "the Fighting Jeweler" himself—and the two were transported to the city morgue.

While "Pete the Polack" was expiring and his friends were lamenting his being shot, Bronx police at the Liccione bank found the clue that would lead to the gang's capture. During the melee inside the bank, one of the bandits had dropped his new straw hat, which bore the label of the store in Manhattan's Chelsea district. The detectives went to the shop, and the proprietor told them that just the previous day three well-dressed young men had come in and purchased straw hats. When the haberdasher described them, the detectives recognized "Frenchy" and began to look for him.

The next day the car the gang had used on the job and since abandoned was found—and it also contained a new straw hat. By what was deemed "inside detective work," investigators learned the second hat belonged to "Pete the Polack."

On July 23, "Frenchy" was walking in Chelsea when three detectives surrounded him and placed him under arrest. Either "Frenchy" started talking or some underworld stoolie ratted out the gang, because three days later Kerrigan was picked up in Rockaway Beach. Within a few hours Hecker and Oberst were also in custody, and police nabbed Mahoney the following day in his furnished room. Jimmy O'Connor was the only gang member who managed to remain free.

The Liccione bank debacle was not the first robbery by the Oberst Gang to excite the press. The first was the July 1 payroll robbery of Roosevelt Hospital. At 9:30 that morning five of the gang entered the cashier's office where Edith Ware, the hospital switchboard operator, was stationed. Edith had just received a call when she saw the first gunman and told the party on the other end of the line to call the cops. It took a couple of verbal exchanges before the male caller understood what was happening. Seeing Edith talking, one of the bandits ran up to her, swearing, and pulled out her phone plug.

A fast-thinking cashier managed to knock the two pay boxes off the counter. One containing more than $10,000 fell into a pile of mail and was overlooked entirely by the robbers; the other fell to the floor, scattering 200 pay envelopes. One of the gunmen saw this and sent the cashier to the floor with a blow to the chest, yelling, "I'm going to murder someone!"[3] He then stuck his gun into the cashier's ribs and walked him and a handful of hospital employees who were lined up to get paid into an inner office.

While this was happening another bandit got down on the floor and started to pick up the envelopes. With the mayhem going on, Edith figured she would be able to place a call unnoticed and once again plugged in her phone in an attempt to call the police. Seeing this, one of the bandits cursed at her and pulled her plug out again, then pressed his gun against her head and started pushing her noggin around. Over the course of the robbery Edith tried a few more times to put calls through, but each time she was cursed and her headset was unplugged.

Finally, when the bandit picking up the envelopes had gathered as many as he could hold, the robbers headed out of the hospital. Before they left, however, three of them loomed over Edith as one of them said, "We'll kill you if you move." Unfazed, the spunky operator replied, "Aw, go along. Nobody's doing anything."[4] Oberst and the gang got away with $11,000.

The gang's second high-profile job was the attempted payroll robbery of the Loft Candy factory, which took place on July 10 and was similar to the Liccione bank caper in that no money was taken and somebody ended up shot. The victim in this case was James Broderick, a rookie cop on his first assignment. He was on plainclothes duty keeping an eye on the area around the candy factory as the company prepared to distribute the payroll.

Two gangsters remained outside the factory guarding the door while four others entered the building, pushing an employee ahead of them. Once inside, one of the robbers pushed the employee against a wall and stood guard while another walked up to the operator and pulled out her phone plug. This time, a gunman stayed with the operator so she wouldn't try to contact the cops, while the remaining two bandits entered the cashier's office.

Before the duo could grab any money, however, three shots were heard from the outside followed by one of the bandits yelling for his pals to get out quick. The robbers beat a hasty retreat, running past Officer Broderick, who was on the ground with bullet wounds to the neck, abdomen, and hip. Correctly surmising that the two men hanging around outside looked suspicious, he had gone to investigate and was shot down. A passing motorist took the policeman to the hospital, where he received a blood transfusion from another officer. Doctors weren't sure if he would live.[5]

Once in custody, all the gang members denied involvement in the botched Liccione bank robbery until "Frenchy" got caught in a lie and confessed. The others followed suit and even admitted to some other jobs as well. The next day they took part in six lineups for other robberies. The first one was for witnesses from the Sunglo-Sills Grocery Company robbery, one of the most infamous heists that year, in which a salesman and female stenographer were shot and killed.

The gang members were shackled together, and the cashier from the company walked up and down the line eyeing each one carefully. After looking at Frankel for a time, she put her hand on his shoulder and said that he resembled one of the bandits. At this the gunman and his cohorts reportedly began to cry. "Please don't say that I killed anybody," Frankel implored. The others began to chime in, saying they were innocent and that it wouldn't be fair for them to be accused of murders they didn't commit. "Well, I am not positive," the cashier told Frankel, "but you certainly look very much like that robber."[6]

Another Sunglo employee identified Frankel but added, "I'm not sure." Then a third employee, a telephone operator who actually had shots fired at her, began to look at the men's faces. Fearing he would be identified for a third time, Frankel moaned, "I don't know anything about this holdup, miss." Much to the gunmen's relief and the detectives' disappointment, the woman was unable to identify them.

"Frenchy" wasn't so lucky in the next lineup when the switchboard operator for the Loft Candy factory was brought in. She looked over all the gangsters and then walked up to him and said, "You are one of the robbers who came into the office with a pistol in your hand and ordered me and other employees there to throw up our hands."

"Don't say that, miss; that's a serious charge," Frankel countered. "There was a policeman shot there, and I had nothing to do with that holdup." But the operator stuck to her guns, saying, "You *are* one of the men that held up our factory."[7]

With the girl's positive identification of "Frenchy," all the bandits were taken to the hospital and paraded in front of the wounded James Broderick. After looking at Hecker, the rookie cop said, "I feel pretty sure that you are the man who shot me in front of the Loft factory." Upon hearing this Hecker turned white and began to cry again. His confederates followed suit. Hecker then told the officer, "Now, mac, you know this might prove to be a murder charge. Please be sure of what you are saying, I didn't shoot you. I had nothing to do with that holdup." Broderick was confident, however, telling Hecker, "The more I see of you, the more convinced I am that you are the fellow who shot me."[8] He was unable to place the others at the crime scene, however.

The prisoners were transferred back to police headquarters and reportedly cried along the way. They next faced witnesses from yet another job, the $6,700 robbery of the City and Suburban Homes Corporation. "Those five men took part in that robbery," one of the witnesses declared without hesitation. "Yes, they are five of them," a coworker concurred. Both women then identified a photo of the deceased Peter Baranowski and agreed that he also was involved. After this, one of the gang admitted to twenty more holdups, including the payroll robbery of the William F. Kenny Construction Company in Long Island City, Queens. The press played up the fact that the gang members had been crying and whimpering throughout the day, and soon the Oberst Gang was dubbed the "Cry Baby Bandits."

The gang was wanted by district attorneys in both the Bronx and Queens. The Bronx indictment came down first, and the two D.A.'s made a deal to turn over the hoodlums to Queens after the Bronx was done with them. After Queens had wrapped up its prosecution, sentencing would be imposed.

The "Cry Babies" went on trial for the Liccione bank job on August 7. The prosecution used their confessions against them, but when the state rested, the bandits took the stand in their defense and stated that they had confessed only because they were tortured by the police. The abuse, they claimed, began with the arresting officers and went all the way up to Inspector Coughlin, the head of the detective division, and the police commissioner.

According to Hecker, at one point during their interrogations at police headquarters when no answers were forthcoming, the inspector had ordered his subordinates to, "take them down and stick some hairpins in them till they're within two inches of their lives, and maybe they'll come through."[9] The bandits went on to name the detectives who had punched, kicked, and beaten them with rubber hoses. When it was Oberst's turn on the stand, he began to discuss the cops' brutality and one of the jurors became agitated and demanded to be removed from the panel. The judge declared a mistrial, and a new jury had to be put together and the bandits retried. In the end, the jury sided with the prosecution and all of the defendants were found guilty on August 19, 1926.

The bandits asked that they be sentenced as soon as possible, and their wish was granted with long terms in Sing Sing. By making this move, the "Cry Babies" believed they could not be put on trial for any of their other robberies. When detectives from Queens came to pick them up, Hecker joked to his mates, "We put one over on them." The officers weren't quite sure what he was talking about, but when they returned to the Queens County Jail with the bandits they were informed that it was illegal to house them there since they already had been sentenced to Sing Sing. The bandits were placed in a van for the ride to Manhattan, from where they would then be shipped to Sing Sing.

Reveling in their glory, the hoodlums sang songs during the trip. Their exuberance was short lived, however, because although it was illegal for them to go anywhere but the prison to which they were sentenced, the Queens D.A. only had to obtain a writ of habeas corpus to get them in the courtroom. The bandits only managed to buy a little time and forced the D.A. to do a little paperwork. In early September they were back in the Queens County Jail awaiting trial for the $2,460 payroll robbery of the William F. Kenny Construction Company.

With five of the seven gang members behind bars and one dead, detectives set their sights on the only one who remained at large: Jimmy O'Connor. It took two months, but they finally got him. O'Connor had fled to northern Pennsylvania and kept on the move. Detectives learned that he had a sweetheart in New York and were intercepting the letters the two were sending each other. At the end of August, Jimmy was in Philadelphia and sent his paramour a letter asking her to join him. After reading the letter, detectives only had to follow her to her man.

On September 5 they boarded the same train as the blonde, bobbed-hair moll and tailed her to O'Connor's rooming house. Two detectives went to the back door while a Philadelphia detective, who had joined them at the station, went to the front door. When the Philly detective burst through the front door, O'Connor tried to escape out the back but ran right into the New York lawmen. As his associates had done back in New York, Jimmy started to cry. "Life is cruel," he told the detectives. "For two months I have waited for her, and then we meet, and now this."[10]

The couple was taken to City Hall, where the girl was released and told to go home while extradition papers were prepared to return Jimmy to New York. Jimmy cried throughout the process and later made an unsuccessful attempt to jump out of a fifth-story window.

O'Connor was returned to the city on the evening of September 9. Earlier that day prison authorities had thwarted a plot to break his confederates out of the Queens County Jail. A keeper making his rounds had spotted a bundle of newspapers under some books in the cell of a convict not affiliated with the Oberst Gang. Investigating the peculiar package, he found a twenty-foot-long rope made out of sheets. Further investigation of the cell turned up two spoons that had been turned into shivs. The plan was for the convict to attack the night guard with the filed-down spoons and use his keys to release all the prisoners on the fifth tier, including the "Cry Babies." They would then use the sheet rope to escape to the street below.

The convict hiding the weapons and the extended length of sheet insisted that he was planning to use them to commit suicide. He said he was going to cut his wrist with the shivs and hang himself with the sheets. But he never did explain how he planned to hang himself from his seven-foot ceiling with a twenty-foot rope.

Sometime between his capture and the start of the trial for the Kenny job, Jimmy O'Connor turned state's evidence. He admitted his participation in all the holdups the gang had been accused of and also gave a full confession regarding the robbery for which he and his former mates were now on trial, conveniently filling in the gaps left by the witnesses.

The second trial for the "Cry Baby Bandits" opened on September 14, and on the first day William Heidman, the company's cashier, stated that a few minutes after receiving the payroll, Walter Heep, an employee of the company, entered the office with his hands over his head, followed by men wearing tinted driving goggles and holding guns. Heidman was able to identify Oberst and Frankel as two of the men.

He was followed on the stand by the company's stenographer who, pointing at Oberst said, "I saw this man and this man [Frankel] at the Kenny company office. I saw Frankel go over to Mr. Heidman and tell him to 'put up your hands.' Frankel ordered me to put my hands over my head and to keep quiet and stay where I was. Oberst walked over to Mr. Heidman's desk and took the money. Frankel then ordered Heidman and Heep to turn their backs to the wall and stay in that position for ten minutes."[11]

On the second day another employee identified Hecker, Kerrigan, and Frankel. Hecker had asked the witness if there was a gun in the office and was told no. A subsequent search of the employee's desk turned one up and Hecker hit the man with it, saying, "You big bum. I thought you said there was no gat here. I ought to shoot you for telling us that."[12] Kerrigan, however, came to the man's rescue and stopped Hecker.

If the gang members who weren't identified by the Kenny employees felt at all relieved, their hopes were dashed later that day when O'Connor's confession tying them all to the crime was read aloud in court. The bandit's statement said that on the day of the robbery the gang had met at a Fourteenth Street flat and that he and Hecker had taken a cab to Long Island City and walked to the company. After the robbery he and Hecker had returned to the Fourteenth Street room where the others were waiting and divided the loot, his share coming to $500. As O'Connor was being escorted from the courtroom after the trial wrapped for the day, Mahoney jumped at him and yelled, "Squealer." The other four gangsters joined him and attempted to pummel their former mate until guards were able to restore order.[13]

When court convened the next day all of the bandits except Oberst and O'Connor took the stand and again claimed that their confessions had been coerced through police brutality. Hecker said that after his arrest the police commissioner had promised he would get off with a light sentence if he would tell what he knew about the Kenny robbery. After he told the commissioner he didn't know anything about it, he said he was beaten unmercifully.

Kerrigan testified that when the D.A. was questioning him, he could hear two of the other bandits screaming as they were being beaten in other rooms. "You'll soon be screaming like those others," he claimed the D.A. told him, "if you don't answer questions and answer truthfully." When it was Mahoney's turn on the stand, he claimed the arresting detective "bounced me up and down like a rubber ball." Frankel stated that he had been held for five days without being able to contact an attorney and that he was beaten each day.[14]

On the last day of the trial O'Connor took the stand and testified about the gang's participation in the crime. As he ended, Hecker jumped to his feet and yelled, "Did you tell the court and the jury that you are dope fiend and a degenerate?"[15] The judge threatened to put Hecker in handcuffs for the remainder of the trial, and there were no further outburst. The trial wrapped up and the jurors were sent to deliberate. They returned in less than an hour, and all the bandits were found guilty.

Hecker, as a second offender, received a life sentence. Oberst, Frankel, Kerrigan, and Mahoney each received forty years, the sentences to be served after those they had received for the Liccione bank job. The five were returned to Sing Sing and put to work shoveling coal. O'Connor wasn't sentenced until a week after his former confederates, and when the judge informed the twenty-one-year-old that he would be spending the next fifteen to thirty years behind bars, he staggered and had to be steadied by court attendants. He no doubt thought that by turning state's evidence he would rewarded with a shorter term. O'Connor later passed out while being prepared for his trip up the river to Sing Sing.

The judge said he felt bad about sentencing the young man to such a long term, but it was the minimum he could hand down. O'Connor's lawyer said he would try to arrange for his client to be housed in a section of the prison where his former gang mates wouldn't be able to get to him. But any worries O'Connor may have had regarding retribution were short lived, for less than two weeks after he arrived at Sing Sing, Oberst and the other four hoodlums were transferred to Clinton Prison in Dannemora.

Seeing Red

"It is all right to steal and murder if you don't get caught."

— Thomas "Red" Moran

Thomas Moran was nuts. Just ask anyone who knew him. His mother would tell you how he used to chase his seven younger brothers and sisters around the house with a knife, laughing at their fear. Michael Cahill, a fellow gang member, would tell of the time Moran got drunk and tried to stab all his friends. His girlfriend Agnes Guilfoyle could chime in with a more peculiar than lethal example: One time before a date he hid mice up his coat sleeve, and once they were in the movie theater he began pulling them out one by one.

At twenty years of age, Moran, who went by the moniker "Red," was a small-time Brooklyn hood who, along with his gang, was guilty of pulling some twenty-five small-time robberies, mostly of cab drivers and stores. His modus operandi was to hail a cab and have the driver take him to a secluded area where he would relieve the driver of his cash and cab. The cab would then be used as the getaway car for the robbery of a store.

Among those in "Red's" gang was eighteen-year-old James De Michaels, whom everyone called "the King." Like many other hoods, De Michaels had a hard-luck story. His parents had died when he was ten, and he and his siblings were sent to an orphanage. When he turned sixteen he moved into a boys home. At eighteen he was living with Moran at a boarding house.

Another member was Joseph Lacurto, who, like Moran, had mental troubles. "I know he is crazy," his father told the press. "There is something wrong with his head."[1] His mother concurred, saying that when he was five he contracted some disease of the head. Although she never actually learned what it was, she said that since that time her boy had never been the same. Lacurto also did jail time in Trenton, New Jersey; however, when he was released, his father, a career employee of the Brooklyn-Manhattan Transit Corporation, set him up with a lucrative job. Not one to maintain a 9-to-5 schedule, Joseph started robbing with Moran. Rounding out the gang were hoodlums Michael Cahill, Robert Donahue, and Robert Tate.

The event that propelled "Red" from common punk to bandit du jour occurred on Friday, November 19, 1926, when he and five associates rented a car for a robbery. After stopping for lunch, they stopped at a store to pick up some pictures of "Red's" girlfriend that he was having developed. One of the men went inside, and while the rest were sitting in the car, police Officer Edward Byrnes approached and asked "Red" for his license, which he produced. The patrolman went away seemingly satisfied. Afterward, Moran's crony returned to the car and reported that the pictures weren't ready yet. This didn't sit well with the mentally unbalanced Moran, who became infuriated.

With Lacurto at the wheel, the bandits pulled out and went on their way. After a short distance Officer Byrnes pulled alongside in a police car, with his partner, patrolman Frank Daszkiewicz, standing on the running board. Daszkiewicz ordered the bandits to pull over, and as they did Byrnes slid to a stop in front of the stolen vehicle, blocking it in. The two cops walked up to the car and ordered the the hoodlums to get out. As "Red" emerged he drew his pistol and yelled, "Hands up!" As Daszkiewicz went for his weapon, "Red" fired two shots into him, then shot Byrnes as the officer reached for his service revolver. As Daszkiewicz was falling, he grabbed Lacurto and held on tightly.[2]

All the bandits took off with the exception of Lacurto, who was stuck in Daszkiewicz's grasp. Within a few moments a good Samaritan came up and helped restrain the bandit. Moran ran into the rear of a building a few blocks away but was quickly dragged out by two sisters who thought he was a burglar. When they wrestled him to the front door, he broke free and ran. "Red" made it to the Brooklyn Bridge, where he jumped into a cab to Times Square in Manhattan. From there he taxied uptown, then back downtown where he took in a vaudeville show and later a burlesque show. He topped the evening off by taking a girl for a cab ride.[3]

Once in custody Lacurto had no problem singing, and soon other members of the gang were rounded up. De Michaels was nabbed while playing checkers, and Robert Tate, who wasn't even in the car at the time of the shooting, was also arrested. Lacurto's aria also included the jobs they had pulled. Even the guy who sold them their guns, Anthony Marchia, found himself behind bars.[4]

Saturday found the most-wanted man in town with the girl he had hooked up with the night before. She must have been nice because "Red" gave her all his money except four dollars and then spent most of Sunday at a restaurant contemplating what to do. That night he rode the subway worrying that his pals might end up going to the chair for his crime, so decided to give himself up the next day.[5] On Monday he returned to Brooklyn and entered the police station on Snyder Avenue to surrender to a detective he knew named Fitzgerald. But when the cop-killer walked up to the front desk and asked to see him, the officer on duty barked, "Fitzgerald isn't here. Get out of here." So he did.[6]

Still wanting to save his buddies, Moran made his way to the Empire Boulevard station where he approached the desk and asked the lieutenant on duty if there were any detectives around. The officer told him to go look for himself. Moran did, but finding no detectives, he went back to the lieutenant, who offered to find one for him. But Moran had had enough. "Oh, I guess you'll do," he told the officer. "I'm 'Red' Moran. I shot those two cops on Hicks Street last Friday; I guess you're looking for me." He then made a complete confession, taking responsibility for the shootings.[7]

An unkempt Moran showed up at court where a reporter for the *New York Times* noted that he, "lacked the steely nerve of a Chapman or the quiet courage of a Whittemore, and appeared what he was—a sulky school boy facing punishment for his crime."[8] Two indictments of first-degree murder were lodged against the youth, and he pleaded guilty to both. However, state law precluded a guilty plea in a first-degree murder case, so to his disappointment "Red's" plea was changed to not guilty. When asked if he had a lawyer, he said no and declared that he wanted to go to the electric chair.[9]

A few days later two court-appointed attorneys, Albert Conway and Peter Smith, showed up at the Raymond Street Jail to speak with Moran but the gunman wasn't interested. They stood outside his cell and introduced themselves. "We are your attorneys, appointed to advise you," Conway told him. "I don't want any attorneys" Moran shot back. "We may be able to help you," Smith said. "I don't want any help," "Red" responded. "I want to die. I want to have it over with as soon as possible."[10] Reluctantly, Moran gave in and answered some questions while refusing to answer others. After their first visit Conway and Smith said they believed Moran was "mentally abnormal."

Psychiatrists were called in to interview the defendant so that an insanity plea could be put forth.

Moran's trial began on January 24, 1927, and "Red" was not happy that his lawyers were going to try to convince the jury he was crazy. As he entered the courtroom he told his guards that he wasn't nuts, he just wanted to be electrocuted. Moran appeared unconcerned during the trial. His lawyer mentioned that mental illness ran in Moran's family, citing six other cases. The fact that he had been discharged from the Navy because he suffered from Jacksonian epilepsy was brought up, as was the fact that he had a plate in his head as a result of being hit by a truck as a child. "Red" sat through his mother's testimony and that of gang member Mike Cahill, all the time muttering his trial mantra, "What's the use of all this?"[11]

As the proceedings progressed, "Red" became more and more belligerent. On the day he was supposed to take the stand he refused to move from his seat. Later he began to drum on the table with a pencil and continued to do so after being ordered to stop. Finally a guard had to come up and take it away from him. His rudeness continued after lunch when he refused to stand when the judge reentered the courtroom. A guard was quick to "help" him to his feet by pulling him up by his shoulders.[12]

"Red's" defense team brought in two psychologists who stated it was their opinion that the gunman was indeed crazy. When asked for specifics, they said "Red" had told them he was not only the best shot in the Navy, but he also could pull radio messages out of the air without any sort of equipment. His superhuman abilities didn't end there: he also stated that all women were defenseless when confronted by his hypnotic powers.[13]

In his closing argument the prosecuting assistant D.A. dismissed insanity pleas as a whole. "I don't believe in medical experts," he told the jury, "and the practice of using them has become such that I do not wonder at the almost universal public sentiment against such insanity defenses as this."[14] The jury concurred, and on January 31, 1927, Moran was found guilty and shipped off to the Sing Sing death house.

Five months after his trial "Red" was back in a Brooklyn courtroom. The previous December while in the Raymond Street Jail he had passed a note to two men being held for a robbery saying that he was the one who had pulled the job. Now that they were on trial, the young killer was brought in to testify that he was the actual perpetrator of the crime. But any hopes the bandits had about Moran coming to their aid were quickly dashed when he took the witness stand. His antagonistic replies did not help their case at all. Samples include:

> PROSECUTOR: You are an inmate of Sing Sing, aren't you?
> MORAN: Don't you know? Everybody else knows.
> PROSECUTOR: What are you there for?
> MORAN: If you don't know, I won't tell you.[15]

Of course his surliness wasn't proof that he hadn't pulled the job. That came when the prosecutor pressed him for specifics on the robbery that he couldn't answer. Flustered, he refused to say who had taken part in the robbery with him, although he did mention that he used thirty-five cap pistols during the heist. Tiring of the Q & A, Moran groused, "I'm sick of this. I'm not going to talk anymore. Take me away! I'd sooner be back in Sing Sing. Besides, it's time for dinner."[16]

Interestingly, during the trial he changed his tune and denied ever saying that he wanted to go to the electric chair. According to Moran, what he really said was that he wasn't afraid to die. His new attitude coincided with a decision by the court of appeals that allowed a retrial of the cop-killer. This was because the judge in the first trial, when charging the jury, failed to mention that they could find him guilty of something other than first-degree murder, e.g., manslaughter, second-degree murder, etc.

Early 1928 found Moran back in Brooklyn's Raymond Street Jail awaiting his retrial. Because he constantly bragged about how tough he was, "Red" was not a favorite with the other prisoners. One inmate in particular who hated Moran was William Reid, who was serving a thirty-day sentence for disorderly conduct. Moran went on and on boasting about how he had beaten up Reid's brother a few years earlier. Finally, Reid could take no more and on February 8, the day before he was to be released, he attacked Moran with a shiv he'd carved from a spoon. Before "Red" was able to wrestle the knife away, he received stab wounds to the neck and body that narrowly missed his lung and kidneys. Moran was taken to the hospital, where it was determined his injuries were non-life threatening. All Reid would say to the jail keepers was that, "Moran got what was coming to him." The glee the other inmates displayed at the news of the attack seemed to confirm it.[17]

Moran's second trial wasn't much different from the first. He sat through most of it with his eyes shut, apparently not carrying one way or the other what happened. One difference in the trial was that six psychologist were called, three testifying for the defense and three for the prosecution. On March 20 "Red" was once again found guilty. "Well, I guess I got the works this time,"[18] was his only comment before being shipped back to the death house.

In November, Moran's counsel attempted to get another trial after "Red's" mother had received a letter from gang member Joseph Lacurto, who was serving a life sentence at Clinton Prison in Dannemora. Lacurto wrote that he and James De Michaels, at the time serving a twenty-year term at Sing Sing, were the actual shooters and that her son had volunteered to take the rap for them.[19] The motion for a new trial was denied, and "Red's" date with the executioner was set for December 14, 1928.

On "Red's" last day he was visited by his brother while his mother and sister hounded the governor for a reprieve that never came. When the guards came to escort him from his cell to the pre-execution chamber, Moran was waiting and said, "I'm ready, fellows; let's go." He then asked for and received permission to shake hands with the other death-row inmates. His final hours were spent with a priest. "I'm game and I'm not worrying a bit," "Red" told him, and he managed to keep his nerve until the very end.

At about 1 a.m. Moran entered the execution chamber puffing on a cigarette and headed right for the chair. Without looking around or speaking, he took a seat and allowed the guards to strap the electrodes to him. At 1:02 a.m. the signal was given and the executioner threw the switch. After six minutes the juice was turned off and "Red's" wasted life was officially declared over.[20]

DISHONORABLE MENTION

1920-1929

Murder in the Pirates Den

At noon on Monday, August 29, 1921, Sing Sing's Catholic chaplain, Father William Cashin, received a most unexpected visitor: William Hoey, a known hoodlum from New York City's West Side. What made the visit even more intriguing was that on the previous Saturday night a New York City cop had been killed, and the authorities were searching for the man who now stood at the chaplain's door.

The murder had taken place in a fenced-in lot known as the Pirates Den on Thirty-ninth Street between Tenth and Eleventh avenues where Hoey was employed as a night watchman. Claiming innocence, Hoey said he wanted to help solve the case, telling the chaplain, "Father, I want you to call up the district attorney in New York and tell him I want to talk with him. I'll go down with you, and I think I can help the police get the man who killed Neville [the murdered patrolman]. I'm afraid to go to the police because they'll beat me up."[1]

Hoey had reason to fear the cops. They knew him quite well. Less than three weeks before the killing he had been arrested for robbery and was currently out on bail. His record dated back to 1914 when he was arrested six times for juvenile delinquency and convicted twice. He spent part of 1916 in the House of Refuge, and on May 18, 1917, he was sentenced to the New York State Reformatory for assault. Two years later, in January 1919, he would again be convicted of assault and robbery and sent to the reformatory at Elmira. While there he was said to have killed another inmate, although a jury found him innocent, and was transferred to Sing Sing. After having time knocked off his sentence for good behavior, he was paroled from Sing Sing but wound up in the workhouse on March 11, 1921, for possessing drugs. Hoey knew that with the murder of their brother officer still so fresh, the police wouldn't be willing to reason with a paroled junkie with a long list of arrests.

The chaplain brought Hoey back to New York City and turned him over to the authorities who, because of Hoey's publicized fears, questioned him without using violence. The chaplain repeated to reporters what Hoey had told him about the murder. Hoey said he had been standing at the gate on Thirty-ninth Street guarding some boxes. Officer Neville approached, and the two men, knowing each other, started talking. As they were conversing, four men approached and Neville pushed Hoey behind some boxes as the quartet entered the lot and made their way into a small shanty. Hoey assumed the patrolman had pushed him behind the boxes because he was afraid the hoodlum would warn the four men that a cop was present. Then, with gun drawn, the cop entered the shanty.

"The next thing Hoey could tell about was hearing two revolver shots." the chaplain continued. "He thought the policeman entering the shanty had fired at the four men. But a second later he saw the policeman stagger from the shanty, take one or two unsteady steps, and fall." The recitation closed with Hoey stating that he had then seen two of the four men run from the shanty, climb the fence, and run off. He didn't say what became of the other two.[2]

Fearing what would happen to him at the hands of the police, Hoey had fled the scene and stayed away from his apartment. He rented a room for the night and went out to his sister's place on Staten Island the next day. He tried to get his sister to escort him to the D.A.'s office, but she refused, saying that she had to care for her kids. She told him go to the priest who was also acting as his parole officer, but since he was out of town Hoey had decided to go to Father Cashin at Sing Sing.

Hoey did indeed help the police find patrolman Neville's murderer. While Father Cashin was conversing with the press, a witness was identifying Hoey as one of the men who had hopped the fence after the shooting. The witness stated that he had run up after the gunfire in time to see Hoey jump the fence. He then said that Hoey had turned his gun on him and said, "Don't you open your mouth,"[3] before running away. The next day, after another witness testified that he had seen Hoey running from the crime scene with another man, he was charged with the murder.

A nationwide search was also initiated for the three men the police said had been with Hoey at the time of the murder. One was another drug addict named John "Soup" Gleason, who was identified as the man who had jumped the fence with Hoey. The other two men were John "the Swede" Lindquist and Albert Lanson.

While in custody Hoey began going through withdrawal and demanded drugs. The prison doctor allowed him to shoot up, and with the narcotics in his system, he transformed back into a tough Hell's Kitchen hoodlum. But when he learned the grand jury had indicted him for the murder, his disposition immediately changed, and keepers stated that he started banging his head on the walls, threw himself on the floor, and cried all night. The prison physician attributed the behavior to Hoey's fear of the electric chair.[4]

On September 9 police came to take him to court so he could answer the murder charge, and when they got to his cell he refused to stand. "What's the matter with you?" one of the detectives asked him. "You're not acting like the tough guy you used to pretend you were." Hoey's response was a pathetic, "Save me! Save me!" The convict was given some drugs and then brought into court, where he broke down and cried and begged for mercy.[5]

About two weeks after Hoey's pitiable display at court, the police found "Soup" Gleason in a place they weren't expecting—the morgue. "Soup" had overdosed while staying with a family friend. At 1 a.m. on September 25, Gleason had stopped at the apartment of a couple who were friendly with his brother and asked if he could spend the night. The couple said he seemed drunk [alcohol was also found in is system], so they gave him a room for the night. At 9:30 that morning the lady of the house went to wake him and found "Soup" sitting upright in a chair, dead.[6]

Hoey went on trial in January 1922 and was found guilty of second-degree murder and shipped off to Sing Sing, but his presence was still felt on Manhattan's West Side. Later that year, on June 4, Tim McIrney, one of the main witnesses against Hoey, was shot by two men in a speeding cab. McIrney's wounds were superficial and he was sent home after being treated. His friends told the press the shooters were no doubt friends of Hoey's out for vengeance. The police, however, said that Hoey was a low-level junkie who had no allegiance of hoods who would be out for revenge.[7] They weren't so sure, however, when four months later, on October 1, another witness, George Swan, was shot and nearly killed.[8] Swan refused to discuss the shooting with police, which leads one to believe that the shooting was a personal matter and not a case of an innocent civilian being gunned down by vengeful gangsters.

Levy's Last Stand

Nelson Levy was bad man. He was arrested eleven times in eight years, and chances are it would have been an even dozen if a detective's bullet hadn't brought his crime spree to an end. His first arrest was on April 29, 1913, for burglary, but the sentence was suspended. Three months later he was shipped off to the reformatory at Elmira for robbery. Unreformed, he pleaded guilty to another burglary on July 25, 1915, but managed to get his five-year term suspended. Levy's knack for avoiding jail continued into 1916 when he was able to get two more sentences quashed, one for burglary and one for possessing a gun. Finally, in June of the same year after yet another burglary charge, a judge realized that Levy just might be a threat to society and shipped him off to Sing Sing for four years.

Levy was released in 1919 and immediately returned to a life of crime. He was picked up three times that year and served twenty days for disorderly conduct. On March 15, 1920, out on bail while awaiting trial for grand larceny, he was again arrested for grand larceny. He made bail then skipped both court appearances, forfeiting both bonds.

All the jobs the bandit may have taken part in during his year and a half on the lam are unknown, but by November 1921 he had made the jump from burglary to armed robbery and had become proficient with a gun. With his brother-in-law Joseph Oates as a new accomplice, Levy stole some company payrolls, but their main targets were United Cigar Store franchises. It was at one of these on December 23, 1921, that Levy made his last stand. Had the holdup been successful it would have been the duo's fourth cigar store job in a week.

At about 8 p.m. Levy and Oates, both suavely dressed in overcoats and caps, entered the cigar store and browsed around as the manager and his assistant waited on the numerous customers. When all the patrons had departed, the manager approached Levy, saying, "Well, young man, what can I do for you?" Whipping out his pistol, Levy snapped, "You can throw up your hands, and be quick about it!" The bandit then hustled the manager to the rear of the store and began tying him up with picture wire.

While this was happening, Oates shed his coat and hat and went behind the counter where, at gunpoint, he ordered the assistant to start wrapping candy. Two customers came in, and Oates sold them some cigarettes. Then about a half-dozen more came in, and the bandit was able to serve them without any problems. Just as he was finishing, a new batch of customers poured in, one of them a regular. The man approached the assistant, but Oates yelled, "Don't bother him now, young man. He is very busy, and I will wait on you." Seeing the fear on the assistant's face, the customer knew something was wrong. As soon as he got his merchandise he left and called the police, telling them he believed the store was being robbed.[9]

In less than five minutes, just as Levy was walking back into the front room, Detectives McCarthy and Connell entered the cigar store with their guns drawn. Assuming that Levy was a salesman, McCarthy asked him what was going on. "Nothing that I know of," the bandit calmly replied. "Do you see anything wrong?" "Well, we heard there was a holdup going on here," McCarthy said. As he and his partner turned toward the store assistant, Levy pulled out his pistol and began firing. The first shot hit McCarthy in the mouth, but he and Connell both returned fire.

Levy didn't even try to find cover—he just stood there, taking aim and firing. His composure paid off as his fourth shot drilled Connell in the ear, knocking him to the floor. Miraculously, the detective was able to get back up, and at this point both lawmen realized Oates now was shooting at them. They fired a volley in his direction, and he fell to the floor with a belly wound. Levy took this opportunity to run past the detectives and out the door.

With Oates out of the way, the detectives staggered outside in pursuit of Levy, who was running down the street. By now everyone in the area had realized a gunfight was in progress and had sought cover, giving the detectives a clear shot. Their guns barked, and Levy fell in a heap as one of the bullets pierced his right shoulder and plowed into his heart. McCarthy and Connell approached the expiring bandit and took his gun. They could tell he wasn't going anywhere, so they made their way back to the store to check on Oates, only to find that he had fled while they were chasing Levy. Witnesses said a car had been waiting for him and it sped off once he was inside.[10]

Oates was in a fix. Suffering from a punctured intestine, he made his way to the apartment of his estranged wife and, with Levy's younger brother, came up with a plan of action. Realizing that a trip to a New York City hospital would result in his immediate capture, they decided to go to New Jersey to seek medical attention. The younger Levy hailed a cab and helped Oates inside. They ordered the driver to take them across the Hudson River, and at 2:30 a.m. Oates checked into the Englewood Hospital, where he was immediately prepped for surgery.

He told the doctors he was the victim of a robbery at the ferry and that a bandit had shot him. A doctor called the local police, who came out and spoke with Oates and the two Levys, who backed up the former's story. The officer, however, noticed that a New York taxi had brought Oates and company to Englewood, and being aware of the cigar store stickup, he reported his suspicions to his superior. The New Jersey authorities got in touch with NYPD headquarters, and Detective Dominick Caso from the Bronx was sent to investigate.

Oates denied any involvement in the robbery, but when Caso told him Levy was dead, the bandit said, "I don't believe it." "If you don't believe it, here's the morning paper." Caso responded, adding a veiled threat: "I've got your wife here, and she is liable to get into trouble."

Realizing the futility of the situation, Oates admitted his part in the cigar store robbery as well as the many others he and his partner had pulled. He also seemed somewhat remorseful about the shooting, saying, "We didn't want to kill anybody unless we had to, but the detectives covered us and there was nothing else to do." He didn't mince words about his pal, however: "I'm sorry old Levy is dead. He knew his business."[11]

The Music Man

Although the press tagged him with a relatively innocuous nickname, "Radio Burglar" Paul Emmanuel Hilton was in fact a lethal character, as the New York Police Department would unfortunately find out. Although he was an admitted music fan, his true passion was baseball, an obsession that would lead to his demise.

Born circa 1900 in the Williamsburg section of Brooklyn, Hilton was orphaned at the age of eleven and spent the rest of his childhood in various institutions including the Catholic Protectory after being arrested in 1909 for delinquency. He started burglarizing at a young age and was arrested on May 22, 1916, but the sentence was suspended. He wasn't so lucky on September 17, when he was arrested for the same crime and sent to the Elmira Reformatory. His speed and athletic ability guaranteed him a spot on the prison's baseball team as a third baseman.

He was released in time to enlist in the Navy during World War I and spent his time at the training station in Newport, Rhode Island, where he was a bugler (he also played the cornet). A little more than a month after Armistice Day, on Christmas Eve 1918, he was back in New York and again was arrested for plying his trade.[*] This resulted in a stay on Blackwell's Island. Upon his release he tried his luck back in Rhode Island but was captured in April 1921 and sent to the state prison in Cranston[**]—just in time for baseball season.[12]

After serving about four and a half years, Hilton was released in November 1925 and returned to New York. He hooked up with George Ebert, an ex-convict whom he had met at Elmira, and used Ebert's name to purchase a car. Shifting between various Bowery flophouses, Hilton began his crime spree on January 30, 1926, when he robbed his first house, in Woodhaven, Queens. He struck again the following night and every couple of nights thereafter, mostly in the same section of Queens. Though he took silver and basically anything that could turn a dollar, mostly he stole radios. More than two dozen successful burglaries later, residents of Woodhaven were going to bed fearful that they might be the next victims of the "Radio Burglar."

---

* At the station he gave the name Frank Merriwell, a fictional baseball player popular at the time in books for adolescent boys.

** This time he bypassed baseball players for cowboys and said he was William Cody from Colorado.

It is strange that Hilton wasn't caught sooner, because he wasn't the type of prowler who hid in the shadows until the coast was clear. Quite the opposite, after a successful heist, he would simply walk to the nearest subway station with the radio under his arm and take it to his fence, Morris Reiff, who owned a radio shop in the East Village. Normally, Hilton would make less than $10 per job, although once he did snatch a radio valued at $200 and was given $15 for it. Later the burglar would complain that Reiff was an even bigger crook than he was.[13]

In the early morning hours of February 26, Hilton let the police know they were dealing with more than just a simple prowler. Patrolman Jacob Biegel was walking his beat at 3 a.m. when he noticed a man slinking through the bushes around a house. Capturing the illusive "Radio Burglar" would be a feather in any cop's cap, so Biegel drew his gun and immediately ran toward the figure. Hilton heard him coming and ran out onto the lawn and started down the street. "Stop! Halt! You're under arrest!" the officer yelled. Hilton came to a standstill and turned around, waiting for Biegel to approach—and in a flash fired two shots from a gun the patrolman never even saw. Hilton made good his escape as Biegel dropped to the ground. Nearby residents came to the officer's aid, and his wounds proved non-fatal.[14]

Less than a week later, Hilton was back in business and successfully raided another thirteen houses before his next run-in with the cops. On March 25 it appeared the "Radio Burglar" had pulled his twenty-sixth robbery when police received word at 3 a.m. that a house was being robbed and rushed to the scene. Officers Arthur Kenny and Frank Donnolly went to cover the rear of the house, and Donnolly had his pistol out as Hilton walked out the back door and told the lawmen he was the home's owner. When Donnolly lowered his gun, the bandit seized the opportunity and drew his own pistol, shooting the patrolman in the neck before running out of the yard with Kenny on his heels.

Hilton distanced himself from Kenny and ducked into an alley but was unable to find an escape route. As Kenny turned into the alley, Hilton yelled, "Don't shoot, I'm a policeman!" and told him that the burglar had run the other way. As Kenny turned to look, Hilton raised his gun and fired a bullet into the patrolman's chest, then beat a successful retreat.[15]

Nearly two weeks would go by before the police would get the clue they needed to capture the "Radio Burglar"—unfortunately, another lawman would be wounded in the process. On April 6 Detectives Charles McCarthy, Richard Siegert, and John Mireau were driving through Woodhaven at about 2 a.m. when they saw a man (Hilton) walking down the street. Suspicious, they pulled over and McCarthy approached the man and asked, "Is this Eighty-seventh Avenue?"

"I don't know; I'm a stranger here," the man replied.

Where do you live?"

"South Brooklyn"

"What are you doing here at this hour?"

"I'm legitimate, I'm Toole from the gas company."

Hilton then produced a wallet he had stolen on one of his jobs containing an I.D. card for a Bernard Toole. As McCarthy took the card, Hilton dropped the wallet, pulled out his gun, and shot the detective in the neck. As McCarthy fell, Hilton fired another shot that missed and then ran away. Detectives Siegert and Mireau gave chase, but the athletic hoodlum easily outran them. McCarthy would survive his wound, but later that day patrolman Arthur Kenny, who was shot on March 25, passed away. Murder was now added to the "Radio Burglar's" list of offenses.[16]

The wallet Hilton dropped would lead to his downfall. Inside were two pawn tickets made out in the name of George Ebert. There were half a dozen George Eberts in New York City, and through the process of elimination investigators came to Hilton's pal from Elmira. They asked the ex-con if he knew anyone who would use his name, and he mentioned Hilton. Ebert wasn't too concerned about turning in Hilton; during their reunion the previous November the latter had stolen some of his clothes. Armed with a name, the police went through their rogues' gallery and found Hilton. His picture was then shown to the detectives who had been shot, and they all identified him as their assailant.[17]

Over the course of about a week detectives investigated Hilton, who managed to pull two more burglaries on April 8 before heading to Providence, Rhode Island, for the weekend. They learned Hilton was a big baseball fan and that he might show up to watch the Giants' season opener at the Polo Grounds on April 13. The information they received proved solid, and at about 2:45 p.m. the subject of their manhunt arrived. Just as Hilton was preparing to enter the ballpark, three detectives jumped on him, two pinning his arms while the third asked, "What's your name?"

Pulling an arm free, Hilton produced an identification card and snapped, "My name is Donnelly." As the detectives began to walk him toward the street, he stopped and asked, "Who are you anyway? I don't know you. Show me something." But before the officers had a chance to respond, Hilton blurted out his familiar line, "I'm legitimate. I'll show you who I am." With that, he jerked his left hand free and went for his gun. The detectives grabbed him before he could get it into action, and they wrestled around for a few minutes before one of them was able to rip the weapon from Hilton's coat. The cops then proceeded to drag their prisoner under the elevated train tracks, throw him to the ground, and beat him into submission.[18]

Once in custody Hilton readily admitted to all the burglaries as well as to killing Officer Kenny and wounding the other policemen. He said he regretted the shootings and that "I only shot to get away." When asked about his predilection for radios during his break-ins, he responded simply, "I like music."[19]

The fact that Manhattan detectives had captured the "Radio Burglar" when thirty Queens detectives couldn't do so was not lost on Police Commissioner George McLaughlin. He commended the Manhattan officers and promoted those who had captured Hilton, while demoting to uniform patrol duty Detectives Siegert and Mireau, who had allowed the bandit to escape after he shot Detective McCarthy.[20] More demotions were impending, since Hilton had been able to prey on the same neighborhood for three months and—adding insult to injury—the majority of the burglaries had taken place within a half mile radius of the Richmond Hill Police Station.

The authorities believed Hilton was crazy, and he probably was. He stayed in top physical condition and considered himself always to be in training. "My only dissipation is cigarette smoking. I'm not interested in women, liquor, coffee, or pie," he told the police. Somewhere in his mind, stealing radios was akin to playing professional baseball, but he was an articulate speaker, which didn't help in the insanity department. When officials admitted to him that they were impressed with how well spoken he was, he told them, "When I was in Elmira Reformatory, we had to attain a scholastic standing of seventy-five percent or draw an additional thirty-day stay in the institution. I passed every term." He did, however, mention that he drew an extra thirty days once when he was caught smoking.[21]

In the end it was determined that Hilton was indeed sane, and ten months later, on February 17, 1927, the fat lady sang for the music fan as he took a seat in the electric chair.

An Englishman in New York

James "English Harry" Wallon was born in Carlisle, England, about 1888 and some twenty years later crossed the Atlantic and ended up mixing with the New York City underworld. Though he rubbed elbows with the notorious "Kid Twist" Zweibach's gang, Harry was a robber, not a gangster. His record shows an arrest in Elmira, New York, in 1913 followed by a short sentence. The next year he was arrested for first-degree robbery and sentenced on November 9 to nineteen years.

After serving about eight years, "English Harry" returned to New York City and he put together a new mob that preyed on gambling joints and nightclubs as well as hijacking liquor trucks. On January 7, 1923, he was again arrested for robbery but beat the rap.[22]

In the spring of 1926 the police department began to follow his gang, and on April 4 five members—Adolph Abraham (known as "Dutch" Adolph), Nicholas Chrisano, John O'Brien, and William "Cockeye" Baker—met in Wallon's room at the Markwell Hotel, then headed to a Midtown gambling room at 2 a.m. to rob the place. Little did they know the NYPD was tailing them.

There must have been a spy at the gambling house, because the gangsters were expecting to find a Chinese merchant who was winning big, but he wasn't there when they went inside. "Where's the Chink?" one of them said. A gambler told them he had just left, so the bandits drew their guns, lined the gamblers up, and robbed them of $300 and some watches. After closer inspection, the thieves gave back all but two of the watches because they considered them cheap.

When the bandits left the building, six detectives were waiting for them outside. The hoods tossed their guns in the street and began running, but the detectives caught up with them. A fistfight ensued which ended with the gangsters being subdued by blackjacks and pistol butts; back at the police station two ambulances were needed to supply medical care to them.[23]

Seventeen gamblers identified the robbers, and a month later Harry plead not guilty and went on trial. After just fifteen minutes of deliberation the jury found him guilty, and on May 5 he received a forty-year prison term. Not wanting to get a dose of the same, his associates quickly pleaded guilty and received shorter sentences.[24]

Harry had the last laugh, however. Sing Sing prison baled its waste paper and sold it to a junkyard, and on May 23, 1929, twenty-seven bales were prepared for shipment. Guards didn't oversee the actual baling process, so Harry slid his diminutive five-foot-one frame into one of the bales. An accomplice did the same. When the delivery trucks arrived, all the bales were slid down a chute to the loading dock where a guard jabbed each one with a pointed rod to ensure no one was hiding inside. Both prisoners escaped detection and neither was hurt, and they were loaded onto the truck and taken to the junkyard.

When they arrived, Harry wiggled free and took off running. His partner, however, was unable to work himself loose and ended up being captured. It appears that Wallon managed to stay free. A search of press reports revealed nothing of his capture, so perhaps "English Harry" returned to his native land, where no doubt they just called him Harry.[25]

Murder at the A & P

A month after the "English Harry" Wallon mob was put out of business, the Baraseck Gang also went under. Not so much a gang as a trio, the Barasecks were nonetheless a desperate and violent crew guilty of fifteen robberies.

The "gang" consisted of twenty-eight-year-old William Baraseck (true name Barszouyk), his twenty-three-year-old brother Kasimir, and twenty-one-year-old John Maxwell, all from Brooklyn. Robbery was their business, with Kasimir serving as the getaway driver and Maxwell and William as the gunmen. They specialized, although not exclusively, in robbing United Cigar shops and A & P stores. Two of their A & P jobs resulted in murder.

The first occurred on January 22, 1926, when at 6:30 p.m. Maxwell and William entered a store and ordered the clerk, Joseph Mullarky, to head to the rear room. In an act of defiance Mullarky picked up a can of peas and hurled it at one of the gunmen. He missed, but Maxwell and Baraseck opened fire, hitting Mullarky once in the head and twice in the stomach. He died a short time later in the hospital.

Eight days later there was more gunplay when the bandits entered a chicken market and began to rob the patrons. The store's proprietor, Morris Summer, went for the bandits with a knife but was was shot in the stomach and critically wounded.

The second botched A & P robbery occurred on February 13. While Kasimir waited outside in the car, William and John Maxwell entered with guns drawn and corralled the staff and customers into the rear room. As William was emptying the tills a woman entered. In an attempt to frighten her, Maxwell pointed his gun in her direction and accidentally pulled the trigger. The bullet struck the woman in the shoulder, and she went into shock and died.

After the shooting William and Maxwell ran out of the store and jumped into the car, but when Kasimir was unable to get it started, the trio jumped out and took off on foot. Maxwell jumped on the running board of a passing cab, pointed his gun at the driver, and told him to stop. "Nothing doing. I have a passenger," the cabby replied. One of the Baraseck brothers caught up with the vehicle, and both gangsters aimed their guns at the driver. "You'll take us or you'll be a dead chauffeur in a minute," one of them told him, and when the cabby refused, both bandits fired into him, killing him. The three thugs then jumped on the back of a truck and ordered the driver to speed off. They stayed on the back of the truck all the way to Times Square, then jumped off and made their escape.[26]

Three months later the trio popped up in Cambridge, Massachusetts, where they and a new member of the gang from that city robbed another A & P of $60. The following day the four hoods were driving through Darien, Connecticut, when a motorcycle cop pulled them over, suspecting they might be bootleggers. Looking inside the car, the officer noticed a pistol, but wanting to take the men by surprise, he pretended not to see it. "Well, I guess you are all right," he said, turning as if to walk to his motorcycle. Once his back was to them, he quickly drew his gun and spun around, jamming the weapon into Kasimir's head. "You keep your hands on that steering wheel, and the rest of you guys put up your hands," he ordered. "The first one of you that makes a wrong move, I'll blow this man's brains out."[27]

The Baraseck brothers and Maxwell were sent to Brooklyn to await their murder trials. They planned an escape but made the mistake of telling their plans to an inmate serving a short term who didn't want anything to do with them. He squealed to the warden, saying, "One day last week one of those guys that did the shooting in the grocery store came to me in the kitchen and asked, 'Which way do you get upstairs from here?' I pointed to the door that leads to the stairs and told him a couple of other things about the layout of the jail, and then I asked, 'What's the idea?' He says, 'You look pretty straight; I'll tell you. We're going to make a break some night next week, and if you do the right thing by us and keep your mouth shut, maybe we'll take you along. But if you open your trap, we'll put you out of business.'

"I asked, 'How are you going to do it?' He answered, 'Three friends are coming to the jail after midnight, and they are going to get in by saying that they want to bail a guy out. But when they get inside they are going to shoot it out until the four keepers are done for, and then they'll let us out and we're all going to beat it. We want you to show us the way out. No funny business, see?'"[28] The warden immediately put extra security measures in place, and the proposed escape never got off the ground.

The three hoods were desperate to break out because they knew they were facing the death penalty—and that was indeed the sentence handed down on June 8. Just before sentence was pronounced, each man was asked if he had anything to say. Since he was only the getaway driver and not one of the gunmen, Kasimir said, "I don't think justice was done to me in my case. I hope I will get justice. I leave it to you."

The judge responded by saying the evidence was convincing, and he sentenced all three to death. "It was not convincing!" Kasimir shouted, as he began shaking and pounded the rail.[29] His protest was in vain, however, and the trio was executed on December 9, 1926.

A Moth to a Flame

A chance meeting in a speakeasy turned a seemingly hard-working, law-abiding everyday Joe into a gun-toting desperado destined for a rendezvous with the electric chair.

Twenty-one-year-old Peter Seiler had everything going for him. Unlike most young people of his day, he was a high school graduate and managed to find steady work. Granted, his jobs probably weren't very exciting. In an era renowned for jazz, bootleg liquor, fast women, and flashy gangsters, Peter first worked as a claims adjuster for an insurance company, then got a clerking position at the post office, and finally another clerking job at the American Railway Express Company.

In late November 1926 Peter was patronizing a speakeasy when he met Walter Tipping. At thirty-three years of age Walter was probably everything Peter wanted to be. Known as "Whitey," Tipping was a professional criminal with a police record stretching back some fourteen years. By the time he was in his mid-twenties he had already spent time at Elmira and had two terms at Sing Sing under his belt. Police knew him as a mild-mannered burglar and didn't consider him particularly dangerous. Tipping and Seiler quickly became good friends and were said to be inseparable. They must of made quite an odd couple, the mild-mannered criminal and the office clerk who craved excitement. Shortly after they got together, Peter quit his job at American Railway Express and joined his new pal in a life of crime.[30]

Over the course of two months Seiler and Tipping took part in three successful robberies. Because of a quick trigger finger, their fourth job would prove to be their last. On January 31, 1927, Tipping, Seiler, a young woman named Grace Peterson, and another couple entered an Upper West Side restaurant. Seiler and Peterson appear to have been an item, even though Peterson was six years his senior and married to man who raised and trained racehorses. At some point during their party, Tipping had the owner of the place write out a note that would allow him and Seiler to enter a nearby speakeasy.

Police Officer James Masterson, off duty and dressed in street clothes, was leaving the speakeasy just as Seiler and Tipping arrived and handed the doorman the note, which simply read "O.K." and was signed by the restaurant owner. The two were allowed inside the joint, where a third bandit, Philip Trainor, was waiting for them. Before Masterson was out of the foyer, he heard someone yell, "Get into the corner and stick 'em up!" In his haste to comply, one of the patrons knocked over a table, sending glasses and bottles crashing to the floor. A woman screamed, and a rough voice replied, "Keep quiet, or we'll kill you all!"

Realizing a robbery was in progress, Masterson drew his pistol and crept back toward the door, but unfortunately for him, one of the gunmen was guarding the entrance and opened fire on him. Wounded in the abdomen, Masterson was dragged to the rear of the speakeasy and forced to stand against the wall with the rest of the victims while the robbery took place. Before leaving with their loot, the bandits helped themselves to Masterson's gun and badge but left behind a very valuable clue—the "O.K." note from the resort up the street.[31]

The case was given to homicide Detectives Thomas Martin and Steven Donohue, the men responsible for bringing in the Diamond brothers for the West End Bank messenger murder (see Chapter 4), as well as John "the Dope" Marino and Frank Daly for the 1925 Mount Vernon trolley car murder (see Chapter 7). Armed with the "O.K." note, the detectives went to the restaurant and questioned the owner. Since the men for whom he'd written the pass had killed a cop and robbed the speakeasy, he was more than happy to name "Whitey" Miller as one of the culprits. He also mentioned that one of the women who had been with them was Mrs. Grace Peterson. The police knew "Whitey" Miller to be one of Tipping's aliases. Grabbing a rogues' gallery, they went to the hospital to visit Officer Masterson, who was able to identify Tipping as one of the bandits before dying. Some of the robbery victims also identified Tipping's mug shot.[32]

The day after the murder Tipping and Seiler left town with Mrs. Peterson and drove approximately 300 miles upstate to the town of Old Forge, where her husband had a cabin in the Adirondack Mountains. Not long after they left, police showed up at the Peterson house and began a stakeout. About a week later detectives got the break they were waiting for. In her haste to leave, Grace hadn't packed properly for an Adirondack winter, and she sent home for a fur coat. The police intercepted the box and got the address of the cabin.[33]

Detectives Martin and Donohue were assigned two more detectives and went to arrest the gunmen. They first stopped in Albany and picked up a couple of state troopers who knew the mountain region and then headed for Old Forge. By speaking with locals, they were able to confirm that the two hoods and Mrs. Peterson were together. At daybreak on February 8, the six lawmen approached the cabin. As they got close a dog started to bark, and they stopped in their tracks until it finished. The damage had been done, though, because Tipping woke up.

When the men stepped onto the porch, a board squeaked, causing them to stop again for a moment, but then they burst through the door. Tipping yelled some obscenities from the bedroom, and agent Martin stuck his hand through the curtain that served as a door and fired a shot. Tipping was ready and shot back, nicking the detective in the wrist. Tipping's room was pitch black, so Martin told his partner, "I'll go out and run around to the window. When you see me there, you fire and I'll fire at the flash of his gun." When he saw Martin by the window, Donohue fired a shot, which the bandit returned. Martin then emptied his weapon in Tipping's direction, but this time there was no return fire.

From Seiler's room came only words: "Don't shoot. We'll give up." The other two detectives burst in and captured the bandit and the Peterson woman without any trouble. Martin and Donohue weren't sure what was up with Tipping. He hadn't fired since Martin emptied his gun, but the room was still too dark to see anything. Not wanting to take a chance, they sent Mrs. Peterson into the room to investigate. A moment later she came back out and said, "He's on the floor, dead." Thinking it might be a trap, both detectives entered the room using Peterson and Seiler as human shields. But she hadn't lied—there on the floor, with a bullet in his right temple, lay Tipping.

Seiler immediately began berating the detectives, saying that if it hadn't been for Mrs. Peterson he would have taken out at least one of them. Apparently, when he had gone for his gun, it fell to the floor, and before he could retrieve it, she had jumped on him. Even though Seiler played the tough guy with the arresting detectives, he refused to accept responsibility for Officer Masterson's murder. The gun he'd been reaching for when Mrs. Peterson tackled him turned out to be the one taken from Masterson during the speakeasy robbery. When asked how it had ended up in his possession, Seiler claimed one of the other bandits had given it to him afterward. When asked who shot Masterson, he put the blame on Tipping.[34]

Seiler was placed on trial that April, and witnesses from the speakeasy testified that he had in fact done some shooting. The speak's owner went even further, stating that Seiler was the one who had shot the policeman and dragged him to the back wall and forced him to stand with the others. When Seiler took the stand, he proclaimed that not only was he innocent of shooting Masterson, but he also had tried to talk Tipping out of robbing the place. He said the robbery hadn't been planned, that he, Tipping, and Trainor had gone there to sell some vermouth, which Trainor was supposed to have. But when Trainor told them he didn't have any, Tipping had said, "Let's stick up this place; there's a good crowd here and we can get a good bunch of money." Seiler said he'd objected but claimed Tipping had threatened to kill him and had thrust a pistol into his hand, forcing him to take part.[35]

The jury didn't see it that way and found Seiler guilty of murder. On December 16, 1927, a little more that a year after leaving his clerking job, he was strapped into the electric chair and reunited with his pal.

Remember Me to Herald Square

On June 17, 1928, Edwin Jerge and a young lady friend were driving up Broadway in a Hudson automobile he had borrowed from a cabaret actress he knew. About forty-five years old, probably no one was more surprised than Jerge that he was still alive.

Originally from Buffalo, the hoodlum had come to the Big Apple by 1914 and was situated on the Lower East Side, where he became associated with members of "Dopey" Benny Fein's gang. He was arrested for pickpocketing on March 13 of that year but moved up to armed robbery within a couple of years.

In 1916 Jerge and Lower East Side gangsters "Little Abie" Beckerman, "Pinky" Fine, and Charles Kraemer journeyed to Chicago and robbed the Washington Park National Bank. The four were arrested, and Jerge turned state's evidence against his cohorts, who were found guilty and shipped off to Joliet state prison. Since that time, Jerge had confided to friends that he knew he would someday get his for being a squealer.[36]

Over the next dozen years Jerge added to his rap sheet. In 1923 he was arrested in Cleveland under the name of Atwater for forgery, and he later spent four years in the federal penitentiary at Atlanta for stealing money orders from a post office in Newark, New Jersey. If vengeance for squealing wasn't enough for him to worry about, by 1928 Jerge was pushing the envelope by preying on members of the underworld. With his partner Charles Crawford and a fake badge, he would pose as a federal agent and shake down speakeasies and bootleggers. On or about June 12, 1928, the duo accosted a Lower East Side drug peddler named Samuel Weissman, better known as "Kitty the Horse," and "arrested" him, taking the bit so far as to handcuff the pusher and walk toward police headquarters. However, before going very far they stopped and accepted a bribe of either $136 or as much as $1,500, depending on the source. A short time later Weissman, and more importantly the drug dealers he worked for, realized that they had been duped by frauds.[37]

And so, on that Sunday afternoon as Jerge and his gal were heading up Broadway, there were any number of gangsters who wanted him dead. However, seeing that he was on a busy thoroughfare in the middle of the afternoon, the hoodlum probably let his guard down and didn't notice that he was being followed by four men in a sedan.

A little after 3 p.m. Jerge came to a red light at Manhattan's high-traffic Herald Square. Seizing the opportunity, the sedan pulled up next to the Hudson, and one of the four men inside stepped onto the running board of Jerge's car and fired three shots through the window into his neck. As the bullets plowed into Jerge, splinters of glass cut his girlfriend's face as she dove for the floorboard. After the third shot, the gunman opened Jerge's door and fired three more rounds, striking him once in the abdomen and twice in the back when he fell over. The killer then stepped back into the sedan and sped to safety.[38]

Had Jerge been found dead in a ditch somewhere, chances are that little would have been said about his murder, but since it was one of the most brazen killings in New York City during that era, the pressure was on the police to solve it. When the narcotics squad was unable to crack the case, there was a shake-up and many detectives lost their jobs. Although boasts were made to the press that a solution was near, their replacements did no better, for while suspicion for the murder drifted back and forth between friends of Beckerman and Fine* and gunmen employed by the drug syndicate that Jerge had ripped off, his murder was never officially solved.

---

* Beckerman and Fine were killed in 1923 when a train struck the truck in which they were hauling bootleg liquor.

14

New York's Most Desperate Criminal

"The worry about being caught and sleeping with a gun under the pillow ain't the easiest thing in the world."

— JAMES NANNERY

n 1926 twenty-two-year-old James Nannery, the man who would one day be known as "New York's Most Desperate Criminal," was running his own speakeasy at East Ninety-second Street near First Avenue. Had he stuck with peddling booze, he might have escaped history's notice, but when he joined up with the McKenna brothers for a series of jobs that spring and summer (see Chapter 9), his destiny was set.

Later that year, with the majority of the McKenna Gang either dead or behind bars, Nannery, described by police as "short, good looking, faultlessly dressed, a typical cake-eater type," hooked up with another gang of bandits. On January 14, 1927, he and his newfound confederates were involved in a botched robbery of the Bronx National Bank in Westchester. The ill-fated heist began at 8 a.m. when ringleader John Bolling and his partner Jack Gormley took up positions outside the bank. The gang was there to steal a payroll that was supposed to be delivered shortly after eight o'clock. Another gang member was standing across the street, while Nannery, armed with a couple of shotguns, stayed in the car with the getaway driver.

For some reason the payroll was delayed, and instead of calling it a day and waiting for the next opportunity, the bandits remained at their posts. At 10 a.m. a mounted police officer who had passed the bank a few hours earlier noticed that Bolling and Gormley were still hanging around outside. He he went back to headquarters to report the suspicious activity, and a group of detectives was dispatched to investigate. When they arrived, Detective Lenihan approached Bolling and said, "We're detectives. Where do you fellas live?" Bolling replied, "We're here on business from Astoria."

Not satisfied, Lenihan asked, "Where do you live, and what is your business?" On the pretense of getting his I.D., Bolling took off his gloves, unbuttoned his coat, reached inside, and quickly pulled out a .38, which he jabbed into Lenihan's stomach before pulling the trigger. The heavens must have been smiling on Lenihan that day, because the pistol misfired, and before Bolling could get off another shot, the fast-thinking detective grabbed the gun and wedged his finger behind the trigger so it couldn't be fired. With his free hand he began to beat Bolling. Gormley went for his gun but was pummeled by the other detectives.

Seeing that the jig was up, the gunman across the street ran to the getaway car and the trio of bandits sped off. Commandeering an auto at the scene, some of the detectives gave chase. Misfortune followed the three hoodlums, as their car stalled at the height of the high-speed getaway. Two of them were able to escape on foot, but the detectives surrounded the car before Nannery had a chance to get out.

Once in custody, Nannery admitted his participation in a couple of other jobs he'd helped pull, saying, "I might as well come across. I'm gonna burn anyway." He told his interrogators he had been involved with the McKennas in robbing Reuben's Restaurant as well as the Reid Ice Cream Company.[1] Convicted of armed robbery, Nannery was sentenced to Sing Sing for a stretch of up to twenty-five years.

When Nannery entered Sing Sing he and a pal named Eddie "Snakes" Ryan were given trusty jobs preparing breakfast for the other prisoners, which meant they were allowed to leave their cells each morning before the general population. There were two head counts each day, the first at 6:30 a.m. when the inmates were released from their cells for breakfast, and the second at 10:30 p.m. when the prisoners were locked into their cells for the night. Nannery and Ryan learned that the armed guards who manned the prison walls were only on duty between the two head counts. On July 16, 1928, Nannery and Ryan were let out of their cells at 5:50 a.m. to report to the kitchen, but when the roll call began an hour later, Sing Sing was short two prisoners.[2]

What at first appeared to be an inexplicable Houdiniesque escape that confounded prison officials turned out to be quite unspectacular. It seems the principal keeper on duty had left his office, which was on the courtyard, unlocked. Seeing their chance, Nannery and Ryan made their way to the courtyard and went over the walls, which they knew were unguarded, and jumped into the Hudson River, swam downstream a couple of miles, and then hopped a freight train into New York City.[3]

The breakout began the Nannery myth, and within a month the escaped felon was being blamed for a string of robberies and murders. On August 23 a company payroll heist occurred that resulted in a blazing shootout between cops and robbers and a high-speed car chase that ended in a crash, with the bandits escaping on foot. The police determined the robbery had all the makings of a "Nannery job," although they did not specify what those were.

Three weeks later the worst of all the crimes laid at Nannery's feet took place. At 3 a.m. on September 13 three men whom police identified as Nannery, Ryan, and a hood named Enrico Battaglia entered Fordham Hospital in the Bronx. Either Ryan or Battaglia had smeared iodine on his hand, and the two men approached an orderly and asked him to get a nurse to dress the hand. When he saw there was no wound, the orderly told the hoods to leave. Ryan and Battaglia retreated to a stairwell to talk things over, then reappeared and demanded that the orderly go for a nurse. The orderly complied and left to go find some help.

Once he was gone, Nannery came inside with a sawed-off shotgun strapped to his arm and concealed by the sleeve of his coat. The three men then made their way to the prison ward of the hospital, where the only patient was a former colleague of Nannery and Ryan's named James Wood. As the hoods approached the guard on duty, Officer Jeremiah Brosnan, Nannery stuck his hand inside his coat and blasted the officer at close range, killing him instantly.[*]

Police initially suspected Brosnan was killed because the gunmen had entered the hospital to free Wood and the guard got in the way. However, they later theorized that the bandits were actually there to kill Wood for double-crossing them. Apparently, Wood was supposed to have been on hand when Nannery and Ryan broke out of Sing Sing, but since he wasn't there the convicts were forced to escape via the river.[4]

Whatever the reason for Brosnan's killing, the heat was on the threesome, and the first to feel it was "Snakes" Ryan. Acting on a tip, detectives began to stake out an apartment near the George Washington Bridge, and on October 8 Ryan was seen leaving the building. As the officers closed in, Ryan immediately bolted toward a stairway leading down to the Harlem River. Hoping to cut him

---

[*] This was a police theory. The murderer of Officer Brosnan was never definitely identified.

off, the detectives jumped in their autos and drove around the building, where they found the gangster stuck knee-deep in mud trying desperately to make another escape by water.[5]

Authorities were unable to prove his part in the Brosnan killing, and Ryan was sent back to Sing Sing to finish out his sentence. Nothing was heard of "Snakes" until November 1930, when he tried once again to escape, this time with guns Nannery supposedly arranged to have smuggled inside. A poorly planned affair, the breakout resulted in a brief shootout in which a guard was wounded and Ryan's accomplice committed suicide.[6]

Five months after Ryan's botched escape, Nannery, who was wanted for some high-profile robberies in New Jersey, was profiled by the *New York Daily News* in its weekly column "What Ever Happened to Justice?" which posed the question: "Why is he still loose nearly three years after busting out of prison?" Nannery correctly assumed the article would generate heat.

Not long afterward two men approached Nannery, who at this time was living with his girlfriend, Patricia, in a well-to-do neighborhood in Parsippany, New Jersey, and confronted him with the article. They were hoping for a payoff, but instead the couple packed up their things and moved. A few days later police raided the empty house, finding only newspaper clippings about the gunman that he had left behind.[7]

Now that they were getting close, the authorities released wanted circulars of the bandit in New Jersey, New York and Pennsylvania. They also managed to get the license plate number of the car he was driving, which was given to every police officer along with the warning that the vehicle's occupant was armed and dangerous.[8]

Two weeks after the *Daily News* column appeared, Nannery drove Patricia into the small town of Dover, New Jersey, on the rainy morning of April 26 so she could go to a pharmacy. The desperado dropped off his girlfriend and pulled into a bus lane to wait for her. Noticing the traffic violation, a local policeman began to approach the car, but when his eyes caught the license plate number and he realized who the driver was, he froze for a moment. Although he knew that Nannery was armed and dangerous, he also knew that if he went back to the police station for backup, he stood a good chance of losing the car.

Deciding to try to take down the bandit himself, the officer drew his pistol and, keeping it hidden under his poncho, approached Nannery and nonchalantly said, "Hey, don't you know you're in a bus lane?" Nannery figured the cop was oblivious to his identity and played along. When the officer asked to see some I.D., Nannery, who had a fake driver's license, thought he'd bluff his way through the situation. But when he reached for his wallet, the cop whipped out his pistol and snapped, "Never mind that. Get out!"[9]

While the rain continued to fall, New York's most desperate criminal was marched through downtown Dover to the police station as an ever-increasing crowd joined the procession. Patricia exited the pharmacy in time to see her boyfriend being led away, and she jumped into the car and sped off. She stopped in the next town to make a quick phone call. All she said was, "Picked up." Then she hit the road again, at some point pulling over to change the car's license plates. It didn't matter, as she was captured just twenty miles from Dover.[10]

Back at the police station, the officers began to process Nannery, who attempted to keep up his gangster bravado by joking at every opportunity. "Can I help?" he asked while being frisked. "Just keep your hands up," he was told. "You'll find a tear gas gun in my vest." They did, and they also found a .45 in each of his coat pockets. This was only part of Nannery's arsenal, however, because a search of the car later turned up a gas mask, a .38, a Thompson submachine gun, and plenty of ammunition for each weapon. Also found on his person was $450 in cash—"getaway money," he called it.[11]

The hood kept up his jocularity throughout the questioning. Name? "James Nannery." Race? "I'm French." (The Irish thug from Hell's Kitchen thought this was particularly funny.) Where do you live? "Oh, just make it anywhere you want. I travel a lot in my business."[12]

Nannery went on to say that he was shocked by his capture. "I never expected to be caught like that. I was ready to shoot it out, and I didn't intend to let anyone take me alive." He confessed that he couldn't believe he'd been duped by a small-town cop. "What gets me is the way the hick flatfoot kidded me with that poker face of his," he told investigators. "I thought he just wanted me for a traffic violation. I was always set to kill myself if I got into a jam with the cops, but this bird was too much for me." He ended cryptically with, "If anything like this happened in New York, the shooting would have started just as soon as the cop started to come toward the car."[13]

Nannery was quickly transferred to the jail at Morristown for safe keeping. To ensure he made it there without incident, five state troopers armed with shotguns joined five local cops in a motorcade of three cars. Upon his arrival, guards armed with shotguns patrolled outside and inside the jail to thwart any breakout attempts.

Since authorities in both New Jersey and New York wanted to prosecute the gangster, he sat in a Jersey cell while the two states fought it out, and at one point even made a "Crime Doesn't Pay" newsreel. In the end it was determined that neither state had concrete evidence Nannery had committed any of the crimes of which he was suspected, so the felon was sent back to Sing Sing to finish out his original sentence plus time added for his escape. He was placed in the death house for safekeeping, and a few months later he and "Snakes" Ryan were sent to Auburn Prison, where escape would be less likely.

Was James Nannery New York's most desperate criminal? Judging by his official record, no. He only had the robberies he admitted to in 1927 and the prison break to his credit, but he also was a traveling arsenal, with at least six guns, a gas mask, and an oxygen tank in case of siege. He told authorities he was a "mental hijacker," meaning that bootleggers fearing his reputation paid him money to leave them alone. One person ventured that Nannery was a hired gun for gangster "Dutch" Schultz, which is possible because there is a link. Nannery admitted to police that he was associated with Enrico Battaglia (suspected with Nannery in the murder of Officer Brosnan at Fordham Hospital), who was chummy with onetime Schultz torpedo "Fats" McCarthy, who eventually turned against the Dutchman by joining the Vincent Coll gang.

There is also evidence suggesting that Nannery may have been associated with "Mad Dog" himself, and with "Legs" Diamond. The fact that Patricia stopped to make the "Picked up" call after Nannery's arrest indicates that they were involved with others. Patricia also went on to tell authorities that the couple had spent a lot of time on the road and stayed a number of times in Acra, New York, "Legs" Diamond's bailiwick, which is not far from where the Coll mob had a couple of hideouts.

One question that has never been answered is whether Nannery actually killed Officer Brosnan. Although there was never any evidence to prove it, it should be mentioned that after his capture, Nannery was reported as having a "shriveled left arm from some old wound sustained after his jailbreak." Could that wound have been caused by strapping a sawed-off shotgun to it and firing?

If judged by his official police record, Nannery may not seem to be deserving of the title "New York's Most Desperate Criminal." But considering the company he kept and the arsenal with which he traveled, if James Nannery wasn't the city's most desperate criminal, he certainly ranked near the top of the list.

Sexy Takes a Ride

*"She was evidently a woman of many acquaintances.
From the information we have at present it certainly does not
seem that she made her money at any lawful trade."*

— Bronx Borough Inspector Henry Bruckman

At approximately 11 p.m. on February 25, 1931, Vivian Gordon strutted through the lobby of her apartment building sporting an expensive mink coat. Underneath she was all dolled up in a black velvet dress trimmed in cream lace. On a finger sat a $2,500 diamond ring and adorning her wrist was a platinum and diamond watch worth $650. With her red hair, the five-foot-four, 125-pound woman was still turning heads at age forty. She was just the type of gal an out-of-town businessman or public official wouldn't mind passing the evening with. If they were married they were a shoo-in, because Ms. Gordon specialized in spending quality time with married men of means and then blackmailing them after they returned home. She also wasn't above supplying some girls for a special event if needed.[1]

Tonight, though, she was on a special mission. Harry Stein, an underworld figure she had known for a handful of years (she had even lent him $1,500 so he could go to Oslo, Norway, for some nefarious reason), got in touch with her and said he had a pigeon on the line who had $250,000 worth of diamonds on him and that he had set it up so they could meet. Vivian knew just how to handle a chump with that kind of loot. She met Harry and the two jumped into a cab to the Bronx for a rendezvous with the mark.

When they arrived, Vivian followed Harry to a seven-passenger Cadillac sedan parked off Grand Avenue. In the back seat sat the sucker with the diamonds. Opening the door, Stein introduced Vivian to the wealthy man. "Where have you been all my life?" the red-haired vixen asked as she slid in next to him. Stein climbed in after her, closing the door. "Drive to Max's place," the man ordered his chauffeur.

But as the car pulled away from the curb Harry punched Vivian in the head and face twice, knocking her to the floorboard. Using his feet, the "pigeon" held her down while Stein pulled out a six-foot length of clothesline from under the seat and forced it around Viv's neck. The chauffeur heard gasping followed by a "cackle." Next he heard Stein say, "She's done now; she's finished."[2]

The chauffeur was ordered to drive into Van Cortland Park, where he pulled over about three to four yards from Mosholu Parkway. With Stein grabbing her feet and his cohort taking her under her arms, they dragged Vivian from the car and dumped her in a ravine. Not ones to let an opportunity to make some easy dough slip by, the killers helped themselves to Gordon's mink coat, expensive watch, and diamond ring before returning to the car.

As the Cadillac pulled away, the murderers discovered one of Vivian's shoes and tossed it out the window. Stein said he wanted to go to her apartment to get his hands on a couple of diaries Vivian was known to keep, but his partner said, "You're nuts," and the journals were never picked up.[3]

Vivian Gordon's predictions had come true. For nearly two years she had written in her diary that she was going to be murdered, and now the onetime streetwalker who had become a high-class, high-rolling extortion queen who prided herself on her fine appearance, was lying dead in a ditch with a clothesline knotted around her neck and her pink silk panties bared to the world.

Vivian's life was a sad one. Her real name was Benita Franklin and she was born in Michigan City, Indiana, in 1891 to parents who were described as well to do. She was a troubled young woman, and her family sent her to a Catholic convent in Ontario, Canada, where she attempted suicide numerous times. After leaving the convent she traveled the East Coast as a chorus girl in a Vaudeville show.[4]

While on tour in 1912 she married a man named John Bischoff and three years later gave birth to a daughter whom the couple also named Benita. The troubled woman, however, wasn't cut out for married life. She left her husband in 1920, when they were living in Philadelphia, and moved to New York City, where she lived with a number of different men. John Bischoff filed for divorce and tried to get custody of little Benita. He finally was successful when his wife was arrested for prostitution on March 9, 1923, and sent to the prison at Bedford, New York, where she would remain until November 1, 1926.[5]

Upon her release, she embarked on a lucrative career in the sex/extortion racket. A few arrests followed, including one in 1927, when she was brought into the station house with several men after a fight had broken out at the Hotel Claridge. Nothing came of it. On March 1, 1930, she and a john checked into the Palace Hotel as Mr. and Mrs. Lemer from New Orleans. Something went wrong, though, because later that night the police were called after she climbed out on the fire escape screaming for help. She and the john were taken into custody, but even though "Mrs. Lemer" had a bruise on her head, she filed no charges.

Three months later, on July 2, a taxi pulled up to a police station and the driver complained that Vivian, as she was now known, had refused to pay him. Left with few choices, she paid the fair but threw in some choice words for the cabbie as she did so. It was obvious to the cops that she had been drinking, so they booked her for intoxication and misconduct, but the charges subsequently were dropped. She was picked up the following month for extortion.

A reporter had borrowed $2,000 from her and paid back all but $200. Vivian said if she didn't receive the rest of the money she would have him arrested for violating the Mann Act, a federal law prohibiting the transport of a woman across state lines for "immoral purposes." The reporter contacted the police and a rendezvous was set up in the lobby of the Hotel McAlpin. When Vivian arrived and took the reporter's money, she was arrested. However, the charge was dismissed the following October 7.[6]

As the Roaring Twenties came to a close Vivian was doing quite well. She was living in a $150-a-month apartment—not bad when the average worker was pulling down $750 a year. In 1929 she formed the Vivigo Corporation and purchased a block of property in Jamaica, Queens, and had thousands more tied up with her lawyer, John A. Radeloff.

About an hour after he dumped Vivian's body into the ravine, Harry Stein placed a call to underworld fence David Butterman but got his wife instead. "This is Harry," Stein told her, "Please wake Dave, I want to talk to him." Butterman was awakened and Stein told him, "I'd like to meet you in the morning; I have something for you."[7]

The two met for breakfast at a place on Broadway and Ninety-sixth Street, and then the killer took Butterman to an apartment on Riverside Drive. A woman greeted them at the door and led them to the kitchen, where Stein showed Butterman Vivian's mink coat, diamond ring, and platinum watch. Butterman passed on the watch and then inspected the coat. He immediately tore out the lining so the coat couldn't be identified and then took some ink to cover up markings on the pelt. As he was doing this he accidentally spilled some ink on the sofa cover. He asked Stein how much he wanted for it, and Stein said, "The boys are asking $400."

Unaware that the previous owner was lying dead in the Bronx, Butterman took the coat and watch to his brother-in-law, William Rosenfeld, who dealt in jewelry. A little while later Stein called to see if he wanted to buy either item. Rosenfeld declined, although he did ask to see the ring. Stein brought the ring over and asked a thousand dollars for it, but Rosenfeld said no and the two men departed. Stein went his way, and Butterman took the coat to a dressmaker he knew named Max Mishkin to have it appraised. Deciding that he didn't want it, he took the coat to a temporary storage site and checked it, and three days later gave the claim check to Stein.[8]

A couple of hours before Stein and Butterman met for breakfast, Vivian's body was discovered by a man on his way to work, and soon the area was crawling with police. Chances are Vivian's murder wouldn't have received much press, but it had two things going for it that made it irresistible to New York journalists. One, it involved a sexy woman, and two (and more important), it was quickly speculated that she was murdered because she had testified against police during the well-publicized investigation by the Seabury Commission into municipal corruption that was going on at the time. The main victims of the corruption were women arrested for prostitution under false pretenses and then forced to pay a lawyer's fee (bribe) in order to escape jail.

Vivian maintained that her arrest on March 9, 1923, for prostitution had been a "frame-up" by the arresting detective, Andrew McLaughlin, and her husband, who wanted to get custody of their daughter. She told her lawyer, John Radeloff, that she was going to contact the crime commission and tell them all about it. Radeloff advised her not to, as the case was eight years old and she could gain nothing by it, but the vindictive Ms. Gordon replied that she was "going to give McLaughlin the needle just to get even."

On January 19, 1931, Vivian sent the following letter to Detective McLaughlin:

> Mr. McLaughlin,
>
> You know doubt recall how you framed Benita Bischoff on March 9, 1923, causing her to be convicted for vagrancy. She is now writing you to tell you that she is going to appear before the vice commission to tell the whole story.
>
> She leaves the rest to your imagination which, she hopes, is as good as it was when you concocted those lies about her in court.
>
>   B.F. B.[9]

McLaughlin received the letter and put it in his coat. He would later testify that he didn't remember the case. Vivian then composed a letter to her former spouse, who had remarried and was living a respectable life in Audubon, New Jersey:

> You know that my conviction was caused by a frame-up between you and Detective McLaughlin. You may think that you have the last laugh, but get this—I am going before the investigation committee this week and intend to tell the whole story of the dirty frame-up. When I am through it will be just too bad for you. Little Benita is old enough now to realize that a dirty trick has been played on me. I intend to go the limit and you know as well as I do that this will mean your finish.[10]

In addition to revenge it appears that Vivian also may have been hoping for some sort of payoff that never came, because it was a full three weeks before she put pen to paper again. Against her lawyer's advice she wrote the following to one of the Seabury investigators on February 7, 1931:

> Dear Mr. Kresel:
> I have some information in connection with a "frame-up" by a police officer and others, which I believe will be of great aid to your committee in its work. I would appreciate an interview at your earliest convenience.
> Very truly yours,
>   VIVIAN GORDON

She received the following reply:

> My Dear Miss Gordon,
> Your letter addressed to Mr. Kresel under the date of Feb. 7 has been turned over to me for attention. I should be glad to see you at the above address on Friday Feb. 20 1931 between the hours of 10 A.M. and 5 P.M.
> Very truly yours,
>   Irving Ben Cooper[11]

Vivian showed up at Cooper's office and, according to Cooper, said she had been convicted as the result of a plot concocted by her husband, who wanted to obtain complete custody of little Benita, and the arresting officers. She said she had been living at a hotel in Manhattan and had given her mail to a man and was planning to stop by his place later that day to pick it up. On her way there, she said, a detective posing as the man's roommate had stopped her and said he was supposed to take her to the friend's apartment to wait for him. Shortly after arriving she had been arrested for prostitution.

Cooper told Vivian she would need to get corroboration for her story, and she told him she would do her best. Less than a week later she was dead. If that weren't damaging enough, the detective in question, Andrew McLaughlin, was conveniently away on a Bermuda cruise when the murder took place and wasn't available for questioning.

After Vivian's body had been identified, the police searched her apartment and read the diaries that her killer, Harry Stein, had wanted to retrieve after the murder. After perusing Vivian's private thoughts, the police quickly arrested her lawyer, John A. Radeloff, and his underworld man Friday, Sam "Chowder Head" Cohen, and held them both on $50,000 bail. "Chowder Head" had a lengthy record, with eleven arrests and three convictions dating back to 1915. More recently, he had been arrested on May 20, 1930, on charges of impersonating a federal officer and attempted extortion.

What led police to suspect the lawyer and "Chowder Head" in Vivian's death were certain entries in her diaries, such as the first entry in the first diary, dated January 1929, which read:

Did not start this diary for reasons other than to remind me of dates—but think—advisedly so—that it's best to put down things as they happen concerning John A. Radeloff—he is not to be trusted—he would stoop to anything.

As well as:

The only man I have to fear is Radeloff. He could get Cohen or henchmen to do away with me.

Vivian recorded her thoughts over the course of the next two years, and the passages pertaining to her lawyer grew more and more incriminating:

Feb. 12, 1929, J.A.R. here—finale—between us. Refused to pay Dr.'s bills . . . If anything happens to me—he is to blame—he has henchmen—don't know when I go to hospital—reckon as soon as he, J.A.R., gives me money for Dr., &c.

Not to mention:

The threat has been made—Sam Cohen—who is client of J.A.R. in a case has brought to J.A.R.'s office—so JAR told me—and he refused to let them do the trick—?? How did they know?? J. and I had a scrap unless he told S. C. and why make a confidant of a common loft thief?

The above information was conveyed to me in my apt. after a reconciliation on Feb. 23—but still I list this information—in case his man (is according to his after statement supposed to have said "We'll take her out somewhere—no one will know what happened to her. Every mark of identification will be missing, especially that ring"—meaning that $2,500 ring I wear.

The following entry seems to indicate that Gordon and Radeloff's relationship went beyond that of client and lawyer.

JAR again hinted—about my getting killed—said "I'd better get my collars and shirts out of here—if you should be killed they'd look for me." There is $18,000 in mortgages of mine in his office.

Why would a lawyer have spare clothes in his client's apartment? Apparently Vivian wasn't happy with being the other woman either:

John A. Radeloff's office—$500—not show up—waited 7½ hours.—phoned his home—went over there—had it out with him—met him as he and wife were going out for walk—read the riot act to him—she didn't say a word—dumb! dumb! dumb!!

This last act may have been the straw that broke the camel's back:

Radeloff said that S. C. had been in to see him within past week. Sam Cohen is one who was to have knocked me off last Winter—I guess JAR is seeking his services now for that deed. JAR would stoop to anything—JA Radeloff is the only one who is really an enemy of mine—because of certain things I have told his wife in retaliation for all the rotten things he has done to me—he was just using me for a good thing. Treating me half civil—a necessary evil—as it were—because he knew that he could borrow money from me—besides—I have a mortgage of $11,330 [$11,000] due to close on Oct. 30. It wouldn't surprise me a bit if he tried to grab that money, no one close to me to put up a squawk if anything occurred. Anything I have done to him—he deserves 100 per cent more.[12]

On March 1, three days after the murder, Andrew McLaughlin returned from his cruise and both he and John Bischoff were questioned by the D.A. and brought before a grand jury. Both men denied any involvement in the murder, and the D.A. gave up the premise that Vivian was murdered to protect crooked cops. The police, glad to be out of the crosshairs, continued to concentrate on Radeloff and Cohen. It turned out that Joseph Radlow, the reporter Vivian had threatened with blackmail to obtain the final $200 of a loan he owed her, was Radeloff's first cousin. After that arrest, Vivian told the assistant D.A., Radlow had swindled her out of $50,000. In addition, another pal of Radeloff's owed Vivian $10,000, and the loan was coming due in less than a month, on April 8.[13]

Although the police felt that Radeloff was responsible for Vivian's death, they lacked the proof to bring him into court, so continued to study her diary. Investigators read an entry from July 1929 that stated she had loaned $1,500 to a Charles Reuben. The word *Oslo* was written next to Reuben's name. There was an entry a few months later naming those who had borrowed money and paid her back, and there was an entry for Harry Saunders for $1,500 with a question mark. Since there was no record of Reuben paying Vivian back, and there were no other loans for that amount, the police deduced that Reuben and Saunders were the same man. They also figured that *Oslo* meant the city in Norway, so they checked the passenger list of a ship that had sailed for there on July 20, 1929. On the passenger list was Charles Reuben, who had sailed with two others, one of whom went by the name of Sam Cohen, although it was determined that the man wasn't "Chowder Head."

Detectives obtained a sample of Reuben's handwriting from the government passport office and took it to headquarters where they compared it with writing samples of hoodlums on file. They eventually came up with a match: Harry Stein. A check of Stein's record showed that he had been arrested in the past for an attempted strangling, and the police immediately put a tail on him.[14]

Stein seldom left his apartment before noon, and when he did leave, he typically went to the Times Square area. One of the places he hung out was a Romanian "tea house" on Sixth Avenue that catered to shady characters. On one visit there Stein was seen talking with another denizen of the underworld named Sam Greenberg (who police later would learn was the man who had sailed to Norway with Stein under the name Sam Cohen). The police then assigned some men to follow Greenberg.

A couple of days later Stein stepped into a phone booth, and the detective tailing him approached and heard him ask for "Harry." Harry wasn't available, but the cops had the call traced to an apartment that was being rented to a Harry Harvey. The police staked out the apartment. Even though they didn't recognize Harvey, the cops figured he was somehow involved in crime since, like Stein and Greenberg, he had no visual means of support.

At about this time police Commissioner Edward Mulrooney received a tip from a source that would never be divulged. The tipster told Mulrooney Stein had showed Vivian's coat and jewelry to David Butterman and William Rosenfeld, and that Butterman had shown the coat to Max Mishkin. The latter three were picked up. With this new information, additional men were sent to follow Stein and Greenberg, and police also tapped "Harry Harvey's" phone. Mr. and Mrs. Butterman quickly spilled what they knew about Stein and Gordon's belongings, and detectives went to the apartment on Riverside Drive where Butterman had inspected the coat and took the ink-stained sofa cover into evidence. They questioned Madeline Tully, who ran the rooming house, but her answers were evasive.

On April 8, 1931, the detective who was listening in on Harry Harvey's phone, intercepted a call between Harvey and Harry Stein. "I've got some money," Stein told him. "It isn't much, but it's something. Where can I see you?" They agreed to meet in Harvey's lobby in fifteen minutes. The detective raced over and witnessed Stein hand something to Harvey but made no move to arrest them. Fearing that word of their questioning the Buttermans, Rosenfeld, Mishkin, and Tully would make its way back to the suspects, police decided to pick up Stein, Greenberg, and Harvey the next day, which they did. Greenberg and Harvey said they knew nothing of the murder, and since the cops had anything to hold them on, they were released.

Both men were shadowed for weeks afterward, during which time police learned that Harvey's real name was Harry Schlitten and that a Harry Schlitten had rented a seven-passenger Cadillac sedan on the night of Vivian Gordon's murder. Schlitten and Greenberg were once again picked up and questioned, and after a time Schlitten broke.

He told the cops he had met Stein six months before the murder, while he was working as a card dealer at the Romanian "tea house" on Sixth Avenue, and that Stein later introduced him to Greenberg. On the day of the murder, Schlitten said, Stein had gone to the restaurant and asked him to rent a car, but when he asked why, Stein had told him, "If I don't get a certain party out of the way, a friend of mine is going to wind up going to jail."[15] Schlitten and a pal obtained the car on the Lower East Side and had picked up Stein and Greenberg on the corner of Norfolk and Rivington. After dropping Schlitten's pal in Midtown, Schlitten said Stein had directed him to continue driving uptown, saying, "You get a thousand or two thousand out of this tonight."[16]

When the car reached 100th Street and Park Avenue, Schlitten said, Stein had gotten out and returned about ten minutes later with a package. Inside was a new clothesline, which Stein had placed under the seat. Schlitten told the cops he was then directed to, "Drive up to the Bronx, and we'll look for a spot." When they were in front of 1601 Grand Avenue, Stein had said, "This looks like an ideal spot." Schlitten said he had then driven Stein back downtown and returned to the Bronx with Greenberg and waited. He said when he asked Greenberg what it was all about, Greenberg had replied, "I know as much about it as you do." He then filled Schlitten in on the scenario that was going to be played out, saying, "When the party comes up with Stein, you are only the chauffeur. If I say, 'Drive to Max's place,' you drive down to the bottom of the hill. The gag of this is, I'm a sucker with a quarter of a million in diamonds; this party is coming up, supposed to take me for them. That's the plot. Get it?"[17]

At about five minutes to midnight, Schlitten said, he had seen Stein approaching with Vivian and exclaimed, "He's got a woman with him," since he had assumed the victim would be a man. "Yes, that is the party that is supposed to go," Greenberg responded. Schlitten said Vivian and Stein had gotten into the car, and after introductions were made Greenberg had ordered him to "drive to Max's place."[18]

The district attorney felt confident in bringing Stein and Greenberg to trial and delegated the prosecution to the chief assistant D.A. Harry Schlitten, having turned state's evidence, was granted immunity and was the prosecution's number-one witness. Not only could he testify that the defendants had killed Vivian, he could also provide a motive. According to Schlitten, the day after the murder Stein dropped in to give him some money. "I was looking at the *Journal*," he stated, "and I said, 'There's your friend "Chowder Head." Then I opened to the picture of Radeloff and said, 'Who's this party here?' Stein said, 'There's the party we done it for, Radeloff. I owe him $1,500. He defended me in a case.'"[19]

On June 22 Schlitten took the stand and told his story. He was followed by Izzy Lewis, who had gone with him to rent the Cadillac, who corroborated Schlitten's testimony regarding the auto. Max Mishkin testified that Butterman had brought Vivian's fur coat to him, and Butterman in turn testified that he had gotten Vivian's articles from Stein. Mrs. Butterman took the stand and described the phone call Stein had made to their apartment after the murder.

Stein testified that he had been at a show with his sister, who backed up his testimony, and Greenberg stated he had been sitting shiva for his mother who had died six days before to the murder. Greenberg's sister also testified on his behalf. In the hands of an average lawyer it might have been curtains for Stein and Greenberg, but they had prepared for the battle of their lives by retaining famed gangland lawyer Sam Liebowitz.

In his summation Liebowitz noted that all the witnesses were underworld characters who could not be trusted, which in itself created reasonable doubt about their testimony. It took the jury just three and a half hours to concur. When the words "not guilty" were uttered, observers in the courtroom reacted with total surprise. As the jurors were leaving the box, Greenberg went up and kissed them on the cheek, thanking them. Stein wasn't as celebratory as he was immediately arrested for another crime.

The chief assistant D.A. called the verdict, "the greatest miscarriage of justice that ever took place in the Bronx." His boss echoed the sentiment, saying it was, "the rankest miscarriage of justice I have ever known. Verdicts like that are responsible for gang conditions in America today. Killers are turned loose scot-free—even with the strongest evidence against them."[20] With the killers exonerated, prosecutors didn't bother going after Radeloff. Vivian Gordon's case officially remains unsolved.

KING OF THE PUNKS

"He is meek, never speaks loudly. Nevertheless, he is one of the most dangerous men we have encountered."
— POLICE COMMISSIONER EDWARD MULROONEY

I n the span of three months Francis Crowley went from being an unknown nineteen-year-old punk from the Bronx with a handful of arrests for auto theft to one of New York City's most notorious killers. Criminally speaking, he achieved nothing. He had no gang to do his bidding; he pulled no big jobs resulting in extreme riches. He did kill a police officer, but then again so did his foster brother and many other hoodlums of the day. What guaranteed Francis a spot in the Big Apple's pantheon of celebrated criminals was his dramatic capture.

Crowley's start wasn't much different from that of any other hoodlum. In 1911 a young immigrant girl took a job as a maid in a well-to-do household. One of the sons there allegedly seduced her and she became pregnant. The family then fired her and she was on her own. On October 31 of that year she gave birth to a son. Whether she named him Francis isn't known, but not long after the child's birth she handed him over to Mrs. Annie Crowley, who ran a baby-boarding house, or "baby farm," as it was known.[1][*] Although she already had a son and three daughters, she decided to raise Francis as her own.[**]

Her new son did poorly in school, and Mrs. Crowley attributed this and other mental deficiencies the boy had to two bad falls he had suffered.[2] The fact that he was a diminutive lad (at maturity he would stand just five feet three) in a tough neighborhood couldn't have helped his disposition. Later on in life his attorney would later label him a "moral imbecile"[3] and a psychiatrist would testify that he had the mentality of a ten-year-old.

Francis was a self-confessed cop-hater. Two reasons were given for this. One was that when he was first arrested as a juvenile, the cops beat him at the station. The other was that his foster brother John Crowley was killed by a police officer.[4]

Brother John was no angel, however. Fourteen years Francis's senior, his police record began the year Francis was born, when he was arrested for assault and sent to the city prison. Upon his release he was rearrested for violating his parole and was sent back. In 1918 he was arrested for burglary and sent to the Elmira Reformatory. The following year he was arrested again for burglary, but the charge was dismissed. John's most serious offense occurred in 1922 when he was arrested for killing his friend James Hayes. The friend's sister helped track down John, but he was able to beat the rap.

The trouble that would eventually cost John his life started on January 15, 1925, when Maurice Harlow, a twenty-seven-year-old cop, was walking his beat and came upon John, who was noticeably intoxicated. When Harlow confronted him, John tried to take the officer's nightstick and hit him with it, but Harlow thumped him over the head and took him to the station. The next day Harlow testified against Crowley in court, and the latter was fined $5. According to police, he threatened to "get" Harlow.

A little over a month later, on the evening of February 21, John and his new wife, Alice, attended a friend's birthday party. The party went late into the night and became a bit too raucous. Officer Harlow was walking his beat, and at 1 a.m. he entered the party and asked everyone to quiet down. Later the Crowleys left the party, and witnesses stated that Harlow was walking by the building as the couple exited. An instant later they heard shooting.

---

* This account is supposedly from Crowley's birth mother, whom the *New York Daily News* quoted the day he was executed. The *New York Evening Journal*, however, stated not long after his capture that records showed his father was John Flood, age thirty-eight at the time of Francis's birth and a frequent guest at the home where Crowley's mother, whom they called Dora Dietz, an immigrant from Austria, worked as a maid. She was, according to the records, thirty-six years old when the boy was born and not quite the ingénue the *Daily News* painted. The *Daily News* stated that Flood was a New York City police officer or detective. The *Evening Journal* listed his occupation as investigator but did not explain what kind of investigator.

** Annie would have eight children in all.

When the police arrived, nobody claimed to have seen the actual gunfight; however, Harlow was found on the sidewalk, clutching his pistol, with a bullet wound behind his right ear. A few feet away was another gun and a trail of blood that led across the street and into a doorway where Crowley was slouched with a bullet through his body. Still alive, he and his wife began to yell at the cops who approached them. Police believed that Crowley had come up behind Harlow and shot him in the head, but before collapsing the officer was able to turn and shoot his slayer. Each man then fired another shot that went wild. Harlow fell where he stood, and Crowley staggered across the street before collapsing. The officer was rushed to the hospital but died en route; Crowley expired a short time later.[5]

At the time of his brother's death, Francis and his foster mother were living at 300 East 134th Street, and Francis fell in with a crowd of Bronx toughs. His first arrest for stealing cars came on May 3, 1929, but the grand jury failed to indict him. Two months later, on July 4, he was again arrested for auto theft and the outcome was again the same. This scenario played out twice more over the course of the year, with arrests on October 21 and November 16.[6]

Francis's burgeoning criminal career was almost sidetracked by love when he went to a dance in Roosevelt, Long Island, and met sixteen-year-old Helen Walsh. Helen came from a good family and didn't like Francis's hoodlum pals, so to please her he quit hanging around with them. Frank (as Crowley was known) fell deeply in love with the teenager (who called him "Shorty"), and in 1930 he asked Helen to marry him. She said no. "She threw me down, and I went to the dogs," Crowley would say later. "I started to drink and went back to the gang in the Bronx, which I had tried to keep away from because Helen disapproved of them"[7]

"Shorty's" ascent to the pantheon of New York's criminal elite began early in 1931. On February 21 he and three of his Bronx cronies tried to crash a dance at an American Legion Hall. All four were forcefully removed from the premises, but before they were hustled out the door a couple of them drew guns and started firing, wounding two people. It was after this episode that Francis decided he was going to become a full-fledged gunman. He went to Philadelphia and purchased two handguns, two sets of brass knuckles, and two blackjacks.[8]

A few weeks after the American Legion shooting, three of the gunmen were arrested and released. Detective George Schaedel of the Morrisania station still wanted Crowley, however, and he began to periodically stop in at 369 Lexington Avenue, where Crowley was known to work. The head of the company was P. J.

Doherty, Crowley's brother-in-law, and each time the detective stopped in, Francis wasn't there.

Schaedel was persistent however, and came back early on the afternoon of March 13 and received the usual report. Schaedel said he would be back later, and when he returned at 4 p.m. and walked into the office, there was Francis. Crowley had no time to respond as Schaedel gave him a quick frisk and pulled a .45 from Francis's hip pocket. The detective was pocketing the handgun when Crowley said, "Wait, you have me wrong; I'll show you identification papers." He then reached into his coat.

Assuming correctly that he was reaching for another gun, Schaedel grabbed Francis, but he managed to wriggle free, draw a .32 and fire two shots, hitting the detective in the leg and stomach. Crowley ran out of the office with the wounded detective staggering behind him. Bracing himself against the wall, Schaedel fired as Francis ran into a stairwell and disappeared. The detective was sent to Bellevue, where he eventually recovered. Crowley was now on the NYPD's radar.[9]

Around this time Crowley struck up a friendship with a truck driver from Ossining, New York, named Rudolph Duringer. Crowley and Duringer would have been quite noticeable when walking down the street together. Unlike his diminutive friend, who weighed about 100 pounds, Duringer, four years Crowley's senior, was of average height but weighed nearly 220 pounds, resulting in his being stuck with the unflattering nickname "Fat." Though they differed in appearance, the two men were similar in that neither of them was overly bright.

They met at a Harlem taxi-dance joint both frequented called the Primrose Dance Palace on 125th Street. Crowley had an on-and-off relationship with one of the dancers there named Billie Dunne. Duringer had a thing for another dancer there named Virginia Joyce Brannen. Virginia, who had moved to New York City from Bangor, Maine, went by her middle name and was known to be a "cut-up" who liked to go to parties and for joy rides. It was also said that she wasn't very discriminating about the men she associated with. As a fellow taxi-dancer would later put it, "Going out with a number of men was necessary, as it is important to be popular in the dancehall game."[10] In the "dancehall game" the girls were given twenty dance tickets they had to sell for a dime apiece, which amounted to at least twenty dances per shift. With all the girls competing for the available guys, it paid to have regular customers.

At about 1 a.m. on April 27, 1931, Duringer showed up at the Primrose with a pal named Robert LeClair (sometimes LeClaire) and the latter's date, Mildred Moore. As was his custom, Duringer asked to dance with Brannen. "Fat" was noticeably intoxicated when they arrived, and once he was on the dance floor with Joyce, he was more clumsy than usual, at one point actually dropping a pistol on the floor. This scared Joyce, who fled upstairs to the dancers' waiting area. Mildred went up and talked her into coming back down.

Wanting Joyce all to himself, Duringer bought all her dance tickets, and she joined the trio at a table where they joked until about 3 a.m. and then left. At some point they hooked up with Crowley, because when they left the dance hall he was driving. They hit a few more speakeasies and went out for breakfast. After dining on ham and eggs they got back into the car and headed toward Ossining. Crowley, who hadn't been drinking, was driving, and in the front seat with him were LeClair and Mildred. Feeling the effects of the evening, the latter was leaning on the former, trying to sleep. Both were asleep by the time they hit Yonkers. In the back were Joyce and Duringer, the dancer having started the drive on "Fat's" lap. LeClair would later describe what happened as the car neared St. Joseph's Catholic Seminary:

> "Millie was sleeping with her head on my shoulder, and I was dozing with my head on hers. Then I heard a shot and looked back. Rudy had a gun in his hand, and Joy was slumped sidewise. She called out, 'My God, take me to a hospital,' or something like that, but Jeez, I don't remember just exactly what happened."

Mildred's version was pretty much the same:

> "I put my head back on Robert's shoulder and I heard him say, 'Millie's fainting' and Fat snapped, 'Shut your mouth. She's all right.' Then it was I heard Joy moan, 'Oh, oh, take me to a hospital.'"[11]

LeClair pleaded with Crowley to let them off at the next drugstore they passed. Crowley pulled up to the curb and let them out at the Seminary pharmacy, telling them he would be back in a few minutes. LeClair and Millie went into the drugstore and bought a seltzer. When they came back out, Crowley pulled up with Duringer but Joyce was gone.

There was short stone wall that bordered the Seminary property, and running along the inside of the wall were thick bushes. At about 10 a.m. two men walking along the wall simultaneously saw a hand protruding from the bushes on the other side. Joyce's body was still warm when the police were called. Yonkers Police Chief Edward Quirk arrived and found the taxi-dancer entangled in the shrubbery, her cheeks pierced by some of the branches. It was his opinion, later backed up by the medical examiner, that the girl was still alive when she'd been tossed over the wall. Later, when asked if she thought Joyce had still been alive when dumped, Millie responded, "I'm sure of it."[12]

Reporters arrived, and with the Vivian Gordon murder still a hot topic, the first thing they asked the police chief was, "Think she may have been one of those girls that were sent up illegally by members of the vice squad?" Quirk replied simply, "Can't tell yet."[13]

Crowley and Duringer were pretty careless with the disposal of Joyce's personal items. They left her purse with her, which contained a photo of the dead girl and two friends, as well as a prescription from a Bangor pharmacy. There was also a piece a paper that had been torn into a number of pieces. It was easy enough for the police to put it back together, and once reconstructed it showed the address 449 West 123rd Street.

Chief Quirk sent some men with the photo to question the tenants of the building. Since most people tended to clam up during murder investigations, the cops were instructed to say the girl had been the victim of a hit-and-run accident. At the address police spoke with Adele McDonald, a Bangor resident and longtime friend of Joyce's who also worked at the Primrose, who identified Joyce from the picture and gave the police her address. They stopped at the dead girl's apartment and spoke with her roommate and went through her belongings. Adele was then taken to the morgue, where she positively identified Joyce.

Detectives also were sent to the Primrose, where the proprietors told them the dancers probably wouldn't talk but gave them the name of a former dancer named Babette who might open up. Babette was found and when asked if there were any special guys who paid attention to Joyce, she told them, "There was a big lummox of man who always used to ask for Joyce. [Adele] McDonald knows who he is, but don't tell her I told you or she'll scratch my eyes out."[14]

At three o'clock the next morning, detectives and the Westchester County district attorney paid a visit to the Primrose. In hopes of getting the girls to talk, the D.A. stopped the dancing and gave a short, graphic speech describing how their friend and coworker had been found brutally murdered and was now lying on a marble slab. Instead of the tears and confessions he was hoping for, the D.A. received only blank stares from the women.

Adele McDonald was working that night, and they took her into an office and pumped her for information about the "lummox." She told them he had been in the Primrose the previous night and told them about "Fat's" clumsy actions. When they pressed her for his name, she said, "I know him only as Rudy. He drives a truck for somebody in Westchester County. But he's not the man you're after. He's just a big good-natured slob who, I'm sure, wouldn't hurt a fly."[15]

Armed with the information the cops went to the license bureau and came up with Rudolph Duringer. A detective was sent to the garage where he worked and learned that "Fat" hadn't shown up since the previous Saturday night, the same night that a Chrysler being stored there was stolen, along with some blankets and a siren from an ambulance.

Detectives were sent to Duringer's mother's apartment and to visit other relatives in the area. The detectives staking out his mother's place stopped two men who approached the apartment, but they turned out to be insurance adjusters wanting to talk to Rudy about an accident in which he'd been involved. The cops took them aside and asked them to try to get some information from the mother about her son. When they returned, the insurance men were able to tell the detectives that Rudy's best friend was a man named Robert LeClair.

As this was going on, members of the NYPD gun squad came across a Chrysler containing two men. The men opened fire on the cops, led them on a chase, and managed to escape, but not before the police were able to get the license plate number of their vehicle. The license was for a Ford registered to one Rudolph Duringer.[16]

Meanwhile, the police were making headway with their investigation. Through a source who was kept anonymous, they were able to pick up LeClair at his job. After his arrest, Millie Moore and LeClair's mother came to the station, and both broke down and told their stories. The police now had another reason to get Crowley. Police also learned through LeClair that at various times Francis had lived on Fourteenth, Ninety-sixth, and Eighty-fourth streets with a girl named Billie Dunne. "But if I were you, I'd play Jamaica, Long Island," LeClair said. "He's got a girl there. Her name is Walsh, and he's really in love with her."[17]

With the shooting at the Legion Hall, the wounding of Detective Schaedel, and now the Brannen murder credited to him, Crowley became one of the hottest criminals in the city. Wanted posters were sent to all surrounding police departments, and the hunt was on. Two Bronx detectives, Dominick Caso and William Mara, went searching for Billie Dunne but only found dead ends.

Crowley and Duringer weren't sitting idly by. On Tuesday, May 5, they entered a garage at 2:20 a.m. and stole a Ford sedan, forcing the night watchman to go with them but dropping him off shortly thereafter.[18] Later that evening Crowley dropped Duringer off and went out to a house in Merrick, Long Island, where he had previously boarded, to visit Helen Walsh. The woman who ran the boarding house, Amanda Davis, and her nineteen-year-old son, Clinton, knew who Crowley was, as did two other male teenagers who were present. None attempted to alert the authorities.

Crowley took Helen and the three teens out driving, and they ended up on what was called "Black Shirt Lane," a desolate road where it wasn't uncommon for young people to go to make out. Once they were parked, Crowley got into an argument with one of the teens who was afraid the outlaw would try to have his way with Helen. Crowley kicked the three youths of his car, and they began the walk back to Davis's house.[19]

Alone in the sedan, Francis and Helen began to discuss getting married again. As they were talking, a police car pulled into the lane. Inside were officers Frederick Hirsch, a twenty-eight-year-old husband and father of four, and rookie patrolman Albert Yodice. Hirsch was supposed to have gone off duty, but since Yodice was new he stayed on. The policemen saw the Ford sedan in the lane and decided to investigate. Yodice and Hirsch approached the car and asked the couple what they were doing. "Just talking," replied Crowley. Not interested in a couple of kids, the cops returned to their car. As the officers walked away Crowley told Helen that he thought Hirsch had recognized him, but Helen said he was just imagining it. He wasn't, though.

When the patrolmen were back at their car, Hirsch, who had a Crowley wanted poster, said to Yodice, "I believe that boy is Crowley."[20] He went back to the Ford for a closer look and, with his gun at the ready, asked Francis for his driver's license. Feigning a move for his wallet, Crowley stuck his hand in his coat and pulled out a pistol. Expecting such a move, Hirsch stuck his gun through the car window and pulled the trigger, but nothing happened. He squeezed the trigger again, and again nothing happened.

By now Crowley had his gun out and pumped four bullets into Hirsch, who fell forward and dropped his pistol into the hood's car. He pushed the mortally wounded officer off the running board, picked up the cop's gun, opened the door, and fired two more rounds into Hirsch with the latter's own gun, which now was working. Crowley started the car and sped off as Yodice fired a volley of shots, one of which pierced the right side of the windshield and two that hit the passenger-side door. Crowley shot back but missed. He drove Helen and himself to Jamaica, Queens, where they ditched the car and hopped a subway into Manhattan.[21]

Police found the car, and because of the bullet holes and the fact that Crowley was wanted for killing Brannen, they claimed he also had killed Helen. "There is no doubt that the girl was killed," the inspector in charge of the investigation told the press. "Crowley must have done it to protect himself. She was the one person who could have convicted him of first-degree murder. He knew that and knew she had to be silenced. I have not the slightest doubt that he shot and killed her and dumped her body out somewhere."[24]

Helen's father told the D.A., "If that little rat has done anything to my girl, I'll kill him with my own hands." Then, as a warning to all cops, he added, "He didn't give Hirsch a chance. He won't give you one. So if you find him, let him have it— before he gets you."[23]

Only Helen's mother seemed confident that her daughter was alive. "Frank Crowley is a splendid young man," she said, "no matter what people say about him being a murderer. He is madly in love with my daughter. They have been sweethearts for two years. Why, he wouldn't harm a hair on her head. She is as safe with him as she would be in my arms. . . . I know he would rather die than see anything happen to Helen."[24]

The answer to whether Helen was alive or dead came soon enough. While searching for Billie Dunne, Detectives Caso and Mara hit pay dirt. They came across a detective's best friend, the anonymous tipster, who told them that Billie Dunne possibly might be found at 303 West Ninetieth Street. The detectives couldn't believe their luck when the tipster added: "And what's more, maybe you'll find Crowley and Duringer there, too."[25]*

On May 7 Mara and Caso drove to the apartment house and parked nearby. Caso sat in the car while his partner grabbed a newspaper out of the back seat, opened it to the classified section, and walked up to the building posing as someone who wanted to rent an apartment. Mara entered the vestibule and saw ten mailboxes, one for each apartment, but he recognized none of the names. On the box for Apartment Ten, however, was a note which read:

> Murray and Red: Do not ring. Helen and I have gone to the store. Will be back shortly — Billie

Detective Mara was intrigued. Did the note refer to Billie Dunne and Helen Walsh? He looked for the building superintendent's buzzer but couldn't find it. Luckily, a tenant leaving the building told him he could find the super in his office around the corner on West End Avenue. Mara found the super and asked if a Billie Dunne was living in either of the buildings. When the super said no, the detective pulled out two pictures, one of Crowley and one of Duringer. Showing the photo of Crowley, he asked the man if he had seen him before. "Why, sure," the superintendent replied, "that's Crowley, the fellow they're hunting for." Mara asked if he'd seen Crowley in the building, and the super said he would have called the police if he had.

Mara then showed him the photo of Duringer and asked the same question. "Why, this man looks like Mr. White in Apartment Ten at our other house," he responded, and then asked to see the picture of Crowley again. This time the super covered Crowley's moppish hair with his hand and took another look. "By God!" he said, "this fellow is up in Apartment Ten, too! He's going under the name of Clark. This picture and the ones in the newspapers fooled me. I've always seen him with a hat or a cap on."[26]

---

* By all accounts Billie Dunne was the reason for the capture. She and Crowley were an item, and both he and Duringer were staying with her. After the Hirsch murder and reconciliation with Helen, Crowley called Dunne and told her he was coming home with a new girl and that she could either clear out or go with Duringer. Not happy with the new arrangement, Dunne showed up for work at the Primrose telling anyone who would listen where Crowley could be found. Someone listened and alerted the detectives.

Wearing some overalls and a cap the superintendent had loaned him and posing as a tinsmith, Mara and the super entered the apartment building where the fugitives were staying. They proceeded up the stairs to the fourth floor and stopped as if conducting an investigation for repair work. The detective went up to the fifth floor to check out the area. The stair landing was right by Crowley's apartment, and down the corridor was another apartment. In the middle was another door, numbered eleven, which appeared to be another apartment but was actually the doorway to the skylight room, which led to the roof. Mara and the super went to the roof, where the detective was able to get the lay of the land. He saw that Crowley's apartment had three windows facing a back area and took notice of the surrounding buildings that had good views of the apartment.

It was now about 3 p.m. Finished with his reconnoitering, Mara and the super went back downstairs and around the corner to the latter's office, where the detective called his lieutenant and gave him the lowdown. In a short time three police sedans containing twelve officers quietly pulled up to three different locations within a two-block radius of the apartment. By ones and twos the twelve men sauntered into the superintendent's office. Six other cops arrived shortly thereafter and a plan was hatched.

The inspector in charge was betting that Crowley and Duringer thought the skylight room was just another apartment, so three detectives were chosen to pose as out-of-town businessmen looking for a room to rent. Someone was sent to get luggage for the cops, while others were detailed to nearby roofs overlooking Crowley's windows. However, they didn't move into position yet, fearing they might be spotted. All exits and approaches to the building were covered, and men were placed in the front apartment overlooking the vestibule so that if Crowley and Duringer weren't in the apartment they could be taken when they arrived.

Once the luggage arrived, the superintendent led the three "businessmen" to the faux apartment. They spoke loudly on their way there to throw off any suspicion should Crowley be listening. The men entered the room and pretended to discuss the place and dickered about price for a bit before agreeing to rent the space. The superintendent thanked them and departed. Successfully in place, the detectives left the door open a crack so they could keep an eye on Apartment Ten.

Getting the cops positioned took about an hour, and while they were discussing what to do next a series of events began to unfold that would result in the greatest police siege in New York history. Detectives in the first-floor apartment saw a young woman enter the building, but since she wasn't Helen Walsh or Billie Dunne, they let her pass so as not blow their cover. The woman walked up the stairs all the way to the fifth floor. Assuming that she was either Walsh or

Dunne, two detectives in the skylight room stepped into the corridor as she reached the landing so they could force their way into Apartment Ten after she opened the door. To their shock, however, the young lady turned and went to the apartment at the other end of the hall.

Despite having shown themselves, the detectives kept up their charade and proceeded down the stairs to the fourth floor, where they cursed their misfortune. The two detectives decided to try to sneak back up the stairs into the skylight room, and as they were slowly making their way there, a man entered the vestibule downstairs and rang the bell for Apartment Ten. The detectives on the ground floor quickly nabbed him, while Mara and two others in the ground-floor apartment started to ascend the stairway to see if anyone from Crowley's apartment would come out to answer the buzzer. The two other detectives on the stairs heard rustling sounds coming from Crowley's apartment, and knowing his propensity to shoot cops, they hurried back down the stairs. Looking over his shoulder, the second detective saw Crowley standing outside his door brandishing an automatic pistol.

Mara and his two companions met the other two detectives on the landing and shouted to the desperado, who responded by firing at the skylight room and running back into his apartment. Moments later he fired another volley through the door. The officers ducked while bullets ricocheted around the corridor. Detective Mara crawled up to the door and fired six shots through it which were quickly answered from inside. After that barrage, Mara hurried through the skylight room to the roof. Realizing that cops were on the landing, Crowley and presumably Duringer began firing through the thin plaster walls, sending the detectives scrambling to the fourth floor amid flying chunks of plaster and mortar. Mara ran across the roof to the West End Avenue building and yelled to the detectives who had been given roof details, "Come on up, fellows. They're in there—both of 'em—and the shootin's started."[27]

One can only imagine what must have gone through the hoodlums' minds when, believing the cops were outside the door, rifle, shotgun, and machine-gun fire began pouring in through the windows behind them. While such overwhelming firepower might have caused most criminals to surrender, Crowley soon appeared at the windows and began exchanging volleys with the officers. Word of the shootout spread across the police teletype, and soon more officers were taking their places on the surrounding roofs. As the sound of the gunfire echoed throughout the neighborhood, thousands of people began to gather in the streets to witness the fight.

Up on the roof, Detective Mara and others returned with an ax and some gas bombs and proceeded to hack away at the floor above Crowley's apartment. The shooting continued, and miraculously no one was seriously hurt as Crowley's bullets slammed into other apartments. At one point the woman from the room across the hall could take no more and ran out into the corridor, but a detective in the skylight room jumped out and grabbed her and brought her to the roof. She was taken to safety and questioned about Crowley, and when the cops were satisfied that she knew nothing about the gunman, she was released.

Hearing the axwork going on above him, Crowley pointed his gun upward and began firing through the ceiling but hit no one. Police returned fire, and Crowley fled into another room. During the melee the police managed to wound the hoodlum three times, once in the wrist and once in each leg. The detectives on the roof managed to chop a sizable chunk out of Crowley's ceiling and began to chuck gas bombs into the apartment, but as soon as one dropped through the hole, Crowley or Duringer would pick it up and throw out the window into the courtyard.

The battle dragged on, and as it was approaching its second hour a group of cops with bulletproof vests began to prepare for a final assault through the front door of the apartment. To drive Crowley away from the entrance before they charged in, the police unleashed a barrage of rifle and shotgun fire that lasted a solid minute. Because of his wounds, the effects of the gas lingering in the apartment, and the fact that he was nearly out of ammunition, Crowley didn't have much fight left. When the cops burst through the door, he surrendered immediately, saying, "I'm shot. I give up. Anyway, you didn't kill me."[28]

When asked what he had done with his guns, Crowley said he'd thrown them out the window. Three pistols, including Hirsch's, were subsequently found in the courtyard. When he was frisked, however, the police found two automatics strapped to his legs. "What do you mean by that?" an arresting officer asked. "What do you expect me to do?" Crowley replied. "I'm going to the chair anyways."[29] Duringer was found in the bedroom, where he'd managed to stuff his 220-pound frame under the bed. Helen was curled up in a corner.

The love of Crowley's life was the first one whisked out of the apartment through the throng of spectators, followed by "Fat." The main attraction was then carried down in a stretcher and transported to Bellevue Hospital, where it was determined that his wounds were non-life threatening. Inside Apartment Ten investigators found some writings the trio had left behind. During the siege when things were looking bleak, both Crowley and his sweetheart had put pen to paper. "Two-Gun's" farewell to the world was a sorry attempt at poetry:

To whom it may concern—I was born on the 31st. She was born on the 13th. I guess it was fate that made us mate. When I die put a lily in my hand and let the boys know how they'll look. Underneath my coat will lie a weary heart what wouldn't harm anybody. I had nothing else to do; that's why I went around bumping off cops. It's a new sensation of its own. Take a tip from me to never let a copper go an inch above your knee. They will tell you that they love you but as soon as you turn your back they'll club you and say: "What the hell." Now that my death is so near as a couple of bulls are at the door and saying, "Come here" I am behind the door with three .38's one of which belongs to my friend who put on weight so quick in North Merrick. He would have got me if his bullets were any good.

There was more, but the final line was smudged with his blood.

Of the three notes that Helen left, the most intriguing was:

To whom it may concern—I bet Legs Diamond dies upon something different from bullets.* I'll see you in heaven if there is such a place. Everybody thinks he's hard but he can't be. He cooked my breakfast this morning and washed my pajamas so I could sleep in them. The only thing that I regret is that I will never see the rest of the world and I wanted so much to travel all over. If I should see Vivian Gordon I will ask her who shot her.** Love to mother, father and sister.

P.S.

Show this to my sister so that she will know that I died singing "Please don't talk about me when I'm gone"[30]

Once in custody Duringer admitted to killing Virginia Brannen. "I heard she was going to marry somebody else," he said. "I was jealous of him."[31] Crowley readily admitted to killing Hirsch as well as shooting Detective Schaedel. He also said he had come close to killing another Bronx police officer whom he despised a few days earlier, but since the officer was with his family at the time, he decided against it. While Crowley was recuperating from his minor wounds and exposure to the gas, Bellevue received numerous phone calls from women who wanted to make sure he was going to be OK.

Since he would be tried in Nassau County for the murder of Officer Hirsch, the following day Crowley was transferred from Bellevue to a hospital in Mineola, Long Island. During the trip Crowley was interviewed by the Nassau County district attorney and told him that he wanted to get the trial over with as quickly as possible. "You know, Frank, it looks like you'll go to the electric chair," the D.A. told him. "Yes, I guess I'll burn," he responded, "but I don't care."[32] During the interview Crowley mentioned that he resented one newspaper's claim that he

---

* "Legs" Diamond would in fact "die upon bullets" seven months later.

** Vivian Gordon was strangled.

was a beer runner for "Dutch" Schultz. "I'm not a member of any gang," he told the D.A. "I work alone." When the discussion turned to the detective he had shot a few months earlier, the wounded hood asserted, "Schaedel was just going to shellac me, and I beat him to it."

"Two-Gun" continued discussing his troubles with the police. "A couple of months ago they tried to hang a hot car on me up in the Bronx that I had nothing to do with. The cops have always been sore on me, and maybe that's why I shot him."[33] Whether "him" meant Schaedel or Hirsch was not determined. Asked if he regretted what he had done, he replied in the negative. The next day, as Officer Hirsch was being buried, Crowley was arraigned for the murder in his hospital bed. When asked how he would plead, he pleaded guilty but was quickly informed that in a first-degree murder case he couldn't do so. "Anything you say," he responded. "All I want is to get my girl out of the jam and get it all over with." And when told that May 18, was the tentative date for the trial, he replied, "Isn't there any way we can get this thing over with before that?"[34]

On May 10 Crowley was deemed well enough to be transferred to the county jail in Mineola. His mother was on hand, and both agreed he probably would receive the death penalty. He told her he would prefer going to the electric chair rather than serving a long sentence. She then asked if he was praying. "Yes, I pray every night," he said. "Good, keep praying," she advised him, "and maybe you will yet get out of your trouble."[35] Later she berated her foster son, who was a lather, for falling behind on his union dues.

On May 26 jury selection began for "Two-Gun's" trial, and he took part in the process, dismissing people because he didn't like the way they looked. Sitting back, chewing gum, he got rid of "baldy" and another man who was "too slick looking."[36]

Crowley's lawyer was going to contend that his client was unstable and had a subnormal mentality and that there was no premeditation when he killed Hirsch. The prosecutor intended to counter the mental claims by bringing to the stand the psychiatrist who had interviewed Crowley at Bellevue and considered him sane. He also was going to argue that while the first barrage the hoodlum fired at Officer Hirsch may not have been premeditated, the final, and probably fatal bullet was fired into the detective with his own gun after Crowley's first shots didn't kill him outright.

The trial began the following day, and a number of young people were on hand to see Crowley, who had become somewhat of a macabre teen idol. He sat there chewing gum and smiling at them while his lawyer told the jury he was an imbecile. Over the course of two days all parties involved in the shooting took their turns on the stand, as did the psychiatrists. On May 29 the lawyers wrapped up and the jury was sent to deliberate. After less than twenty-five minutes they returned a guilty verdict.

A few minutes later Crowley, who was handcuffed to a deputy sheriff, was led from the courtroom. As they passed Crowley's mother the doomed young man pulled back on the cuffs so he could stop to kiss her goodbye. This action caused the policemen and bailiffs to rush him, and Crowley began to flail about trying to hit the officers with his elbows. After about half a minute he was dragged and pushed out of the room.[37] After the trial Crowley was assigned three deputy sheriffs to protect him from the Nassau County police, who may have wanted to get some payback for Hirsch before the killer was sent off to the death house at Sing Sing.[38]

On Monday, June 1, Crowley appeared in front of the judge, snapped his gum, and smiled as the judge pronounced sentence, saying the killer would "be put to death in the manner prescribed by the law in the week of July 5, for the murder of patrolman Frederick Hirsch." Upon hearing that, a woman let out a muffled scream and Crowley said, "Thank you, Judge."[39]

As he was waiting to be transferred, Crowley asked his lawyer if he could take the rap for the murder of Virginia Brannen as well. He also said that if he'd had a couple of machine guns the outcome of his capture may have been different. Crowley was then loaded into a car with two other prisoners and driven to Sing Sing. Upon arrival he was a little less boastful when talking with the assistant principal keeper. He told him, "I just defended myself; that's all I did to get this deal."[40] Crowley, now prisoner #84567, was strip-searched and a three-and-a-half-inch knife carved out of a spoon was found in his sock. "What's the idea?" asked the keeper. "Try and guess," Crowley responded.[41]

The same day Crowley was transferred to Sing Sing, Duringer was sitting in a Bronx courtroom listening to Millie Moore tell the story of Virginia's shooting. Prosecutors also read his statement, made after his capture, in which he claimed he had killed her because he was jealous that she was going to marry another man. Detectives Mara and Caso then testified.

The next day Robert LeClair took the stand and was followed by Duringer, who spent four hours on the hot seat trying to save his neck. With the electric chair on this mind, Duringer said that, following Crowley's advice, he had lied in his confession. He claimed he hadn't shot Virginia out of jealousy—she had brought about her own death accidentally.

"Come on, let's have some excitement," Duringer quoted her as saying, which had led "Fat" to pull out his pistol and shoot through the floorboard of the car. Afterward, he claimed, Virginia had grabbed the gun and pulled it toward her, and that's when it went off. As for throwing her over the wall, that had been Crowley's idea, he said. Crowley had decided not to go the hospital because the police were after him, and because his judgment was impaired by booze, Duringer had agreed to dump her body.[42]

The jury didn't buy Duringer's story, and he was found guilty of murder in the first degree. On June 8 he caught the train for Ossining and joined Crowley in Sing Sing's death house.

Crowley whiled away the remainder of his life engaging in artistic pursuits. He drew pictures of the death house and other prison buildings and showed an aptitude for working with his hands by constructing various buildings out of cardboard. His prize creation was a standing bridge.[43]

A nineteen-year-old gunman at Sing Sing at the time was Patrick O'Brien, who was serving a twenty- to forty-year sentence for an armed robbery he had committed the previous January. O'Brien was able to get Crowley to agree to take the rap for that robbery, saying that he [O'Brien, who supposedly resembled Crowley] had been arrested in a case of mistaken identity. O'Brien was granted a new trial, and both he and Crowley were brought to the Bronx. With four armed guards around him, Crowley sat on the stand cracking his gum while the prosecutor questioned him. Though he took responsibility for the crime he wasn't familiar with the facts of the case, and O'Brien was again found guilty. Both were returned to Sing Sing.[44]

On December 10, 1931, his twenty-sixth birthday, Duringer was scheduled to "ride the lightning." Family members spent most of the day petitioning the governor to commute the sentence but to no avail. "Fat's" only gripe was that he didn't want to die on his birthday and if possible until after Christmas. They allowed him to share his last meal with Crowley, who laughed and said, "I'm in a great spot. I get half the dinner."[45] Crowley's joviality wasn't shared by his friend, who reportedly cried during the meal. Duringer's old pal Robert LeClair showed up for a final visit, but the condemned man refused to see him. At 10 p.m. his family came in for the last time and bid him farewell.

A few minutes after 11 p.m. Duringer, who after nearly seven months of inactivity had ballooned up to 260 pounds, a fact that garnered him the title of heaviest man to be executed at Sing Sing, walked through the door and was strapped into the electric chair. At 11:08 p.m. he was pronounced dead.

The holidays came and went, and on January 21, 1932, it was Crowley's turn to take a seat in the electric chair. The day before the execution Helen petitioned the court to allow her to visit her boyfriend for the last time, saying, "I have been told his dying wish is to see me. Unless I can grant that wish, I will never be happy." Her request was denied. The prison stated that she had been mistaken about his dying wish.

When told that Helen wanted to see him, Crowley, who had heard, among other things, that since his incarceration she had been seeing a cop, responded, "The hell with her. She wants to sell her story to the papers." When told that she wouldn't be seeing him, Helen broke down and cried. Speaking to reporters, she said, "Wasn't it awful that Frank would say a thing like that about me? And why doesn't he write me? I heard from him at first, but he hasn't answered my last two letters." When a reporter asked if she was going to the funeral, she said, "No. If he doesn't want to see me when he is alive, then he surely won't when he is dead."[46]

On his final day Crowley allowed only his family to visit him. Helen still stuck around the prison and sent a message into him saying,

> Dear Shorty,
> I am with you to the end. Do you want to see me? I am waiting. You have been misinformed about the cop. Won't you see me?
>
> Love, Helen.

Convinced that Helen was just trying to get the final chapter for a tabloid story, Francis still refused to see her.

His final meal consisted of roast turkey, salad, rye bread, ice cream, an orange, tea and five packs of chewing gum. He also ordered a box of candy for his mother and a box of cigars to pass out to the other death house inmates as well as the guards he liked. His second and final visit with his family that day commenced at 5 p.m. and lasted for four hours, and then Crowley was led back to his cell for his final two hours of life.

At 11 p.m. he entered the death chamber escorted by the prison chaplain and the principal keeper, followed by ten officers. The priest was praying and Crowley was uttering the appropriate responses. Once inside, the condemned killer was heard to say, "I don't mind it." He planted himself in the chair without any assistance and said, "My love to Mother, and tell Mrs. Lawes [the warden's wife] I appreciate all she did for me." Then, recognizing one of the guards who had followed him in, he waved and said, "How is it, Sarge?"[47]

Once he was strapped in the chair Crowley commented that he didn't think the straps on his leg were tight enough. Then he once again said, "Give my love to Mother." At 11:02 p.m. the switch was thrown, and five minutes later he was pronounced dead. The straps had been tight enough.

COLLEGE BOY

"I think it did me good."

— ROY SLOANE, WHEN ASKED ABOUT HIS PRISON EXPERIENCE

R oy Sloane should not be in this book. Whereas most gangsters and desperadoes came from the mean streets of the poor Irish, Jewish, and Italian
neighborhoods and had little opportunity and meager outlooks on life, Roy
came from a good background and had the brains and opportunities to lead a
productive, law-abiding life. His weakness, however, was stealing cars.

Roy's upbringing wouldn't lead one to believe he was headed for the underworld. His father was a minister, and his mother, who held three degrees, had
authored a number of books. She also was the founder of the National Arts and
Crafts Institute in Washington D.C., and worked for the Department of Labor.
Perhaps it was their divorce that caused Roy to go astray, or perhaps it was just
his penchant for Nash automobiles. Either way, by the age of sixteen young master Sloane had his first run-in with the police for stealing a car.

When he was seventeen he was enrolled in Carnegie Institute of Technology
in Pittsburgh, but when he wasn't hitting the books, he was hitting the streets
looking for a car to steal. Soon he was wanted in Pittsburgh and was arrested in
Akron, Ohio. Sent back to Pennsylvania, he spent a short time in jail. Upon his
release he joined his mother in New York City and enrolled in Columbia University. Once again he chose the streets over the library and was soon stealing cars.

In June 1926 he stole an auto in Mount Vernon, a town just east of Yonkers, and was arrested that fall. On November 31 he was released on $3,000 bail, and shortly thereafter agents of the Department of Justice (precursor of the FBI) showed up with a warrant for his arrest for attempting to sell the car he had stolen the previous June in another state, which was a federal crime.

The very night he was released on bail two detectives were cruising in Brooklyn when they saw Roy drive by. They pulled him over, took him to the police station, and ran a report on the car he was driving. Sure enough, it was hot, stolen that day in Mount Vernon. He told the detectives that the car was given to him by "a fellow in Brooklyn." He was found guilty of auto theft, and since he was a second offender he received a ten-year term in Sing Sing.[1]

Roy had no intention of serving out his sentence. Putting his brain to work, he began to study law to see if there wasn't a legal way to get out of his cell. Hedging his bets, he also began to plan an escape. He was determined to get out, legally or illegally.

In December 1927 a search of Roy's cell turned up an old valve wheel that he had fashioned into a set of brass knuckles. Normally, possessing brass knuckles was a misdemeanor, but criminal law stated that if the possessor had been convicted of a felony then having the weapon was in fact a felony, and therefore seven more years were added to his sentence.

Sloane managed to finagle a new trial and represented himself. He brought two Sing Sing inmates with him who testified that they actually had stolen the car and that Roy was framed. The jury believed their story as well as the well-spoken Sloane, and his conviction was overturned. However, because of the brass knuckles affair, he still had seven years to serve, so it was back to Sing Sing.[2]

Since legal means had gotten him only so far, Roy opted to try something illegal to get him the rest of the way. Toward the end of 1929 Sloane, no doubt using the skills he'd acquired at the Carnegie Institute of Technology, devised a method of escape. In a nutshell, he was going to get out of his cell and knock out the power to his entire cell block, which would douse the lights and cause all the cell doors to open. Then, in the pandemonium that would surely follow, he and his confederates would make their escape.

Brought into the scheme were James Nannery's old pal Edward "Snakes" Ryan; Joe "Babe" Pioli, gunman and killer of "Big" Bill Brennan; and another convict named Walter Frelig. However, before the plan could be put into action the guards got a tip, and on November 13, 1929, they put the kibosh on the escape. Inside Frelig's cell they found Roy's blueprints for the tools he was going to need to knock out the power. In another cell they found a wooden key, a model of the one used to open all the cells, which prison officials figured was going to be smuggled out so that a metal one could be forged and smuggled back in. Sloane, Ryan, and Pioli were placed in the death house for safekeeping, and Frelig was transferred to Clinton Prison. (Since he was the only one of the four transferred, one wonders if the transfer wasn't for his own protection. Was he the leak?)[3]

It was rumored that a gun had been smuggled in for the breakout, so Sloane's cell, originally built circa 1826, was taken apart stone by stone. Authorities didn't find a gun, but they did find a spoon that had been modified into a key that was able to open the cell door.[4]

Another year would pass before Sloane's next bid for freedom. His illegal attempt had failed, so it was back to the legal approach—and this time it worked. Sloane and his lawyer argued that the time Roy was now serving stemmed from a felony conviction for the brass knuckles found in his cell in 1927. They contended that since his original conviction for car theft had been overturned, his conviction on the weapon charge was actually a first offense, thus making it a misdemeanor punishable by a year in prison, which he had served three times over. The court agreed, and Sloane was back on the streets in time for Christmas 1930.[5]

"I think it did me good," Sloane said, when asked about his prison experience as he posed for pictures with his mother and lawyer upon his release. The lawyer was so impressed with Roy's intelligence that he put him to work as a clerk in his law firm. It was also said upon his release that while in prison Sloane had come up with an invention that would revolutionize the aircraft industry. The future looked bright for the twenty-six-year-old, but no matter how sincere he may have been about going straight, he soon hooked up with some actual gangsters.

Most likely the hardened criminals he approached were friends of men he had met in Sing Sing, like Edward Ryan and Joe Pioli. One convict he supposedly was trying to help get released was a tough guy named John McDermott, who, among numerous other crimes, had been arrested in 1929 for the murder of ex-Mafia member and racketeer Frankie Marlow.[6]

On February 18, 1931, about two months after his release from Sing Sing, Roy, a twice-convicted ex-con named Jack Geller, and another man whose name was never learned entered the Karos & Stein jewelry manufacturing shop on the tenth floor of a building on the corner of Fifth Avenue and Forty-sixth Street. Once inside, the three men pulled out pistols and proceeded to tie up both Karos and Stein and two of their employees with picture wire and tape. One of the bandits had succeeded in grabbing about $8,000 worth of jewels when the sirens of a fire truck were heard.

Thinking it was the police, one of the bandits shouted, "The cops are on to us. Let's get out!" The three men fled and the victims began to yell. The hoodlums ditched the jewels and pistols and began to run down the stairs. One of them hopped out of a fifth-floor window and made his escape over the neighboring rooftops. Someone on the tenth floor heard the Karos & Stein victims yelling and sounded the alarm, which caused the building to go into shut-down mode.

An elevator boy began to close the gate to the Forty-sixth Street exit when Geller ran up and tried to push his way through. The operator grabbed him and was dragged outside where an approaching cop saw the scuffle and nabbed the thief. Sloane was trapped in the lobby with numerous other people. Nattily attired in a blue suit and a chesterfield coat topped off with a bowler on his head, Sloane approached one of the cops and tried to talk his way outside. He seemed a little to anxious to exit the building so the policeman took him upstairs, where Karos, Stein, and their employees identified him as one of the bandits.[7]

Sloane was able to raise the $20,000 needed for bail and was back on the streets. What he was doing for money is a matter of speculation, but he frequently hung out at a speakeasy known as the Mad Dot Boat Club. As his trial date drew near, Roy learned he was in trouble with his underworld pals. In fact, he was literally "on the spot."

On May 12, 1931, as he was getting ready to go out for the evening, he sat down and wrote his mother a letter. In it he said that he had just learned that a certain gang leader wanted him dead because he was afraid that Sloane, in an attempt to save his own skin in the upcoming trial, might go to the authorities and turn state's evidence against him. He wrote that he was going to meet with two of the gang members that night and that if anything happened to him, she should hand the letter over to the police.[8]

Seven hours later, at about 11 p.m., three men (whom the press alluded to as being Italian) entered the Mad Dot and began drinking. After a while one of them went to the phone and made a call. After he hung up he made another call and was heard to say, "He's coming up." He then returned to his friends and said, "He'll be here in a minute." As if on cue, Sloane showed up and joined the group. According to the bartender, Sloane seemed uneasy with the fellows and told him not serve them anything harder than beer. Sloane and the men chatted for a bit, and then the trio left.

A short time later Sloane exited the building with another man, but before they took many steps a maroon sedan pulled up and its back door flew open. Two shotguns blasted, and Sloane dropped to the ground with wounds to the abdomen and groin. The man he'd left the building with, who was suspected of being a "spotter" for the hit men, dove to the pavement and then ran away. As the car containing the gunmen drove off, Sloane struggled to his feet and staggered down the street and around the corner before collapsing. A cop responding to the sound of the shotgun blasts found him and took him to the hospital, where he died an hour later.[9]

Among items police found on his body were a fake mustache and a badge. Was Roy posing as a Prohibition agent or a cop and shaking down bootleggers? They also found keys to a Nash that was parked across the street from the Mad Dot as well as a driver's license that identified him as John McDermott, the convict in Sing Sing he was supposedly trying to help get out.[10]

Roy's mom turned over the letter to the police, but they did nothing with it. Three months after the murder the letter came to public attention, and the police stated that a number of the men named in the letter had left the city after the murder so they couldn't be questioned. The cops also believed the man Sloane claimed was a powerful gang leader with political connections was nothing more than a common car thief, and they didn't push the matter.[11]

It Came from Massachusetts

*"Listen, you may feel a little bad after you knock off the first
one, but after you've bumped one guy, what difference does it
make how many more you knock off?"*

— LEONARD SCARNICI

The Midwest wasn't the only section of the United States to feel the wrath of bank robbers during the early years of the Depression. New York City and the surrounding area also had their fair share. Just as cities like Chicago and St. Paul were havens for bandits, so to was the Big Apple.

One such gang of robbers was headed by a psychopath named Leonard Scarnici, who, although he was born in the Big Apple, first made his mark in the underworld in Springfield, Massachusetts. Like many hoodlums, his reputation was built on rumor and considerable hearsay. The official record shows he was a robber and killed at least three men, probably a few more, but by the end of his life he was called one of gangland's most proficient hired guns. It is unknown whether his reputation was deserved, or if the police simply found him to be a convenient solution to some unsolved murders.

Leonard was born on January 12, 1906, in Manhattan's Little Italy, the first child of recently arrived immigrants from Sicily. Soon after the boy's arrival the family moved to Springfield, where Louis, the family patriarch, worked as a carpenter. Three more children followed, two girls and another boy. The Scarnicis struggled to get by on Louis's intermittent pay. Like other poor kids, Leonard got two educations, one from school and one from growing up in the streets. He was a bit of a paradox. The principal of his school referred to him as a "bad product of an unwholesome home environment," and the adjectives used by his teachers included "vulgar," "ill-mannered," "foul-minded," "physically dirty," and "ill-kept." Despite this he was an above-average student who apparently never had to study because he was able to retain what was discussed in class.

Tragedy struck the Scarnici family in 1914 when Leonard's mother died during childbirth. His father sent the two youngest kids to live in a children's home while he attempted to raise Leonard and the oldest daughter himself.

By the time Leonard was fourteen his father had become a moderately successful contractor. He wanted his son to graduate from high school and attend college, but halfway through the ninth grade Leonard, who by this time was reportedly staying out until at least midnight each night, informed his father that he was through with school. Unable to change his son's mind, Louis put him to work as a carpenter. But steady work did not diminish Leonard's wild streak, and he soon found himself in trouble with the law.

On May 12, 1922, an outsider came into his neighborhood, and Leonard proceeded to beat up the man. He was charged with assault and battery, but the case was dismissed. The judge suggested that Leonard join the National Guard and take his unbridled energy into the boxing ring. This the young man did, and for a while it kept him out of trouble, or at least out of police custody.

In 1923 Louis Scarnici remarried and started a new family. Feeling like an outsider, Leonard stayed away from home more and more, drinking and carousing. One writer states that at this time Leonard and some pals were gang-raping girls. Whether that is true is a matter of conjecture, although there is no doubt he was sexually active. In April 1924 a girl went to the authorities claiming that Leonard was the father of her baby. The young hoodlum was hauled into court and found guilty of "bastardy" and ordered to pay child support to the tune of $16 a month. After two months of non-payment, Leonard found himself in the hoosegow for the first time.

Although his term was only thirty days, it proved to be a life-changing event. His cell mate was a truck driver for a Boston bootlegging operation who set him up with a job after his release. At the young age of eighteen Leonard set his carpentry tools aside and began to haul illegal booze. He moved out of his father's house and roomed with a fellow gangster in the making.[1]

Over the course of the next couple of years Scarnici worked his way up to body-guard for the bootlegging ring's top brass, and in 1927 he got his first contract to kill. A small-time bootlegger from his hometown of Springfield had gotten into a shouting match with one of Scarnici's bosses. During the verbal battle the hood-lum's chauffeur, Frank Wilson, yelled some particularly insulting remarks, and the Boston big shot decided he had to be taught a lesson. Since Leonard was from that city and actually knew Wilson, he got the job.

On April 27, 1927, Wilson disappeared and Scarnici was arrested for murder. While in custody he confessed in the presence of Springfield's chief of police, a stenographer, and Wilson's mother but then refused to sign the statement. Since there was no corroboration—or body, for that matter—Scarnici was released.[2]

For reasons that are unclear, Scarnici decided to return to the city of his birth. The date of his arrival is unknown, but he came to the attention of the police when he was arrested on March 2, 1930, for possessing burglar's tools. He did a short stretch and was released. He then decided that Connecticut might be a more convivial locale, so he and two others, David Reiner and Morris Shapiro, traveled to the town of Salisbury, where they robbed the post office on October 13, 1931.[3] Scarnici was arrested and ended up serving six months. Back on the streets, he was arrested for another robbery in New Haven. Released on $10,000 bail, he skipped town, but not before wreaking more havoc on July 27, 1932.

On this day Scarnici and two others pulled into a gas station/general store in the town of Woodbridge and attempted to rob the proprietor, Louis Albino. The owner's son, John, came to his father's assistance, and Scarnici shot him. Then he turned the gun on the father and shot him too before retreating to the car. As the bandit car pulled away, Louis Albino staggered out to the store's porch as his son ran to the road to get a look at the car. John was able to give police a description of the bandits and their auto before both he and his father succumbed to their wounds.[4]

Scarnici returned to New York City, where he kicked his career up a notch by moving into bank robbery. His core gang included: Anthony Reino, whose record consisted of four arrests between 1929 and 1931, when he was shipped off to prison for impersonating a revenue agent; Charles Herzog, who had five arrests dating back to 1919; Philip Zeigler, a Sing Sing alum with a whopping fourteen arrests dating back to 1916; and Fred Plentl, whose only offense was an arrest in 1927 for felonious assault with a knife.

There were others involved in the bank jobs, including Manhattan tough guys Marcel Poffo, the man credited with getting "Dutch" Schultz started in his criminal career, and his longtime partner Max Parkin. Although authorities felt he took part in numerous bank jobs, Leonard admitted participating in just two.

The first took place in Brooklyn on September 1, 1932, and almost cost Leonard his life, ironically by his own hand. At about 1:30 p.m. two cars pulled up in front of the Bensonhurst National Bank. While one man stayed with the cars, one guarded the door and six others entered the bank, where Scarnici put a gun to the vice president's head and made him take him into the vault. When they entered the vault a teller stepped on a button that caused its door to close. Believing that he was locked in for good, Leonard told the bank officer that he was going to kill both of them. Luckily for the two, Herzog saw what had transpired and pointed his Thompson submachine gun at the teller and made him reopen the door.

As this was taking place, the other four men rounded up the rest of the employees and customers and told them to gather in a corner. One customer misunderstood the order and stood still and was knocked over the head with the butt of a pistol. The thieves ended up getting $300 from depositors, while two other bandits jumped over the partitions and cleaned out the teller cages. The robbers fled with a take of $5,000 after ordering the victims not to call the cops.[5]

Although he didn't admit taking part in the heist, Scarnici was later identified as one of the bandits who took part in the December 15, 1932, robbery of the Bank of Manhattan. Having done their homework, the robbers knew the bank had no alarm system and that the only way to call for help was by telephone, so before entering they made sure the phone lines were cut. As one man remained at the wheel of the getaway car, four men entered the bank and immediately pulled out pistols and a sawed-off shotgun. There were no customers, so the robbers split into two groups to cover the bank employees. One of the bandits grabbed a chair and climbed over a seven-foot partition to let his partner into the teller cages. As this was happening one of the other gunmen told the employees, "Keep quiet; keep your hands up. One false move and we'll let you have it."

At one point one of the men produced a hand grenade and threatened to blow up the bank if anyone attempted to interfere with the robbery. After two of the gunmen were admitted into the vault and had taken what they could, they yelled to the others that they were done. The man with the grenade threw his ordinance as he was backing out of the bank, but it turned out to be just a teargas bomb. As gas filled the bank, some staff attempted to call the police but to no avail.[6]

A few weeks later, in early January 1933, Poffo and Parkin were arrested for stabbing a detective. They were represented by famed gangland lawyer Sam Liebowitz and were released on bail paid by "Dutch" Schultz. Both Poffo and Parkin were rearrested for the Bank of Manhattan job. Parkin was identified by bank employees as the man who had thrown the teargas bomb, but Poffo was released and then rearrested after witnesses claimed he had been involved in another bank robbery. Both failed to show up for trial in the stabbing incident and forfeited their bail.[7]

The final bank heist for Poffo, Parkin, and Scarnici, and the one that would lead to the demise of all three, took place outside New York City in the upstate town of Rensselaer on May 29, 1933. At noon six men entered the bank, one of them carrying a package wrapped in paper. Once inside, the man ripped off the paper, revealing a machine gun. Aiming the weapon at the eleven people in the bank, the gunman yelled, "Come on, get into that back room, all of you." The other five bandits drew pistols and forced the victims into a room behind the teller cages. However, one employee managed to step on an alarm button before leaving his post.

When the alarm went off at the police station, two detectives went to investigate. The lookout saw them coming, and as the two officers approached the bandits fired a volley through the front door. Both detectives were wounded, one mortally, but as they feebly returned fire, all of the bandits managed to escape.[8]

Less than two weeks later, on June 10, a police officer in Harrison, New York, was making his rounds when he came across two bodies lying in the road. They turned out to be Poffo and Parkin. Each had been shot in the stomach, and their heads and faces had been worked over with a knife.[9]

By July 1933 Scarnici and Reino had a rendezvous in the Bronx as well as a couple of rooms at a boarding house in the town of Mount Kisco, located about thirty miles north of New York City. Around the end of August New York detectives located Scarnici and his gang and began to shadow them. The cops never said how they found the hoodlums or how they discovered they were bank robbers, but the answer may be found in the kidnapping of John J. O'Connell Jr.

O'Connell, the nephew of two of Albany's Democratic political bosses, was snatched on July 7, 1933, and held for twenty-three days in Hoboken, New Jersey, before being released after a $40,000 ransom was paid. One of those arrested was an Albany underworld figure named Manny Strewl. Not long after he was taken into custody the police learned about Scarnici and his gang. There was speculation that Strewl may have used Scarnici as a bargaining chip for himself, or that Scarnici had a relationship with the Albany underworld and had been been tailed by police after he was seen with Strewl during the O'Connell investigation.[10]

Regardless of how the police became aware of Leonard and his mob, after following the gang for about three weeks and learning their haunts, the police decided to make their move. On the night of September 19, 1933, a dozen detectives stationed themselves around the gang's Bronx hideout. As men stood on the fire escape and in the hallways, a detective knocked on the apartment door. Anthony Reino opened the door and quickly slammed it in the detective's face.

The cops forced their way inside, and as they were doing so Scarnici tried to throw a .38 pistol and two pairs of handcuffs out the window but was stopped by a detective. Scarnici, Reino, and Philip Zeigler surrendered without any trouble. In addition to the items Leonard was trying to jettison out the window, police found gauze, goggles, and adhesive tape, which caused the cops to believe they had nailed O'Connell's kidnappers. A short time later detectives picked up Charles Herzog in his Brooklyn apartment and Fred Plentl at his Harlem residence.

Early the next morning two New York detectives, assisted by two Mount Kisco police officers, a state trooper, and a Department of Justice (FBI) agent, raided the Mount Kisco hideout. The raiding party broke into the house and found Leonard's wife, Eleanor, in one bedroom and Reino's wife, Emma, in another. More importantly they found the gang's arsenal, which consisted of a machine gun, three shotguns, a Luger, and three .38 pistols as well as thousands of rounds of ammunition.[11]

Once the gang members were in custody, John O'Connell was brought in to see if he could identify them as his kidnappers. Although he said that Scarnici and Reino resembled the men who had snatched him, he wasn't 100 percent sure and since the charges were so serious he didn't put the finger on them. He did, however, say the handcuffs in their possession were the very ones he had worn during his captivity. He said he was able to recognize them from a rust spot in a certain place.[12]

For some reason, while the rest of the hoodlums remained mum about their activities, Scarnici talked up a storm, or rather, wrote up a storm in the form of a confession. He went into detail about the Bensonhurst National Bank job, saying, "I went straight to the man behind a sign which read 'vice-president.' I stuck my gun to his temple and ordered him to take me into the vault." Once the teller on the outside had closed the vault door, he said he told the bank officer, "I am going to kill myself. But I am going to take you with me." When the door was opened and he saw that Herzog had saved him, he thanked his comrade, saying, "Charlie, you are the gamest fellow in the world to get me out. I thought I was gone."[13]

In his confession he also admitted taking part in the Rensselaer bank job, although he denied firing the shots that killed the detective. However, he didn't have a problem with taking credit for other murders. He openly discussed the murder of the father and son who were killed at their filling station in Woodbridge, Connecticut. "We killed them because they didn't get their hands up quick enough," he said. He also stated that he, Reino, and Plentl had killed Poffo and Parkin for double-crossing them on the Rensselaer job. The police, however, kept asking him about the O'Connell kidnapping, but he kept denying involvement, at one point yelling, "You've got me for five murders. What more do you want?"[14]

Not satisfied with just five murders, the police were hoping to clear up other high-profile gangland executions. They surmised that Scarnici may have been the machine gun-wielding hit man who took out Vincent "Mad Dog" Coll in February 1932. They also claimed that Scarnici may have played a part in the double murder of William Price and Edward Flanagan, two gangsters found stuffed in sacks in the back seat of a car in Brooklyn.

If things weren't bad enough for Scarnici, Margaret Wilson, the mother of his first murder victim, Frank Wilson, came to New York trying to get him prosecuted for the six-year-old slaying. "Thank God they've got him at last," the sobbing mother said. "He told me with his own lips that he killed my Frankie." She showed detectives old newspaper articles about the killing. She then showed them pictures of her son being removed from a shallow grave on October 30, 1931, along with an autopsy report that stated Frankie had been buried alive. Though touched by the grieving mother, detectives told her she really needed to bring it up with the police in her home state.[15]

To help place Scarnici at another bank job, detectives brought in two boys who identified the hoodlum as one of the men they had seen entering the Savings Bank of Richmond Hill in Queens on August 5, 1932. "We were playing in front of the bank," one of the kids explained to the court. "He had a machine gun in his hands and was leading the other men into the bank when he saw us. He said, 'Mind your own business, kids, and I'll give you a buck.'" At this time the other kid chimed in, "Yeah, but he didn't give us the buck."[16]

None of Scarnici's gang went on trial for the O'Connell kidnapping. However, Leonard, Reino, and Herzog stood trial that December for the murder of the detective at the Rensselaer bank. On December 16, 1933, Reino and Herzog were acquitted and the jury was divided on Scarnici.

Believing their client couldn't get a fair trial in Rensselaer County, Scarnici's lawyers were granted a change of venue to the town of Schoharie for his retrial. The move proved fruitless, however, because on February 23, 1934, after two hours of deliberation, Scarnici was found guilty. Three days later he was sentenced to death in the electric chair. During sentencing he was asked if he had anything to say. Referring to the judge, Scarnici said, "I want to thank you personally for being direct and fair." But while answering some routine questions for a court clerk, he stated, "I still say I'm innocent of killing James Stevens [the detective], regardless of the outcome of this case."[17]

The month after Scarnici's conviction it was Reino and Herzog's turn. Although absolved of the Rensselaer job, they were not as fortunate in their trial for the Bank of Manhattan robbery. Witnesses stated that Reino had been one of the men toting a machine gun during the robbery and that Herzog held a teller at bay while others looted the vault. Witnesses also identified Scarnici through a photograph as a participant. On March 21, 1934, both were convicted and sentenced to from twenty to forty years in Sing Sing.[18]

Interestingly, as the judge sentenced the two men he read from a report stating that in addition to the murders of Poffo and Parkin, Scarnici and his gang were responsible for killing three more of their confederates—Red Harrison, Joseph Calligari, and Frank Russo. The bodies of the two men, both in their thirties, were found March 18, 1933, in Westchester County by a farmer a short distance from the highway on a remote road known as Green Lane between the towns of Bedford Hills and Mount Kisco.

Both men had been shot twice in the chest and once in the forehead, leading police to believe that a machine gun had been used. The killers had a macabre sense of humor, because the dead men had been carried over a small stone wall and placed near a tree that had a sign which read, "No dumping."[19] Other than close proximity to Mount Kisco, where Scarnici and Reino would rent rooms later that year, no reason was given why authorities believed them to be victims of the gang.

Leonard Scarnici was originally sentenced to be executed on April 15, 1934, but this date was staid by the court of appeals. The next date set was January 17, 1935, but two weeks before Leonard was to be put to death his lawyer petitioned the governor of New York, claiming that Leonard was a "victim of the Prohibition era" and that "society has something to answer for his condition. His frame of mind was built up by society's attitude to Prohibition." The lawyer also argued that Leonard was "morally insane and sick mentally."

The district attorney who prosecuted him told the governor that any questions had been answered during the trial and had been viewed by the court of appeals. He assured the governor that "Scarnici had a fair and impartial trial, and there are no circumstances that should move you to grant clemency."[20]

The governor was going to let them strap Leonard in the chair, but when his execution date arrived Scarnici said he could offer information about the still-unsolved O'Connell kidnapping. Eager to clear Albany's most notorious case, the governor granted a four-week stay of execution, which subsequently was extended to March 25 and finally to June 27, 1935.[21]

Leonard, however, had nothing of value to add to the case, so his lawyers came up with a new angle. They claimed Leonard's rights had been violated because the wording of the charge against him had been altered between the first trial and the second. Because of this, the killer was allowed to do something no other condemned man in Sing Sing history was permitted to do on his execution day: leave the prison.

Accompanied by four guards, one of whom was toting a machine gun, Leonard was placed in a car. "It's nice to see the sun again," he told the guards before remaining quiet during the trip to the federal court building in New York City. For eight hours his lawyer argued for a new trial while Scarnici sat in a rear office chewing gum as more than a dozen detectives stood guard nearby. In the end the judge found that none of Leonard's rights had been violated, and he was sent back to the Sing Sing death house.[22]

Scarnici was scheduled to be the second prisoner executed that night. The first was a roadhouse owner named Eva Coo, who had been found guilty of murdering a man. A couple of minutes past 11 p.m., as Eva was being escorted from her pre-execution chamber, she stopped in front of Leonard's cell. "Goodbye, Scarnici," she said. Leonard stood up and said, "Goodbye. Keep your chin up." About five minutes later, Eva Coo was dead. Then it was Scarnici's turn.

He entered the death chamber smoking a cigarette. Taking a final drag, he flicked the butt to the side before sitting down. He was quickly strapped into the chair, and as the mask was being placed over his head he asked, "Warden, can I say a word?" The warden motioned to the guards to remove the mask, and Scarnici said, with a small smile, "I want to give out a message to the people of Albany. They double-crossed me, but I'm a better man than they are. I thank you, Warden." The mask was then placed back over his head and the current applied. Four minutes after entering the room, he was pronounced dead.[23]

It was assumed that Leonard's last words were directed at Manny Strewl and other Albany hoodlums who may have turned him in to gain favors with the police.

19

BRIDE OF THE MAD DOG

"Get those hands up, you mug!"
— LOTTIE COLL TO ROBBERY VICTIM

One would think that after spending a year as the moll of one of New York City's most desperate and hunted gangsters and getting out with not only your skin intact but a small prison sentence would have been enough to make most women do everything possible to walk the straight and narrow. Lottie Kriesberger Coll, however, was not most women. It was a gangster's life for her, but after her husband Vincent was machine-gunned in a West Side phone booth she was no longer satisfied with just playing the hoodlum's girl, she went on her own crime spree.

As with many gangsters, information about Lottie's early days is hazy. Sources have her being born Charlotte Moran. In 1933 she claimed to be twenty-five years old, although authorities said she was thirty-one. Her police record supports the latter as it shows she was arrested for robbery on November 21, 1919, and had already married her first husband, Joseph Kriesberger. Although she is mostly remembered as gangster Vincent Coll's beloved, Lottie dwelled in the underworld long before she became the "Mad Dog's" wife, and the men she was involved with throughout her youth had the habit of ending up on a mortuary slab.

There was no jail time for Lottie's first offense. She had a softy judge who dropped the charges hoping that young Charlotte would mend her wicked ways. She didn't. A year later, on December 4, 1920, she was again arrested for burglary and again was discharged. Her arrests were probably for helping her husband Joseph, who was a silk robber. He also wasn't above making a buck off of his wife—Kriesberger dolled up his spouse and put her to work in a dance hall where she mixed with New York City's tougher elements.[1]

The sexy dancehall siren caught the eye of Adolf Romano, a mobster involved in the ice racket, and soon Mr. Kriesberger was history, literally. After Romano made his move on the girl, we hear nothing more about hubby number one. Lottie began to shack up with Romano in his Harlem apartment at 405 East 117th Street and all was peaceful for a while, but the love-struck Romano was not Lottie's only suitor. A young man by the name of Sam Medal was also smitten with the young beauty.

Medal is a bit of an enigma, whereas Lottie and the company she kept grew up in the poverty-ridden neighborhoods of New York City. Medal was a graduate of Columbia Law School. He was an orphan but had received financial support from his wealthy older brothers. Although he had brains and money, Medal was attracted to the darker side of life, and a relationship blossomed between him and Charlotte. Before they could be together, however, something would have to be done about Romano.[2]

On July 8, 1927, Lottie was in the hospital recuperating from an operation when Medal came to visit her. During the visit a fight broke out between them, and the college graduate lit into her for her continuing association with Romano. The hot-headed Medal reportedly had to be physically removed from the hospital after spitting in the girl's face.[3]

Later that day twenty-seven-year-old Romano was driving along Morris Avenue in the Bronx. Either because it was raining or because he was possibly looking for an address, he was driving slowly. As he approached 140th Street three men, each armed with a pistol, ran out of a doorway and jumped onto the running board of his car. Five bullets were fired into Romano killing him. The gunmen leapt from the gangster's car and fled as it careened down the street for a block before jumping the curb and crashing into a fence.[4]

A witness said he had seen Medal near the murder site five minutes before Romano drove by, but when the police went to question him, he couldn't be found. Medal went on the lam and managed to stay away for about six months, but he either surrendered to police through his lawyer or was captured in January 1928 and put on trial for Romano's murder.

In an attempt to establish a motive for the murder, prosecutors called Lottie into court and questioned her about the fight between her and the defendant. Like a good moll, Lottie lied and said she had been delirious at the time and had no recollection of the incident. Medal was acquitted of the murder and quickly left town to avoid any reprisals by Romano's mobster pals.[5]

Between 1928 and 1931 Lottie's life is sketchy, but one reporter attaches her to a West Village bootlegger named Patrick "the Link" Mitchell. If this is correct, then the romance was short lived because "the Link" had a significant portion of his head blown away in a Greenwich Village speakeasy on May 20, 1928.[6]

Exactly how and when Lottie hooked up with the man she would forever be linked with is also a mystery. One writer says they met at an East Side dance hall, but whatever the truth might be, by early 1931 Lottie and Vincent Coll were an item. In the spring of that year Coll was waging war against Bronx beer baron "Dutch" Schultz as well as making enemies of powerful mobsters Owney Madden and Ciro Terranova. As a result, Lottie's man was now the most-wanted gangster in town, a fact not lost on the couple.

On October 4, 1931, two days after the Coll gang bumped off a Schultz employee, a dragnet went out over the city. Coll's crew were arrested at a number of different locations, and Coll himself was traced to the Cornish Arms Hotel. Learning that Coll was in Room 501, the police went upstairs and began a stakeout. After three hours Coll and a confederate stepped out of the room and were immediately arrested. During the arrest Coll asked if they could go down to Room 404 to tell Lottie what happened and to say that he was all right. The cops said they would handle the task themselves and shipped Coll and company off to the station house.

The detectives burst into Room 404 showing their badges, and Lottie, thinking the worst, asked, "Where's Vince?" "In good hands," one of the detectives replied. We got the whole mob." Relieved, Lottie said, "Oh, I thought something happened to him." A search of the room turned up a .38 pistol in a makeup bag, so Lottie was charged with violating the Sullivan Law. It was put down as a misdemeanor, and she was released on bail pending trial.[7]

That December, Coll went on trial for what was called the "Harlem Baby Massacre," a drive-by shooting gone awry in which the intended victim was unhurt but a five-year-old child was killed and four other kids were wounded. However, he was acquitted on December 29, and less than a week later, on January 4, 1932, Coll and Lottie went to Albany and were married. A month later, she was a widow.

On February 8, 1932, Lottie and Vince were once again at the Cornish Arms Hotel on West Twenty-third Street. A little before midnight Coll had to make a call and left the room and went across the street with an associate to the London Chemist Drug Store. Little did Vince know but his companion had betrayed him and was setting him up to be killed. A few moments after he entered a phone booth to make his call a machine-gun-wielding hit man entered the store and calmly made his way to toward the booth. Trapped, with no way out, "Mad Dog" could only stand there while his killer sprayed him with bullets.

A little more than ten minutes after her husband had left Lottie received a phone call telling her that "Vincent was hurt." Knowing where he was, she quickly ran across the street into the drugstore and found a small crowd gathered around her bullet-riddled husband. "Vince! Vince!" she screamed as she knelt next to him and refused to move until the police arrived. It was never determined who informed Lottie about her husband's murder. She would only say that she had received an anonymous call, but undoubtedly the caller was Coll's double-crossing companion who had entered the store with him.[8]

Three weeks after Vincent's death Lottie appeared in court in her mourning clothes to face the gun charge from the previous October. She pleaded guilty, and as she was being led to a cell to await the sentencing hearing all the trauma of the past few months caught up with her and she collapsed. She was taken to the prison ward at Bellevue to recuperate.[9]

She stayed in the prison ward four months, and during this time an old pal, Sam Medal, back in the city and running a restaurant called Conti's on the West Side, began to pay her visits. In June she was deemed healthy enough to appear in court for sentencing and received a term of six months in the workhouse. However, the four months she had spent in Bellevue were taken off her sentence, and she was back on the streets on August 18, 1932.[10]

Whether the relationship between Lottie and Medal was rekindled will never be known. But if it was, it was a short romance because three weeks after Lottie was released, Sam joined the ranks of her former loves and was taken for a ride.

On September 6 Sam, who lived with his sister, called her from Conti's and said he would be home late because he had to take care of some business.[11] It was the last time she ever heard from him. He was last seen leaving his restaurant with two strangers and had $4,000 in his pocket.[12] Detectives sought out "Dutch" Schultz for questioning because three months earlier, on June 5, the police station near Medal's restaurant had received a phone call saying the Dutchman was about to be rubbed out inside Conti's. A contingent of plainclothes detectives was sent out, and they found Schultz and his main torpedo, Bo Weinberg, in the establishment having dinner. The gang leader was none too concerned with the report about his impending demise, but the detectives brought him and Bo in for an all-night Q & A session, just in case.[13]*

---

* New York thought the mystery of Sam Medal's disappearance was solved that fall. On October 16 a body matching Medal's general description was found along Swan Lake in the upstate town of Liberty with bullets in the head and chest. On November 2 two of Medal's brothers were summoned to try to identify the remains. One was able to do so; the other was not. A third brother was summoned but couldn't make a positive I.D. New York authorities finally arrived with copies of the missing man's fingerprints, and they did not match those of the corpse, so what happened to Medal still remains a mystery.

With her past acquaintances either dead or in prison, Lottie sought out new companions. Around the beginning of 1933 she met a twenty-two-year-old punk named Al Guarino, who also went by the name Thomas Pace. It appears that a relationship blossomed between them, and in the spring Guarino introduced her to his pal, twenty-three-year-old Joseph Ventre. About this time the trio formed a mini-gang, and Lottie, who had the most underworld experience, was the brains of the outfit. Throughout May 1933 Lottie, sporting a blonde wig, and her two gun-toters pulled a series of small-time robberies in the Bronx that netted a meager $15 to $130 per job. After a month Lottie reportedly told the young hoodlums that she was tired of "the five-and-ten-cent-store stuff" and wanted to go after "big game."[15]

Ventre suggested as a victim Isadore Moroh, a shylock who also dabbled in jewelry. Ventre and Guarino had met him at a dice game where he had given Ventre $5 because he thought he was homeless. A plan was devised whereby Ventre would approach Moroh and ask him to come to the trio's car to talk with Ventre's friend about the Elmira Reformatory. When he did, they would force him into the back seat and rob him.

At 10:30 p.m. on June 21 Lottie and her two henchmen parked their car on Wheeler Avenue in the Bronx. Diagonally across the street from where they parked, four young women stood in front of an apartment building talking. As Ventre drove around the block to the corner of Elder and Westchester avenues, where Moroh conducted business, Guarino got out and went down the street to wait for his partner to return with the mark. Ventre found Moroh and asked him if he wouldn't mind talking to a friend about "the El" (Elmira Reformatory). Moroh agreed, and Ventre led him back to the car where they found Lottie.

Lottie told them that "the friend" had gone to make a phone call and would be back shortly. In the meantime Lottie asked the jeweler if he would be interested in buying a two-and-a-half-carat diamond. "You never saw one," Moroh snapped at the moll. Then Ventre asked him if he could change a thousand-dollar bill. "You've never seen one of them either," he said to the punk he had just ten days before given $5.

After a few minutes Moroh said he had to leave, but at that point Guarino walked up to the car with his coat collar up and his hat pulled over his face. Lottie leaned over the seat and opened the back door, saying, "This is a stickup." Ventre tried to force Moroh into the back seat, and from there the plan fell apart. "I kicked the door shut and swung at Ventre," Moroh said later, "then I grabbed Ventre and shoved him in front of Guarino."

Successfully breaking away, Moroh ran up the street, zigzagging as Guarino fired four shots at him. Although no bullets struck Moroh, one did rip through the cheek and out the back of the head of one of the young women chatting in front of the apartment building across the street.[16] After the botched robbery Lottie and her two cohorts moved from their room in the Bronx into a Midtown Manhattan hotel.

Just as the Moroh debacle was taking place, a number of robbery victims in the Bronx picked Lottie's photo out of the rogues' gallery and identified her as the woman in the blonde wig who had robbed them. Police then put out the word that she was wanted, and some underworld informants said she could be found at the Dixie Hotel on West Forty-second Street. Detectives arrived at the hotel and showed Lottie's mug shot to the desk clerk and were told that she was in Room 601.

Furnished with keys to the room, the detectives let themselves in and looked inside a closet, where they found three guns in a suitcase. They found Ventre asleep in one bedroom and Lottie and Guarino asleep in another. All were forced awake at gunpoint and allowed to get dressed. While getting ready Lottie said that she wanted to "powder her nose" and reached for her purse. One of the detectives grabbed the handbag and removed the .32 pistol that was inside. "Go to hell," Lottie yelled as the detective shoved her into the bathroom and told her she could finish getting ready in there.[17]

Reinforcements were called, and all three bandits were taken to the Fifty-seventh Street Station, where robbery victims came forward and identified them and some of the loot from the jobs. Detectives also noted that the trio seemed very anxious about something besides the robberies. Ballistics reports were conducted on the guns found in the hotel, and it soon became obvious what the trio was worried about. The three were indicted for the murder of the young Bronx woman, and once the word got out Moroh turned himself over to police and filled in the story.[18]

Guarino admitted that he had done the shooting, saying, "I am very sorry that it had to happen. It was an accident. I got excited and fired a shot." However, he fell short of implicating his gal and friend, saying "I refuse to answer" when questioned about either of them. It was to no avail, though, because all three went on trial and all three went to jail.

Because he had done the shooting, Guarino was sentenced to twenty years to life. Ventre was given seven and a half years, and Lottie's time in the criminal spotlight ended with a term of six to twelve years. She served a little more than nine years before being paroled on July 2, 1943, and slipping into obscurity.[19]

20

The $427,000 Payday

The police announced that the case had been "broken"
and that the round-up of the gang of bandits who
staged the robbery with unprecedented daring and skill
would be only a matter of days.

— *NEW YORK TIMES*, FIVE YEARS BEFORE THE CASE WAS CLOSED

August 21, 1934, was a typical day at the Rubel Ice Plant in Brooklyn. Peddlers showed up with their carts to pick up their supply of ice to sell, while across the street people played tennis and neighborhood children loitered about. Little did the Brooklynites realize that they would soon witness the most lucrative cash robbery in history up to that time. The bandits themselves didn't even know how big it would be, but they did know they had an ingenious plan which, if executed with precision, would garner them thousands of dollars in a few minutes.

The gunmen knew that every Tuesday an armored car arrived at the ice plant to pick up the weekly earnings. The only trouble was they didn't know at what time it would arrive. The armored car's drivers didn't know either, because their routes were changed each week for security reasons. Until they got into the vehicle and opened their itinerary, they had no idea in which order they would be making their stops.

Assuming that the Rubel plant would be the first stop, the gangsters prepared themselves. Nobody seemed to notice when five extra ice peddlers took up positions around the plant. Across the street by the tennis courts stood one of the plan's originators, John J. "Archie" Stewart, along with former "Legs" Diamond gang member Percy "Angel Face" Geary. Near the loading platform stood John Oley and John Manning, each with a Thompson submachine gun in his cart covered with canvas. Up the street John Oley's brother Francis also was posing as an ice peddler.[1] Geary and the Oleys had worked together before. The previous April 12 they had been indicted for kidnapping John J. O'Connell Jr. (see Chapter 18), a prominent resident of Albany, New York, whom they had snatched the year before and successfully ransomed for $40,000. Around the corner were the two getaway cars, one to carry the money and the other to carry the bandits. One was driven by Bernard McMahon, who, like Geary, was a former "Legs" Diamond associate; the other was driven by Joseph Kress.[2]

A little after noon the armored car passed McMahon and Kress and pulled up to the ice plant. Armored cars of the day were vulnerable when the front door was open, because there was access to the rear of the truck from the passenger compartment. The gunmen knew this, so when one of guards, William Lillienthal, swung the door open and jumped out, the bandits went into action. Before he could close the door, Stewart and Geary, armed with pistols, accosted the guard and led him into the plant's office while John Oley and Manning covered the driver and the guard in the rear of the armored car with their machine guns.

McMahon and Kress quickly pulled up in the getaway cars and started to load the money.[3] It was fortunate for the bandits that the ice plant hadn't been the day's first stop for the armored car. There was so much money inside that McMahon and Kress had to remove the back seat of their car to make room for the hoard. A signal was given and the bandits piled into the cars and took off. They didn't know it at the time, but the take would amount to a little over $427,000. The time it took to get it was just three minutes.[4]

The ingenuity of the robbery itself was reflected in the gang's escape plan. Knowing that the police would have all tunnels, bridges, and ferries from Brooklyn locked down in short order, the bandits knew escaping by car would not be a viable option, so instead they drove nineteen blocks to the Brooklyn waterfront, where two speedboats were waiting. Manning the boats were their owner, former rumrunner Thomas Quinn, and John Hughes and Stewart Wallace. Quinn and Hughes appear to have been brought in on the job because they had the boats, and it Wallace's duty to stay with them to make sure they didn't back out and leave the gang stranded.[5]

The two sedans pulled up, and the money and guns were transferred to the boats. So far lady luck had smiled on the gangsters, but one bandit's fortune was about to take a turn for the worse. As Bernard McMahon was loading a sawed-off shotgun into a boat he bumped up against the side and the gun discharged, blowing off his left kneecap.[6]

Once everyone and the loot were aboard, the boats sped around Coney Island and came ashore at Jamaica Bay in Queens, where two cars and a truck were waiting for them. After the gang was done with the boats, they were taken out into the bay and sunk.[7]

The rendezvous was a boarding house on Manhattan's West Side run by Madeline Tully, the same woman who had harbored Vivian Gordon's killer, Harry Stein (see Chapter 15). The money was transported in the truck along with two of the bandits, one of whom was still toting a machine gun. The money carriers had a moment of anxiety when they heard a police siren behind them and were forced to pull over, but they breathed a sigh of relief when the cops whizzed past them to answer a call.[8]

The gang converged on Tully's rooming house, and Dr. Harry Gilbert, a physician not above catering to the underworld, was summoned for McMahon. The wounded gangster was plied with alcohol to help ease the pain, but after about three days gangrene set in and he died.[9] To dispose of his body the gang obtained a trunk, but McMahon proved too big to fit inside. It was determined that his legs needed to be removed, so with the help of Dr. Gilbert the amputation process began.[10]

As they were cutting McMahon's legs off at the knees, the door buzzer began sounding. One of the gangsters went to check and saw a cop standing in the foyer. The officer was speaking with a woman and accidentally had leaned against the buzzer. The bandit alerted him to the situation and the policeman apologized and left.[11] The gangsters then continued with their gory work. On Monday, August 25, New York became aware of McMahon's demise when a curious pedestrian saw blood leaking from a trunk that had been left on a sidewalk.[12]

Sixty-two detectives were assigned the task of solving what was at the time the biggest cash robbery in history. From the get-go the police said they knew who the perpetrators were and it would just be a matter of rounding them up.[13] This is difficult to believe in view of the fact that they were unable to link McMahon to the job. Their first clues came when they found the boats at the bottom of the bay and were able to raise them.

Even though the boats were registered under a false name, police were able to trace them to Thomas Quinn through "former bootlegging channels." Quinn, however, had skipped town three days after the job was pulled and spent time in West New York and Paterson, New Jersey. Authorities staked out his house and his usual haunts and they finally nabbed him on Manhattan's West Side on November 15. His first words were, "I don't know nothing about this."[14] He admitted that he owned one of the boats and was part owner with Hughes of the other. His alibi was that two men had hired the boats for a fishing a trip. He said that although he was with them, they pulled into shore to get some food and when he came out of a coffee shop he saw his boats leaving without him. The next day he heard about the robbery and his friends had advised him to leave town.[15]

Quinn was held as a material witness, and police once again stated that the gang would be rounded up in a matter of days. But the investigation came to a standstill. After remaining in jail for about five months, he was finally released in March 1935 on $5,000 bail.

Months went by without arrests in the case, and the press let go of the story. The police did have a list of bad guys they wanted to question, however, and on that list was John "Archie" Stewart, one of the planners of the heist. They got their chance nearly two years later when Stewart took part in a botched bank robbery on May 11, 1936, in the upstate burg of Pine Bush. Also taking part in the robbery was fellow Rubel bandit Stewart Wallace and three other desperadoes—"Dutch" Charlie Rickleff, John Mahoney, and a third man who managed to remain anonymous.

After the robbery, state police caught up with the bandits in the town of Wortsboro and a gunfight ensued in which Wallace was wounded and captured. The shootout continued when the four remaining robbers sped off with the police following them. The troopers overtook the bandits' car outside Middletown, New York, and the gunmen escaped into the woods. Stewart and Mahoney stuck together, and Rickleff and the other bandit went their own way.

Two days later a truck driver witnessed Stewart's capture. "I saw two men walking into the road," he said. "They were unshaven and dodged into the bushes when they saw me. A moment later they came out and hailed me for a ride. Just then I saw a car with two troopers coming. I went on a little way and stopped. When the men saw the troopers," the trucker continued, "they ran back in a field of high grass. They [the troopers] shouted at the men to stop, and when the men kept running, the troopers opened fire. Both of the men fell about seventy-five yards away."[16]

Refusing to be taken alive, Mahoney put his pistol to his head and pulled the trigger. With bullets in both legs and a broken hip, Stewart was captured and taken to a hospital where he was kept under heavy guard. New York detectives came out to question him about the armored car robbery but learned nothing. They said Wallace wasn't a suspect in the case.

One of the other bandits who apparently wasn't on the detectives' list of suspects was John Manning. About two months later, on July 9, Manning was walking in East Harlem at 9:20 p.m. when he was shot to death. Though there were several people about, no one claimed to have witnessed the murder.[17] If the police actually did suspect Manning had been a participant in the heist, they kept it mum, as his killing was treated as just another gangland execution.

"Angel Face" Geary and the Oley brothers were hunted by New York City detectives, for the armored car robbery and by federal G-men for the O'Connell kidnapping. After nearly three years the break the authorities were waiting for came on January 20, 1937, when Francis Oley was arrested in Denver, Colorado. Exactly how he came to be captured is in question. New York City authorities said they got the tip from a prisoner at Clinton Prison in Dannemora who was brought to the city to be questioned about another case. Denver authorities, however, stated that Oley was identified by a resident who had seen his picture in a crime magazine. Either way, Oley and his wife were arrested. Oley maintained that it was a case of mistaken identity.

A major clue to rounding up the rest of the gang came when Oley's five-year-old daughter mentioned some letters from Uncle John.[18] Through evidence found in Francis Oley's abode, brother John, Percy Geary, and Harold "Red" Crowley, a gangster who had taken part in the O'Connell kidnapping, were traced to their apartments in Brooklyn. Working together, G-men and New York detectives arrested all three men without any trouble on the same night.

The first one they got was Geary, who was nabbed while walking out of his apartment at approximately 8:10 p.m. on January 31. Oley was taken sometime between 2 a.m. and 3 a.m. His building was surrounded and an agent posing as the building superintendent knocked on his door. Awakened from his sleep, Oley appeared at the door wearing pajamas. Realizing he'd been duped, Oley made a dash for the fire escape, but agents and detectives were there waiting for him. Simultaneously, Geary and Oley's confederate Crowley was also tricked into being captured when a patrolman knocked on his door and told him his car lights were on. When he went outside three plainclothes officers grabbed him.[19]*

The FBI held the gangsters and prepared their kidnapping case, much to the chagrin of the New York detectives who had to admit it would be very difficult to have witnesses from the Rubel robbery identify the gunmen. The feds

---

* Like the apprehension of Harry Brunette three months earlier (see Chapter 21), the capture of Oley, Geary, and Crowley was a combined effort of the G-men and the NYPD. Both sides were complimentary to each other in the press until a few days afterward when the feds refused to turn over the bandits to the police so that they could interrogate them about the Rubel Ice Plant job. After that the police stated that the treatment wasn't fair, considering that they were the ones who had received the tip that led to the arrests.

did, however, allow detectives to bring in Thomas Quinn, who identified John Oley as one of the men who had fled in his boats.[20]

On August 12, 1937, Geary, Oley, and six of their confederates were found guilty in the O'Connell kidnapping case. Geary and Oley were sentenced to seventy-seven years each and shipped off to Alcatraz. Francis Oley had cheated the government out of its victory by hanging himself in prison the previous April 2.

The gangsters appealed their convictions and were sent to the Onondaga County Penitentiary outside Syracuse to await word on a new trial. If their motion were denied, they would go straight back to Alcatraz. Not wanting to leave their fate to the courts, John Oley, Geary, and "Red" Crowley broke out of the Onondaga jail on November 16.

The official version of the breakout was that Geary had managed to saw through his bars and keep them in place with chewing gum. The jail's superintendent said the desperado had let himself out of his cell about 2:45 a.m., made his way upstairs, and hidden while awaiting the night guard making his rounds. As the guard approached, ringing a bell as he did every hour to signal all was well, Geary jumped out with a pistol and said, "Go ahead, ring it." The guard complied. Geary then marched him at gunpoint to the office where the other guards were stationed and told him to call the others and "tell them that Oley is hanging himself." When they rushed out, Geary captured them and took them back to his tier to release Oley and Crowley. The trio helped themselves to whatever money the officers had and forced one of them to drive them to Syracuse.[21]

When word of the escape got out, 350 state troopers surrounded the city as local authorities and a number of G-men—who had been given orders by an angry J. Edgar Hoover to shoot to kill—began the search.[22] The escaped convicts apparently hadn't planned on such swift action by the authorities. Once in the city, they forced a man at gunpoint to drive them out of town. Before they had gone very far they saw a roadblock and made their hostage turn around and take them to his house, where they forced his mother to cook them something to eat. Once sated, the bandits left.

Later that day they took refuge in an abandoned house but were interrupted by a man who was looking it over to rent. According to the man, who was a janitor at a boarding house, the trio surprised him with their guns and one of them said, "We want to get a room." He said that he could fix them up where he lived. "How about eats?" one of them inquired. "I'll get you some eats, too," the janitor promised. He got the escapees situated and brought them some food and booze, that latter of which he partook with them "to give them the idea I would go along." Then he left and went to the authorities to turn them in.[23]

The authorities arrived at the janitor's room and found the key in the outside door and let themselves in. Still eating, Oley and Crowley surrendered without a struggle while Geary leapt out a window and made his escape.

After all the prison staff had been questioned about the breakout, the only statement issued by the state Commission of Corrections said, "We've found a number of discrepancies in the different stories." Back in custody, Oley and Crowley told a different tale about the escape. "It was as easy as getting out of a paper bag,"[24] they said, adding that they didn't actually have any guns but had used pipes, and that Geary never sawed through the bar in his cell but had found one that was loose and was able to break it. The part about the chewing gum was true, though.

FBI Director Hoover was no doubt displeased that the local authorities had captured the men and not his agents. To add insult to injury, Oley said, "These local cops are lots smarter than G-men." In reference to his pal still on the loose, Oley was complimentary yet practical, saying, "Geary, he's the smartest of all, but I imagine we'll be seeing him soon in Alcatraz."[25] Oley didn't realize how soon, for Geary was taken without trouble the very next day when he was found hiding in a parking attendant's booth, bedraggled and unable to walk well because of an injury he had sustained when jumping out of the janitor's second-story window.[26] Both he and Oley were sent to Alcatraz.

With Oley and Geary on "the Rock," the investigation into New York's most famous unsolved robbery once again came to a standstill. Police got the tip they had been waiting years for when in 1938 a prisoner being questioned in Brooklyn said the cops were being "foolish" by questioning him about the small-time crime when he could discuss "bigger things, like the armored car job."[27] Although the convict wasn't part of the gang, it appears that John "Archie" Stewart had done some talking in prison. The Brooklyn hood was pumped for what he knew, and then the authorities went to question Stewart. When they told Stewart another gang member had already squealed, he began to talk. Shortly after interrogating "Archie," authorities flew to San Francisco on October 2 to question Oley and Geary.

After questioning the convicts, the cops picked up Quinn again, along with Dr. Gilbert, the physician who had worked on the doomed McMahon, and Madeline Tully, the underworld landlady who had been released the previous month after serving two and a half years for harboring the Arsenal Gang (see Chapter 23). Stewart made a full confession. Three of the participants in the heist—McMahon, Manning, and Francis Oley—were dead. Manning reportedly was killed because he was angry about how the gang had dealt with his pal McMahon and they were afraid he might squeal.

With Stewart as their prime witness, authorities in New York City were finally able to bring the $427,000 armored car job to a close. Indicted for the robbery were Thomas Quinn, John Hughes (who was indicted in absentia since he was still at large) Stewart Wallace, Oley, Geary and John Kress, who had been arrested since the robbery and was serving a sentence for possessing a machine gun. Madeline Tully and Dr. Gilbert were arraigned as accessories after the crime.

Since Oley's and Geary's terms at Alcatraz were to run until 2014, prosecutors didn't bother with them, leaving Quinn, Kress, and Wallace to face the music. "Archie" Stewart was the star witness, and he gave the inside story of the robbery. In his summation Burton Turkus, Wallace's defense counsel and future Murder Inc. prosecutor, painted the chief witness as "a human cobra if I ever saw one. He says he wants immunity from prosecution for the armored car robbery. He's a liar. He has made a deal to tell this cock-and-bull story to get released from prison where he is serving thirty to sixty years for bank robbery." Quinn's and Kress's lawyers beat the same drum. After thirteen hours of deliberation the jury decided that "Archie" Stewart was indeed telling the truth and found the three defendants guilty.

On July 19, 1939, after nearly five years, Brooklyn authorities were finally able to close the books on the $470,000 armored car robbery when Quinn and Kress were sentenced to ten to thirty years each and Wallace a flat thirty. Or were they? In their haste to solve New York's biggest robbery, prosecutors weren't too particular about who took the rap. After sentencing, Stewart Wallace, who Burton Turkus declared was the victim of lies spewed by "Archie" Stewart, the "human cobra," addressed the court. "I want to make a statement," he said. "I'm guilty of this crime, but these two men [Quinn and Kress] are not. For the record I want to state that there were not ten men involved but only nine, and these men are not two of the nine men who committed this crime. I'll have more to say on that later."[28]

But later never came.

21

FBI vs. NYPD

*"A couple of New York cops could have accomplished
all the federal men did with half the fuss."*
— NEW YORK FIRE COMMISSIONER JOHN McELLIGOTT

During the 1930s the FBI battled hoodlums like John Dillinger, "Baby Face" Nelson, and "Pretty Boy" Floyd, but in the closing days of 1936 Director J. Edgar Hoover found himself in war of words with the Big Apple's police department after he and his New York City office captured a wanted fugitive in a headline-grabbing shootout.

The wanted man was twenty-five-year-old Harry Brunette. Though his criminal career ended on New York's Upper West Side, he originally came from Green Bay, Wisconsin, where he worked briefly as a librarian before becoming, as the FBI labeled him, "one of the most dangerous criminals of his day."[1]

The crime spree that ended in a shootout began on July 12, 1936, when Brunette and his hometown pal and fellow jailbird Merle Vandenbush escaped from an Ohio prison farm where both were serving a sentence for assault to rob. With their newfound freedom the duo returned to their native Wisconsin on August 19 and robbed the state bank at Seymour of $5,600. They followed this with another bank job in the town of Ripon on October 2.[2]

Somewhere along the line Brunette met a young woman from Manhattan named Arlene LaBeau. That fall he and Vandenbush moved to the Big Apple and

hid out in Arlene's Upper West Side neighborhood. On November 11 the desperadoes headed back west with Brunette's moll in tow in a car bearing Michigan
plates. As they sped through Somerville, New Jersey, they caught the eye of State
Trooper William Turnbull, who pulled them over. When the officer approached
the car he found himself facing the business end of a handgun. Relieved of his
pistol, the trooper was bound and gagged and forced into the back seat of the
bandits' car, where they covered him with a blanket and some luggage.

A little over an hour later they pulled over on a quiet road outside Freemans-
burg, Pennsylvania, and released the trooper. The trio then headed to Philadelphia and left their car in a parking garage and stole another for the remainder of
the trip back to Wisconsin. Turnbull hitched a ride with a farmer to the police
department in Bethlehem, Pennsylvania. Since the trooper had been taken
across a state line, the kidnapping became a federal offense and the FBI was
notified. Given some photos to go over, Turnbull was able to identify Brunette
and Vandenbush.[3]

On November 17, six days after kidnapping Turnbull, the bandits robbed a
bank in the town of Monroe, Wisconsin. On Thanksgiving Day, Brunette and his
moll got married and returned to Manhattan, where they rented an apartment.[4]

On December 1 the owner of the parking garage in Philadelphia where the
bandits had ditched their car called the police after realizing the automobile had
been abandoned. The vehicle was turned over to the New Jersey State Police,
and a dusting for fingerprints turned up one of Vandenbush's. More important,
however, authorities found a receipt from a New York City repair shop. The Jersey police's next stop was the 100th Street Police Station, where they asked the
NYPD for assistance in the case. At the repair shop employees identified
Brunette and Vandenbush as owners of the car.[5]

Detectives began to canvass the neighborhood, and since the bandits' car had
Michigan license plates it had been noticed by residents, who told the police it
had belonged to Arlene LaBeau's boyfriend. Arlene's family lived on 105th Street,
and a stakeout was set up that included Trooper Turnbull, who was able to identify Arlene as the woman involved in his kidnapping. Brunette's moll was followed to 102nd Street where she eluded police.

At this point the FBI was brought into the fold, and a door-to-door search for
the fugitives was conducted. A New York detective and New Jersey state trooper
located a rental agent who recognized Brunette's photo and said that Brunette
and LaBeau had rented an apartment posing as Mr. and Mrs. Lake. Authorities
were given access to the building, and men were placed in the apartment above
Brunette's and possible avenues of escape were noted. The cops also began a
stakeout in an apartment across the street.

The NYPD, New Jersey State Police, and the FBI made an agreement regarding Brunette's capture. It was determined that all three agencies would take part

in the bandits' apprehension and that Brunette would be taken to New York police headquarters to be put into lineups to determine whether he had taken part in any robberies in the city. At first the FBI balked at the latter proposal but then acquiesced.

Stakeout reports showed that Brunette slept during the day and stayed up nights. The law enforcement agencies involved decided the arrest would take place at 2 p.m. on December 12, believing the desperado could be taken then without much fanfare or risk to human life. The evening before the arrest two New York detectives and two New Jersey state troopers were on stakeout detail, and at approximately 1:30 a.m. on the twelfth both detectives went to a coffee shop, telling their counterparts to come and get them "if anything breaks."

Moments after they left, J. Edgar Hoover showed up with ten agents, some armed with Thompson submachine guns, and began to surround Brunette's apartment. Shocked that the raid was taking place eleven and a half hours early, the state troopers asked Hoover why he wasn't waiting for the designated hour. The director only shrugged his shoulders and continued about his business. One of the troopers ran to get the New York detectives, but by time they returned it was too late—the federal agents were already involved in a firefight with Brunette.

When the feds knocked on Brunette's door and ordered him to surrender, the bandit answered by firing through the door, which caused the surrounding agents to open up with their machine guns. As bullets flew, a large crowd began to gather to witness what many thought might be another "Two-Gun" Crowley-like spectacle. The New York cops, who were supposed to take part in Brunette's capture, began to arrive but were reduced to crowd-control duty.

Things got more chaotic when an agent threw a gas bomb through a window, starting a fire. Now smoke and bullets were coming out of the windows. After a bit Brunette's door opened and the agents stopped firing as Arlene limped into the hallway with a slight flesh wound to her thigh. One of the G-men picked her up and carried her upstairs, and then the gunfight resumed. Responding to a call about the smoke and flames, the fire department showed up. Hoover told them what was taking place, but the firefighters were determined to douse the flames. The director told them he couldn't guarantee their safety and refused to order his men to hold their fire. Some firefighters gained access to the roof from a neighboring building, but as they made their way downstairs they were stopped by an FBI agent with a Thompson who ordered them to "stick 'em up."

Running low on ammo and trying to avoid the fire, Brunette hid inside a closet. Firemen finally were able to get a hose into the apartment building and went to knock down Brunette's front door, but Hoover reportedly tried to intervene since he wanted his G-men to be the first ones to crash into the apartment. The firefighters prevailed, and moments later Brunette came out and surrendered. "What a brave bunch of guys," the desperado sneered at the agents as they closed in on him.

Not all the headlines Hoover and the FBI received after Brunette's capture were the type the director was seeking. A day after the story broke the *New York Times* reported on its front page that, according to the New York and New Jersey police, the FBI had broken its agreement with them and raided Brunette's apartment so the bureau would get all the glory. The cops also criticized the federal agents' performance, saying that if they had waited until the agreed-upon time Harry Brunette most likely could have been taken without any shots being fired or putting innocent bystanders in danger. They also said there was a chance that if the FBI had not acted so rashly, the lawmen may have been able to capture Merle Vandenbush as well.[*]

Hoover responded that no agreement with New York and New Jersey police had been violated and that the FBI had learned where Brunette was living through other channels. He also said that "emergency circumstances," which he did not specify, forced the FBI to move when it did. Hoping to put the issue to rest, the director reminded everyone that, regardless of the methods used to capture Brunette, the important thing was "this embryo Karpis or Dillinger is in custody," and that the American taxpayers had gotten what they paid for.[6]

However, the situation didn't go away as Hoover wished. The following day New York Fire Commissioner John McElligott and Police Commissioner Lewis Valentine ganged up on him via letters to each other that were released to the media. McElligott fired off his letter to Valentine first, saying in part:

> It occurs to me that members of the New York Fire Department are exposed to sufficient hazards in the line of duty without the added hazard of placing them in the line of gunfire and without adequate defensive equipment. I should say too that the use of a bomb capable of igniting the contents of a building is very short sighted and should be given serious consideration in future activities.[7]

Valentine responded that the commissioner's concerns were justified, adding:

> However, the action referred to was taken without the consent, and as a matter of fact, contrary to plans carefully considered and agreed upon by

---

[*] This wasn't the first time the FBI had received bad press for a seemingly reckless performance in New York City. The previous March 13 agents captured bank robber Eddie Bentz in a Brooklyn apartment house after lobbing a tear-gas bomb into an apartment containing a woman and three children. In all, eight families were affected by the gas. The G-men, however, got their man and the headlines.

the New York police, the New Jersey state troopers, and members of the Federal Bureau of Investigation who were working with us on the case. These plans, if adhered to, I am convinced would have resulted in the capture of the prisoner concerned without unnecessary danger to persons lawfully in the vicinity, law enforcement officials, and the officers and men of the fire department.[8]

I have made it a rigid policy to prohibit melodramatic raids on the hiding places of criminals. They are unnecessary, although they do bring bigger headlines in the newspapers. We [the NYPD] are concerned with capturing lawbreakers and not with publicity. In a matter of departmental routine, members of our force frequently arrest criminals as desperate as Harry Brunette is alleged to be, yet always without fanfare, spectacular or unnecessary gunplay."

Commissioner Valentine cited his department's successful yet uneventful capture of the Arsenal Gang (see Chapter 23) as an example.[9]

By the time the two letters were made public Hoover was already back in Washington. The head of the FBI's New York office, Rhea Whitley, defended his chief by reiterating what Hoover had said about there being no deal and that federal agents had traced Brunette to his hideout, not the local authorities.

Hoover attempted to put the issue to rest by issuing a statement in which he described Valentine's comments as "kindergarten stuff" and said the NYPD had only itself to blame because had the detectives (who went to get coffee) not abandoned their post, they could have been in on the arrest.[10]

22

Messing with the Mob

Not all hoodlums made their living robbing civilians. Some preyed on other members of the underworld. From a criminal's point of view, this avenue of banditry had both positive and negative aspects. On the one hand, you didn't have to worry about the cops poking around, because when gangsters were ripped off they didn't run to the police. On the other hand, underworld denizens settled their own scores and didn't bother with jurisprudence. If you stole from them and they found you, you died.

One group of desperadoes who played this dangerous game evolved in the Bronx and was led by a hot-headed, cocaine-addicted cop-killer named Al Stern. Stern (often Stein) had the appearance of a bookworm and was nicknamed "Teacher." But this moniker was a bit ironic, as both he and his gang proved inept at pulling jobs and lacked knowledge of the underworld—which resulted in half the gang being shot down in the streets by Mafia gunmen.

Second in command was Harold Brooks, known as "the Shake." At thirty-one years of age he was an ex-convict who also dabbled in bookmaking. He had three arrests dating back to 1928 for minor offenses and in June 1931 was arrested in Seattle for robbery under the name of Harry Goodman and sentenced to a term of five to six years. Next he appeared in New York as a policy man and a collector for a shylock ring before becoming involved with Stern.

The gang's first recorded failure occurred on July 9, 1935, when its members tried to rob a gambling resort called the Cloyden Club in Linden, New Jersey. Actually a mansion, the Cloyden Club was in full swing when the hoods pulled up in two sedans. Posing as gamblers, Stern and Brooks made their way to the front door, and when the doorman opened the portal to admit the duo, four more gangsters quickly approached with guns drawn. Realizing what was about to happen, the doorman slammed the door shut as the hoods tried to blast their way inside, wounding the doorman in the process. The casino was prepared for this type of trouble, and guards inside quickly returned the fire, forcing the would-be robbers to beat a hasty retreat to their vehicles and flee the scene empty-handed.[1]

After the Cloyden Club debacle the gang next decided to try its luck at kidnapping. Gang member Benny Holinsky believed he had the perfect victim, twenty-nine-year-old policy racketeer Baptiste "Bart" Salvo, who could likely be ransomed for $25,000. One thing Holinsky didn't know or possibly forgot to mention was that Salvo was a mob guy connected with Vincent "Jimmy Blue Eyes" Alo and Charles "Lucky" Luciano.[2]

On August 19 Brooks, Stern, Holinsky, and gang member Fred Miller drove to a used car dealership on Gunhill Road and White Plains Avenue in the Bronx that Salvo used as a headquarters. They parked near the dealership, and after a while a car pulled up and man stepped out whom Holinsky identified as Salvo. The quartet returned to their apartment and dropped off Holinsky—who wouldn't take part in the snatch because Salvo would recognize him—and picked up the other four members of the gang: Edward Knott, Leo Aaronson, Lewis Ellbrock, and Frank Dolak.

Four of the hoods piled into a Buick and returned to the dealership, followed by the other three gangsters in a Chevrolet truck. They waited about half an hour for Salvo to emerge, and as the racketeer was walking to his car they closed in behind him. Realizing that something was about to happen, Salvo made a dash for his car, but the gangsters grabbed him before he could make it. Salvo put up a fight but was quickly subdued after Brooks whacked him on the head with his pistol butt. The hoodlums quickly loaded the dazed Salvo into his own car, and with Brooks at the wheel they returned to their apartment.

After they unloaded Salvo, Brooks and Aaronson took the mobster's car to the corner of Jerome Avenue and Echo Place, where they called Salvo's partner,

Tommy Milo, from a drugstore and informed him that they had kidnapped his associate and would release him after twenty-five grand was paid. As proof that they had Salvo, Brooks told Milo where he could find his car.

Brooks and Aaronson returned to the hideout and found the gang a bit befuddled because the kidnap victim said he wasn't Bart Salvo. Holinsky was summoned to verify that they had snatched the right man. After Salvo was blindfolded and Holinsky came in and made a positive identification, all were relieved to learn they had indeed kidnapped the right man.[3]

The next day Brooks called Milo to arrange the ransom but was shocked when Milo offered to pay just $1,500 for his associate's return, a far cry from the $25,000 the gang was expecting. Brooks kept Milo on the line long enough to get him to commit to $2,500, then he went back to the hideout and reported to Stern. Upon hearing the news Stern went ballistic and said that if Milo didn't come up with all the money by the next day, they would cut off Salvo's ears and send them to him.

When Brooks called the following day, Milo upped his offer to $5,000, which Brooks refused. Back at the hideout, Salvo, not wanting to lose his ears, begged his captors to give his friends another day to scare up the money. He said if they would let him talk to Milo, he would fix everything.

Stern agreed, but there was a problem. The apartment didn't have a phone, which meant the gang would have to escort Salvo to the drugstore to use the phone there. Despite protestations by Brooks and the rest of the crew, the policy man was taken to the pharmacy by two gang members who followed closely on his hells in case he tried to make a break. Salvo placed a call, then told his captors a substantial payoff would be made the next day. Back at the hideout, Stern agreed to give Salvo's cohorts until the next morning but told Salvo he would be killed if the offer wasn't high enough.

When Brooks called the next day, Milo told him the most they could pay was $9,000. Stern found this acceptable, and a plan was made to exchange Salvo for the money. The bookie was loaded into the back of the Chevy truck with three of the gangsters, while Stern sat up front with Brooks, who was driving. After a while they passed under a bridge on the edge of the Bronx where a car containing a single man was parked. The truck came to a halt, and Stern jumped out and ran back to the vehicle, where the man handed over the nine grand. Stern returned to the truck, and Brooks drove around for another hour before Salvo was released.[4]

Flush with cash, the gangsters went on a spending spree. Brooks, Miller, and Ellbrock all bought new furniture and lived high on the hog for about a week, which was enough time for the mob to learn their identities.

Brimming with success, Stern and his gang began planning their next crime, and on the afternoon of August 30, 1935, Dolak and Holinsky picked up Miller at his apartment to discuss the new job. With Holinsky at the wheel, Miller on the passenger side, and Dolak in the back, the gangsters turned onto Third Avenue in the Bronx and began heading uptown when Dolak announced they were being followed, possibly by cops. Holinsky pulled up to the curb, and when the pursuing vehicle pulled alongside three men armed with pistols jumped out. Miller knew instinctively that the men weren't cops and jumped out of the car, rolled on the sidewalk, then got up and started to run as one of the gunmen fired shots in his direction.

Untouched by the bullets, Miller managed to get away, but Holinsky and Dolak weren't as fortunate. Trapped in the car, they were sitting ducks for the other two gunmen, who shot them both numerous times. The two men lingered in the hospital for a few hours but died without telling the cops anything.

During the investigation an officer who was familiar with the victims knew that Aaronson was a pal of theirs and brought him in for questioning. After enduring hours of the third degree, Aaronson broke down and admitted that he and the two dead men were part of a gang. He went on to name the other members and also said that he felt the shooting was the result of the attempted robbery of the Cloyden Club. The veteran detective, however, knew a mob hit when he saw one and pressed for more info, which wasn't forthcoming.

Now that the police were armed with the names of the surviving gang members, it was a race between them and the Mafia to round up the survivors before the mob could wipe them out. They stopped by Miller's apartment, and he surrendered without any protest, happy that the cops had found him before a hit squad. During the arrest the detective made a mental note of all the new furniture Miller had acquired.

Luck was on Ellbrock's side as well, and he was brought in at about the same time as Miller. Both men gave the attempted robbery at Linden, New Jersey as the probable reason for the shooting of the their partners. The detective in charge still didn't buy it and interviewed some underworld contacts and learned that a policy man had been kidnapped and ransomed the previous week. Remembering the new furniture in Miller's apartment, the detective checked all the furniture stores and learned that Miller, Ellbrock, and Brooks, who was still at large, all had purchased new furnishings.

Working on a hunch, he then went back to Aaronson and told him that he knew all about the kidnapping so he might as well come clean. Once again Aaronson cracked and admitted that the gang had kidnapped a policy guy but he was unsure of his name. A book of mug shots was brought out and he picked out Salvo, who was arrested immediately. Salvo, however, turned out to be no help because he refused to admit he had been kidnapped. He maintained this stance even after Miller and Ellbrock joined Aaronson in singing. Since he refused to admit that he was a victim, the police charged him as an accessory to his own kidnapping and held him on $50,000 bail.

In the interim the mob missed out on another of the gang members. Edward Knott was picked up by authorities in a bar after walking into a trap. He tried to get away but received a superficial gunshot wound to the shoulder.[*] The two remaining gang members, Brooks and Stern, managed to elude police and the mob for a time.[6]

It took over a month but the mob beat the cops to Brooks. They caught up with him in Harlem on October 15. At 12:40 p.m. "the Shake" was loitering about, apparently waiting for someone, supposedly Stern, when a black sedan pulled up and a man jumped out and fired six shots into him. The gunman quickly got back into the car and made a successful escape. Brooks was taken to a nearby hospital and was questioned by detectives regarding the shooting but lived up to the gangster code for the final two hours of his life and disclosed nothing.[6]

For self-preservation Stern moved to Newark, New Jersey. According to witnesses, he had hit rock bottom by his last week. A good Samaritan from Newark said that he saw him on the afternoon of October 20, begging for money on the street and that he was "very pale" and "his face was twitching." The man followed him for a bit and then offered to help him. He said Stern told him that he hadn't eaten or had a place to sleep for several days. When the man offered to help him, Stern reportedly dropped to his knees and begged him to find him a place to sleep. Stern's benefactor took him to a boarding house where he knew the proprietor. He told her about Stern's circumstances and paid for a week's rent. The landlady also described Stern as "pale and shaky." The following day Stern came downstairs and refused breakfast, saying he was on a liquid diet. After that, nobody saw much of him.[7]

With three of his gang dead[**] and the rest in police custody, Stern realized he was at the end of his rope. To make matters worse, the heat was turned up to boiling that week when on October 23 New York gangster "Dutch" Schultz and three of his men were gunned down in a Newark tavern and first reports named Stern as the killer, which lead to his picture being plastered all over the

---

* On January 6, 1936, those in custody for the kidnapping went on trial. Aaronson, the witness for the state, received no jail time. His three cohorts, however, all got fifty years to life, and Salvo, who believed he undoubtedly would be acquitted, was also sent away.

** There were actually two more associates who were killed as a result of the kidnapping: Irving Amron and Abraham Meer. Both were slain September 16, 1935, by Murder Inc. killers as a favor to Alo. The connection to the Salvo case wasn't made until after the Murder Inc. trials of the 1940s.

newspapers. Knowing that no matter who got him first, the cops or the mob, it was certain death—either by legal execution for the killing of the police officer or illegal execution by Mafia gunmen—Stern decided to be his own executioner. On October 24, 1935, he sat in his room and put pen to paper:

> Darling: This is goodbye. Life is not worth living without you. One who loves you more than life.

Below his signature, he added:

> Please take it as I would want you to.
> Remember the lilacs.

He then devised a noose with his necktie, tied it around an open gas jet, and saved the mob the trouble of having to kill him.[8]

DISHONORABLE MENTION
1930-1940

The Out-of-Towner

At 6:15 a.m. on October 7, 1930, a cop walking his beat in upper Manhattan came across a parked car. Knowing it wasn't there when he had passed the same spot thirty minutes earlier, he stopped to inspect it. Peering in the window he saw nationally sought gunman and confidence man Herbert Irving Roberts with bullet holes in his left cheek and left temple. That Roberts knew he was about to die was apparent because his own pistol was next to him with the hammer cocked, but he'd never gotten a chance to fire it.

His criminal record dated back to 1912 when he was first arrested in Seattle, Washington. He racked up a number of arrests on the West Coast before heading east and getting arrested in Cincinnati in 1924 for mail fraud and in Detroit in 1926 for robbery. On February 13, 1927, he and a partner named John Morgan robbed a cafeteria in Richmond, Virginia. While attempting to break into a second safe, however, they were scared off when an electrician showed up to do some work. The police wired their descriptions to the police in Washington, D.C., and the next day both were nabbed at Union Station.

Both men were subsequently sentenced to fifteen years in the Virginia State Penitentiary at Danville. Roberts remained in prison until July 3, 1928, when he placed a dummy in his bed and managed to escape by climbing the wall. Circulars were sent all over the country, but he remained at large until his discovery in the back seat of the sedan.[1]

Detectives linked him with the criminal underworlds in New York, Chicago, and Miami. A key found on the dead man led detectives to an Upper West Side hotel where it was learned that he had checked in with his wife on September 22 under the name of J. A. Rogers. Inside the room they found a large amount of expensive clothing, all of which, including the suit Roberts was wearing, bore labels from stores in Montreal. They also found a set of golf clubs, two pistols, and a fountain-pen tear-gas gun with extra cartridges. Mrs. Roberts was not there, having left the previous week for Chicago. There was, however, a letter from an actress in the city named Shirley LeMon.

Ms. LeMon was brought in for questioning and said she had met the Robertses, whom she knew as the Rogerses, while performing in Miami and a friendship blossomed. The actress told of overhearing a phone conversation between Mrs. Roberts and her husband when they were in Miami regarding a gangster who had just been killed in Chicago, and afterward Mrs. Roberts had said the dead Chicago gangster was one of her former boyfriends. She said she had heard Al Capone's name mentioned as well as those of other gangsters then in the Windy City. Because she feared being "bumped off," after her interview with the detectives she was lowered by a rope from a second-story window of the police station to avoid being seen by newspaper photographers who were loitering in front of the building.

Even though the death car, which was stolen from a man in the Bronx, had been sitting for less than half an hour when found, an autopsy showed that the gangster had been dead for at least eight hours. Roberts's car was discovered in a garage near the hotel where he had been staying, and inside the trunk was a complete set of burglar's tools. Since all his clothing was from Montreal, police believed that Roberts also had been involved in bootlegging with underworld characters from New York, Chicago, and Florida.[2]

Road Kill

Early on the morning of May 9, 1931, the night watchman at the Seeley Bottle Works found a horribly mangled body in front of the plant. The victim had been stabbed in the face, back of the neck, and hands thirty nine times, but death didn't come until he had been thrown into the street and run over a few times with a car. His head and face had been crushed, there was a tire track across his chest, and mutilations on his leg proved that one of the wheels was missing a tire and he'd been run over by the rim. Although the man was known to police, they couldn't identify him because of the severity of the disfigurement. But a check of fingerprints showed the victim was Vincent Gaffney, well known on Manhattan's West Side since the 1910s when he ran with the Gophers gang.

On March 31, 1918, at the age of twenty-one, Gaffney plead guilty to the murder of Charles "Chick" Tucker and was sent to Sing Sing for a twenty-year stretch. Because of a technicality in sentencing, he was sent to the Tombs to serve his time until he could be returned to Sing Sing.

While in the Tombs Gaffney befriended a trusty named John Callahan who had access to all areas of the prison. Callahan informed the Gopher that the bars in the kitchen window on the fifth floor were held in place by only four screws.

Gaffney devised a plan, and during an exercise period he had Callahan sneak him a suit of khaki clothing worn by trusties. He also got the word out to some fellow Gophers to have a car and some guns waiting. On June 12, 1918, at about 3:30 in the afternoon, while all the inmates were heading out to the courtyard for exercise, Gaffney donned the khakis and walked unmolested to the fifth-floor kitchen where he and Callahan removed the bars from the window. Gaffney mounted the sill and leapt over the alleyway, dropping twenty feet to the roof of the women's prison next door. He jumped down another fifteen feet to an extension of that building, made a leap of ten feet to another structure, then finally dropped twenty feet to the sidewalk and got into a waiting getaway car.

The police were oblivious to the escape until Callahan made his jump. He wasn't as athletic as his partner and broke his leg on his first rooftop. Still determined, he made the second jump, but before he could make the third the police had him in their gunsights and forced him to surrender. By this time Gaffney and the other Gophers were racing uptown.

About a half hour after the alarm went out across the city Detectives Patrick Flood and George Whitney, who had arrested the gangster for murder the first time, saw him back in Gopher territory with two others in the getaway car, which had stalled. Gaffney saw the two detectives emerge from a streetcar and immediately pulled out a pistol and started shooting. The detectives returned fire and a running gunfight ensued which resulted in the wounding of two children. Gaffney ran into a tenement and made his way to the roof. The detectives followed and once again the trio exchanged shots. Gaffney ran to an adjoining roof and entered the building, made his way to the backyard, and finally lost the detectives after jumping a fence.[3]

Even though a police dragnet was cast over the West Side, Gaffney managed to escape and stay hidden for over a month, but on July 20 he was traced to a west Harlem apartment. Police were positioned around the building and on the roof, then a detective entered the apartment, where Gaffney was found clad only in his underwear. The wily Gopher wasn't about to surrender, though, and he grabbed his gun and jumped out the window onto the fire escape. An officer on the roof began to fire at him, and the two men exchanged shots until the gangster reached the first story and entered a window. Gaffney jumped into an air shaft leading to the cellar and then miraculously disappeared. The officers had to explain to their superiors and to the public how a man clad only in underwear had escaped from them.[4]

Gaffney managed to elude the police for three months but was finally captured on Saturday, October 19, when police learned he was attending a dance in North Bergen, New Jersey. They followed a girlfriend of his over from New York, and when they knew for sure the gangster was at the dance the officers alerted New Jersey police. Working together, New York and New Jersey authorities set up a cordon of officers outside the dance hall while three detectives went inside.

The cops had a man tell Gaffney that some friends wanted him at the front door, and when the Gopher showed up detectives quickly fell on him and took him into custody before he had a chance to draw his gun. Unexpectedly, the gangster surrendered without a fight and said he was actually glad they had caught him. "Now I can sleep at night," he said. "Ever since I escaped from you in that Harlem flat I have not had a sound night's sleep because I was always expecting some cop to knock at the door and try to shoot me. Now I can sleep, and you can take me back to the Tombs, or Sing Sing, or any other place you want."[5]

Gaffney was given a twenty-year sentence and sent back to Sing Sing where he held considerable sway. Three times he was transferred from the prison, but each time he was able to have himself sent back through political pull. The third transfer was from Dannemora on August 13, 1925, and two days after his arrival Gaffney was the catalyst of a prison riot between rival gangs that resulted in several convicts being injured, including one whose stomach was slashed and another who had part of his nose cut off.[6] Even though he was the cause of the riot, Gaffney was paroled after serving just eleven years of his sentence.

After his release he appeared to go straight. He left the Hell's Kitchen district where he'd spent his youth running with the Gophers, and lived with his new wife and child in Astoria, Queens. Police said, however, that before his murder there were rumors he had opened a speakeasy on the Upper West Side and was trying to muscle in on territory claimed by West Side and Long Island bootleggers.[7]

Judging by the condition of his corpse, it appears the murder was more personal than business. If a rival gangster had wanted him out of the way, a few bullets would have sufficed, but whoever killed Vincent Gaffney seemed to have a score to settle, hence the numerous stab wounds and the use of the car. Two other viable theories are that he was murdered by friends of Charles "Chick" Tucker, whom he murdered in 1918, or by members of the rival gang he'd battled in prison, who possibly were the same men.

Cab Ride from Hell

On August 21, 1931, a run-of-the-mill payroll robbery snowballed into possibly the deadliest firefight ever in New York City when two bandits engaged numerous detectives, patrolmen, and enraged citizens in a motorized gun battle that zigzagged for twelve miles through the Bronx and Washington Heights. Though reports vary, what is certain is that by the time the chase ended eighteen people had been wounded, a third them fatally.

The payroll heist began at 3:45 p.m. when Lloyd Fomnhoff pulled up to the rear of the Mendoza Fur & Dyeing Works with the company's $4,619 payroll. Serving as guard was Officer Walter Webb. As the men were alighting from the car twenty-five-year-old John Prechtl and his nineteen-year-old accomplice Martin Bachorik ran up and demanded the money. Webb went for his gun and was immediately shot down, a bullet piercing his badge and going into his heart.

The bandits forced Fomnhoff out of the car and sped off with it and the money. A short time later, either by design or because of an accident of some sort, the gunmen ditched the car and stole an abandoned taxicab, which they drove to an elevated subway stop. Running up to the station, they hurried back down a few moments later and jumped into a different taxi, this one driven by Herbert Hasse. One witness stated that one of the bandits put his gun to Hasse's neck upon entering the vehicle.

As Hasse's cab sped through the Bronx it caught the attention of motorcycle cop Edward Churchill, who was talking with another cop, Ed Worrell. Churchill gave chase as Worrell looked for a car to commandeer so he could do likewise. As Churchill attempted to pull over the bandit car, the gunmen let loose a barrage that knocked the officer from his bike with a fatal wound. Seeing the murder of Churchill, nearby police and citizens alike began to pursue the bandits. Vincent Hyde, a fireman who had seen the motorcycle officer fall, grabbed the patrolman's gun and opened fire on the fleeing taxi. Moments later the car with Officer Worrell pulled up and the fireman jumped on the running board with him and continued the chase. It was short lived, however, because bandit bullets perforated one of the car's tires and they had to stop to grab another vehicle.

Cab driver William Nugent had begun to follow the bandits and was flagged down by Detective Kily, who jumped onto the running board while another patrolman piled into the back seat. "Now get those bums!" one of the cops told Nugent. Another cabbie, Nicholas Klein, joined in the fracas and followed the bandits until a bullet in the arm knocked him out of the chase. Hasse's cab sped past patrolman Francis McPhillips, who commandeered a cab driven by Jacob Siegel. McPhillips fired at the bandits from Siegel's running board until he was picked off by the gunmen. Another bullet hit Siegel in the arm (or jaw, depending on the source) and he to was knocked out of the pursuit.

Hearing the shooting, patrolman David Lewis stepped into the street with his gun drawn as Hasse's cab approached, but a bullet to the chest (or face, depending on the source) ended his involvement. With bullets flying from a number of cabs, some approaching police weren't sure who the bandits were. At one point a police car joining the pursuit opened fire on Nugent's cab until the detective on the running board and the patrolman in the rear were able to identify themselves.

Hasse crossed from the Bronx into Manhattan and whizzed by yet another patrolman, Michael Lyons, who commandeered a cab driven by Rubin Katz and gave chase as Hasse made his way to Riverside Drive and headed up toward the tip of Manhattan. They reached Dyckman Avenue, took that to Broadway, and headed south before Lyons and Katz were wounded, ending their parts in the drama. After this Hasse seems to have been undecided as to where to go, for he started to circle the same three streets. This allowed the pursuing vehicles and officers on foot to close in. Finally, on the second loop a truck backed out and forced Hasse to stop, at which point the authorities descended on the cab and emptied their weapons. Hasse and Prechtl died at the scene, and Bachorik succumbed en route to the hospital.

After examining the car, police determined the bandits had fired seventy-one shots. In addition to the previously mentioned dead and wounded, a four-year-old girl was killed during the melee and both her parents were wounded. Other injured parties included a thirteen-year-old boy who was shot in the arm, a woman who received a bullet in the leg, and a young lawyer who attempted to chase the bandits but was sidelined after a bullet pierced his windshield and glass cut his face. Not until after the fight did Vincent Hyde, the firefighter who picked up Officer Churchill's gun and joined in the pursuit, realize he was wounded in the chest.

Before the gun smoke cleared, the question arose whether Herbert Hasse was one of the bandits or an innocent man executed by the police. The cops of course swore that he was one of the bandits, and one of the patrolman involved in the final shooting stated he had taken a .32 revolver with all shots fired from the hack's pants pocket. Hasse's wife was quick to jump to his defense. "He was no bandit," she told the press. "He was the best man in the world, the best husband a woman ever had."

What about the .32 pistol police said they found in his pocket?

"He never owned a gun, never. He didn't even know how to shoot one," she replied.

As proof of Hasse's innocence she pointed out their cheap, dingy apartment.

"Surely if Herbert had been a gangster it stands to reason we wouldn't be so poor. Why, I haven't got a cent in the house to buy food for the children (two-and-a-half-year-old Herbert Jr. and his nine-month-old sister, Claire), let alone bury him. Do you think we'd be living in this dump if we weren't poor?"[8]

In the investigation that followed, police admitted there was no conclusive evidence that Hasse had known the bandits or had anything to do with the robbery. They also said it was the opinion of sixteen of the seventeen witnesses questioned (thirteen were civilians) that Herbert had ample opportunity to escape the gunmen. Some witnesses claimed he'd had a chance to get away when the bandits ran up to the elevated train station but had sat there and waited for them to come back down. Other witnesses, however, said the bandits had arrived at the subway stop in another taxi but when they came back down they jumped into Hasse's cab, where the previously mentioned witness stated he had seen one of the gunmen stick his pistol against the driver's neck.[9]

It seems likely that Hasse was not involved and was yet another victim of the gunmen. Chances are the bandits ran up the elevated train to catch a subway train to freedom and when one wasn't to be had they ran back to the street to find an alternative form of escape. They jumped into Hasse's cab and threatened to kill him if he didn't drive. With fifteen people dead and wounded by the time the vehicle finally came to a stop, the police weren't about to give anyone in that cab an opportunity to surrender.

A Bugs' Revenge

Like Herbert Irving Roberts, Robert Carey was an out-of-towner who came to New York City looking for prosperity but instead found violent death. Also like Roberts, Carey had left his mark in other parts of the country. He was originally from St. Louis, where he was a member of that city's premier gang, Egan's Rats, but the entire Midwest was indeed his oyster. Police in Detroit wanted him for the murder of hoodlum Charles "the Rat" Snyder, cops in Toledo wanted him for killing one of their own, and in Los Angeles he was suspected of pulling a train robbery. But it was his role in seven murders in Chicago that would win him infamy.

The Chicago slayings took place on February 14, 1929, and were considered a massacre—the St. Valentine's Day Massacre to be precise. Carey was one of a handful of St. Louis gangsters who took part in the grisly mass killing by, according to police from Detroit, procuring the police uniforms used by the gunmen.

Three years later Carey was on the East Coast with his moll Rose Sanborn working at extortion and counterfeiting. The couple had put in some time in the Washington, D.C., area, where Rose would lure well-to-do men—possibly even two U.S. Senators—into "unspeakable poses" and Carey would take pictures with a hidden camera. The couple moved to Manhattan's Upper West Side with their incriminating photos, 112 to be exact, as well as a printing press that Carey used to produce fake five-dollar bills.

A neighbor in the building saw the "Sanborns" at 11 p.m. on Friday, July 29, 1932, on his way to work. The next morning the neighbor saw the light was still on and thought it odd since it was daytime but didn't act until the following morning when he saw the light still burning. Thinking that something might be wrong, the neighbor got a patrolman and together they tried Carey's front door but found it locked. Across the hall was an empty apartment, so they went through a window and into Carey's apartment.

In the hall next to the bathroom they saw Rose's body. She had been shot three times, in the chest, head, and arm. In the bathroom drooped over the tub was Carey with a single shot to the head. Though a pistol was found at Rose's feet, police declared that it was a murder/suicide.[10] Seven decades would pass before an alternative theory arose.

While researching her books on Chicago North Side gangsters Dean O'Banion and George "Bugs" Moran, author Rose Keefe was able to interview a man who had worked for the gangsters as a truck driver during Prohibition. He mentioned that he had run into an inebriated Moran at a bar one evening in the winter of 1932 and after discussing the victims of the St. Valentine's Day Massacre, Moran mentioned that he had just returned from the coast where he had partly evened the score by taking care of Robert Carey. The former beer runner had never heard the name before and kept the comment to himself until his interview with Ms. Keefe.[11]

See Spot Die

Feared by all, trusted by none, and hated by many." That was the way the *New York Times* described Joseph Leahy, reputedly the last member of the Gophers gang still alive and not in prison (with the exception of Vince McCormick, "Bum" Rodgers's pal, who joined the Foreign Legion to escape the NYPD).

Thirty-six-year-old Leahy, called "Spot" because of his many freckles, had been involved with the Gophers back in the pre-war days and served in a leadership role with Vincent Gaffney. He was arrested for the first time on June 18, 1915, on a concealed weapons charge after a cop noticed a piece of lead pipe bulging under his coat; he received a suspended sentence. He was arrested another twenty-one times for just about everything, including homicide, and although police suspected he had taken part in a dozen murders he only served jail time for five minor offenses.

When Prohibition rolled around, Leahy began selling "cut" gin for $15 a case to cordial shops. He also provided protection to these shops and West Side crap games for $25 a night. His résumé also included performing strong-arm work for mobsters Larry Fay and Owney Madden.

"Spot" carried a gun, but the police said he was more proficient with a knife, or if no weapons were available he would break a glass on a table and use that. Though he wasn't the big shot he pretended to be, the police did agree that he was the toughest man in Hell's Kitchen and that even "Legs" Diamond and Vannie Higgins avoided messing with his alcohol business out of fear.

In addition to being the number-one suspect in the deaths of his wife and mistress, Leahy also was thought to be the killer of the man who supposedly murdered his sixteen-year-old brother, Francis. Francis was reportedly killed in a gang fight in 1925 while "Spot" was in prison. Shortly after his release the man suspected of Francis's murder was himself knocked off.

By 1933 Leahy was living in a $12-a-week hotel called the Manhattan Towers and had been reduced to being a bouncer for several speakeasies. Still playing the big shot, however, he bragged that he was Owney Madden's right-hand man. Of course nobody believed it, but nobody was dumb enough to question him about it either.

The end of the line for the Gopher came on October 1 after a long night of drinking. He was last seen alive staggering around Broadway at 3 a.m. When Bobby Gleason, proprietor of the Tonawanda Social Club, locked the doors to his second-story speakeasy and started down the stairs, he saw Leahy lying at the bottom of the stairwell with his throat slit. Because Gleason's piano player and bartender had left the Tonawanda an hour before the proprietor and the victim was not yet present, the time of death was said to be sometime between 5:30 and 6:30 a.m. Since "Spot" Leahy had such a sordid past and was, as the *New York Times* said, "hated by many," the police didn't even attempt to seek a motive for the murder.[12]

Much Ado About Nothing

On Sunday, March, 15, 1936, New York City was faced with another gangland killing. The victim was a West Side hoodlum named Charles Butler, who was cut down by three shotgun-wielding men in a passing sedan. Not long afterward police got an underworld tip that they might find the killers living in a rooming house on the Upper West Side.

Detectives investigated the tip over a couple of days, and seven of them made their move on the house in the early hours of St. Patrick's Day. The officers staked out the front of the building, and when a couple emerged they swarmed in on them. The two, however, were innocent boarders of the establishment who agreed to let the detectives in the front door. At the inner door the detectives were greeted by underworld landlady Madeline Tully, who had housed Vivian Gordon's slayer, Harry Stein, as well as armored-car bandit Bernard McMahon in his last torturous hours. When asked who was living in the building, Mrs. Tully gave some fake names, which the police didn't buy.

Pushing her in front of them, the detectives went to the first apartment and made the landlady knock, "Who is it?" came a voice from inside. "It's me, Mrs. Tully," she replied. The door was opened and, pushing Mrs. Tully ahead of them, the detectives rushed in with pistols in hand. A total of five men were taken totally by surprise as they sat eating breakfast unable to get to any of the three pistols, two repeating rifles, or three sawed-off shotguns in the room. Across the hall two women were found cooking more ham and eggs. After they were questioned Frank Peraski, the man who opened the door, was sent for. When he entered the kitchen he made a quick dash for the window. One of the detectives saw a .45 on the sill and yelled out a warning to one of his partners who managed to knock the hoodlum out with a single blow of his blackjack. Two more of the gang were arrested in an upstairs apartment without any fuss.

At the station police were able to identify the catch:

- Frank Peraski, 31, said to be both the gang's leader and gunsmith. No prior record.
- Joseph Heel, 32, a record of over a dozen arrest including one for murder.
- Frank Campbell, 26. six arrests, wanted since August 1934 on suspicion for the Rubel Ice Plant robbery.
- Albert Ackalities, Sing Sing alumni with six arrests wanted since June 13, 1935, for parole violation.
- Michael Kane, 23, four arrests. Suspect in a murder and was wanted in both New York and New Jersey.
- Joseph Devine, 33, five arrests. Was sentenced to Sing Sing in 1928 for ten to thirty years for homicide.
- John Ryan, 42, half a dozen arrests going back to 1914. Also a Sing Sing alumni, he was arrested twice in his career for impersonating a federal officer. Like Kane and Ackalities, he was also a "wanted" criminal since 1931.
- The two women arrested cooking for the gang were Peraski's wife Mary and his sister Jean Martin. Mrs. Tully was also brought in.

The aforementioned weapons found in the apartment were only a portion of the gang's arsenal. A safe belonging to the hoodlums was found in a third-floor closet, and when it was opened the authorities were shocked to find four machine guns, another repeating rifle, two automatic pistols, a hand grenade, 10,000 rounds of ammo. As a result, the press dubbed the captives "the Arsenal Gang."

Police Commissioner Valentine described the hoods as a "desperate mob" and assured the city the arrests were the "most important since the taking of the

Whittemore Gang" and that they "prevented a series of the most bloody gang killings." Police Inspector Kear said he was "morally certain" the Arsenal Gang had murdered Charles Butler over the hijacking of a fur truck and also laid a number of robberies in several surrounding towns and states at the gang's feet.

Moral certitude and accusations aren't enough to put people in prison, so in the end New York put the gangsters on trial for possessing a machine gun. Prosecutors felt that was the safest option for getting them behind bars, and it proved to be so. Six of the gunmen received seven- to fourteen-year sentences. Kane got off with a three and half to seven years, while Devine had twelve years added to his sentence for a previous homicide charge. Both Jean Martin and Mary Peraski were sent to the Bedford Hills Prison for Women for one and half to seven years and two and a half years respectively.

Mrs. Tully pleaded that she was a victim of circumstance and had no idea that her lodgers were a mob of desperadoes. She maintained this stance even though a Christmas card sent to her by Vivian Gordon's murderer, Harry Stein, was found in the same safe that contained the gang's arsenal.[13]

Gangster Holiday

A gang of seven desperate gunmen from New York's West Side were hiding out at a cottage along the Pequannock River in Mountain View, New Jersey, and on June 23, 1935, were captured as a result of their own amusements.

The gang included, John "Peck" Hughes and Edward Gaffney, who police erroneously believed had orchestrated the $427,500 Rubel armored car robbery of 1934, and twenty-six-year-old Louis Balner, reportedly a onetime member of Detroit's infamous Purple Gang. The gang also consisted of twenty-eight-year-old gunman Joseph McCarthy; Arthur "Scarface" Gaynor, arrested ten times since 1922 for robbery and murder; twenty-nine-year-old James "Ding Dong" Bell, who was nursing a bullet wound to his shoulder and had been shot and wounded on two other occasions in New York City; and Frank Fox, who although he didn't have a record, admitted to his participation in a kidnapping.

The gangsters spent most days swimming, canoeing, sunbathing, and racing around in their vehicles, which neighbors found most bothersome. For the most part their neighbors considered them polite fellows if not a little rambunctious and devilish. In one instance they "borrowed" some cement blocks from a neighbor's house to build a barbecue pit, and when the neighbor protested they apologized so sincerely that she allowed them to keep the blocks as long as they promised to return them when they were finished. The hoods used another neighbor's driveway as a shortcut to their cottage, and when he complained they once again offered sincere apologies and took to making their own crude entrance.

But it was the racing of cars that drove the neighbors crazy and eventually led to the gang's capture. The gangsters would apologize whenever they received a complaint about the racing and refrain from doing so for a short period. But they continued to speed about, and finally one neighbor mentioned it to a local policeman making his rounds. The officer went to the cottage and took down the license plate numbers of the three vehicles—a Studebaker, a Dodge, and a Ford truck.

A check of the plates showed that the ones on the Studebaker and Dodge had been reported stolen. The Studebaker also fit the description of the car involved in the shooting death of James Gaynor, the younger brother of gang member Arthur "Scarface" Gaynor, who had been killed the previous March in Hoboken. The Dodge fit the description of a car that had been used in a number of New York City crimes, and even the Ford fit the description of a truck that had been used in a $50,000 fur hijacking.

Two New Jersey state troopers began to stake out the cottage, and after a few days they called in four New York detectives who joined the watch party and immediately recognized a number of the hoodlums. The lawmen studied the comings and goings of the gang for about two weeks and devised a plan to arrest them all early on Sunday morning, June 23.

As the gangsters spent that Saturday night in the cottage playing cards, seven sedans containing thirty-two police officers pulled up. The cops, most armed with rifles, surrounded the house while two sharpshooters were placed on the far side of the river to thwart any attempt at an escape by boat. The card game broke up in the early morning hours of June 23, and all the gangsters went to bed except Balner, who was given guard duty. As his buddies fell off to sleep the former Purple Ganger stepped out onto the screened porch and began a game of solitaire with his rifle at hand. As the minutes ticked away Balner had a hard time staying awake and finally, a few minutes before 5 a.m., his head dropped for the last time and he was sleeping as soundly as the men he was supposed to be protecting.

Seizing the opportunity, the police crept up and removed some screens to the house and entered. Not wanting to take any chances they knocked out Balner with blow to the head with a pistol butt. Then they entered the two bedrooms where the rest of the gang was sleeping two to a bed and woke them up, shouting, "Stick 'em up! It's the police!" The groggy gangsters quickly responded with, "Don't shoot! Don't shoot!" and surrendered without a fight.

The cottage next door was raided, and George Maiwald and his wife were also arrested. Maiwald had a record dating back to 1924 and was said to be the man who set the gangsters up with the cottage and took care of the place for them.

The arsenal the police uncovered was quite impressive and included a Remington and a Winchester rifle, three .38's of various makes, a .45 inscribed with "I will right all wrongs," two .32 Smith and Wesson revolvers, a Savage automatic pistol, two Luger automatic pistols with elongated barrels, a tear-gas gun complete with tear gas, and, more disturbingly, mustard-gas bombs. There was also enough TNT to blow up a large building.

Once in custody the gang was separated and questioned relentlessly while ballistic tests were done on the firearms in the hope that some murders might be solved, namely the killings of Thomas Protheroe and George Keeler. Although the high-profile murders the police were hoping to clear up remained unsolved, two murders that went unnoticed by the press were cleared off the books: James McCrossin, who was shot in his car at Twenty-fifth Street and Second Avenue on December 20, 1934, and John Adobotto, who was killed the previous February on the corner of Washington and Houston streets. Armed with this knowledge the police went back to the gangsters, and two of them, whom the authorities didn't name, made full statements.[14]

Disgruntled Co-Worker

Like any occupation, banditry can bring together two personalities that just don't click. Such was the case with the gang of robbers who had the audacity to attack a department store during business hours.

The gang probably consisted of five men, possibly a few more, but subsequent events would lead to the naming of only four of them. The leader of the gang was Isador Lipschitz, who, by the end of 1936 was the subject of a wanted flyer for his participation in a restaurant holdup. Lipschitz's record went back to at least World War I when he went AWOL. He was arrested in Paris following the Armistice and sent to the jail on Governor's Island from which he escaped. Recaptured, he was sent to Leavenworth for seven years.

Another member of the gang was Fred Dunn, who had several arrests dating back to 1922 when he was arrested at the age of fourteen and spent six months in the Washington State Reformatory. Six more arrest would follow in as many cities around the country. The first was in Indianapolis in 1924 when he was arrested for grand larceny. Next he was arrested in Seattle and served another six months. Nineteen twenty-eight found him in San Quentin after being apprehended in Los Angeles for grand larceny. He served a year and headed east where he was arrested for the same thing in Newark, New Jersey, in 1932. His sentence was suspended, and he was later captured in Queens for grand larceny and served more time. In June 1936 he was seized in New York City by the Treasury Department for counterfeiting but was out of prison by the end of the year.[15]

As 1937 rolled around, Dunn was living on the Upper West Side with his teenage wife, Sally. The two had met in Sally's hometown of Williamsport,

Pennsylvania, where the gang would sometimes stay. The couple lived in the building's basement apartment, but Fred introduced two gang members to the super who then rented them a room on the main floor on Christmas Day. This room became the rendezvous for the gang for the upcoming robbery.

The target was Barney's Department Store in Manhattan's Chelsea district. In addition to Lipschitz and Dunn, the gang included Dunn's friend Larry "La La" Mullins and Michael Prochorchick. There was at least one other man and possibly one or two more. At about 8 p.m. on January 2, the gang entered the store, leaving one man at the front door to stand guard. Two gangsters went straight to the cashier's office and proceeded to rob the safe and take the company payroll as well as keep the cashier away from the switchboard so no calls could be placed from the store.

Counting employees and customers, there were approximately a hundred people in the store. While the cashier's office was being looted the rest of the gang, consisting of at least two men with machine guns, proceeded to herd all the shoppers and workers to the back of the store. Most people were unaware there was a robbery in progress until they either saw a guy with machine gun coming through the racks of clothes or heard one of the gunmen, most likely Dunn, yell, "This is a holdup. Get in back and don't anybody make a false move or you will get plugged."[16]

The store's proprietor, Barney Pressman, was in the back and oblivious to what was going on until his wife came back and told him they were being robbed. "Impossible," he said, and went to see what all the fuss was about. He ran into Dunn, who, angered that he was going in the wrong direction, kicked him in the shins and ordered him to the rear of the store with the others. When everyone was in the back Dunn started to rob each individual. While he was helping himself to wallets, jewelry, and anything else of value, Lipschitz came up and yelled at him, "Didn't I tell you to let the little stuff alone? We're after the big dough."[17] Soon the bandits were gone. The entire episode lasted about eight minutes.

The gangsters returned to their Upper West Side rendezvous to split the loot. When they entered the room they turned on the radio at high volume so neighbors couldn't hear them speaking. The dough was tossed onto a table, but it only amounted to $700. Immediately accusations were made that somebody was holding out. Moments later the building's super heard shooting over the sound of the radio. As he was walking down the stares to investigate, he saw three men hastily leaving the apartment. He went down and looking in saw "La La" Mullins sitting in chair trying to stem the flow of blood was from his face. "Get a doctor," Mullins muttered. The super ran to the street to get help, and when he returned "La La" was gone but he found Dunn dead on the floor with a single shot through his heart.[18]

The cops arrived and found some of the money and checks taken from Barney's. Since Dunn lived in the basement, they waited for Sally to come home. When she arrived she was taken into custody and under questioning was able to name the other three members of the gang. In discussing Lipschitz she said, "He had a terrible temper and he'd fly off the handle for no reason at all. I think they got into an argument over the money, but I really don't think Fred was killed deliberately." She also gave them a sound tip: Lipschitz and Prochorchick had dates that weekend in Williamsport.[19]

The New York police alerted authorities in Williamsport that the wanted robbers might be there. Sure enough, they heard back that Lipschitz and Prochorchick were staying at a hotel in town. A carload of detectives was sent at once. A stakeout of the hotel was set up, and the cops watched as the bandits stepped out and entered the diner next door. The detectives followed them inside with their guns drawn and the duo surrendered without trouble.

Lipschitz was found with a little less than $700 and said that was all the gang had stolen (Barney's claimed about $11,000 in cash and another $6,700 in jewelry had been taken). Other than that, he said no more. Prochorchick stated that Dunn was killed when an argument broke out about the small amount of money, but he added that he was in the bathroom at the time and hadn't seen who did the actual shooting.[20]

After the double arrest the story was forgotten. Seeing that there was still about $17,000 unaccounted for, it may have been a happy ending for the unknown fifth gang member.

Pesticide

On December 8, 1939, thirty-two-year-old David Beadle, known along the West Side waterfront as "the Beetle" and "the Brow," walked into the Spot bar on the corner of Forty-sixth Street and Tenth Avenue and ordered a glass of water. He had a headache and needed something to wash down an aspirin. "The Beetle" had grown up in the Hell's Kitchen district and prior to Repeal in 1933 was a rum-runner, but by this time he had moved into the dock rackets. And while he continued to "work" on the mean streets of his youth, he now resided in Queens.[21]

Violence was nothing new to Beadle. His reputation was made on April 25, 1930, when he took on the Lawlor brothers, and not since the Daltons were shot to pieces in Coffeyville, Kansas, have three brothers fallen so fast before an enemy's gun. The Lawlors, however, were not trying to rob a bank when they were gunned down, not that they were above robbing and killing. The brothers had police records and were not unfamiliar with prison, but they were actually toiling in the Hell's Kitchen speakeasy owned by their brother-in-law Bartley Cronin.

The youngest, twenty-three-year-old Lawrence, was behind the bar when "the Beetle" entered and began waving a pistol around. Knowing the violent history of the Lawlor brothers, the customers began to inch their way to the door as Lawrence began to chastise Beadle. "The Beetle" began gloating about his toughness, which enraged Lawrence even more. Finally the youngest Lawlor could take no more and came out from behind the bar and went for the gunman. Beadle shot the young man in the heart, and he dropped in the doorway between the bar and the back room.

Hearing the shot, brothers Michael and William came out of the rear room and, seeing their prostrate brother, jumped over him and rushed Beadle, who quickly fired another fusillade, of which three bullets found their mark. Michael was struck in the head and chest and William was critically wounded in the stomach. Beadle made a hasty exit but was later picked up by the police. Lawrence was dead before the authorities arrived, and thirty-year-old Michael, known as "Bootsy," who had been questioned as a suspect in 1921 during the Hoey case (see Chapter 13), died at 11:15 p.m. in Bellevue Hospital. William was taken to Roosevelt Hospital, where he wasn't expected to survive. He refused to answer any questions, which didn't surprise the police, because on the previous August 23 he had been shot in the groin and refused to say anything.[22]

Over nine years later "the Beetle" stood at the bar washing down an aspirin. When he finished he stepped back out onto Tenth Avenue where his brother was waiting. He had only gone a few steps when four men walked up to him and one of them fired five shots into his body. Three men were eventually arrested for the murder but were exonerated. "The Beetle" simply took his place in the lexicon of murdered waterfront thugs.

We Only Kill Each Other (Most of the Time)

We only kill each other." So said Benjamin "Bugsy" Siegel to a contractor who was afraid to work with the mobster for fear of being put on the spot. Siegel's reply wasn't entirely true, however, as evidenced by the murders of five men, none of whom were members of organized crime.

Gerard Vernotico and Antonio Lonzo appear to have been members of a small-time gang of robbers, but both were killed not for being involved in crime but because Vernotico happened to be married to a woman coveted by Vito Genovese, the second-most powerful gangster in New York, if not the country.

Vito was head over heels in love with Vernotico's wife, Anna, and the two were most likely having an affair. Perhaps Anna was old-fashioned and didn't believe in divorce, or maybe Vito just didn't want to wait for one. Whatever the reason, Genovese put out a contract on the small-time desperado and it was carried out on March 16, 1932, by Mafia soldiers Petey Muggins and Michael Barrese.[23]

Vernotico and Lonzo were bludgeoned over the head and then strangled with clothesline in a third-story apartment at 159 Prince Street. Their bodies were dragged to the roof of an adjoining building at 124 Thompson Street, where they were subsequently found. A blood trail led back to the murder apartment, where police found some papers burnt in the sink, more bloodstains, and a crowbar. Police said a witness had heard fighting in the apartment earlier that morning, but no other information was forthcoming.[24]

Twenty-eight-year-old Vernotico had a record dating back to 1917, and Lonzo was out on bail with an assault and robbery case pending against him. Both men had been acquitted the previous April on grand larceny charges. Twelve days after the murder Anna and Vito were married.

The murders of Vernotico and Lonzo are discussed in the book *The Valachi Papers*, and mob turncoat Joe Valachi gives the reason for the killing. Also in the book Valachi discusses the first contract he was given as a member of Charles "Lucky" Luciano and Vito Genovese's crime family. It was to bump off a twenty-two-year-old nobody named Michael "Little Apples" Reggione.

One of six brothers, "Little Apples" was not a big underworld power. In fact, his sole jail sentence was handed down on January 9, 1930, and that was for third-degree robbery. But unfortunately for him, according to Tony Bender, Valachi's lieutenant, he was the younger brother of two men who had messed with Luciano and Genovese a few years earlier and were knocked off as a result. And now that "Charlie Lucky" and Vito were at the top of their power, they didn't want to take a chance that Reggione, recently released from the prison in Elmira, New York, would attempt to avenge his brothers.[25]

Genovese gave the contract to Bender who in turn handed it over to Valachi. Valachi learned that Reggione hung out at a certain coffee shop in Harlem, so he began stopping by the place and eventually started talking to the twenty-two-year-old ex-convict. After a few days Valachi hatched a plan to eliminate "Little Apples" under the pretext of going to a crap game. On the evening of November 25, 1932, Reggione was lured to a tenement not far from the coffee shop where two of Valachi's buddies, Petey Muggins and Johnny D, were waiting.

Reggione was walking in front of Valachi and when he entered the building two bullets ripped into his jaw and another tore into his neck. When the police found him he was still clinging to his cigarette holder, which contained a smoldering cigarette.[26]

The death of Michael Reggione has been written off as an insurance hit for Luciano and Genovese; however, although two of his brothers were gunned down, the murders didn't take place until *after* "Little Apples" was slain.

When Michael's death was covered in the press there was no mention of any of his brothers being killed. In fact, two of them, James a.k.a. "Chip Chip," and Louis, who went by "Fat Elevator," were in prison at the time of his murder.

James was about thirteen years older than his brother Michael, and had racked up a total of eleven arrests dating back to 1905. He did jail time for various burglaries and robberies and in 1926 was sent to Sing Sing for a term of fifteen years after a robbery conviction. He was serving this term when Michael was killed. After serving eight years of this sentence James was paroled around December 1934.

On May 23, 1935, the thirty-eight-year-old ex-con left his home and journeyed to lower Manhattan, where he stopped at a relative's home and asked his twelve-year-old niece to go for a walk with him. The two went to a place, and James asked his niece, Mary Sedano, to go inside and ask for a man named Eddie Bow. His niece complied and upon entering the establishment was told that Bow wasn't there. She then went back to her uncle and the two began to head up town. As the two passed a vacant lot containing a billboard, a gunman jumped out from behind the sign and started blasting away at James. According to Mary, her uncle quickly pushed her aside and began to tussle with the gunman but quickly collapsed after sustaining three bullet wounds. Chances are Reggione knew he was in trouble and that was why he had picked up his young niece, hoping that a gunman wouldn't attempt anything while he had a child in tow.

In the news stories following James's death, mention was made of his brothers Michael and Louis, who was serving time in Atlanta, but there was no mention of any other brothers who had been killed before Michael, just as there were none mentioned when "Little Apples" was put on the spot.[27]

The same month that Gerard Vernotico and Antonio Lonzo were killed thirty-nine-year-old Louis "Fat Elevator" Reggione was convicted of counterfeiting and shipped off to prison. After serving eight years he was paroled from the federal penitentiary at Lewisburg, Pennsylvania, in April 1940 and returned to Manhattan. Four months later, on August 26, he was walking in Little Italy with his brother Joseph. It was just before 2 a.m. when two men who had been following them fired eleven shots at the pair. Five found their mark in "Fat Elevator," and he dropped dead into the gutter.

The day after the murder the press mentioned that Louis was the brother of the previous slain Michael and James, but just as when the latter two were killed, there was no mention of any other Reggione brothers being murdered. In fact, the *New York Times* stated their were six Reggiones, the three deceased and Joseph, who was with Louis when the latter was killed but didn't appear to be a target himself, and brothers John and Tom, who were incarcerated at the time.[28]

Given what is now known about the Reggiones, the question begs to be asked: Why was twenty-two-year-old Michael "Little Apples" Reggione killed in the first place? Even though Genovese told Bender that Reggione was the brother of two men he [Genovese] and Luciano had murdered, that appears to have been fictitious, since he was the first of three brothers to be put on the spot.

The answer to the question may lie in the murders of Gerard Vernotico and Antonio Lonzo. In 1932 "Little Apples" lived at 125 Thompson Street, which would have been directly across the street from No. 124, where the bodies of Vernotico and Lonzo were found. *The Valachi Papers* states that Petey Muggins, one of the murderers of the two men, told Valachi there had been some witnesses but they had been "straightened out."

Is it possible that Michael knew something about the murder or was somehow involved, or more likely, was "Little Apples" a member of the murdered duo's robbery gang, and Vernotico and Lonzo were the "brothers" Genovese was talking about? After all, Harlem is a long way from Thompson Street, so Michael was avoiding his neighborhood for a reason. This scenario seems plausible, seeing that Genovese didn't want to advertise the fact that he had murdered two guys in order to get married. So, not wanting to take a chance that Reggione wouldn't avenge his partners, he concocted the story about the brothers as the reason to have him hit. James and Louis Reggione, on the other hand, may have fallen victim to the insurance hit, considering that they were both killed shortly after leaving prison.

APPENDIX I

And in the End ...

Chapter 1 / "Gentleman Gerald" and the Dutchman

The night of the Hance murder, Charles "One Armed" Wolfe was arrested at his mother-in-law's house and carted off to jail. On November 19, 1925, he was convicted of murder in the first degree and received a life sentence and was shipped off to the Indiana State Prison to serve his term.

❧

After serving more than four years in prison, Walter Shean was paroled on May 2, 1929, and apparently managed to stay out of trouble after that.

❧

Frank Grey, Chapman's accomplice in the escape from the Atlanta Federal Penitentiary, finished his sentence and returned to New York City. A career criminal, Grey, whose real name was probably Shaeffer, spent time in a number of the Empire State's penal institutions. In 1911 he was convicted of grand larceny and sent to the prison at Elmira. Two years later he was sent to Sing Sing for two and half years for burglary. Nineteen sixteen found the crook in the New Jersey State Penitentiary for blowing a safe in Newark.

On August 7, 1929, Bronx detectives were making the rounds for known criminals and suspicious persons when they ventured into what they called a "meeting hall" of gangster "Dutch" Schultz (true name Arthur Flegenheimer). Inside they found Grey, another hoodlum named Abraham Grout, and the Dutchman himself, and all three were taken into custody. Schultz was released on $1,000 bail, but Grout and Grey were held, the latter being wanted in the Big Apple for pick-pocketing and in Newark for forgery.

Grey next popped up on January 7, 1934. He and another guy were standing in front of a bar on Manhattan's West Side when, at 2 a.m., a taxicab pulled up containing a number of gunmen who opened fire on the duo. Grey and his pal took off running while the cab followed them and the gunmen continued firing. After a brief chase Grey pitched forward on the sidewalk while his buddy continued running. With Grey down the taxi took off and disappeared into the Broadway traffic.

When the coast was clear, people came out of their hiding spots as well as restaurants, nightclubs, and other buildings and gathered around Grey. They rolled him over and it appeared he had fallen and cut his head and was unconscious. An ambulance was called and the crowd was told that what they thought was a cut was actually a bullet wound and that the man was dead. An examination showed he had also been hit under the left armpit.

What Grey was involved in is unknown, but when killed he was "shabbily dressed" and only had a few dollars on him. At the end, his record listed fourteen arrests and five convictions.

After escaping from Atlanta with "Dutch" Anderson, Ludwig "Dutch Louis" Schmidt went his own way. On April 16, 1924, he and three confederates were attempting to rob a freight train in Newburgh, New York, when a railroad detective came across them and a shootout ensued. "Dutch Louis" was hit three times, and his pals drove off leaving him to his fate. He was captured and hospitalized and after about a week his true identity was learned and he was sent back to the Atlanta Federal Penitentiary.

"Dutch Louis" finished his term at Atlanta on October 8, 1931. He was immediately rearrested by immigration officers who were working to have him deported to Germany. The deportation didn't come along soon enough, however, because about eight months later he and four others attempted to rob a garage in Knoxville, Tennessee, and he was once again shot by a cop. After this encounter, "Dutch Louis" faded into history.

Chapter 2 / Let's Misbehave
Shortly after arriving at Sing Sing, Ed was allowed a transfer to Auburn Prison so he could be closer to Cecilia. Once there he was given a job working on an embossing machine making license plates. On August 21, 1924, his hand got caught in the machine and he lost four fingers. Eventually he would have to have his entire hand amputated. Ed's health problems didn't end there, though. The years went by and he was once again transferred, this time to Clinton Prison in Dannemora, where he contracted tuberculosis and spent the remainder of his time in the T.B. ward.

Aside from Ed's health issues, the Cooneys' imprisonment passed uneventfully, and with time off for good behavior both were paroled in late 1931 after serving seven years. At first they went to stay with Ed's mother, but around Christmas of that year Ed received $12,000 from the state as a result of the accident that had cost him his hand. With their newfound wealth the Cooneys moved to the suburbs of Long Island and started a family. They had two sons, Ed Jr. and Patrick. All was going well until Ed's tuberculosis crept back into the picture. Most of the money they had left went toward his medical bills and was long gone by time the disease claimed him on May 30, 1936.

Chapter 3 / Ma Flanagan's Boys
Gang member John Little was a lifelong criminal whose recorded crime career began in 1913 when at the age of twelve he was arrested for burglary and sent to the Elmira Reformatory. The following year he was sentenced to six months for petty larceny. He was discharged on an attempted robbery charge in May 1916 but still hadn't learned that crime doesn't pay, because just three months later, on August 25, he was arrested for robbery and sent to Sing Sing for a five- to ten-year stretch.

After being shot in the mouth during the Phipps holdup, Little was sent to the hospital ward at Bellevue where on January 10, 1922, he and two other inmates sawed through the bars in the ward and slipped into the hospital courtyard, where they were met by two gangster colleagues and ushered into a waiting taxi that had been commandeered at gunpoint. A statewide manhunt commenced, but Johnny was able to elude capture for five months before finally being nabbed in Newark, New Jersey.

Little was sentenced to fifteen years at New York's Clinton Prison where he eventually became a trusty and received a job in the boiler room, which allowed him access to the prison yard.

One night in early June 1928 while working the late shift, Little made his way into the yard with an improvised ladder, scaled the prison wall, and fled into the woods. This escape only netted him ten days of freedom, however, and soon he was back inside with a new life sentence.

Amazingly, Little was put back to work in the boiler room and began to serve his time not realizing that another attempt at freedom, albeit legal, was just around the corner. In July 1929 a riot broke out in the prison, and during the melee marauding inmates charged the boiler room in an attempt to blow up the equipment. Little and three others held them at bay until the riot could be quashed. Because of their bravery in the face of danger, Governor Franklin D. Roosevelt pardoned the four convicts on July 16, 1930, saying, "I am commuting the sentences of these four men, solely as a reward for services rendered by them during the riot at Clinton Prison. Such assistance to the state and to the forces of law and order not only entitles these men to consideration from the state but indicates a desire on their part to become useful members of society." So Little was once again back on the streets of New York.

It appears Little recognized what a good break he got and attempted to stay out of jail. He began singing at saloons and actually did some minor radio work, resulting in the sobriquet "Singing" John Little, but found himself in police hands once more when he was arrested on November 19, 1930, for carrying a gun but managed to have the case dismissed.

After his last run-in with law nothing was heard of Little until April 19, 1931, when his body was found in Queens with two bullets in the head. The police determined he had been killed in Manhattan and then dumped in Long Island City amid the many warehouses. Though they had no actual proof, police were confident that he was killed as a result of his participation in quelling the riot at Clinton.

Chapter 4 / Two Worthless Diamonds
After Nick "Cheeks" Luciano, the man who ratted out the Diamond brothers and John Farina in the West End Bank job, perjured himself in Farina's retrial he was sent to Sing Sing for about three years and released sometime in 1929. Fearing the friends of the men he'd testified against, Luciano understandably kept clear of his old haunts in New York and lived in Bayonne, New Jersey. His existence in New Jersey, however, was a lonely one and against the advice of his parents he started once again to hang out in the Big Apple.

On Sunday night, December 7, 1930, Luciano was invited to a small dinner party at a grimy Lower East Side restaurant. His parents pleaded with him not to go, but after nearly a year of seclusion in Bayonne, Luciano gladly accepted the invitation. The party, consisting of four other men and three women, was going well and all seemed to be having a good time when at 4 a.m. an undetermined number of men entered the restaurant and made their way to the back room where Luciano and his cohorts were having their fun. The men approached the party and pulled out pistols. Knowing Luciano's history, the men and women who were a moment before partying with him all quickly vacated the premises and left "Cheeks" to his fate. Once they had him isolated, the gunmen opened up and perforated the squealer with twenty bullets, bringing closure to the West End Bank debacle that had begun seven years earlier.

Chapter 6 / Bum, Ice Wagon, and Killer LLC
With Rodgers behind bars and Cunniffe dead, the only participant from the Welfare Island prison break still at large was Vincent McCormick. Because of the company he kept, police believed he was involved in the Elizabeth, New Jersey, job and redoubled their efforts to locate him. Their search came to and end in late October 1928 when it was discovered, through a letter to a girl, that the bandit had joined the French Foreign Legion and was currently in Morocco. A spokesman for the Legion informed detectives that it was their policy not to ask questions of its soldiers or give out information about them. In short, no, they could not have him back.

After the Elizabeth mail truck job, two of the perpetrators were arrested on other charges. Canice Neary was picked up for carrying a gun on January 14, 1927, and sent to Welfare Island, and William Fanning, arrested on the same charge, was serving a seven-year stretch in Brooklyn when detectives had their first breakthrough. Frank "Ghost" Kiekart was traced to a Baltimore boarding house and arrested on December 7, 1927. While in custody he spilled the beans about the Bellmore Bank job of 1924. Shortly after this, police acting on "an anonymous" tip picked up Ben Haas in Weehawken, New Jersey, just as he stepped off the ferry.

Over the next few months Haas and Kiekart, looking at a murder charge, began to cut a deal for themselves and word made its way back to Neary, who then decided to make like Rodgers, Cunniffe, and McCormick before him and escape from the island. Like his predecessors, Neary was also a trusty working in the hospital area. At some point between 7 and 9 p.m. on May 2, 1928, he disappeared. It was thought that some accomplices had come by in a boat and picked him up. Police mentioned that he always had large sums of money but denied the rumor that he was allowed free run of the island.

Neary brought about his own downfall when four months later, on September 10, 1928, he and two companions were speeding in Manhattan and their car collided with a hearse. Instead of dealing with the situation, the hoodlum and his pals immediately drove off, but two cops who saw the crash jumped on the running boards of a car and ordered the driver to pursue Neary. During the chase the police opened fire, which was returned by Neary's confederates. The gun battle continued until Neary's auto crashed into another. His pals jumped out of the car and escaped, but Neary kept trying to restart the vehicle. As the sedan containing the police pulled up, Neary fired at it and hit the civilian driver in the wrist. The police quickly fell onto the escaped convict and beat him into unconsciousness.

With Kiekart and Haas testifying for the prosecution, Neary and Fanning went on trial for the murder of John Enz, the driver of the mail truck, and were found guilty on January 31, 1929, and sentenced to life at hard labor. Neither man showed any emotion when the verdict was read, but as they were being escorted out Fanning sneered to reporters, "I hope those two dogs who testified against us are satisfied now."

The next member of the robbery gang to be picked up was Daniel Grosso, who sprayed the cabin of the truck with the machine-gun bullets that killed John Enz. Since the holdup he had been involved in bootlegging in New York City as well as acting as bodyguard and gunman for the mob. He was arrested on June 30, 1929, for killing New York gangster Frankie Marlow six days earlier when the police received a tip about two gunmen who lived in Queens (Grosso and his then-partner Nicholas McDermott), just ten minutes away from where Marlow's body was found.

Police got word that a woman visitor was going to be stopping by the apartment, and two detectives went to the roof and climbed down the fire escape to the second floor where they peered through the window. They saw Grosso sitting in a chair and McDermott lying on a bed, both still in their pajamas. Two other detectives then knocked on the door. Assuming that it was the young woman, Grosso opened the door and then quickly tried to slam it after seeing the detectives. Just then the two officers from the fire escaped yelled from behind, "Hands up!" Grosso immediately raised his while McDermott started to rise off the bed.

Climbing in the window, a detective trained his gun on McDermott and said, "Put your hands up, and if you make a move you'll be killed." The men surrendered and a search of the apartment turned up two .38's and fifty rounds of ammunition for .38s and .32s (the caliber of the gun that killed Marlow). The police also found a pair of binoculars mounted on a swivel in a window. When asked about it Grosso said, "Oh that? We used that to get a slant on anybody we suspected. You see, I've been in the beer-running business lately and I've got a lot of enemies." Grosso then asked one of the detectives, "Say, will you do me a favor? Hit me on the head with the butt of your gun, will you?" When the detective asked why, the gangster answered, "Well, you know, the mob won't think me tough getting a pinch like this." After the detective declined, Grosso then offered him a $20,000 bribe to let him go. This also was declined.

Things looked bad for Grosso and McDermott from the get-go. Two witnesses picked them out of a lineup and said they had seen them moments after Marlow was dumped from a car. Police specialists felt certain that the .32-caliber bullet taken from Marlow's head was from the same batch found in the gangsters' apartment. It also came out that Grosso and McDermott used to work for Marlow, and since that time the two had been receiving money and protection from another source who police said was an enemy of Marlow. Knowing that New Jersey wanted him for the mail truck robbery and that his case was hopeless, Grosso told reporters, "I know they have a great deal on me. I know they have enough on me to burn me. But I'm not talking, see?" He then said that if he were sentence to die in the electric chair, he would take the secret of Frankie Marlow with him. On April 11, 1931, Grosso kept his word and was the only member of the robbery crew to be executed.

⌒⌒⌒

Kiekart and Haas were sentenced for their participation in the mail robbery, and no doubt Neary and Fanning were tickled to death when in 1935 the latter identified the former as the killer of Ernest Whitman during the Bellmore Bank Robbery. Sentenced to death, "the Ghost" lucked out, however, because a week before he was scheduled to ride the lighting, his sentenced was commuted to life in prison.

Chapter 7 / The Daly Show

Two years after the Mount Vernon trolley car murders it seemed the case was closed. Since his testimony cleared up the crime Marino received a five-year sentence, but because of tuberculosis his term was cut short and he died after serving only a year. Both Frank Daly and David DeMaio were executed, and it appeared the other three bandits would go unpunished. However, two years after the fact two detectives were walking in lower Manhattan when one of them spied a familiar face in a restaurant. "That's Solly Cheesecake; he's wanted for murder," one of them said. They entered the restaurant and took Salvatore Melito (Solly's real name) into custody. As soon as they were outside Cheesecake wrangled himself loose and took off down the street. The detectives pulled out their guns and fired a fusillade in the bandit's direction, winging the gunman. Unfortunately, another bullet struck a nine-year-old girl in the head, killing her. Cheesecake rounded a corner and disappeared, but the detectives picked up a trail of blood and found him hiding in a building. The bandit ended up receiving a twenty-year term for his participation in the trolley job.

Another two years would pass before the fifth bandit came to the attention of the authorities. After the murder Jimmie Lipso fled to Italy, where he was arrested for another murder in 1929. Though the Italian government refused to extradite him, he reportedly received a long sentence.

After Lipso's arrest five of the six trolley murder participants were accounted for and the crime was forgotten. Almost a quarter century would pass before it came back to public attention. In August 1953 a union official was murdered and the subsequent investigation showed that one of his locals had a contract with Yonkers Raceway and had received some of the $200,000 in labor extortion kickbacks plaguing the track. Investigators learned that nearly three dozen of the union's employees had criminal records and planned to fingerprint all workers to search their backgrounds. Hearing this, the fifty-three-year-old parking lot supervisor, George Florea, quit. He wasn't out of work long, because he was also a member of the AFL Union of Operating Engineers and was immediately put to work running a compressor. Authorities were still interested in him, however, and took his fingerprints.

A background search was done and Mount Vernon authorities were notified that Joe Mazza, the sixth bandit from the trolley car murders, was now known as George Florea. The aging bandit was arrested, sent to Mount Vernon, and booked on a first-degree murder charge. He admitted knowing four of the gunmen involved but denied taking part in the slaying. With the passage of twenty-eight years there were only a small number of witnesses left, and seeing there are no other mentions of the affair in the press, it appears that nothing came of the arrest.

Chapter 8 / The Candy Kid

"Reese, Reese, I won't leave you. I can't live without you," Margaret "the Tiger Girl" Whittemore cried to her doomed husband before his hanging. Turns out Margaret was able to live without Reese, for she remarried on January 20, 1929. This time, however, she made her vows to a Baltimore salesman as opposed to a hoodlum.

Whittemore's early rumrunning pal, "Chicago Tommy" Langrella, reportedly was put out of business permanently in 1926. His body, it was said, was found in New Jersey

The last member of the gang to be arrested was wheelman Nate Weinzimmer, who managed to evade capture during the gang's roundup and beat it back to his hometown of Cleveland, Ohio. New York police traced him to his home on February 27, 1927, and tried to bring him back, but he fought extradition. He was released on $50,000 bail while the courts decided his fate. When they decided against him he hightailed it to St. Louis but was captured around the first of December and sent back to the Big Apple, where he was found guilty of driving the getaway car during the Goudvis robbery.

For his participation in the Whittemore Gang, Anthony Paladino was deported to Italy.

The Kraemer brothers received forty-year sentences and were sent to Clinton Prison at Dannemora, New York. By the fall of 1927, with accomplices on both the inside and outside, Leon Kraemer was working on a plan to break out. He had a shipment of six pistols, 200 rounds of ammunition, and roadmaps of the Adirondack Mountains sent to the industrial department of the prison; however, there was a squealer in the midst and the contraband was seized. The warden had the six convicts working in the industrial department transferred. Leon was undeterred and went back to work. In late October another shipment of guns and ammunition was smuggled into the prison, but once again the warden was informed and the weapons were seized. The second time, Leon figured out who the snitch was and on November 7, with a knife fashioned from a spoon, attacked him in the exercise yard. Guards were able to restrain Kraemer before he could inflict any serious injuries.

It took about five years, but Leon Kraemer finally escaped from prison. By 1932 he had been transferred from Clinton to Great Meadow Prison in Comstock, New York, where he befriended the warden's chauffeur, inmate Thomas Burke. Guards at the gates were used to seeing Burke come and go and never questioned him. On August 23, 1932, Leon jumped into the rumble seat of a coupe owned by the warden's son, and Burke drove them through the gates to freedom. The coupe was found abandoned in Saratoga, New York. Brother Jacob left prison feet first, having succumbed to tuberculosis in Dannemora in 1930.

Leon managed to elude police until the evening of June 8, 1933, when police received a call regarding gunshots. They arrived at a well-furnished apartment and found Kraemer sitting in chair reeling in pain from bullet wounds to the chest and leg. A search of the apartment turned up a vast arsenal of rifles and pistols. Three blocks away twenty-year-old George Schaefer was found with two bullet wounds in the stomach. Police were certain Schaefer was living with Kraemer, but the former died without answering any questions and the latter was taken to Bellevue Hospital, where he recovered without spilling anything and was returned to prison. Interestingly, scarcely two weeks earlier, on May 29 at 9:30 p.m., traffic came to a halt on a Lower East Side street when a large sedan came to an abrupt stop. A door was opened and Joe Trop, the fence for the Whittemore Gang, was thrown unconscious to the street. Four men then stepped out of the car and, in front of hundreds of witnesses, shot Trop twice in the head and twice in the body, pulling off what the police considered to be one of the city's "most brazen murders."

Police speculated that Kraemer and Trop may have been put on the spot because they were longtime friends of beer mogul "Waxey" Gordon, whose gang was currently being decimated by rival gangsters. There was speculation that Kraemer had bumped off Trop and the latter's friends had caught up with him, and that Kraemer and Schaefer actually had gotten into a fight and shot each other. Either way, Trop and Schaefer were dead and Kraemer went back to Dannemora and stayed until his release on September 13, 1949.

Six months after Leon Kraemer walked out of Dannemora, "Baltimore Willie" Unkelbach was found dead on March 8, 1950, in a hobo jungle. He was forty-nine years old and broke.

Any sadness or misgivings Richard's father, Rawling Whittemore, may have had were short-lived as the fifty-nine-year-old patriarch of the Whittemore clan was struck and killed by an automobile on November 4, 1926, less than three months after his son swung into eternity.

Chapter 9 / Red Scare

The first instigator of what would end up being the bloody Tombs debacle was Peter Heslin, said to be a friend of "Bum" Rodgers, who was convicted of killing a cop on April 5, 1926. On that evening Heslin was hiding in a doorway armed with two .45's and surprised four Italian men who came by. Heslin barked, "Hands up!" in Italian. Patrolman Charles Reilly heard the robbery taking place and was able to creep up behind Heslin and jump on him. The two wrestled and Heslin managed to get a hand free and shoot the patrolman twice. Reilly, who had a reputation for being able to handle tough guys, made a final grab at the bad man. Heslin fired again but only managed to hit himself in the leg.

Reilly was unable to hold his man and Heslin hobbled off. One of the Italian victims fetched two more cops who returned and called an ambulance for Reilly, who died before it arrived. With flashlight in hand, one of the officers followed a trail of blood across the street into a tenement and up to a fourth-floor apartment where the gunmen appeared to have tried to gain access. The trail then led to the roof, down the stairs, and out back. Police followed the blood trail to a friend's apartment and found Heslin in bed. The apartment's occupants said the bandit had arrived a half hour earlier saying he'd been shot in a fight.

Heslin was convicted on May 31, 1926, and placed in the Tombs until he was transferred to the Sing Sing death house. It was there that he befriended the McKennas and the botched escape with John Hogan took place. Heslin kept his date with the electric chair and was executed on July 21, 1927. When he entered the death chamber he announced to witnesses, "I was planted on circumstantial evidence. You are now watching an innocent man die."

Chapter 10 / From Maiden Lane to the Tombs

Within five hours of the ill-fated Tombs breakout police arrested Amberg's older brother, Oscar, a thirty-two-year-old self-described painting contractor, and Hyman's twenty-four-year-old pal Robert Weiner and charged them with supplying the guns that were used in the botched escape. Weiner and Oscar Amberg were chosen as fall guys because of their actions the day of the escape. Especially Weiner, who was seen at the Tombs just prior to the escape in a roadster he'd rented for the day with a fake driver's license. A pedestrian passing the Tombs when the gunfight broke out saw a man, later identified as Weiner, run from the prison, jump into a roadster, and take off. He took down the license plate number and gave it to police who then traced it back to Weiner.

Amberg admitted he had gone with Weiner to get the car and to a photo studio to get a picture to alter the driver's license. He said he'd then been dropped off at Third Avenue and Forty-second Street where he jumped a subway to the Bronx to check on a painting job. Supposedly, Weiner was going to the Tombs to visit Hyman, so Oscar gave him $20 to give to his brother. Weiner and his girlfriend drove to the prison, but when he wasn't allowed to see Hyman they left. This was about twenty minutes before the breakout, according to Weiner. The police contended that Weiner was alone and waiting with the car to drive the convicts to safety but took off after the gunfire erupted and it was obvious they weren't going to make it out.

Weiner had visited Amberg a number of times at the Tombs, the final time being a few hours before the escape. He initially was questioned at the detective bureau by the chief and then escorted to the basement for further questioning with blackjacks and pieces of bicycle tire. According to Weiner, "There were seven or eight policemen. They started kicking me all over. They kicked me in the ribs, They pulled my hair out and tried to stuff it in my mouth. They broke my nose. When I saw the only way to get out of another beating was to talk, I did." Weiner said he told the detective in charge, "If you want me to tell you a story, I will. I'll say yes to anything." The beatings stopped as the detective announced, "All right, boys, he has confessed." The detective then told him, "Now, whatever the boss asks you, say yes to."

Weiner signed a confession which stated that a week before the escape he had thrown two pistols over the prison wall at the behest of Hyman Amberg. The confession said that three days later he visited Amberg, who told him he had received the guns, although the name of the person who supposedly delivered them was never learned. Since the guns that Weiner supposedly threw over the wall were used in the killings during the breakout, Weiner and Oscar Amberg were put on trial for murder. Oscar was acquitted since there was no proof tying him to the guns used in the murder. Weiner wasn't so fortunate. Because of his signed confession he was found guilty on March 17, 1927, and shipped off to the death house at Sing Sing where he was scheduled to "ride the lightning" on May 2. A stay was given while the defendant prepared an appeal.

The resulting shake-up of at the Tombs after the murders of the warden and the guard was severe. The bribing of prison personnel came under the spotlight, especially after a prisoner testified that he had seen a gun in Amberg's cell but was not surprised because Hyman seemed to enjoy certain privileges, such as his cell remaining open while all the others were locked. It wasn't uncommon for Amberg to be away from his cell up to an hour at a time. One of those who began to feel the pressure was "Old Tom" Colton, who had smuggled in money and whiskey to the McKennas. So worried was he that he slashed his wrist that summer in a suicide attempt. He survived and moved to Cold Spring, New York, to recuperate. That October an investigator for Weiner's lawyer went to the hotel where "Old Tom" was staying to serve a subpoena and was told the old man had just slit his throat and was at the hospital. The investigator rushed to the hospital, but the aged jailkeeper was dead.

At Clinton Prison in Dannemora, John McKenna learned of Colton's suicide and wrote a letter to Weiner's lawyer stating that he had some information the attorney might find beneficial. McKenna was brought down and told the court that as far as he knew Weiner had nothing to do with the guns used by his brother, Berg, and Amberg. He stated that he had seen his brother pay Colton to smuggle the guns in, and that he was hoping to take part in the escape himself before being sent up. Warned that he was incriminating himself, McKenna didn't expand much further. He did say they had arranged for a number of cars to be on hand waiting to drive the escapees to safety. When asked why he hadn't offered this information during the first trial, he responded, "I didn't care at the time about Weiner's case. I was upset over Mike's death, and they were hard on me at Clinton Prison." It should be mentioned that Hyman's brother Joe was also at Dannemora at this time. Perhaps he played a part in the affair as well.

Even with the new information given by John McKenna, the court upheld Weiner's original conviction and refused to grant him another trial, so he was sent back to the death house. His lawyers took the case to the court of appeals, which reversed the decision because his confession had been given under duress. Without the confession the state had no case, and Weiner was released. After thirteen months in the death house, Weiner walked out of Sing Sing a free man on May 10, 1928.

Robert Weiner wasn't through with crime, though. Later that year, on December 5, he was acting as lookout while two confederates were preparing to the blow the safe of a furniture store. Little did they know that three detectives had been trailing them for three months and were watching and waiting for them to finish before arresting them. Before they had a chance to blow the safe, however, a patrolman came walking by and Weiner gave the alarm. The three bandits tried to run away but were grabbed by detectives. On February 26, 1929, Weiner and his cohorts were sentenced to the maximum three years for violating the Sullivan Law and unlawful entry. It was far less time then the detectives were hoping for, but since the hoods never finished blowing the safe, it was the best the court could do.

By 1932 Weiner was out of prison and involved in organized racketeering. On August 31 of that year he was picked up after threatening a pharmacist who balked at joining the City Pharmaceutical Association, which investigators said consisted of several hundred druggists who handed over about $2,000 a month in dues. For a $5 membership fee and $2 in monthly dues, a pharmacy owner could expect "protection against cut-rate stores and a list of cosmetics, the price of which is to be boosted." While in custody Weiner denied the "pharmaceutical association" had anything to do with the rash of window breakings and stink-bomb throwings plaguing Brooklyn's drugstores at that time.

Weiner needn't have worried about his arrest. An investigation into the pharmacy racket netted nothing for the authorities. Out of twenty pharmacists who were subpoenaed, only about six bothered to show up in court and, because of threats made by gangsters, they wouldn't give any evidence.

Weiner dropped from view in April 1935 when, on the twentieth, he and perhaps three other men reportedly were arguing about "dope." One thing led to another, and Weiner drew his gun and shot one of his cohorts in the throat twice. Another confederate then whipped out his pistol and sent a bullet into Weiner's throat. Both wounded men were taken to Bellevue Hospital in serious condition.

Spring 1927 found George Cohen in Manhattan's low-security West Side Prison, where he had been residing for a number of months. Since he had become so useful as a state's witness in other cases he was kept in the city jail rather than any of the state prisons. His pals at West Side included Whittemore Gang alumnus "Baltimore Willie" Unkelbach, who was also a valuable witness, having appeared against his own gang members as well as giving information that led to the arrest of other thieves and drug dealers, and McKenna Gang member John Werner, who had been there after being arrested for participation in the General Baking Company the previous May. These three men all occupied cells on the third tier and spent all their free time together.

West Side Prison only had four keepers on duty. One, Dennis O'Reilly, walked the prison with a large key ring at his side. The prison chapel was being renovated, and one of the aforementioned three inmates saw O'Reilly unlock the front door of the chapel to admit some workers. They decided that if they could get O'Reilly's keys and make their way to the chapel, they could open the door and again breathe the fresh air of freedom.

The keeper had a wonderful rapport with the convicts, and when he went to open the trio's cells at 9 a.m. on May 29 he wasn't expecting any trouble. Unkelbach's was the last of the cells he opened, and once all three were in the hall they jumped on the keeper and tried to tie and gag him. O'Reilly started yelling and put up more of a fight than they were expecting, so although they hated to do it, they took the guard's blackjack and his key ring and knocked him unconscious.

The other prisoners on the tier began to holler, which was a common occurrence so second-tier keeper James McShane didn't think anything unusual was happening on the floor above him. He decided to go up and take a look anyway and was quickly locked in a cell. McShane began yelling to the other keepers, and this got the rest of the inmates going. Their hooting and hollering caused first-tier keeper Gustave Hicks to go upstairs to see what all the ruckus was about, and as he entered a corridor he heard the door shut behind him and the lock click. With three of the four keepers locked up and the other inmates in an uproar, Cohen, Werner, and Unkelbach made their way to the chapel knowing that the one remaining keeper, William Dwyer on the main floor, would likely call for reinforcements because of the pandemonium on the tiers.

As the nervous escapees kept trying key after key looking for the right one, a rookie cop outside heard the hoopla and came inside the jail, as did one of the institution's van drivers. As the convicts kept up the key game, Werner got the jitters and ran down to the main-floor corridor where the van driver yelled, "Throw 'em up!" Thinking fast, Werner said, "They're trying to escape. I wanted to warn you." Thinking Werner was a stoolie, the cop and driver didn't bother with him.

Giving up on the chapel door, Cohen and Unkelbach ran into the corridor hoping for another avenue of escape. Keeper Dwyer and the cop saw them and chased them back into the chapel, where they surrendered without a fight. McShane and Hicks were released, and O'Reilly was rushed to the hospital with fractures of the skull and jaw. When the guards were questioned, Werner was found out and faced the music with his cronies.

All three agreed to answer any questions, but before giving any information Cohen said, "But first I want to know how Dennis [O'Reilly] is. I hope that we didn't hurt him much." When told how serious the keeper's wounds were, Cohen began to cry. "Oh my God," the repentant convict said, "don't tell me that. Dennis was awful good to me. I wouldn't have anything happen to him for anything." When officials asked why the three had beaten O'Reilly if they were so fond of him, they said they hadn't intended to beat him, only to tie him up, but he'd started to fight back.

Someone pointed out to the gangsters that their plot was doomed from the beginning because although they saw O'Reilly unlock the chapel door, the key he used was not on his ring—it was a separate key that was kept in an office.

After spending almost five years in jail for his part in the Rodack killing, Benny Mintz, the wheelman for Hyman Amberg's gang of jewel robbers, was put on the spot in a Brooklyn speakeasy. On October 19, 1931, Mintz, now twenty-eight, was in a saloon with his brother-in-law. After the pair had been drinking for a number of hours, two men entered and approached Mintz's table and asked him to step into the back room for a talk. No sooner had the ex-convict set foot inside the room than pistol fire echoed throughout the saloon. With guns in their hands, the two men walked back into the bar area and yelled for everyone to keep quiet as they made their way outside to a waiting automobile and escaped. 'Twas the end of Benny Mintz

Who put Mintz on the spot is anyone's guess. A logical choice would be Joey and Louis "Pretty" Amberg, Hyman's notorious siblings, who surely wanted revenge for his squealing on their brother. It also could have been friends of William Dorsch, whom Mintz had killed in April 1926.

Chapter 11 / Don't Cry Out Loud

Police rookie James A. Broderick, who was shot by Cry Baby Bandit Leo Hecker in the Loft Candy payroll debacle, survived the shooting and benefited from his ordeal. When he went before the grand jury he was applauded at the conclusion of his testimony and the jurors encouraged the police commissioner to reward him for his courage. After recuperating, the rookie officer was given a thirty-day vacation and promoted to detective second grade. His celebrity also won him free police equipment. Police officers had to buy their own gear, and when he showed up at a supply store to buy .38-caliber bullets, a holster, and whistle, he was recognized by other cops in the store.

When they told the proprietor who he was, the store owner wouldn't accept any money from him. "You just take those things with my compliments," he told Broderick when he tried to pay for his items. "Any young fellow who has the nerve to stand up before wild-eyed gunmen as you did is welcome to anything I've got." But the praise couldn't help the detective two years later when a sixteen-year-old girl charged him with attacking her. The once-lauded detective was suspended from duty and placed behind the bars of his own precinct house on October 28, 1928.

Chapter 13 / Dishonorable Mention 1920-1929

Murder in the Pirates Den: John "the Swede" Lindquist and Albert Lanson were subsequently exonerated for the murder of Officer Neville when it was determined that Hoey had acted alone in shooting the patrolman.

After spending thirty-four years in prison William Hoey decided that he hadn't received a fair trial and deserved to be exonerated. He obtained the trial transcripts and wrote out the entire proceedings in longhand and followed this up with his arguments, namely discrediting the chief witness against him as well as the prosecutor. He also threw in some biblical quotes to help prove his point. His pleas, however, fell on deaf ears and nothing was done. Not to be discouraged, he wrote out the entire proceedings in longhand again the next year and restated his arguments. Again nobody was interested.

Chapter 14 / New York's Most Desperate Criminal

Nannery confederate Enrico Battaglia had been wanted by the police ever since the 1928 murder of Officer Jeremiah Brosnan in the prison ward of Fordham Hospital. With the subsequent arrest of James Nannery and Eddie "Snakes" Ryan, Battaglia was the only suspect still at large, although the police also wanted to question gunman and Vincent Coll associate Edward Popke, known as "Fats" McCarthy, about the murder.

On October 19, 1931, Officer John Broderick was walking his beat on Manhattan's Upper West Side when he saw Battaglia and followed him to a brownstone apartment. Broderick called for backup and three detectives, Edward Willi, James De Ferraro and Guido Pessagno were dispatched to help bring in the wanted man.

The detectives and Broderick arrived at the brownstone and rang the doorbell, which was answered by the landlady. The detectives identified themselves and explained why they were there. The landlady, perhaps hoping to tip off her murderous tenants, exclaimed loudly, "No police are coming in here to search my place!" The cops entered anyway and searched the parlor, then started to make their way upstairs. The landlady called out, "Well, can't you shut the door!" At this, Broderick went back down the stairs and shut the door, a move that may have saved his life.

His partners found the apartment door where they figured Battaglia would be and knocked. There was no answer, so they forced the door open. As they rushed inside, Battaglia, "Fats" McCarthy, and an unknown gunman opened fire simultaneously. Pessagno and Willi immediately dropped to the floor wounded, the former mortally. De Ferraro, a step behind his companions, rushed in with his gun blazing, but he too fell in a storm of lead unleashed by the trio of desperadoes. With the detectives down, "Fats" and the unknown gunman leapt over their victims and ran for the stairs leading to the roof, followed by Battaglia. However, before the latter had a chance to get there, Officer Broderick made his way to the third floor and dropped him with a single, fatal shot. "Fats" and his confederate escaped over the rooftops.

Detectives said Battaglia was a member of the old "Snakes" Ryan gang, and his record showed that he had been arrested for the first time on July 16, 1923, for burglary but beat the rap. A month later he was arrested for attempted robbery and received a suspended sentence. A year later, on August 4, he was discharged for violating the Sullivan Law, but his luck ran out on July 21, 1925, when he was sentenced to a two-and-a-half- to five-year term for robbery.

Nannery's pal Eddie "Snakes" Ryan still had one more moment in the spotlight. Paroled from prison in 1950, Ryan went back to the underworld where it appears he became involved in the labor rackets as a gunman. At about 4:10 p.m. on August 28, 1953, "Snakes," now forty-six with gray hair, entered a Bronx apartment building with a handkerchief over his face so the doorman couldn't recognize him and rode the elevator up to the fifth floor. Moments later the doorman heard a series of shots and then Ryan came running out of the stairwell with a pistol in his hand. Lying dead in the fifth-floor hallway was thirty-five-year-old Thomas Lewis, president of Local 32-E of the Building Service Employees International Union. He had held the post for the past twelve years.

The doorman followed Ryan outside and ran up to a traffic cop and yelled, "Catch that man! He just shot somebody!" The cop drew his gun and began to chase Ryan, yelling for him to stop. Ryan responded by shooting at him, and a running gun battle ensued. "Snakes" ran for a car that appeared to be waiting for him, but when a shot from the cop clipped him, the car sped off without him. Ryan turned and fired one more time, missing the officer, whose next round found its mark in the hoodlum's head. Ryan dropped to the pavement and died faceup with his gun in his hand. This murder would lead to the capture of Joe Mazza, the sixth and last member of the gang responsible for the 1925 trolley car murders in Mount Vernon.

Nannery appears to have led a crime-free life after being released from prison. And a long life it was. The young man who, when last heard of, was making his living with fast cars and Tommyguns died May 12, 2001, at age ninety-six, almost four months to the day before the 9/11 terrorist attacks.

Chapter 15 / Sexy Takes a Ride

Vivian Gordon won a posthumous victory with regard to Detective Andrew McLaughlin, the vice squad officer who she claimed framed her in 1923. Although he was exonerated of Vivian's murder, he was called to the stand during the Seabury investigation when officials learned that between November 18, 1928, and December 31, 1930, McLaughlin had managed to bank $35,800—an amazing feat considering his salary during this period was $3,000 a year. Claiming that his Constitutional rights were being violated, he refused to answer any questions about how he had obtained such a large sum. The court responded by taking his badge. Almost twenty years later, on June 6, 1950, the former detective, now the father of a police officer and suffering from depression and an undisclosed illness, took his son's regulation police pistol and sent a bullet through his brain.

Any sense of satisfaction Vivian may have gotten from McLaughlin losing his badge no doubt would have been trumped by the sorrowful news of her sixteen-year-old daughter Benita's suicide. With her mother's sordid history making front-page news, the young girl couldn't face her peers. On March 3, about a week after her mother's murder, Benita, who also kept a diary, made her final entry:

I can't face the world any longer. I'm going to end it all.

With that, she went into the kitchen and asphyxiated herself with gas.

After the Gordon trial some bright agent at the Department of Justice began to look into the trip to Norway that Stein and Greenberg had made. Since they had sailed under false identities, Stein as Reuben and Greenberg as Samuel Cohen (he was not an American citizen and had borrowed the real "Chowder Head" Cohen's birth certificate to make a phony passport) both men were arrested for passport fraud on November 20, 1932. Stein would have been arrested too, but he was already behind bars.

During the Gordon trial a Mrs. Lola Baker saw Stein's picture in the newspaper and went to the police station because she had a story to tell. On April 11, 1930, Stein, posing as a bond salesman, stopped by her house to scope out her jewelry to see if she would be a good target. He returned that evening under the pretense of making a sale, and once inside he grabbed her and shoved a handkerchief doused with chloroform in her face. Lola passed out and Stein began to steal her jewelry. After a few moments Lola regained consciousness and pleaded with the hoodlum not to hurt her. When she started to struggle, Stein said, "I hate to do this, but I'm desperate." He then punched her in the face and fell on her with both knees, breaking a couple of her ribs and knocking her out. When she awoke she was missing about $2,000 worth of jewelry. Stein went on trial for the robbery and on October 29 was found guilty and sentenced to twenty-five years in prison. He served less than twenty years.

On April 3, 1950, Stein, now fifty-two, and two cohorts robbed a *Reader's Digest* truck in Chappaqua, New York, of almost $5,000, in the process fatally shooting a messenger on the truck. The bandits were traced through their getaway car's license plate and captured on June 8. Stein confessed to taking part in the crime and was sentenced to death. Though he was granted a number of stays, Stein's luck ran out and he finally took a seat in the electric chair on July 9, 1955.

Chapter 17 / College Boy

One of those involved with Roy Sloane in the failed breakout from Sing Sing in November 1929 was Joseph "Babe" Pioli, who was not unknown to New Yorkers. He had escaped from the same prison in 1927 while serving a sentence for committing one of the most infamous Big Apple murders of the early 1920s.

Born circa 1896, Pioli was a lifelong criminal and borderline psychopath. His first arrest came at age eight, and he spent some of his childhood in the House of Refuge and logged two stays at the Catholic Protectory. At seventeen he was shipped off to Sing Sing for the first time to serve a sentence of twenty-seven months for assault. He was sent back in 1918 for four and a half years after being arrested for burglary.

Pioli's relations didn't have much to do with him after his return to society; however, his mother tried to remedy the situation at the end of 1923. Thinking the approaching New Year might signify a new start, she invited her wayward son to the family's New Year's Eve party. Exactly what time "Babe" showed up wasn't recorded, but when he got to his mother's house he was already intoxicated. Some family accounts have him kissing everyone and wishing them a Happy New Year, then whipping out his pistol and firing at random. Others have him arguing with his older brother Santo and then whipping out his gun. Trying to keep the peace, the mother stepped between the two and was rewarded with a bullet in the belly. "Babe" kept firing at his brother. Whatever the scenario, at about 2 a.m. on January 1, 1924, his mother lay on the floor writhing in pain and Santo was dead.

Early on the morning of June 15 Joe was at the Club Tia Juana, which was partly owned by former boxer Bill Brennan. Well known in his day, Brennan had fought Jack Dempsey twice, most recently on December 14, 1920, when he went twelve rounds with the champ. Now retired at the age of thirty, he was cashing in on his success as a cabaret owner.

With Pioli was Terrence O'Neill and another man and woman, possibly his girlfriend. Pioli got into an argument with the girl and they stepped into the hallway where "Babe" berated the girl for how she was dressed. Brennan approached and told them to quiet down and beat it. Pioli called the former pugilist a "dirty dog" and let it be known that he wasn't afraid of him. Sticking his hand in his pocket, he told Brennan, "If you want to try to punch me, go ahead, try it." A waiter stepped between them and got Brennan to go back into the bar while Pioli and his party left.

At about 4 a.m. Pioli and O'Neill returned to the club. Pioli stayed in the hallway while O'Neill went in and asked Brennan if he could see him outside. Brennan walked into the hallway. The club's cashier stated that he saw O'Neill take a swing at Brennan and that the ex-boxer pushed him away. Then he heard someone say, "Give it to him," and a shot rang out. Brennan's sister, who was in the club with a friend of his, a cop named James Cullen, ran to the hallway in time to see Pioli fire a second shot into her brother. Shirley grabbed either Pioli or O'Neill by the sleeve but was knocked down and a shot was fired at her. Another shot was fired at Cullen, which went through his neck. He managed to chase the men another twenty feet before collapsing. Seeing that her brother was about to expire, Shirley asked him, "Do you know who they were, Bill?" "I don't," he replied, before becoming unconscious. He died before he could be placed in an ambulance.

Meanwhile, the gunmen ran down the stairs and found the door locked, so they broke the glass with the butts of their guns. Hearing the shattering glass, a nearby cop, Lieutenant John Haggerty, figured robbers were at work and ran to the scene where he grabbed both men, who then beat him with their pistols. They knocked the officer to the ground and kicked and stomped him until he was unconscious. The gunmen then jumped on the running board of a car containing three men who were leaving on a fishing trip and forced them to speed away. A taxi driver who witnessed the getaway hollered to a cop who was arriving on the scene and told him to jump in. They pursued the getaway car and after a short chase forced the hoodlums to the curb. Haggerty captured the pair, who had disposed of their guns.

Pioli plead guilty to manslaughter and was sent back to Sing Sing to serve twenty years. Like most long-term convicts he was transferred to Clinton Prison in Dannemora to serve out his sentence, but for some undisclosed reason he was transferred back to Sing Sing on February 12, 1927. Less than a month later he and another convict who also had been transferred from Dannemora disappeared from the prison in the middle of the day. He was last seen at about 4 p.m., but when there was a head count two hours later, he and his confederate were gone.

A little over a month later, on April 24, Pioli gave himself up in San Diego, California, reportedly because he feared he would commit another crime. Although Sing Sing Warden Lewis Lawes quickly applied for his extradition, Pioli had a change of heart and managed to escape again. This time the gunman remained at large until February 4, 1929, when two members of the Elizabeth, New Jersey, Police Department found him drinking in saloon. He was returned to Sing Sing where, as a self-proclaimed student of Houdini, he vowed he would once again escape.

In a way Pioli did escape. After serving just eight more years he was paroled on October 16, 1937, but his freedom would be short-lived. It was stipulated in his parole that he must live at home while working at a job he procured at a garage. Within months he was rearrested for doing neither.

Chapter 18 / It Came from Massachusetts
Eleanor Scarnici, Emma Reino, and Fred Plentl were released in April of 1934.

Though Leonard Scarnici took credit for killing Marcel Poffo and Max Parkin, another theory was that they were killed on the orders of "Dutch" Schultz. In addition to the fact that Poffo and the Dutchman had been friendly, the *New York Herald* reported that the $20,000 bail put up for Parkin after the Bank of Manhattan job had been paid for by Schultz and since Parkin had jumped bail the Dutchman was out twenty grand and meted out his own justice. One fact that supports this hypothesis is that when Poffo and Parkin were found, they collectively had over $1,100 in cash on them. It would seem that if bank robbers had killed them, they would have taken their rolls; professional gunmen characteristically would not do so.

Poffo and Parkin's history went back to at least 1929 when they were arrested as part of an eight-man robbery gang. Police got a tip on one of the gang's "drops" and arrested Louis "Monk" Kaplan. They took him to the station and returned and arrested Anthony Wilk. While searching the premises they came across a piece of marble behind the sink that was loose. Removing it, they found five pistols and a collection of burglary tools. After the two initial arrests a group of detectives raided the gang's second hideout and apprehended Sam Kantrowitz, James Mack, George Bemis, Nathan Finder, and Harry Gordon. Later that afternoon they nabbed Poffo and Parkin.

Prior to the double murder, police raided a Bronx apartment at 1433 College Avenue and arrested Solomon Schepnick and Irving Blauner who were in possession of an arsenal that included a tear-gas pistol and a Thompson submachine gun that the police believed had been used in two bank robberies. The significance of the raid is that both Schepnick and Blauner, who were indicted as a result of the police search, gave Poffo's address as their own, which means they were most likely part of the same gang. Blauner would later be described as an "understrapper" for the Scarnici gang. His job was to store the guns and run errands for the mob.

It was never fully disclosed whether Scarnici took part in the O'Connell kidnapping. During the trial the abovementioned Solomon Schepnick appeared as a witness and stated that in February 1933 he attended a meeting during which Manny Strewl and Percy Geary (two of the men on trial) discussed the job with Phil Zeigler and Leonard Scarnici. He also identified two other men in attendance: Al Fisher and Benny Holinsky (later killed after engineering the kidnapping of Mafia bookie Bart Salvo).

After the execution Leonard's body was claimed by his brother Thomas. Thomas had his own brief moment in the crime spotlight ten years later when he was extradited from Springfield, Massachusetts, for taking part in a Brooklyn robbery in which $27,000 worth of jewelry and furs were stolen from a residence.

Chapter 20 / $427,000 Payday

Upon sentencing, gang member Stewart Wallace stated that Thomas Quinn and Joseph Kress were not involved and that he would discuss this later. Whether because of this or perhaps for another reason, Kress was able to get the court of appeals to dismiss his sentence and he was released in March 1941.

Seven weeks later, on April 24, he was again in custody after he and two others took part in a robbery gone awry. Whether he was courageous or crazy is up for debate because the victim of the robbery was to be Frank Erickson, probably the biggest bookmaker in New York City and right-hand man of Mafia bigwig Frank Costello. The plan was to waylay Erickson in his suite at the New York Athletic Club. Police suggested that the bookmaker may have used this location as a payoff headquarters where up to $100,000 in cash could be on hand. Kress and his two confederates, Lyman Finnell, a thirty-eight-year-old ex-con from California, and Stephan Catlan, who at age thirty-six already had three convictions under his belt, never even made it into Erickson's suite. The trio was blocked from entry, not by gun-toting gangsters on the syndicate's payroll, but by a fifty-two-year-old chambermaid.

The bandits somehow made it past the front desk and went to the nineteenth floor, where Erickson conducted his business. When they got off the elevator the trio saw the chambermaid, Catherine O'Brien, and demanded that she let them into Erickson's room. She said no, and they followed her into a room and tried to forcibly take her keys. The chambermaid managed to knock one of the men down and ripped a button off of Kress's coat while wrestling with him. Mrs. O'Brien then was felled by a pistol butt to the head but managed to knock a phone off the hook and yell to the switchboard operator for help. A bellboy ran out and got two cops. While one of the cops was on the phone calling for backup, the gunmen ran out of the building and the chase was on. A running gun battle ensued in which one of the cops was injured.

Finnell jumped into a car and ordered the driver to step on it. Instead the driver pulled the keys out of the ignition and ran off. Then gunman then jumped into the rear of a chauffeured car and told the woman inside, "No one will get hurt if I can get away." Like the driver of the previous car, the chauffeur jumped out and ran. Taking matters into his own hands, Finnell climbed into the driver's seat. Traffic was thick and he only managed to go a few feet before one of the cops jumped on the running board. Not wanting to face the music, Finnell put his gun to his head and pulled the trigger. A cab driver who witnessed the gunplay followed Kress, who dodged into an antique store and then calmly walked out and nonchalantly hailed a cab. The taxi driver who had been tailing him told three cops which cab the gunman was in, and he was taken without any trouble. Catlan was apprehended later.

On November 12, 1941, a judge sentenced Kress to a term of seven and a half to fifteen years for his bungled robbery, telling him, "I look upon you as one of the finest examples of the fact that crime doesn't pay. You come of a decent family, but you have been 'cutting the corners' of the law for a long time—and getting away with it. I think you are one of the cleverest crooks ever to be arraigned before me, but the law finally caught up with you."

After serving eighteen years in Alcatraz John Oley was transferred to the federal penitentiary at Atlanta, where he served two more years before being paroled on December 5, 1957. Technically he wasn't eligible for parole until July 1958, but because of good behavior and a medical condition he was released early. He resided with his wife in the upstate New York town of Ballston Spa.

Chapter 21 / FBI vs. NYPD

Two months after his partner Harry Brunette was captured, Merle Vandenbush, who had since been labeled "Public Rat No. 1" by J. Edgar Hoover, was apprehended about forty miles north of New York City after robbing a bank. On February 25, 1937, Vandenbush and a confederate named Anthony Rera entered the Northern Westchester Bank in the upstate town of Katonah at 2 p.m. Dressed as mechanics, complete with grease smeared on their faces, the duo entered the bank and, pulling out .38's, announced to the five people there, "This is a stickup." The five were herded into a safe and ordered to lie down. A gate dividing the safe was closed. Just then a customer walked and was forced to lie down in the front section. The bandits scooped $17,600 into a shopping bag and ran out to their car and sped off. They ditched their car a short distance away and jumped into the trunk of a coupe driven by Anthony's cousin, George Rera, and headed toward the Big Apple.

The news of the robbery spread quickly, and area policemen began to set up road blocks. Twenty-two minutes after the job was pulled George found himself in one of these in the hamlet of Armonk about twelve miles south of Katonah. Three officers were on duty, and when they saw the coupe coming through town Patrolman Gerald Hendricks stepped out into the street and stopped it. George posed as a brush salesman on his way to New York City, but his behavior seemed suspicious, so the cop went to the rear of the car and opened the trunk. Vandenbush and Rera were waiting for him with their .38's, so he jumped back and closed the trunk lid before warning his partners. George tried to jump out of the car and run, but one of the cops had him covered. The two other policemen drew their revolvers and ordered the trapped bandits to drop their guns. Once they heard the clank of metal on metal, the lawmen opened the trunk and took both bandits into custody.

At first Vandenbush gave an alias, but as the cops were taking his fingerprints he blurted out, "I might as well tell you now as later," and admitted his true identity. FBI officials requested that he be taken to their New York City office, but the local D.A. denied extradition saying he would be prosecuted locally. Two weeks later, on the eve of trial, Vandenbush and the Reras all pleaded guilty to the robbery. "Public Rat No. 1" was sent to Sing Sing for a term of forty-five to seventy years. Anthony Rera, whose previous record included a $200 fine in Akron, Ohio, for bootlegging, followed by a sentence of one to twenty years in the same city for having a stolen car, and a seven-year stretch in Sing Sing for an armed robbery in the Bronx, received a like sentence.

Chapter 22 / Messing with the Mob

On October 15, 1935, just hours after Harold "the Shake" Brooks died, police were faced with another gangland shooting undoubtedly related to the previous one. The victim was Irving "Red" Blauner, the "understrapper" for the bank-robbing gang led by Leonard Scarnici. Blauner was taken for a ride and lived (for how long isn't known) but refused to say who did it. All that he told the police was that he was in a car and when it reached Seventy-first Street and Central Park West he was shot twice, once in the neck and once in the chin. His would-be killers kept him in the car as they drove through the park and then dumped him out at the southwest corner of the Metropolitan Museum of Art, where he was found by a woman who heard his groans and called a policeman thinking he was the victim of a hit and run.

The police figured that Blauner was involved with Brooks and the Al Stern gang. There are two details that support this: one, one of the detectives working the case positively identified him as a good friend of "the Shake"; and two, Blauner was wanted by New Jersey police for the botched robbery attempt by the Stern gang at the Cloyden Club.

APPENDIX II

Chapter 1 / "Gentleman Gerald" and the Dutchman

Chapman lived with aunt and uncle at 171 East 107th Street

In 1911 Chapman said he lived at 134 East 124th Street

Chapman arrested October 28, 1911, at 212 West 129th Street

In early 1920s Chapman lived at 12 Gramercy Park

In early 1920s "Dutch" Anderson lived at 20 Gramercy Park

Opium den Anderson frequented was at 61 West 142nd Street

Frank Grey arrested at "Dutch" Schultz's "meeting hall" at 3468 Third Avenue, Bronx

Frank Grey resided at 2474 Grand Avenue, Bronx, at time of his death

Chapter 2 / Let's Misbehave

(All addresses are in Brooklyn unless otherwise noted.)

Cecilia lived at 439 Franklin Avenue

Cecilia and Ed's first place was at 252 Madison Street

They also lived at 461 Franklin Avenue

After first robbery they moved to 1099 Pacific Street

Garage where Ed worked was at 1057 Atlantic Avenue

Ed's mother lived at 887 Dean Street

Cecilia was born at 38 East Fourth Street, Manhattan

Family then moved to 171 Essex Street, Manhattan

Cecilia lived with a sister at 97 Prospect Place

Cecilia worked at two laundries, at 25 Dean Street and 566 DeKalb Avenue

First robbery: Roulston grocery, 289 Seventh Avenue

Second robbery: A & P, 451 Ralph Avenue

Third robbery: Bohack store, 267 Brooklyn Avenue

Fourth robbery: Weinstein drugstore

Fifth robbery: Jopsey drugstore, 311 New York Avenue

Sixth robbery: Fishbein's grocery, 341 Albany Avenue

Seventh robbery: Bohack store, 320 Lafayette Avenue

Eighth robbery: Butler grocery, 80 Third Avenue

Ninth robbery: Weiss drugstore, 371 Sumner Avenue

Final robbery: attempt at National Biscuit Company, 1000 Pacific Street

First Florida residence was 125 Ocean Avenue, Jacksonville

Chapter 3 / Ma Flanagan's Boys

Horton Ice Cream Company located at 205 East Twenty-fourth Street

Frank Flanagan and "Lightning Harry" lived at 248 East Fifty-fifth Street in 1921

Tom Flanagan lived at 129 East Twenty-sixth Street in 1919

Tom Flanagan lived at 346 East Forty-eighth Street at time of death

Joseph Flanagan lived at 86 Amsterdam Avenue in 1922 and was arrested at 797 Eighth Avenue same year

Phipps Houses located at 243 West Sixty-third Street

John Little lived at 208 East Forty-eighth Street in 1921

Joseph Flanagan found dead at 796 Third Avenue

Chapter 4 / Two Worthless Diamonds

Diamond family home located at 1959 Eighty-fourth Street, Brooklyn

Diamond brothers also stayed in furnished room at 141 East Twenty-seventh Street

Diamond Wood Company (box factory) located at 315 East Twenty-second Street

Anthony Pantano lived at 8738 Bay Parkway, Brooklyn

John and Angelo Farina's bungalow (gang rendezvous) located at 2712 Williamsbridge Road, Bronx

John Farina captured at 81 Jefferson Street, Hoboken, New Jersey

Nicholas "Cheeks" Luciano lived at 438 West Broadway

Chapter 5 / Urban Cowboys

Frank Tessler lived at 621 Barretto Street, Brooklyn

The Rothermel brothers at 1471 Second Avenue

Louis Austen lived at 4913 West Third Street, Coney Island, Brooklyn

Rose Hameline lived at 523 East Eighty-second Street

Peter Stroh lived at 206 Stanton Street

Moe Auswaks lived at 753 Jackson Avenue, Bronx

Gang drop located at 79 Fourth Avenue

Abe Peskoff's shop located at 160 West Twenty-fourth Street

Dr. Jacob Lane's office located at 210 East Seventeenth Street

David Brownstein lived at 353 East Fifty-eighth Street

Fred Rothermel hung out at bakery at 1141 Second Avenue

Among jobs pulled by the gang: office of Dr. Harry Batzes, 113 East Second Street; store of Jacob Schulman, 24 Avenue B; drugstore of Phillip Bassin, 1758 East Tremont Avenue, Bronx; drugstore of Charles Bushel, East 172nd Street; pool room of Anton Renner, 325 East 162nd Street; drugstore of Michael Taub, 783 Southern Boulevard; drugstore at 1566 Minford Place; drugstore of Harry Silver, 932 Morris Avenue; Hardware store of Robert Sesfeld, 1293 St. Lawrence Avenue

Chapter 6 / Bum, Killer and Ice Wagon, LLC

"Bum" lived with in-laws at 222 East Ninety-fifth Street

"Bum" captured in 1925 at 161 East 118th Street

During February-March 1926 "Bum" hid out at 407 East Seventeenth Street

"Bum" captured in 1926 at 4274 Third Avenue, Bronx

"Bum" and McCormick assaulted Florence Hart at 1495 Park Avenue

Cunniffe lived at 453 West Forty-sixth Street

Vince McCormick lived at 442 East 135th

Cunniffe and Crowley killed at 257 Highland Avenue, Highland Park, Michigan

Frances Harris, Cunniffe's moll, lived at 210 Clark Place, Elizabeth, New Jersey

Canice Neary lived at 320 East Twentieth Street

Benjamin Haas lived at 556 West 181st Street

Frank Kiekart captured at 2334 Gilman Terrace, Baltimore, Maryland

Chapter 7 / The Daly Show

David DeMaio lived at 229 Union Street, New Rochelle

Gang met at Daylight Bakery, 2093 Third Avenue

John Marino arrested at 767 East 149th Street, Bronx

Mary Rooney lived at 163 West Sixty-sixth Street

Joseph Mazza lived at 15 Twain Street, Baldwin, Long Island, in 1953

Daylight Bakery located at 2093 Third Avenue

Edna Baltimore lived at 210 East 114th Street

John "the Dope" Marino arrested leaving 767 East 149th Street, Bronx

David DeMaio lived at 229 Union Avenue, New Rochelle

Frank Daly lived at 213 East Eighty-first Street

Chapter 8 / The Candy Kid

Whittemores and Goldberg lived at 201 West Eighty-ninth Street

Bernard Mortillaro lived at 576 East 187th Street, Bronx

Pasquale Chicarelli lived at 852 Eighth Avenue

Anthony Paladino lived at 78 Mulberry Street

"Baltimore Willie" Unkelbach captured at 150 Manhattan Avenue

Unkelbach's drug dealer lived at 313 Manhattan Avenue

Gang Rendezvous/Jake Kraemer flat located at 108 West Eightieth Street

Joseph Trop lived at 156 Second Avenue

Paladino and moll shared apartment at 396 Street, Marks Place, Brooklyn

Robert Ernst jewelry store located at 566 Columbus Avenue

Folmer Prit Jewelry store located at 90 Nassau Street

Albert Goudvis robbed in front of 14 West Forty-eighth Street

Lindhous Jewelry Company located at Thirteenth Street and Sixth Avenue

Ross Jewelry Store located at 290 Grand Street

Chantee Club located at 132 West Fifty-second Street

Chapter 9 / Red Scare

John McKenna lived at 157 West Eighty-eighth Street

Mike McKenna lived at 149 Meserole Avenue, Brooklyn

McKenna and Nannery arrested at Wheelman's club, 177 West Eighty-eighth Street

James Nannery lived at 108 West Eighty-second Street

Reuben's Restaurant located at 2270 Broadway

Hofbrau Haus located at 1680 Broadway

Carjacked Grossman in front of 344 Riverside Drive

Dumped Grossman in tenement at 160 East Eighty-fifth Street

John Werner lived at 447 East Seventy-seventh Street

William Reichel lived at 308 East Ninety-fourth Street

American Baking Company located at 540 East Eighty-first Street

Reid Ice Cream Company located at 9 West 144th Street

Harry Lucasik lived at 2110 First Avenue

Peter Powers lived at 1713 Third Avenue

Peter Heslin caught inside 2040 First Avenue

Chapter 10 / From Maiden Lane to the Tombs

Maiden Lane robbery took place at 15 Maiden Lane

Sol Brofman lived at 632 East Eleventh Street

Cohen and Brofman hideout at 561 Madison Avenue

Cohen's Chicago address 4241 Roosevelt Road

Robert Berg's Chicago Address 5107 Kenmore Street

Robert Berg arrested in Chicago at 5201 Winthrop Avenue

Hyman Amberg gave two addresses when arrested 120 Amboy Street and 403 Rockaway Parkway, both Brooklyn

Mintz lived at 481 Alabama Avenue, Brooklyn

Card game where Mintz was wounded 293 Sutter Avenue, Brooklyn

Mintz captured after leaving doctor's office at 143 East Twenty-first Street

Isadore Alderman lived at 1441 Broadway

Robert Werner a.k.a. Weiner lived 512 Rockaway Parkway, Brooklyn

Oscar Amberg lived at 2620 Beverly Road, Brooklyn

Rodack "the Fighting Jeweler's" shop located at 3630 Broadway

A. Simms & Company located at 2426 Grand Concourse, Bronx

Raphael Kleinman robbed in restaurant at 113 Norfolk Street

Jacob Woldar pawnshop at 274 Grand Street, Brooklyn

Jacob Levin pawnshop at 171 Lenox Avenue

Herman Goldberg pawnshop at 91 Eldridge

Sam Brill shop at 34 East Broadway

Chapter 11 / Don't Cry Out Loud

Phillip Oberst lived at 341 West Forty-ninth Street

Bernard "Frenchy" Frankel lived at 550 Tenth Avenue

Jimmy O'Connor lived at 759 Tenth Avenue

Peter Mahoney lived at 254 West Sixteenth Street

John Kerrigan/Ward lived at 312 Spring Street

Leo Hecker lived at 146 East Eleventh Street

Liccione Bank located at 590 East 187th Street, Bronx

Oberst arrested at 301 West Thirteenth Street

Roosevelt Hospital located at Fifty-ninth Street between Ninth and Tenth avenues

Chapter 12 / Seeing Red

(All addresses are in Brooklyn.)

"Red" Moran and James De Michaels roomed at 154 Dean Street

"Red's" family home was at 1205 Nostrand Avenue

Moran gang stopped to have film developed at 55 Fulton Street

James De Michaels arrested at 1375 St. John's Place

Moran shot officers Byrnes and Daszkiewicz in front of 172 Hicks Street

Robert Tate lived at 1888 Pacific Street

After shooting the police officers Moran ran into 62 Clark Street

"Red's" girlfriend Agnes Guilfoyle lived at 578 New York Avenue

William Reid lived at 1963 Homecrest Avenue

Moran gang robbed Joseph Tracer's drugstore at 107 Prospect Park S.W., $60 taken

Moran gang robbed Ted Rasmussen's lunch wagon at 732 Fifth Avenue, $40 taken

Chapter 13 / Dishonorable Mention 1920-1929

Hoey lived at 425 West Thirty-fifth Street

After murder of Neville, Hoey ran into 524 West Thirty-ninth Street

Spent the night of the murder at a room in 324 East Nineteenth Street

Hoey's sister lived at 144 Lane Avenue, Arrochar, Staten Island

John "Soup" Gleason lived at 447 West Forty-sixth Street and was found dead at 348 East Twenty-eighth Street

United Cigar store where Levy met his doom located at 880 East Tremont Avenue, Bronx

Joseph Oates lived at 120 East 119th Street

Robberies pulled by Levy and Oates: National Wet Wash Laundry at 1471 Wilkins Avenue, Bronx, 10/14/21, $2,800 taken; Caswell Motor Company at 651 West 125th Street; United Cigar Store at 2432 Eighth Avenue, 12/21/21; United Cigar Store at 1789 Southern Blvd, Bronx, also 12/21/21; United Cigar Store at 361 Lenox Avenue

"Radio Burglar" Paul Hilton's robberies, all in Queens: 8019 Ninety-First Avenue, 1/30/26; 8714 88th Street, 1/31/26; 10807 103rd Avenue, 2/3/26; 3316 Flushing Place, 2/3/26; 10613 103rd Avenue, 2/6/26; 7422 Jamaica Avenue, 2/6/26; 9111 St. Charles Court, 2/10/26; 8629 Ninetieth Street,

2/10/26; 233 Beach Twenty-third Street, 2/14/26; 113 Beach Eighty-fifth Street, 2/17/26; 9133 Eighty-fourth, 2/19/26; 10230 Ninety-First Avenue, 2/20/26; 9419 Ninety-fifth Street, 2/26/26 (Officer Biegel shot); 10215 Eighty-sixth Street, 3/3/26; 236 Ninety-Fifth Avenue, 3/5/26; 10544 131st Street, 3/11/26; 10546 131st Street, 3/11/26; 11416 100th Avenue, 3/11/26; 8835 Seventy-fourth Place, 3/13/26; 8829 Seventy-fourth Place, 3/13/26; 10153 Ninety-seventh Street, 3/17/26; 10155 Ninety-seventh Street, 3/17/26; 10810 103rd Avenue, 3/19/26; 10318 109th Street, 3/19/26; 8415 101st Street, 3/23/26; 9033 Seventy-eighth Street, 3/23/26 (Officers Donnolly and Kenny shot); 11911 109th Street, 4/8/26; 11714 107th Avenue, 4/8/26

"English Harry" Wallon gang arrested after robbing gamblers at 55 West Forty-sixth Street

Both Baraseck brothers and John Maxwell lived at 937 Jefferson Avenue, Brooklyn

Killed Joseph Mullarky, clerk at A & P, 486 Dean Street, Brooklyn

Robbed and critically wounded proprietor of the Summer live chicken market at 6224 Seventeenth Avenue, Brooklyn

Seiler and Tipping killed Officer Masterson at Speakeasy at 214 West 103rd Street

Walter Tipping lived at 532 West Fifty-third Street

Peter Seiler lived at 207 East Eighty-third Street

Edwin Jerge killed at intersection of Thirty-sixth Street and Broadway

Samuel "Kitty the Horse" Weissman lived at 223 East Second Street

Chapter 14 / New York's Most Desperate Criminal

James Nannery lived at 822 Second Avenue, Astoria (1927)

John Bolling lived at 46 West Eighty-third Street, Astoria

Jack Gormley lived at 140 West Fifty-fifth Street

Westchester branch of Bronx National Bank located at 32 Westchester Square, Westchester

Chapter 15 / Sexy Takes a Ride

Vivian Gordon lived at 156 East Thirty-seventh Street, no. 30

Gordon arrested by Detective McLaughlin in 1923 at 124 West Sixty-fourth Street

Chowder Head Cohen lived at 1255 Stratford Avenue, Bronx

Morris Levine lived at 1240 Washington Avenue, Bronx

Sam Greenberg lived at 11 Rivington Street

Madeline Tully lived at 294 Riverside Drive

David Butterman lived at 629 West 173rd Street

Harry Stein arrested at Eightieth Street and West End Avenue

Greenberg arrested at Norfolk and Delancey

Levine arrested Fourteenth Street and Second Avenue

John Radeloff lived at 916 Carroll Street, Brooklyn

Radeloff's office located at 66 Court Street, Brooklyn

Harry Schlitten lived at 300 West Forty-ninth Street

Schlitten hired death car from 123 Suffolk Street

Tea House Stein hung out at located at 1030 Sixth Avenue

Chapter 16 / King of the Punks

Officer Maurice Harlow arrested John Crowley for the first time in front of 222 East 104th Street

Officer Harlow interrupted, leading to shootout at 1812 Third Avenue

After being shot, John Crowley crawled into vestibule at 1803 Third Avenue

John lived at the Crowley family home at 300 East 134th Street (1925)

Shootout between Francis and Detective Schaedel at 369 Lexington Avenue, nineteenth floor

At time of Schaedel shootout Crowley family home was at 134-26 231st Street, Queens

Crowley was most likely living with a sister and brother-in-law next door at 134-28

Primrose Dance Palace located at 322 West 125th Street

Virginia Brannen lived at 386 East 136th Street

Helen Walsh lived part time with her mom at 69 Nassau Street, Brooklyn

Duringer lived at 12 Broad Avenue, Ossining

Robert LeClair lived at 905 Summit Avenue, Bronx

Mildred Moore lived at 1775 Townsend Avenue, Bronx

Police siege at 303 West Ninetieth Street

Chapter 17 / College Boy

Roy's 1926 address 583 Riverside Drive

Roy and mother's 1931 address 547 West 123rd Street

Karos & Stein Jewelry store located at 562 Fifth Avenue

Jack Giller lived at 2933 Thirtieth Street, Coney Island, Brooklyn

Mad Dot Boat Club located at 251 Dyckman Street

Chapter 18 / It Came from Massachusetts

Fred Plentl lived at 62 East 115th Street

Mount Kisco house located at 152 Kisco Avenue

Anthony Reino lived at 611East 182nd Street, Bronx

Philip Zeigler lived at 1037 Bedford Avenue, Brooklyn

Charles Herzog lived at 1525 Charlotte Street, Bronx

Scarnici, Reino and Zeigler captured at 1448 Webster Avenue, Bronx

Addresses for Marcel Poffo (all Bronx): 1031 Freeman Street (1929), 1308 Union Avenue (January 1933), 1547 Longfellow Avenue (June 1933)

Addresses for Max Parkin (all Bronx): 1451 Wilkins Avenue (1929), 1466 Morris Avenue (January 1933), 1455 Sheridan Avenue (June 1933)

Chapter 19 / Bride of the Mad Dog

Sam Medal's restaurant located at 147 West Forty-seventh Street

Medal lived at 1442 Harrod Avenue, Bronx

Medal also kept a suite at the Hotel St. Moritz, 50 Central Park South

Thomas Pace lived at 154 East 112th Street

Joe Ventre lived at 1861 Wallace Avenue, Bronx

Robbed Harry Guth's store located at 1166 Woodcrest Avenue, Bronx

Robbed Morris Adler's store located at 1810 Archer Street, Bronx

Isadore Moroh lived at 1101 Manor Avenue, Bronx

Mollie Schwartz was killed in front of 1175 Wheeler Avenue, Bronx

Lottie, Pace, and Ventre arrested at Dixie Hotel, 225 West Forty-second Street

Chapter 20 / $427,000 Payday

Rubel plant located on Bay Nineteenth Street between Cropsey and Bath avenues

Gang rendezvoused at Madeline Tully's rooming house at 322 West Ninetieth Street to split money

Bernard McMahon taken to Madeline Tully's apartment at 334 Riverside Drive, where he died

McMahon treated by Dr. Harry Gilbert of 11 West Sixty-ninth Street; he also assisted in amputating McMahon's legs.

McMahon's lived at 546 East 146th Street

Trunk containing Bernard McMahon lfound in front of 154 West Seventy-fourth Street

Thomas Quinn lived at 52-20 Forty-sixth Street, Queens

John Manning lived at 340 West Eighteenth Street and was killed in front of 336 East 108th Street

Percy Geary arrested at 2525 Bedford Avenue, Brooklyn

John Oley arrested at 142 St. Paul's Place, Brooklyn

Harold Crowley arrested at 78 East Forty-second Street, Brooklyn

Madeline Tully lived at 519 East Eighty-third Street (1938)

Chapter 21 / FBI vs. the NYPD

Brunette captured at 304 West 102nd Street

Arlene LaBeau originally lived at 2754 Broadway

Chapter 22 / Messing with the Mob

Benny Holinsky lived at 1308 Union Avenue, Bronx

Frank Dolak lived at 1771 Fulton Avenue, Bronx

Dolak and Holinsky killed at 174th Street and Third Avenue, Bronx

Leo Aaronson lived at 1636 Washington Avenue, Bronx

Edward Knott lived at 990 Cauldwell Avenue, Bronx

Irving Blauner lived at 264 East 180th Street

Harold "the Shake" Brooks killed at 120th Street and Madison Avenue

Bart Salvo lived at 645 East 222nd Street, Bronx

Stein found dead at 474 Fifteenth Avenue, Newark, New Jersey

Chapter 23 / Dishonorable Mention 1930-1940

Vincent Gaffney lived at 500 West Fifty-third Street (1918)

Gaffney shot Charles Tucker at Fifty-first Street and Tenth Avenue

Escaped from police in his underwear form 307 West 118th Street

In 1931 Gaffney lived at 32-14 Thirty-second Street, Queens, and was found dead in front of 635 West Fifty-fourth Street

Mendoza Fur & Dyeing Works located at 712 East 133rd Street

John Brecht lived at 1125 Tinton Avenue

Herbert Hasse lived at 315 East 159th Street

Bob Carey and Rose Sanborn found dead in second-floor apartment at 220 West 104th Street

Spot Leahy found dead in front of 2744 Broadway

Leahy lived at Manhattan Towers Hotel located at 2166 Broadway

Arsenal arrested at Madeline Tully's rooming house located at 322 West Ninetieth Street

Barney's Department Store located at 111 Seventh Avenue

Fred Dunn killed at 11 West Sixty-fifth Street, first floor; lived with wife in basement apartment

In 1931 David Beadle lived at 597 Tenth Avenue

Speakeasy where he killed the Lawlors located at 500 Eleventh Avenue

Lawrence and William Lawlor lived at 545 West Forty-ninth Street

Michael Lawlor lived at 1387 Third Avenue

In 1939 Beadle lived at 43-21 193rd Street, Queens

Killed walking out of bar at 651 Tenth Avenue

Gerard Vernotico lived at 191 Prince Street

Antonio Lonzo lived at 305 East Twenty-eighth Street

Both found dead on roof of 124 Thompson Street

Michael "Little Apples" Reggione lived at 125 Thompson Street

Little Apples killed inside 340 East 110th Street

John "Patsy Chip Chip" Reggione lived at 2467 Belmont Avenue

Reggione stopped off at 184 West Broadway before being killed in front of vacant lot

Louis "Fat Elevator" Reggione lived at 174 Thompson Street (1932) and 282 Mulberry Street (1940) and was killed outside 284 Mulberry Street

NOTES

Chapter 1 / Gentleman Gerald and the Dutchman

1. *New York Times*, 4/6/26, pg. 1
2. *New York Times*, 10/29/11, pg. 1; *New York Times*, 8/23/22, pg. 17
3. *New York Times*, 11/3/25, pg. 1; 11/6/25, pg. 1; 7/8/26, pg. 7; 8/23/22, pg. 17
4. *True Detective Mysteries*, November 1929; *New York Times*, 8/17/22, pg. 17
5. *Buffalo Morning Express* 12/2/21, pg. 1; *Buffalo Daily Courier* 12/2/21, pg. 1
6. *New York Herald*, 7/6/22, pg. 1; *True Detective Mysteries*, December 1929
7. *New York Tribune*, 7/6/22, pg. 1
8. *New York Times*, 3/28/26, pg. 18
9. *True Detective Mysteries*, November 1929, December 1929, January 1930
10. *True Detective Mysteries*, January 1930; *New York Herald*, 7/5/22 pg. 1, 7/6/22, pg. 1; *New York Tribune*, 7/6/22
11. *New York Times*, 7/4/22, pg. 1
12. *New York Herald*, 7/5/22, pg. 1, 7/6/22, pg. 1
13. *True Detective Mysteries*, Jan 1930; *New York Herald*, 7/5/22, pg. 1, 7/6/22, pg. 1

14. *New York Times*, 8/24/22, pg. 13
15. *True Detective Mysteries*, January 1927; *New York Times*, 3/28/23, pg. 1
16. *New York Times*, 3/28/23, pg. 1
17. Ibid., *True Detective Mysteries*, January 1927; *New York Times*, 3/29/23, pg. 21
18. *New York Times*, 3/29/23, pg. 21
19. *True Detective Mysteries*, November 1929; *New York Times*, 4/5/23, pg. 1, 4/6/23, pg. 1
20. *True Detective Mysteries*, November 1929; *New York Times*, 4/5/23, pg. 1
21. *True Detective Mysteries*, November 1929; *New York Times*, 4/7/23, pg. 1
22. *True Detective Mysteries*, February 1927
23. *True Detective Mysteries*, October 1929
24. *New York Times*, 12/31/23, pg. 1
25. *New York Times*, 3/28/25, pg. 1
26. Ibid.
27. *New York Times*, 3/31/25, pg. 1, 4/3/25, pg. 1
28. *New York Times*, 3/31/25, pg. 1
29. *New York Times*, 10/13/24, pg. 1, 4/3/25, pg. 1

30. *New York Times*, 11/18/24, pg. 2
31. *New York Evening Journal*, 1/19/25, pg. 1
32. *New York Times*, 1/19/25, pg. 1, 8/15/25, pg. 1
33. *New York Times*, 1/20/25, pg. 1, 1/19/25, pg. 1
34. *New York Times*, 1/22/25, pg. 10
35. *New York Times*, 2/14/25, pg. 6, 4/6/26, pg. 1, 2/6/25, pg. 1
36. *New York Times*, 2/14/25, pg. 6
37. *Time*, April 13, 1925
38. *New York Times*, 3/28/25, pg. 1
39. *New York World*, 8/15/25, pg. 1
40. *New York Times*, 8/15/25, pg. 1
41. *New York Times*, 3/31/25, pg. 1
42. *New York Times*, 4/1/25, pg. 1
43. *New York Times*, 4/3/25, pg. 1
44. *New York Times*, 4/5/25, pg. 1
45. *New York Times*, 4/8/25, pg. 23
46. *New York Times*, 4/5/25, pg. 1
47. *New York Times*, 7/3/25, pg. 4
48. *New York Times*, 7/3/25, pg. 4
49. Ibid.
50. *New York World*, 8/15/25, pg. 1; *New York Times*, 8/15/25, pg. 1
51. *New York Times*, 8/23/25, pg. 24
52. *New York Times*, 11/3/25, pg. 1
53. *New York Times*, 3/16/26, pg. 1
54. *New York Times*, 4/6/26, pg. 1
55. Ibid.
56. *New York Times*, 4/7/26, pg. 1
57. *New York Times*, 4/6/26, pg. 1; *Real Detective*, October 1931
58. *New York Times*, 4/7/26, pg. 1

Chapter 2 / Let's Misbehave

1. *New York American*, 4/28/24, pg. 1; *New York American*, 4/29/24, pg. 1
2. *New York American*, 4/30/24, pg. 6; *New York Times*, 4/16/24
3. *New York American*, 4/30/24, pg. 6
4. Ibid.
5. Ibid.
6. *New York American*, 5/1/24
7. Ibid.
8. *New York American*, 5/2/24
9. Ibid.
10. *New York American*, 5/3/24; *New York Times*, 4/23/24, pg. 1
11. Ibid.
12. *New York American*, 5/3/24
13. *New York Times*, 4/23/24, pg. 1
14. *New York American*, 5/5/24, pg. 6
15. *New York Times*, 4/23/24, pg. 1, 3/6/24, pg. 1; *Actual Detective*, February 1938
16. *New York Times*, 4/22/24, pg. 1
17. *New York American*, 5/6/24; *New York Times*, 5/6/24, pg. 1
18. *Actual Detective*, February 1938
19. *True Detective Mysteries*, July 1924; *New York American*, 5/7/24
20. *New York American*, 5/7/24
21. Ibid.
22. Ibid.
23. Ibid.
24. *New York American*, 5/7/24, 5/8/24; *New York Times*, 4/2/24, pg. 21; *New York Evening Journal*, 4/23/24
25. *New York American*, 5/8/24
26. *Actual Detective*, February 1938; *New York Times*, 4/21/24, pg. 1
27. *New York Times*, 4/22/24, pg. 1
28. Ibid.
29. *New York American*, 5/8/24
30. *New York American*, 5/8/24; *New York Times*, 4/16/24
31. *Actual Detective* magazine, February 1938
32. Ibid.
33. Ibid., *New York Times*, 4/22/24, pg. 1
34. *New York American*, 5/9/24; *Actual Detective* magazine, February 1938; *True Detective Mysteries*, July 1924
35. *New York Times*, 4/22/24, pg. 1
36. Ibid.
37. Ibid.
38. *New York American*, 5/9/24
39. *Actual Detective* magazine, February 1938; *New York Times*, 4/23/24, pg. 1
40. *New York Evening Journal*, 4/23/24, pg. 1
41. *New York American*, 4/28/24, pg. 1
42. *New York American*, 5/10/24
43. *New York Evening Journal*, 4/23/24, pg. 1
44. Ibid.
45. *New York American*, 5/10/24
46. *New York Evening Journal*, 4/23/24, pg. 1
47. *New York Times*, 4/27/24, pg. 1, 4/29/24, pg. 1
48. *New York Times*, 4/29/24, pg. 1
49. *New York American*, 4/28/24, pg. 1
50. *New York Times*, 4/25/24
51. *New York American*, 4/28/24, pg. 1

52. *New York Evening Journal*, 4/23/24, pg. 1
53. *New York Times*, 4/25/24
54. *New York American*, 4/28/24, pg. 1
55. Ibid.
56. *New York Evening Journal*, 5/6/24, pg. 1
57. *New York Times*, 5/7/24, pg. 1
58. Ibid.
59. Ibid.
60. Ibid.
61. *Brooklyn Daily Eagle*, 4/22/24 p 1
62. *New York Times*, 5/7/24, pg. 1
63. Ibid.
64. *New York Times*, 5/8/24
65. *New York Times*, 5/9/24, pg. 12
66. *New York Times*, 5/10/24, pg. 28
67. *New York American*, 5/10/24

Chapter 3 / Ma Flanagan's Boys
1. *New York Evening Journal*, 6/9/15; *New York Times*, 6/9/15
2. *New York Times*, 8/12/21
3. *New York World*, 11/18/29
4. *New York Herald Tribune*, 11/18/29, pg. 2
5. *New York Times*, 12/29/20
6. *New York Times*, 5/25/21
7. *New York Herald*, 7/12/21; *New York Times*, 8/12/21
8. *New York Herald*, 12/23/21; *New York Times*, 12/23/21
9. *New York Times*, 3/12/22
10. *New York Times*, 6/21/22
11. *New York Times*, 7/6/22, 1/19/23
12. *Behind the Green Lights*, Willemse, Cornelius
13. *New York Times*, 12/1/22
14. *Behind the Green Lights*, Willemse, Cornelius
15. *New York Herald Tribune*, 11/18/29, pg. 2; *New York World*, 11/18/29

Chapter 4 / Two Worthless Diamonds
1. *New York Times*, 11/15/25, pg. 1; *True Detective Mysteries*, February 1930
2. Ibid.
3. *New York Times*, 11/26/23; *True Detective Mysteries*, February 1930
4. *New York Times*, 11/26/23
5. *New York Times*, 11/27/23; *True Detective Mysteries*, February 1930
6. Ibid.

7. *True Detective Mysteries*, February 1930; *New York Times*, 11/29/23
8. Ibid.
9. *New York Times*, 12/9/23, pg. 1
10. Ibid.
11. *True Detective Mysteries*, February 1930; *New York Times*, 2/9/24
12. *New York Times*, 3/4/24, pg. 21
13. *New York Times*, 5/1/25; *True Detective Mysteries*, February 1930

Chapter 5 / Urban Cowboys
1. *New York Times*, 10/29/25, pg. 27
2. *New York Times*, 10/19/25, pg. 1
3. *New York Times*, 11/6/25, pg. 25
4. *New York Times*, 3/20/19, pg. 8
5. *New York Times*, 12/5/20, pg. 10
6. *New York Times*, 10/18/25, pg. 1; *New York Times*, 10/29/25
7. *New York Times*, 10/19/25, pg. 1
8. *True Detective Mysteries*, November 1926; *New York Times*, 10/18/25, pg. 1; *New York Evening Journal*, 10/17/25
9. Ibid.
10. *New York Times*, 10/18/25, pg. 1
11. Ibid.
12. Ibid.
13. *New York Times*, 10/19/25, pg. 1
14. Ibid.
15. *New York Times*, 10/18/25, pg. 1
16. Ibid.
17. *New York Times*, 11/6/25, pg. 25, 3/11/26

Chapter 6 / Bum, Killer, and Ice Wagon LLC
1. *Official Detective* magazine, June 15, 1937
2. Ibid.
3. *New York Times*, 5/2/10, pg. 18, 5/10/10, pg. 1
4. *Official Detective* magazine, June 15, 1937; *New York Times*, 10/17/26
5. Ibid.
6. *New York Times*, 7/14/24
7. *New York Times*, 11/3/26
8. *New York Times*, 11/2/26, pg. 1
9. *New York Times*, 4/5/24, pg. 1
10. Ibid.
11. Ibid.
12. *New York Times*, 1/20/25
13. *New York Times*, 3/8/25
14. *New York World*, 7/1/25, pg. 4;

New York Times, 7/1/25, pg. 8
15. *New York Daily News* 12/15/25, pg. 2;
    New York Times, 12/15/25
16. *New York Herald Tribune,* 10/5/26,
    pg. 1; *New York Times,* 10/5/26
17. *New York Times,* 10/6/26, pg. 1
18. *New York Times,* 10/15/26, pg. 1
19. *New York Times,* 11/1/26, pg. 1
20. *New York Times,* 11/26/26, pg. 1
21. Ibid.
22. Ibid.
23. Ibid.
24. *New York Times,* 11/27/26
25. Ibid.
26. New York Post 11/25/26
27. *New York Times,* 11/27/26
28. *New York Daily News* 1/15/31, pg. 2

Chapter 7 / The Daly Show
1. *True Detective Magazine,* August
   1930
2. Ibid.
3. Ibid.
4. Ibid.
5. Ibid.
6. *Bridgeport Telegram,* 8/21/25, pg. 1
7. *True Detective Magazine,* August
   1930
8. *New York Times,* 10/17/25, pg. 1
9. *New York Times,* 11/28/25, pg. 5
10. *New York Times,* 6/25/26, pg. 6
11. Ibid.
12. *New York Times,* 8/17/26, pg. 4
13. *New York Times,* 8/20/26, pg. 2

Chapter 8 / The Candy Kid
1. *Official Detective Stories,* July 15,
   1937
2. Ibid.
3. *New York Times,* 3/20/26, pg. 1
4. *New York Times,* 3/24/26, pg. 1
5. *New York Times,* 3/24/26, pg. 1,
   8/13/26, pg. 1
6. *New York Times,* 3/24/26, pg. 1
7. *Official Detective Stories* July 15,
   1937
8. Ibid.
9. *New York Times,* 3/20/26/, pg. 1
10. *New York Times,* 3/26/26, pg. 2
11. Ibid.
12. *New York Times,* 3/30/26, pg. 1
13. *New York Times,* 3/26/26, pg. 2
14. Ibid.

15. *New York Times,* 12/3/25, 3/26/26/, pg. 2
16. *New York Times,* 3/26/26, pg. 2
17. *New York Times,* 12/24/25, pg. 2,
    3/26/26, pg. 1
18. *New York Times,* 1/12/26, pg. 33, *New
    York Times,* 3/26/26, pg. 1
19. *New York Times,* 3/21/26, pg. 1
20. *New York Times,* 3/20/26, pg. 1
21. New York Post 3/22/26
22. *New York Times,* 3/26/26, pg. 1
23. Ibid.
24. Ibid.
25. *New York Times,* 3/27/26, pg. 1
26. Ibid.
27. *New York Times,* 4/1/26, pg. 1
28. *New York Times,* 4/2/26, pg. 1
29. *New York Times,* 4/7/26, pg. 2
30. *New York Times,* 4/15/26, pg. 29
31. *New York Times,* 4/22/26, pg. 1
32. *New York Times,* 4/28/26, pg. 1
33. *New York Times,* 4/30/26, pg. 1, 5/1/26,
    pg. 1
34. *New York Times,* 4/30/26, pg. 1
35. Ibid.
36. *New York Times,* 5/2/26, pg. 1
37. *New York Times,* 5/22/26, pg. 1
38. *New York Times,* 8/13/26, pg. 1
39. Ibid.
40. Ibid.
41. *New York Times,* 8/14/26, pg. 4
42. *New York Times,* 8/13/26, pg. 1,
    8/14/26, pg. 4
43. *New York Times,* 8/17/26, pg. 23

Chapter 9 / Red Scare
1. Indictment 153546 People of State of
   New York Against Michael McKenna
2. *New York Times,* 11/4/26, pg. 2
3. *New York Times,* 3/9/26, pg. 25
4. *New York Times,* 3/23/26
5. Indictment 153546 People of State of
   New York Against Michael McKenna
6. *Master Detective Magazine,* November 1935
7. Indictment 153546 People of State of
   New York Against Michael McKenna
8. *New York Evening Post,* 6/29/26
9. *New York Times,* 7/11/26, pg. 14
10. *New York Times,* 7/15/26, pg. 14
11. *New York Times,* 7/26/26, pg. 1
12. *New York Evening Journal,* 7/31/26,
    pg. 1; *New York Journal American,*
    7/31/26, pg. 3

13. *New York Times*, 11/24/27, pg. 17
14. *New York Times*, 9/13/26, pg. 1
15. Ibid.
16. *New York Times*, 11/24/27, pg. 17

Chapter 10 / From Maiden Lane to the Tombs
1. *New York Times*, 5/21/27, pg. 21
2. *New York Times*, 12/9/26, pg. 16
3. *New York Times*, 7/20/26; Indictment 167034 People of the State of New York against Samuel Schwartz
4. *New York Times*, 7/22/26, pg. 1
5. Ibid.
6. *New York Times*, 10/17/25
7. *New York Times*, 12/4/25, pg. 25
8. *New York Times*, 12/28/25, pg. 17
9. *New York Times*, 2/1/26, pg. 4
10. *New York Times*, 2/17/26, pg. 23; *New York Times*, 8/29/26
11. *New York Times*, 2/18/26, pg. 25
12. *New York Times*, 7/23/26, pg. 1
13. Ibid.
14. Ibid.
15. *New York Times*, 5/21/27, pg. 21
16. *New York Times*, 8/28/26, pg. 1
17. *New York Times*, 5/4/27, pg. 27
18. *New York Times*, 8/28/26, pg. 1, 8/29/29
19. *New York Times*, 8/29/26
20. *New York Times*, 10/14/26, pg. 4, 10/15/26, pg. 2
21. *New York Times*, 11/4/26, pg. 1

Chapter 11 / Don't Cry Out Loud
1. *New York Times*, 7/28/26, pg. 1
2. *New York Times*, 7/23/26, pg. 1
3. *New York Times*, 7/2/26, pg. 1
4. Ibid.
5. *New York Times*, 7/11/26, pg. 19
6. *New York Times*, 7/29/26, pg. 1
7. Ibid.
8. Ibid.
9. *New York Times*, 8/10/26, pg. 1
10. *New York Times*, 9/6/26, pg. 17
11. *New York Times*, 9/15/26, pg. 31
12. *New York Times*, 9/16/26 29
13. Ibid.
14. *New York Times*, 9/17/26, pg. 23
15. *New York Times*, 9/18/26, pg. 19

Chapter 12 / Seeing Red
1. *New York Times*, 11/23/26, pg. 1

2. Ibid.
3. *New York Times*, 11/24/26, pg. 25
4. *New York Times*, 11/23/26, pg. 1
5. *New York Times*, 11/24/26, pg. 25
6. Ibid.
7. *New York Times*, 11/23/26, pg. 1
8. *New York Times*, 11/24/26, pg. 1
9. Ibid.
10. *New York Times*, 11/27/26, pg. 19
11. *New York Times*, 1/26/27, pg. 8
12. *New York Times*, 1/28/27, pg. 40
13. Ibid.
14. *New York Times*, 2/1/27, pg. 29
15. *New York Times*, 5/20/27, pg. 21
16. Ibid.
17. *New York Times*, 2/9/28, pg. 27
18. *New York Times*, 3/21/28, pg. 15
19. *New York Times*, 11/10/28, pg. 19
20. *New York Times*, 12/14/28, pg. 22

Chapter 13 / Dishonorable Mention 1920-1929
1. *New York Times*, 8/30/21, pg. 1
2. Ibid.
3. Ibid.
4. *New York Times*, 9/10/21, pg. 2
5. Ibid.
6. *New York Times*, 9/26/21, pg. 5
7. *New York Times*, 6/5/22, pg. 20
8. *New York Times*, 10/2/22, pg. 3
9. *New York Times*, 12/24/21, pg. 1
10. Ibid.
11. *New York Times*, 12/25/21, pg. 13
12. *New York Times*, 4/14/26, pg. 1
13. Ibid.
14. *Official Detective* magazine, January 1939
15. Ibid.
16. *New York Times*, 4/14/26, pg. 1
17. Ibid.
18. Ibid.
19. Ibid.
20. *New York Times*, 4/15/26, pg. 29
21. *New York Times*, 4/16/26, pg. 7
22. *New York Times*, 4/5/26, pg. 1, 5/24/29, pg. 14
23. *New York Times*, 4/5/26, pg. 1
24. *New York Times*, 5/6/26, pg. 12
25. *New York Times*, 5/24/29, pg. 14
26. *New York Times*, 5/9/26, pg. 1
27. *New York Herald Tribune*, 5/9/26, pg. 1
28. *New York Times*, 6/7/26
29. *New York Times*, 6/19/26

30. *New York Times*, 2/9/27, pg. 1
31. *New York Times*, 2/1/27, pg. 1
32. *New York Times*, 2/10/27, pg. 48
33. Ibid.
34. *New York Times*, 2/9/27, pg. 1
35. *New York Times*, 5/3/27, pg. 13
36. *New York Times*, 6/19/28, pg. 13
37. *New York Herald Tribune*, 7/4/28;
    New York Times, 7/14/28, pg. 8,
    7/15/28, pg. 21
38. *New York Times*, 6/18/28, pg. 1

**Chapter 14 / New York's Most
Desperate Criminal**
1. *New York Times*, 1/14/27, pg. 1
2. *New York Times*, 7/16/28, pg. 1
3. *Startling Detective Adventures*,
   August 1931; *New York Daily News*,
   4/12/31, pg. 60
4. *New York Daily News* 4/12/31, pg. 60
5. *New York Times*, 3/1/29, pg. 16
6. *New York Daily News*, 4/12/31, pg. 60
7. Ibid.
8. *Startling Detective Adventures*,
   August 1931
9. *New York Times* 4/27/31, pg. 1
10. *Startling Detective Adventures*,
    August 1931
11. *New York Times*, 4/27/31, pg. 1
12. *New York Daily News*, 4/27/31, pg. 3
13. *Startling Detective Adventures*,
    August 1931

Chapter 15 / Sexy Takes a Ride
1. *New York Times*, 3/3/31, pg. 1
2. *True Detective Mysteries*, November
   1931
3. Ibid.
4. *New York Times*, 2/27/31, pg. 1
5. *New York Times*, 2/28/31, pg. 1
6. *New York Times*, 2/27/31, pg. 1,
   2/28/31, pg. 1
7. *True Detective Mysteries*, November
   1931
8. Ibid.
9. *New York Times*, 3/2/31, pg. 1
10. *New York Times*, 2/28/31, pg. 1
11. *New York Times*, 2/27/31, pg. 1
12. *New York Times*, 3/3/31, pg. 1; *True
    Detective Mysteries*, November 1931
13. *New York Times*, 3/3/31, pg. 1
14. *True Detective Mysteries*, November
    1931
15. *New York Times*, 6/23/31, pg. 1

16. Ibid.
17. *True Detective Mysteries*, November
    1931
18. Ibid.
19. *New York Times*, 6/23/31, pg. 1
20. *New York Times*, 7/1/31

Chapter 16 / King of the Punks
1. *New York Daily News*, 1/22/32, pg. 6
2. *New York Times*, 1/22/32, pg. 40
3. *New York Times*, 5/29/31, pg. 13
4. *New York Times*, 1/22/32, pg. 40
5. *New York Times*, 2/23/25, pg. 1
6. *New York Times*, 5/7/31, pg. 3
7. *New York Times*, 5/9/31, pg. 1
8. *New York Times*, 5/29/31, pg. 13
9. *New York Times*, 3/14/31, pg. 20
10. *True Detective Mysteries*, April 1932
11. Ibid.
12. Ibid.
13. Ibid.
14. Ibid.
15. Ibid.
16. Ibid.
17. *True Detective Mysteries*, April 1932
19. *New York Times*, 5/7/31, pg. 3
20. Ibid.
21. Ibid.
22. *New York Times*, 5/9/31, pg. 1
23. *New York Times*, 5/7/31, pg. 3
24. *New York Daily News*, 5/7/31
25. Ibid.
26. *Master Detective*, August 1932
27. Ibid.
28. Ibid.
29. *New York Times*, 5/8/31, pg. 1
30. Ibid.
31. Ibid.
32. Ibid.
33. *New York Herald Tribune*, 5/9/31, pg. 1
34. Ibid.
35. *New York Times*, 5/10/31, pg. 6
36. *New York Times*, 5/11/31, pg. 6
37. *New York Times*, 5/27/31, pg. 23
38. *New York Times*, 5/30/31, pg. 1
39. *New York Times*, 5/31/31, pg. 16
40. *New York Times*, 6/2/31, pg. 60
41. Ibid.
42. Ibid.
43. *New York Times*, 6/3/31, pg. 20
44. *New York Herald Tribune*, 1/22/32
45. *New York Times*, 12/3/31, pg. 10
46. *New York Herald Tribune*, 12/11/31

47. *New York Daily News* 1/21/32, pg. 2
48. *New York Times*, 1/22/32, pg. 40

Chapter 17 / College Boy

1. *New York Times*, 12/2/26, pg. 16;
   Brooklyn Standard Union 5/12/31;
   New York Times, 5/13/31
2. *New York Times*, 11/14/29, pg. 25
3. Ibid.
4. *New York Times*, 11/19/29, pg. 16
5. *New York Times*, 12/5/30, pg. 27,
   12/6/30, pg. 38
6. *New York Daily News* 5/13/31, pg. 2;
   New York Times, 12/6/30, pg. 38
7. *New York Times*, 2/19/31, pg. 21
8. *New York Times*, 8/3/31
9. *New York Herald Tribune*, 5/13/31,
   pg. 4; *New York Times*, 5/13/31;
   Brooklyn Standard Union, 5/13/31
10. Ibid.
11. *New York Times*, 8/3/31

Chapter 18 / It Came from Massachusetts

1. *Official Detective Stories* magazine,
   February 1, 1937
2. Ibid.; *New York Daily News* 9/23/33,
   pg. 3; *New York Times*, 9/23/33
3. *Official Detective Stories* magazine,
   February 1, 1937
4. *New York Times*, 7/28/32, pg. 11
5. *New York Times*, 9/2/32
6. *New York Times*, 12/16/32
7. *New York Times*, 1/17/33; *New York
   Herald Tribune*, 6/11/33
8. *New York Times*, 5/30/33
9. *New York Times*, 6/11/33
10. *New York Evening Journal*, 9/21/33,
    pg. 1
11. *New York Times*, 9/21/33, pg. 1
12. Ibid.
13. *New York Evening Journal*, 9/21/33,
    pg. 1
14. Ibid.
15. *New York Daily News* 9/23/33, pg. 3
16. *New York Daily News* 9/24/33, pg. 28
17. *New York Times*, 2/28/34, pg. 20
18. *New York Times*, 3/22/34, pg. 9
19. *New York Daily News* 3/20/33
20. *New York Times*, 1/5/35, pg. 12
21. *New York Times*, 1/18/35
22. *New York Times*, 6/28/35, pg. 1
23. Ibid.

Chapter 19 / Bride of the Mad Dog

1. Arrest record, *Actual Detective*, April
   6, 1938
2. *Actual Detective*, April 6, 1938
3. Ibid.
4. *New York Times*, 7/8/27
5. *New York Evening Journal*, 9/19/32
6. *Gangster City*, Downey, Patrick
7. *Actual Detective*, April 6, 1938
8. *Gangster City*, Downey, Patrick
9. *Actual Detective*, April 6, 1938
10. Ibid.
11. *New York Evening Journal*, 9/19/32,
    pg. 1
12. *New York Times*, 9/19/32, pg. 36
13. *New York Evening Journal*, 9/19/32,
    pg. 1
14. *New York Times*, 6/27/33, pg. 1
15. *New York Times*, 2/24/34, pg. 30
16. *Actual Detective*, April 6, 1938
17. *New York Times*, 6/28/33, pg. 44
18. *New York Times*, 7/3/43, pg. 15

Chapter 20 / The $427,000 Payday

1. *New York Times*, 6/29/39, pg. 7
2. Ibid.
3. Ibid.
4. *New York Times*, 8/22/34, pg. 1,
   6/29/39, pg. 7
5. *New York Times*, 11/4/38, pg. 3
6. *New York Times*, 10/11/38, pg. 52
7. *New York Times* 11/21/34, pg. 1
8. *New York Times*, 11/8/38, pg. 33
9. *New York Times*, 8/27/34, pg. 4
10. *New York Times*, 10/22/38, pg. 34
11. *New York Times*, 11/8/38, pg. 33
12. *New York Times*, 8/26/34, pg. 1
13. *New York Times*, 11/22/34, pg. 44
14. Ibid.
15. Ibid.
16. *New York Times*, 5/14/36, pg. 3
17. *New York Times*, 7/10/36, pg. 9
18. *New York Times*, 2/3/37, pg. 48
19. *New York Times*, 2/2/37, pg. 46
20. *New York Times*, 2/5/37, pg. 1
21. *New York Times*, 11/17/37, pg. 1
22. Ibid.
23. *New York Times*, 11/18/37, pg. 1
24. Ibid.
25. Ibid.
26. *New York Times*, 11/19/37, pg. 3
27. *New York Times*, 10/11/38, pg. 52
28. *New York Times*, 7/18/39, pg. 12

Chapter 21 / FBI vs. NYPD
1. *New York Times*, 12/16/36, pg. 1
2. *Startling Detective Magazine*, March 1937
3. Ibid.
4. Ibid.
5. *New York Times*, 12/16/36, pg. 1
6. Ibid.
7. *New York Times*, 12/17/36, pg. 4
8. Ibid.
9. Ibid.
10. *New York Times*, 12/21/36, pg. 17

Chapter 22 / Messing with the Mob
1. *Startling Detective Adventures* November 1936; *New York Times*, 11/20/35, pg. 18
2. *Gangster City*, Downey, Patrick
3. *Startling Detective Adventures* November 1936
4. Ibid.
5. Ibid.
6. *New York Times*, 10/16/35, pg. 18
7. *New York Evening Journal*, 10/26/35, pg. 2
8. *New York Times*, 10/27/35, pg. 1

Chapter 23 / Dishonorable Mention 1930-1940
1. *Danville Bee*, 2/14/27, Havre Daily News 10/8/30
2. *New York Times*, 10/8/30
3. *New York Times*, 6/13/18, pg. 1; *New York Herald*, 6/13/18

4. *New York Times*, 7/21/18
5. *New York Times*, 10/20/18
6. *New York Times*, 8/10/25
7. *New York Times*, 5/10/31
8. *New York Evening Journal*, 8/22/31, pg. 2; *New York Times*, 8/22/31, pg. 1; *New York Herald Tribune*, 8/22/31, pg. 1
9. *New York Times*, 9/2/31
10. *New York Times*, 8/1/32, pg. 34, 8/2/32, pg. 34
11. *The Man Who Got Away*, Keefe, Rose
12. *New York Times*, 10/2/33
13. *New York Times*, 3/18/36, pg. 1, 3/19/36, pg. 3, 5/5/36, pg. 52
14. *New York Herald Tribune*, 6/24/35; *New York Times*, 6/24/35; *New York Daily News* 6/27/35
15. *New York Times*, 1/3/37, pg. 1, 1/6/37, pg. 1
16. *New York Times*, 1/3/37, pg. 1
17. *New York Times*, 1/4/37, pg. 34
18. *New York Times*, 1/5/37, pg. 2
19. *New York Times*, 1/6/37, pg. 1
20. Ibid.
21. *New York Times*, 12/9/39, pg. 8
22. *New York Times*, 4/26/30
23. *The Valachi Papers*, Maas, Pete
24. *New York Times*, 3/17/32, pg. 11
25. *The Valachi Papers*, Maas, Pete
26. *New York Times*, 11/26/32, pg. 9
27. *New York Times*, 5/24/35, pg. 15; *New York Daily News*, 5/24/35, pg. 24
28. *New York Times*, 8/27/40, pg. 23

Resources

Books

Downey, Patrick, *Gangster City*, Barricade Books, 2004

Gentry, Curt, *J. Edgar Hoover: The Man and the Secrets*, W. W. Norton & Co., 2001

Keefe, Rose, *The Man Who Got Away*, Cumberland House, 2005

Maas, Peter, *The Valachi Papers*, Harper-Collins 1968

Pasley, Fred, *Not Guilty!*, G. P. Putnam's Sons, 1933

Poulsen, Ellen, *The Case Against Lucky Luciano*, Clinton Cook Publishing, 2007

Willemse, Cornelius, *Behind the Green Lights*, Alfred A Knopf, 1931

Magazine Articles

True Detective Mysteries, "My Escape from Atlanta Prison, Part I," Gerald Chapman, January 1927

True Detective Mysteries, "My Escape from Atlanta Prison, Part II," Gerald Chapman, February 1927

True Detective Mysteries, "The Untold Truth About Gerald Chapman's Escape," William McKinnon as told to Fred Denton Moon, October 1929

True Detective Mysteries, "The Real Truth About Chapman–America's 'Super Bandit,' Part I," David Lindsay, November 1929

True Detective Mysteries, "The Real Truth About Chapman–America's 'Super Bandit,' Part II," David Lindsay, December 1929

True Detective Mysteries, "The Real Truth About Chapman–America's 'Super Bandit,' Part III," David Lindsay, January 1930

Real Detective, "I Saw Gerald Chapman Hanged," Lowell M. Limpus, October 1931

True Detective Mysteries, "The Real Truth About the Killing of 'Dutch' Anderson," C. D. McNamee, September 1933

Time, April 13, 1925

True Detective Mysteries, "How We Caught The Bobbed-Haired Bandit, Detective William J. Carey as told to Allan Van Hoesen, July 1924

Actual Detective Stories of Women in Crime, "Get the Bobbed-Haired Bandit!," Richard Hirsh, February 1938

True Detective Mysteries, "The Clue of the Maroon Car," Alan Hynd, February 1930

True Detective Mysteries, "On the Trail of New York's Cowboy Bandit," Detective Lieutenant Richard F. Oliver as told to Isabel Stephen, November 1926

Official Detective Stories, "Bum Rodgers–Big Shot With Clay Feet," Larry Logsdon, June 15, 1937

True Detective Mysteries, "Eight Lives for $300," Captain Michael I. Silverstein, head of the detective bureau, Mount Vernon, N.Y., as told to Guy Stewart Jr., August 1930

Official Detective Stories, "Born To Be Hanged," Larry Logsdon, July 15, 1937

Master Detective, "Smashing the McKenna Gang–New York Terrorists," November 1935

Official Detective Stories, "Long Island's One Man Crime Wave," Paul Kamey, January 1939

Startling Detective Adventures, "How I escaped from Sing Sing–James Nannery," Vincent deP. Slavin, August 1931

True Detective Mysteries, "Behind the Scenes of the Vivian Gordon Case," Alan Hynd, November 1931

True Detective Mysteries, "Unraveling the Riddle of the Weird White Hand," Edward J. Quirk, chief of police, Yonkers, N.Y., as told to David Lindsay, April 1932

The Master Detective, "The Inside Story at Last of the Killer Crowley Capture," Alan Hynd, August 1932

Official Detective Stories, "Rise and Fall of Racket Barons–Leonard Scarnici, Professional Assassin," Henry Vincent, February 1, 1937

Actual Detective Stories of Women in Crime, "She Tried to Be Queen of the Underworld," Dr. Louis L. Lefkowitz, assistant medical examiner for the City of New York, and Richard Hirsh, April 1938

True Detective Mysteries, "Lottie Coll–New York Gun Girl," Sylvester Ryan, chief assistant district attorney, Bronx County, N.Y., as told to Richard Hirsh, May 1935

Startling Detective Adventures, "The Last of the 'Legs' Diamond Mob," December 1934

True Detective Mysteries and Famous Detective Cases, "Solving New York's Great $427,000 Armored Car Holdup, Part 1," Francis C. Preston, October 1937

Startling Detective Adventures, "Kidnap Showdown," Mackenzie Griffin and Lawrence Flick Jr., March 1937

Startling Detective Adventures, Smashing the Sinister 8," Dodd Moran, November 1936

Master Detective, "The Thin Man and the Arsenal Mob, Part II," Assistant District Attorney William O'Rourke as told to Michael Stern, July 1937

NEWSPAPERS

New York Times

New York Daily News

New York Tribune

New York Herald

New York Herald Tribune

New York Evening Journal

New York American

New York Journal American

New York Post

New York World

New York Daily Mirror

Brooklyn Daily Eagle

Brooklyn Standard Union

Bridgeport (Conn.) Telegram

Frederick (Md.) Post

Danville (Va.) Bee

Havre (Mont.) Daily News

DISTRICT ATTORNEY RECORDS

Indictments 138434, 123181,125603, *The People of the State of New York against Thomas Flanagan*

Indictments 125400, 125401, 125441, *The People of the State of New York against Frank Flanagan*

Indictment 164893, *The People of the State of New York against Joseph Flanagan*

Indictment 1643981?, *The People of the State of New York against Richard R. Whittemore, Jacob Kraemer, and Leon Miller otherwise known as Leon Kraemer*

Indictment 153546, *The People of the State of New York against Michael McKenna*

Indictments 165952, 166066, 166078, 167529, *The People of the State of New York against John McKenna*

Indictment 167531, *The People of the State of New York against James Nannery*

Indictment 166059, *The People of the State of New York against Peter Powers*

Indictment 165562, *The People of the State of New York against John Werner*

Indictments 166006, 168952, 167529, *The People of the State of New York against Henry Lucasik*

Indictment 165562, *People of the State of New York against Walter Gee*

Indictments 166663, 166711, 166664, 167221, 167222, *The People of the State of New York against Benjamin Mintz*

Indictments 167034, 167368, *The People of the State of New York against Samuel Schwartz*

Indictment 166663, *The People of the State of New York against John Doe, otherwise known as "Aldy" true name Isadore Alderman*

Indictments 167436, 167437, *The People of the State of New York against Robert Weiner*

Indictment 138828, *The People of the State of New York against William Hoey*

Indictment 187463, *People of the State of New York against Harry Stein*

Indictment 227803, *The People of the State of New York against Silvio Ventre, Lottie Coll, and Thomas Pace*

Indictment 119873, *The People of the State of New York against Patrick Tevan, Vincent Gaffney, and John Sheehan*

Indictments 208264, 208265, 208473, *The People of the State of New York against Frank Peraski*

Indictment 208264, *The People of the State of New York against Madeline Tully*

Indictments 155522, 155541, *The People of the State of New York against Joseph Pioli*

MISCELLANEOUS RECORDS

U.S. Census 1900 and 1910

Richard Reese Whittemore's death certificate

James Nannery's Sing Sing Prison receiving blotter

James Nannery's Auburn Prison receiving blotter

Francis Crowley's Sing Sing Prison receiving blotter

Index